The History They Tell:

Oral History from Native American and First Nations People Regarding the Battle of the Little Bighorn

Lance J. Dorrel

With research and contributions from

Donovan Taylor

The History They Tell: Oral History from Native American and First Nations People Regarding the Battle of the Little Bighorn by Lance J. Dorrel with research and contributions from Donovan Taylor

Cover Art by Linda Haukaas (saakuah1@gmail.com)

Cover and Interior Design: Matthew Wayne Selznick (https://www.mwsmedia.com)

Paperback ISBN: 979-8-218-44434-1
Also available as an e-book.

Also by Lance J. Dorrel

A Dance with Death: An Irish Soldier of Fortune at the Little Bighorn

Cover Art: Linda Haukaas

Linda Haukaas, Sicangu Lakota, is an enrolled member of the Rosebud Sicangu Lakota Tribe.

Haukaas holds a MCRP, College of Architecture, University of Nebraska.

Haukaas has been a practitioner of pictography / ledger art since 1975. Inspired by her grandfather's pictographic tipi, shown to her in a photo by her paternal grandmother, she was determined to begin her pictographic journey.

Haukaas is considered the initiator of the ledger art genre among Plains Native women. This traditionally male art form typically overlooked women's role in society which Haukaas sought to change. Her representation of Lakota women in their daily lives is often filled with emotion.

Haukaas' ledger art works have been acquired by over 12 museums including: the National Museum of American Indian, Heard Museum, British Museum, Plains Indian Ledger Art collection and the New Mexico Museum of Art.

Email: saakuah1@gmail.com

Leave me the truths of other days

- Frederick Remington

Dedication

This book is dedicated to all those who shared with us the stories passed down to them for safekeeping. In remembrance of those who have made their way through the Milky Way and to the Camp on the Other Side...

Crow people: Grant Bulltail and Fred Lefthand.

Cheyenne people: Tim Lame Woman Sr., Leroy Whiteman, Cleve Little Bear, Gilbert Whitedirt, Alberta American Horse, Keith Spotted Wolf, Steve Littlebird, Ruthie Shoulderblade, Eddie Whitedirt, and Ann Strange Owl-Raben, her husband Dayton Raben, and their nephew, Al Joe Strange Owl.

Blackfeet People: Ernie Heavy Runner.

Lakota people: Marce`ll Bull Bear and my dear friends Garvard Good Plume Jr. and Sam High Crane.

And to those who made the ultimate sacrifice in June of 1876, so that their people might live.

Table of Contents

Author's Notes

This book features new and unheard stories from Native American and First Nations People from Canada pertaining to their involvement at the Battle of the Little Bighorn. The stories relate to the people that came and merged into an encampment that consisted of many camps which settled next to the Little Bighorn River by June 24th, 1876.

With the help and guidance of many, many native elders and historians in the United States and Canada, it is time to put forth a better understanding of who these people were and why they gathered in what is present-day southeast Montana that June of 1876.

These long-kept stories are the Native American and First Nations People's history. We simply followed their trial and let the stories guide us to other amazing stories, some of which were in the historical record, and others that have never before been told.

Sadly, many Native American and First Nations People today do not know, nor had they ever heard of, some these stories. Therefore, we did our absolute best to record what we were told verbatim, and then research to see if anything similar was documented before and elsewhere.

We have been guided by the oral history shared by the Native American and First Nations People who keep this history. We have made it our focus to be guided by this untold history as a form of evidence versus preconceived notions. We did our best to follow each trail until it could take us no further. We'd both like to think that when history was shared with us, those who shared knew we would follow it up with dogged determination.

We hope our endeavor will show that when it comes to history involving Native Americans and First Nations People in whatever the context, one should seek their input instead of relying solely on the written record. With that being said, Donovan and myself know just how lucky and blessed we have been on this journey. With great knowledge, that being the stories shared with us, comes great responsibility. On this journey we had been instructed to be "good human beings," in our stewardship of the information received. Our way to honor those who shared, their families, the stories, and those who were in the encampment in June of 1876 is to make sure this information is preserved and made known. Additionally, it is important the information always helps the Native American People and First Nations People today.

~

Writing Native American and First Nations Peoples tribes and bands names in their native language can be challenging. For the sake of clarity, modernized versions are used for consistency and considerations of readability.

When quoting individuals, I use the exact spelling as it was put down in writing at that time.

In this book, mention is made of some tribes' sacred covenants. The stories, and the importance of the roles they played prior to, at the Battle and afterwards, have not been previously discussed as they are in this work. Donovan and myself considered how and what we should include when sharing the stories told to us over the course of countless conversations. After consulting with the keepers of some of the covenants, all agreed the stories need to be told so the truth is known.

Lance J. Dorrel
Missouri
March 2024

Introduction

"Lightning in my Bones"

Our tale began at the Little Bighorn Battlefield National Monument, Crow, Agency, Montana. It was here, through mutual contacts, that I was fortunate enough to meet Donovan Taylor. A member of the Northern Cheyenne Tribe, Donovan belongs to the Dog Men, also called Dog Soldiers, warrior society. Today, he has the honored position of Drum Keeper for the Dog Soldiers.

Much like me, Donovan Taylor is a seeker of the old ways of the Native American Plains People, as well as the First Nations People of Canada. Donovan's earliest memories are filled with an intense interest in the Battle of the Little Bighorn. His home is only a few minutes' drive from the Battlefield, and his formative years were spent learning from Cheyenne elders as they shared their knowledge and stories. From his father's family, he had learned three of his immediate ancestors sacrificed for the Cheyenne people that day!

Together, we embarked on a quest to find what was left of the stories from Donovan's people and other Native American and First Nations People concerning what happened at the Little Bighorn. How many important pieces of the Battle still remained secret and hidden? What else was out there? The more we thought of it, the clearer the answer: We had to find those who knew the oral stories. We hoped to hear what had been passed down from generation to generation. It was the only way to find the hidden truths of what happened that day at what has become America's most famous battle and greatest mystery… one in which the victors do not play the leading role.

Donovan taught me to have patience, as there is a right way to ask for information from Native People, and there is an obligation on the part of the person asking. After schooling me on traditional protocols and procedures, this Cheyenne man adopted me as his brother.

~

From my time on the Battlefield and around the Northern Cheyenne Reservation, coupled with Donovan's connections, we got a jump start in our journey thanks to knowing Linwood Tallbull, Dennis Limberhand, Leroy Whiteman and Gilbert Whitedirt. These Northern Cheyenne men educated us and helped us meet people. One in particular, Leroy Whiteman, paid close attention to the findings that directly resulted from his help. Not only was he curious as to what our research found, he worried over my well-being. He had warned me, "You are going to get lightning in your bones and it will be hard for you to let go."

Many of the stories come from the descendants of those who were there, in present-day Montana, that June of 1876. These people made up the coalition of tribes and bands that inflicted the greatest military defeat on the United States Army in its history to that point in time.

There are stories shared with us from Cheyenne and Lakota people that add to the existing narrative and these, alone, are intriguing. However, it was the willingness of Arapaho, Cree, Blackfeet, Gros Ventre, Nakoda, Nakota, Yankton, Yanktonai, Sisitunwan and Santee Dakota People to share their histories, many of which have never before appeared in written form until now, that we present proudly. Some of the stories we were told are simply not in the historical record when it comes to many of these tribes and bands being at the Battle of the Little Bighorn.

At times it was as if this journey consumed us. Each story led to another, and to other people who might know more. This would happen in waves; maybe two or three, even four, new contacts made in a week, all with valuable stories and trails that had to be followed. We had to keep going and chase each tale, not only for those who had shared with us, but for those who had been in that encampment on the Little Bighorn River in 1876. So much had been written about the warriors that day, and not much else has been told of the others. New pieces came to us to add to the historical record, many of which have never been discussed in public, let alone put on paper.

Leroy's words were never far from my thoughts, especially after he passed away. I now believe he knew all along what would happen.

As we continued on and met more gracious people, the message was always the same: They were honored we had found them and wanted to talk to them. Happy that we wanted to hear their stories, all who shared wanted us to get these stories recorded so they would be kept and retold. They were afraid their people would either forget, or had never been told. The other recurring message was poignant and simple regarding what to do with the information shared with us: "Be a good human being."

Lastly, we met Faron Iron, a member of the Crow Tribe and owner of land that sits between the National Park Service parcels that make up the Little Bighorn National Battlefield. Faron took us to places not many people have seen nor been. From these excursions and vantage points, we were able to gain a better understanding of how the landscape played a pivotal role in the Battle's outcome. The trips were also immensely helpful for putting the newly shared oral stories into context and determining how they matched up with the written records, maps, testimony and archeological evidence.

~

Donovan and I have let the stories tell just what happened. We simply listened and investigated aspects of the Battle told to us or others from oral stories, and followed their trails. Our effort was to clearly convey what was shared, from whom the story was told, and who and where the stories told of. We pursued the information shared and the outcome, regardless if it didn't fit the accepted stories or theories about one of America's greatest mysteries.

This book is an informative and straightforward investigation from the victorious side and perspective. This book is not about Donovan and myself. We do not prescribe to one theory or narrative. We hope that by providing the stories, readers and researchers will use the information to continue their own research.

The stories that follow deviate from the standard narratives of how the Battle happened. This doesn't mean the historical record is wrong. Instead, let the oral stories be looked upon as new ways to look at old evidence. It just may be that these stories are how certain parts and episodes did indeed play out. They were just never known until now. These stories elevate the study of this Battle.

The oral stories center on the individuals and their actions who were there. Some are more specific with locations, deeds, and times than others. These stories not only ascribe names to certain deeds, they explain why parts of the battle unfolded as they did. They give meaning to the standard narrative, but more so, they bring the real story to life from those who lived it and witnessed it.

In some cases, the stories may reflect known facts, theories, maps and archeological evidence in the historical record. If the stories led us to look at the evidence in new ways, with new theories suggested, we state so. Past researchers and their trails were followed, acknowledged, and are discussed in this work.

We hope these new pieces of evidence will be valuable to readers, and researchers whether new or well-versed in the subject of what happened at America's most famous Battle. Our hope is that future writers and historians, especially the younger generations and those who are Native American and First Nation, will pick up or expand where our efforts leave off and fall short.

This battle was not just fought by warriors and soldiers, it was fought by a deeply profound and highly articulate people. There is a sacredness and spirituality to these stories and to this Battle that non-Native People have never understood and cannot comprehend. The Native American and First Nations People are a people who have had their history decimated and a campaign of genocide waged on them for centuries. Our hope is that this book brings some healing and pride to all those people still living, and that it encourages them to do great things, just as their ancestors and people did. It was their victory, and these are their stories. It is time the deeds of the victorious remain silent no more and their victorious voices are heard.

1
The Historical Record

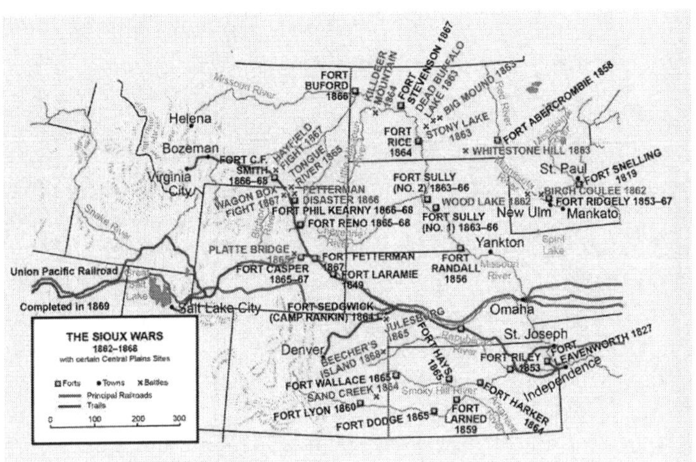

There are a wealth of sources to consult when studying the Battle of the Little Bighorn.[1] What follows is a brief overview of the historical record of events prior to the Battle.

The historical record shows that those who gathered for ceremonies and ultimately ended up at the Battle of the Little Bighorn in what is present-day Montana are said to be a coalition of Native American People. Falling under the Siouan linguistic stock, these people are commonly referred to as the Sioux. They were the Eastern Dakota, known as the Isanti (Santee), which we will refer to as the Santee Dakota throughout this work. The Santee Dakota were comprised of the Mdewakantonwan, Wahpekutetonwan (Wahpekute), Wahpetonwan (Wahpeton) and Sisitunwan (Sisseton). It should be noted here that Sisitunwan people do not adhere to this designation regarding their people as Santee Dakota.[2] The Western Dakota, known as the Wiciyena, comprised of the Ihanktunwan (Yankton) and the Ihanktunwanna (Yanktonai). Also present were the Thithunwan (Teton) Lakota, comprised of seven tribal bands. They are the Oglala, Sichangu (Sicangu), Hunkpapha (Hunkpapa), Mnikhowozu (Miniconjou), Sihasapa (Blackfeet or Blackfoot), Itazipcho (Sans Arcs) and Oohenunpa (Two Kettles).

Cheyenne People and a few Arapaho People are said to be present at the Battle of the Little Bighorn as well. There is seldom mention of any First Nations People, these being the indigenous people from Canada, or other tribes being at the Little Bighorn.

~

For so long, many of the tribes and their bands had put their belief, faith and trust in traditional spiritual leaders and peace chiefs, who they believed could keep them free from harm from the United States government. They were sadly mistaken, and many of their kinsmen paid dearly for it with their lives.

Lakota people had deadly encounters with the United States Army at such places as Ash Hollow, also called the Battle of Blue Water Creek, in western Nebraska. The Santee Dakota fought the U.S. Army in Minnesota, in what is called the U.S.-Dakota War of 1862. There was also the White Stone Hill Massacre in present day North Dakota, in 1863. Add to the mix the plight of their long-time allies, the Cheyenne, who had been attacked and their people massacred at Sand Creek in present day Colorado, the Washita, in present day Oklahoma and at Summit Springs in present day Colorado

Arapaho, Blackfeet and Nakota (Assiniboine), who are at times referred to as Nakoda, were also victims. Twice, Arapaho people were attacked and massacred by the U.S. Army in present-day Wyoming. In what is now present-day northern Montana, Blackfeet people were caught unsuspecting of attack by the U.S. Army and were subsequently burned alive in their tipis. And lastly, a band of the Nakota (Assiniboine) were attacked in their very own beloved Cypress Hills of Saskatchewan, Canada, because white wolf hunters thought they had stolen their horses. Those are just four cases from a long list of attacks by the United States Army on Native People.[3]

By the summer of 1876, the peace chiefs had either been killed or replaced by more militant war chiefs and warrior societies. With these war chiefs and warriors came a hardened people to what is present-day southeast Montana. They were filled with great resolve and determination not to have their way of life taken away. They had to make their stand now, for their people and for all those who had sacrificed so they could have just such a chance at the old way of life. They were, essentially, a Native Peoples coalition.

~

The United States Army had hoped to catch these Native People and put an end to their days of roaming the Plains. The American government's intent was to drive the Native American People onto reservations and get the American West settled once and for all. A military campaign was put into effect and three army units put into the field by early Spring of 1876. One U.S. Army unit, positioned in what is present-day-central Montana and led by General Alfred Terry, was to come from the west. Terry was the campaign's overall commander. The unit from the south came from present-day Wyoming and was led by General George Crook.

Most stories center around the unit from the east, out of present-day North Dakota, with its reputation as the best fighting unit on the northern plains. This would be the United States Seventh Cavalry, led by General George Armstrong Custer.

George Custer had risen through the ranks of the Unites States Army with a highly decorated record for achievements during the American Civil War as a cavalry commander. Custer and the Seventh were thought to be the strongest and most capable fighting force on the Northern Plains.

The U.S. Seventh Cavalry consisted of 12 companies, and this military campaign would be the first time they would all be in the field together. Arikara, and a handful of Lakota, scouts rode with the Seventh as well. Civilian frontiersman hired as interpreters and scouts, packers for the mule train and a few others, brought the total force to over 640 men.[4]

General Custer and the Seventh Cavalry were no strangers to campaigns attempting to subdue Native American People. The U.S. Army and Custer learned that it was a daunting task to even find the Native People on the Plains, let alone bring them to a pitched battle of any sorts. They had skirmished with Lakota warriors on the Northern Plains near the present-day city of Billings, Montana, in 1873. The fight had not amounted to any substantial action.

~

On June 6th, a Sun Dance was held at the Deer Medicine Rocks site in present-day southeast Montana. At this ceremony, the Hunkpapa Lakota Holy Man and war chief, Sitting Bull, had a vision of soldiers falling upside down into the encampment. This vision was interpreted as meaning a great victory was soon to follow for the coalition of tribes over the United States Army.[5]

On June 16th, scouts from camps of the Native Peoples coalition spotted the U.S. Army unit coming from the south. After they reported their discovery back to the leaders, it was brought to council and a plan of action was put forth to leave the Army alone. Young warriors and others would not abide. When the leaders of the different tribes and bands knew they could no longer keep their warriors back, it was decided to send out a party to engage the Army in the field and away from the people.[6] Sitting Bull, in his weakened condition from the Sun Dance, would ride with the large contingent of warriors. However, it was the renowned Oglala war chief Crazy Horse who was asked to led the warriors in battle.[7]

After traveling most of the night, the warriors of the Native Peoples coalition, numbering between 800 to 1,000 warriors and consisting of Arapaho, Cheyenne, Lakota and possibly some Dakota warriors, stopped in the early morning hours of June 17th near Rosebud Creek, also in present-day southeast Montana. They were in separate groups, but well within proximity to communicate and coordinate. Later in the day, this force engaged the U.S. Army unit led by General George Crook. Crook's forces consisted of 1,000 U.S. soldiers, supplemented by 300 Crow and Shoshoni warriors.[8]

What followed was called the Battle of the Rosebud. Very little has been written about this epic event from the perspective of the Native Peoples participants. What should be noted at this point in our story are three key points from the Battle of the Rosebud and how they pertain to the Battle of the Little Bighorn.

One, while the Battle of the Rosebud is said to be a stalemate of sorts, the Native Peoples coalition broke off the fight and moved back to find their people confident they could whip any Army on a battlefield.

Two, the battle had effectively neutralized one of the three U.S. Army units sent to engage them. Crook and his forces retreated to the south. The other two U.S. Army units in the field, one under General Custer coming from the east, and other under General Terry coming from the west, were unaware that Crook and his army could no longer be depended on for reinforcements.[9]

Three, the biggest point to remember here from the oral history shared to us is that the Native Peoples coalition suffered many casualties at the Battle of the Rosebud. The oral history told to us said that both warriors and horses being wounded at the Rosebud was a significant event. The impact of the wounded on the Native Peoples coalition was felt and had to be dealt with. This is an extremely important fact to keep in mind, when reading chapters 9 and 12, which discusses camps for the wounded from the Battle of the Rosebud and who were defending these camps.[10] While these stories did not give exact numbers of wounded warriors and horses, there are glimpses of it in the historical record. The historical record says anywhere from only 16 to 20 Lakota warriors were killed or later died from wounds suffered here. Cheyenne numbers are said to be only one killed. However, some sources put the number of wounded warriors at anywhere from 100 to 400, with 150 to 180 horses wounded or killed.[11] It should be noted, too, that while the Native Peoples coalition was confident and felt triumphant, they knew Sitting Bull's vision of soldiers falling into the encampment had not yet been fulfilled.[12]

~

By the evening of June 24th, 1876, General George Custer had positioned the U.S. Seventh Cavalry to strike the Native Peoples coalition encampment that had now settled on the banks of the Little Bighorn River. The coalition had only arrived and set up their camps earlier in the day. At this point in time, Custer, for his part, had no idea as to the location of the other two U.S. Army units.

In the early morning hours of June 25th, General Custer had been taken to what is called the Crow's Nest, an area the Crow People used to scan the landscape for enemies. So far, Custer had managed to keep his unit hidden. He waited for word from his scouts, who were to reconnoiter the Valley of the Little Bighorn and give him much-needed information on the encampment's exact whereabouts and size.

The scouts found the massive encampment on the Little Bighorn River and, in the early morning hours, tried to show Custer the sizeable horse herds. He then learned that his command had been seen by Native People, presumably, those from the coalition encampment.

General Custer decided to press the attack and strike the coalition encampment in broad daylight. The reasoning was, it was thought the Native People who had spotted the Seventh Cavalry would have by now alerted the encampment, which would scatter.[13]

The historical record tells us that General Custer divided his 12 companies into four parts. The first unit, which consisted of three companies, plus the Arikara scouts, two Crow scouts and the civilian frontiersmen, came to 175 men under the command of Major Marcus Reno.[14] This unit would ford the Little Bighorn River. They were to proceed up the Valley of the Little Bighorn River and move across the flat plain that ran parallel to the river. Reno was to attack and drive back any Native People his unit encountered along the way.

The second unit, under Captain Frederick Benteen, with three companies totaling 115 men, was to move to the West.[15] Benteen was to fully scout and protect the Seventh's left flank, in case of any satellite encampments in this area.

The third unit, under Captain Thomas McDougall, consisted of one company and extra soldiers pulled from the other companies to guard the mule pack train. His strength was 135 men.[16] The pack train had the extra ammunition and supplies for the entire Seventh Cavalry.

Finally, the fourth unit, under the direct command of General Custer, consisted of five companies. The headquarters unit was here too, bringing the number of troopers riding with Custer at 221 men. Four Crow scouts and one civilian scout, Mitch Bouyer, rode with Custer as well.[17] Bouyer was part Santee Dakota and he was married to a Crow woman.

The historical record states General Custer and his command did not cross the Little Bighorn River at this time. They instead followed the terrain leading to the bluffs above the river. Why Custer and his command would choose a route that ran parallel to the river and were at times 300 feet above the river, instead of supporting the Reno command, has been subject to conjecture since the Battle ended. It is believed Custer hoped to find another suitable crossing further down river and cross into the encampment. This move to the bluffs may have also been in response to a report of a party of warriors on these bluffs.[18]

~

The Native Peoples coalition encampment on the banks of the Little Bighorn River was now in the sights of the Seventh Cavalry. Exactly how many people were in the encampment, the U.S. Army's intelligence could not say. That hardly mattered now. The U.S. Army and United States Government had never anticipated an encounter with the multitude and combination of seasoned warriors they were about to face. Besides underestimating the fighting force of the Native American People and those First Nations People who had come from Canada, the U.S. Army had failed to fully grasp the cultural and spiritual components carried by these people. The people the U.S. Army hunted firmly believed they were forever secure and safe, always under the watchful eye of their creator and spirit helpers.

Our focus in the next chapter is to now look at the encampment and the camps within it on the Little Bighorn from the perspective of Native American and First Nations People. In doing so, we take you the reader, back to a time rarely discussed when accurately telling who the Native American and First Nations People at the Little Bighorn were. This is the first time the following story of an ancient alliance of Native People has ever been told. This history goes so far back in time, that today, few if any know it.

Notes

1. Brust, James S., Pohanka, Brian and Barnard, Sandy. *Where Custer Fell*; Donahue, Michael. *Where the Rivers Ran Red*; Donovan, Jim. *A Terrible Glory*; Gray, John. *Centennial Campaign*; Stewart, Edgar I. *Custer's Luck*; Liddic, Bruce R. *Vanishing Victory*; Greene, Jerome A. *Evidence and The Custer Enigma: A Reconstruction of Indian - Military History*.

2. See Albers, Patricia C. 761 - 776. Handbook of the North American Indians, 2001 Vol 13, part 2 of 2. Personal communications with Vine Marks - Sisitunwan Dakota, Akisa Peters Manning - Sisitunwan Dakota, Cody Seaboy - Wahpekute Dakota.

3. Ewers 1958: 249 - 251; Michno 2003; Liberty, Margo and Wood, Raymond 2011.

4. Gray 1988: 293 - 297. Donovan 2008: 139 - 200.

5. For accounts pertaining to Sitting Bull's vision there are a wealth of sources to consult. These are only a few to read. Marquis 2003: 191 - 192; Powell 1981: Vol 1, 947 - 953. Utley 1993: 136 - 139; Vestal 1965: 148 - 151; Viola 1999: 54 - 55.

6. Vestal 1976: 152 - 153; Powell 1981, Vol 2: 954 - 956; Utley 1993: 140; Bray 2006: 205 - 207.

7. For information pertaining to Crazy Horse being chosen to lead the Lakota contingent at the Battle of the Rosebud, I have utilized the stories shared to myself from Chris Dixon. See Utley 1993: 140 and Vestal 1976: 152 - 153.

8. Personal communications with Chris Dixon, Wallace Bearchum - Cheyenne, Keith Spotted Wolf - Cheyenne, Donovan Taylor - Cheyenne, Lindwood Tall Bull - Cheyenne, Bill Goggles - Arapaho. For an in - depth analysis pertaining to the results of the Battle of the Rosebud and how they affected the Battle of the Little Bighorn, readers are encouraged to read: Mangum, Neil C. *Battle of The Rosebud: Prelude to the Little Bighorn,* Chapters X and XI; Vaugh, J.W. *Indian Fights: New Facts on Seven Encounters,* Chapter 4.

9. Ibid.

10. The number of Native American casualties from the Battle of the Rosebud and of wounded horses were a consistent part of the story told to this writer. Many individuals shared this part of the story to this writer. They are as follows: Garvard Good Plume Jr. - Oglala Lakota, Harold Salway - Oglala Lakota, Rick Two Dogs - Oglala Lakota, Basil BraveHeart - Oglala Lakota, Victor Douville - Sicangu Lakota Tribal Historian, Cal Thunder Hawk - Sicangu Lakota, Doug War Eagle - Minnikojou Lakota, Keith Spotted Wolf - Cheyenne, Wallace Bearchum - Cheyenne, Chris Dixon and Inkpa Mani.

11. For accounts on the number of Lakota and Cheyenne casualties and wounded horses from the Battle of the Rosebud see: Utley 1993:141; Marquis 2003: 202 - 203; Vaughn 2016: 193 - 218. Bourke 1971: 316. Kill Eagle in Graham 1953: 52; Young Two Moon in Greene 1994: 30; T. Powers 2010: 189.

12. Personal communications with Garvard Good Plume Jr. - Oglala Lakota, Harold Salway - Oglala Lakota, Rick Two Dogs - Oglala Lakota, Basil BraveHeart - Oglala Lakota, Victor Douville - Sicangu Lakota Tribal Historian, Cal Thunder Hawk - Sicangu Lakota, Doug War Eagle - Minnikojou Lakota, Keith Spotted Wolf - Cheyenne, Wallace Bearchum - Cheyenne, Chris Dixon and Inkpa Mani.

13. Kuhlman 1951: 41 - 46; Stewart 1955: 273 - 278; Gray 1988: 293 - 297; Donovan 2008: 161 - 221

14. Ibid.

15. Ibid.

16. Ibid.

17. Ibid.

18. Personal communications with Mike Donahue, Faron Iron and Chris Dixon. Kuhlman 1951: 151 - 159; Hammer 1976: 97; Donahue 2018: 158, 311.

2
An Ancient Alliance

The information for this chapter came from the following people: Basil BraveHeart - Oglala Lakota, Garvard Good Plume Jr. - Oglala Lakota, Rick Two Dogs - Oglala Lakota, Harold Salway - Oglala Lakota, Lakota Tribal Historian Victor Douville - Sicangu, Lakota Sacred Pipe and Bundle Keeper Arvol Looking Horse, Paula Looking Horse, Joanne Pompana - Hunkpapa Lakota/Seneca/Iroquois, Chico Her Many Horses - Oglala Lakota, Frenchy Dillon-Crow, Ben Rhodd - Potawatomie, Devin Oldman - Arapaho, Bill Goggles - Arapaho, Chester Whiteman - Cheyenne, Vernon Sooktis - Cheyenne, Dwight Bull Coming - Cheyenne, Ernie Heavy Runner - Blackfeet, Jimmy Stgoddard - Blackfeet, James Desjarlais - Nakota / Cree, Jim Red Eagle - Nakota / Lakota, Ken Shields - Yankton / Lakota, Alvin WindyBoy Sr. - Chippewa Cree, Rod Alexis - Stoney Nakoda, Dennis Paul - Stoney Nakoda, Rhonda Funmaker - Ho Chunk, and Tribal Historian Peter Gibbs - Sicangu Lakota.

Some of the enduring questions surrounding The Battle of the Little Bighorn are: just who were the Native People there, and what are some of the histories and stories of these people? The historical record gives little detail on the Native American People, and even less regarding the First Nations People from Canada. When reading this work, one should keep an open mind to what these stories reveal. Stay the course with the oral history, especially if it doesn't conform to the established theory or data. Focus on the information told. The Native American and First Nations People have their own history.

Labeled "militants" or "hostiles," the Native American and First Nations people who had gathered in present-day Montana by early June of 1876 simply wanted to live as their ancestors had since time immemorial in the northern plains across the Western United States and up into Canada.

Native American People were in danger of having their freedom taken away from them for good in 1876. How long they had been there and their ties to the land did not matter to the United States government. Told to give up their free way of life and where to live, those who would not consent moved where the traditional summer ceremonies would be held. They simply wanted to continue to follow what was left of the fast-diminishing buffalo herds and stay as far away from the white man as humanly possible.

There was more to this than is told in the standard narratives. With the help of Native elders and historians, a more complex and long-kept secret now comes to light. This was a gathering of an ancient alliance.

Let's first look at all these tribes and their bands not as separate groups, but as one people. Moving forward we will call them "The People." Now, we present that all The People were one people. They all came from, and were part of, the same indigenous people who were in either one or two groups on the North American Continent. There was one language. There were no tribal designations.

This is not a story, but the history of many Native American and First Nations Peoples, one that goes back so far very few ever knew it existed, and even fewer know of it today.

Eventually, The People dispersed in the form of bands. For some time, despite the breakup and wide scattering of The People an alliance held together thanks to the ancient common ceremonies, star knowledge, and spiritual practices that guided their lives. Today, it's unknown how long this alliance endured.

Because these bands dispersed and then grew so fast, different languages developed. The bands had been instructed by their Holy People, those who were the intercessors with the Star People and Spirits, to name all things they encountered as they moved across the continent. They named the animals, the plants, the birds, the land and its features. However, in doing so, they named all things differently. Disagreements developed over hunting territory and other resources. Warfare soon came into play and became common.

A reunification of the bands came about, but to this day little is known regarding the intricate details of who organized it and what exactly happened. Star knowledge and spirituality were, again, paramount components. What the ceremonies exactly were, what was given, as in the example of sacred covenants and from whom they initially were given by, to and where, is subject to debate depending on what tribe or band you ask. The stories say that for some time, all reunited and the bands put down their weapons and acted like, "good human beings."

The coming of the white man saw a return to warfare; this time, over the fur trade, metal weapons, guns and the horse. Oral history kept vestiges of the old alliance, alive, and bits and pieces were recorded, but for the most part, full knowledge of the history was ignored or brushed aside by European colonizers in order to more quickly establish a new prevailing theory: there was little evidence the People had a developed, articulate culture on the continent.

What I have been told is that the descendants of The People from the Ancient Alliance were meeting in present-day Montana in the general vicinity of where they had once roamed for centuries and received instruction on how to live. It is pondered by these elders and historians now that those who gathered in June of 1876 were not only there for ceremonial purposes, they met with intent to rekindle and begin preparations aimed at preserving the old and sacred ways.

This is not some revisionist theory from these elders and historians. This history is known and has been kept by many tribes and their bands.[1]

~

What follows is, by necessity, an incomplete attempt to accurately describe who some of the People were and where they had come from prior to merging into the encampment along the banks of the Little Bighorn. As we move forward, the history we'll present is derived from research following up on oral stories shared with us from families and individuals of the tribes and bands who were at the Little Bighorn.

Notes

1. Personal communications with Chico Her Many Horses - Oglala Lakota, Frenchy Dillon - Crow/Oglala Lakota, Arvol and Paula Looking Horse, Victor Douville - Sicangu Lakota Tribal Historian, Garvard Good Plume Jr. - Oglala Lakota, Rick Two Dogs - Oglala Lakota, Basil BraveHeart - Oglala Lakota, Rod Alexis - Stoney Nakoda, Dennis Paul - Stoney Nakoda, Alvin Windy Boy Sr. - Chippewa Cree, Jimmy Stgoddard - Blackfeet, Ernie Heavy Runner - Blackfeet, Michael Black Wolf - Gros Ventre, Chester Whiteman - Cheyenne, Dwight Bull Coming - Cheyenne, Donovan Taylor - Cheyenne, Wallace Bearchum - Cheyenne, Vernon Sooktis - Cheyenne, Keith Spotted Wolf - Cheyenne, Harold Salway - Oglala Lakota, Devin Oldman - Arapaho, Bill Goggles - Arapaho, Ben Rhodd - Potawatomi, Iris O'Watch - Dakota/Nakota, Jim Red Eagle - Nakota/Lakota, Joanne Pompana - Hunkpapa Lakota/Iroquois/Seneca, Ken Shields - Yankton/Lakota, Tommy Christian - Nakota/Dakota/Lakota, Ozzie McKay - Santee Dakota, James Desjarlais - Nakota/Cree, Catcher Cuts The Rope - Gros Ventre, Rhonda Funmaker - Ho Chunk, and Peter Gibbs - Tribal Historian Sicangu Lakota.

3
Santee Dakota, Sisitunwan, Yankton and Yanktonai

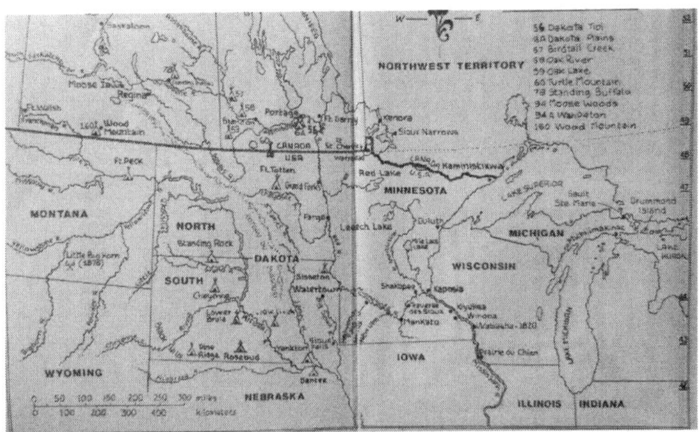

Map courtesy of Gontran Laviolette, *The Dakota Sioux in Canada,* The Marian Press, 1944.

The history told to us on the trail we followed for this chapter on the Santee Dakota, Sisitunwan, Yankton and Yanktonai came from the following people: Mitchell BigHunter - Santee Dakota, Dianne Desrosiers - Sisitunwan Dakota, Ozzie McKay - Santee Dakota, Terry Was'te s'te - Santee Dakota, Vine Marks - Sisitunwan Dakota, Akisa Peters Manning - Sisitunwan Dakota, Cody Seaboy - Wahpekute Dakota, Ben Rhodd - Potawatomie, Victor Douville - Sicangu Lakota Tribal Historian, Iris O'Watch - Nakota/Dakota, Tom Shawl - Nakoda, Tommy Christian - Nakota/Dakota/Lakota, Ken Helgeson - Nakoda, Rod Alexis - Stoney Nakoda, Calvin Bear First - Yanktonai/Santee Dakota, Ken Shields - Yankton/Lakota, Jalen Atchico - Yanktonai /Nakota, Mike Turcotte - Nakoda, Larus Longie - Chippewa Cree, Joanne Pompana, Paula and Arvol Looking Horse and Peter Gibbs - Tribal Historian

Sicangu Lakota. Independent researchers: James Ritchie, Louis Garcia, Inkpa Mani and Bob Saindon.

This part of the investigation focuses on the Santee Dakota, Sisitunwan, Yankton and Yanktonai People and their involvement at the Battle of The Little Bighorn. These people take a back seat to their more famous kinsmen, the Lakota, whose place at the Little Bighorn has been firmly entrenched in the historical record.

The Santee Dakota, Sisitunwan, Yankton and Yanktonai appeared in only a handful of accounts and a few maps. For the most part, they have stayed hidden and kept off the historical record. These people were no strangers to deadly encounters with the United States Army. Until now, how, and from where, some of these people came to the Battle has never before been put in written form.

Oral history shared with me states that the place of origin for the Santee Dakota is Mille Lacs Lake, north of Minneapolis, Minnesota, known as Mde Wakan to the Santee Dakota and interpreted as Spirit Lake / Mystery Lake / Mysterious Lake/Sacred Lake / Holy Lake or Lake of the Great Spirit / Great Spirit Lake. The Dakota's spirits came into the lake from Star People fleeing the stars. The spirits then emerged from the lake and lived there. They are the Eagle Nation.[1]

The Santee Dakota were made up of the following people:

Mdewakantonwan, who are said to be the original gens and are known as the Spirit or Sacred Lake people.

The Sisitunwan, known as the Medicine People.

The Wahpekute, known as the Leaf Archers and as the people who protected the Spirit People (Mdewakantonwan).

The Wahpeton, known as the Village in the Leaves, warriors of great ability. They protected the Medicine People (Sisitunwan) and the Spirit People (Mdewakantonwan).[2]

Lakota oral history shared with me states the Lakota came from the stars and the Maghpia Oyate (Cloud People) then emerged from within the Black Hills with the buffalo. Other oral stories shared with me tell that the Yankton left the Santee Dakota at Mille Lac. After some time, the Lakota separated from the Yankton in the vicinity of Teton Lake, Minnesota, and Lake Traverse, Minnesota.[3]

While the historical record seems to agree on where the Lakota separated from the Yankton, there is a considerable side story to the Santee Dakota history. It should be noted here that the Sisitunwan and Wahpeton bands do not adhere to the standard narrative that they are part of the Santee. Their oral history is much more complex, and documented sources show ties to the Yanktonai and possibly the Nakota (Assiniboine) as well. Some Native American historians say there is evidence that shows a connection to the Hunkpapa Lakota as well.[4]

History shared by Santee Dakota, Sisitunwan and Lakota people tell of migrations and histories seldom mentioned in the historical record. The historical record shows Siouan speaking people in the Central Mississippi Valley region of the United States. Plus, migrations to the American southwest and or from the American south, as well as to and from the east coast seaboard, into the Ohio Valley, up to the state of New York and into Canada.[5]

~

Our investigation into a Santee Dakota presence at the Battle of the Little Bighorn begins first with those Santee Dakota who had remained in Minnesota prior to 1862. Before this time, the Lakota, Yankton and Yanktonai had moved west and onto the northern plains. They had by now fully adopted the buffalo and horse culture for which they were noted.

To the west, northwest and into Canada, other Siouan speaking people can be found. The historical record refers to these people as the Nakota and Nakoda. Both, at times, are called Assiniboine, and the Nakoda are called Stoney, as well. Some sources say the Nakota (Assiniboine) broke off the Yankton, the majority say it was from the Yanktonai.[6]

Before this time, and for possibly hundreds of years, Santee Dakota people had traveled back and forth from the Minnesota Territory and onto the American Plains, down into what will be later known as the southern states region of America, as well as up into the Canadian territories, to hunt, trade and form alliances. It is possible the Nakota (Assiniboine) and Nakoda (Assiniboine) were the northernmost vanguard of this migratory group. These people knew no boundaries, and as a result of these journeys into new lands their culture developed into warrior societies. They also formed close ties to certain bands of Algonquin-speaking people, some of whom would later become the Cheyenne tribe.[7]

By the 1840's, the impact of non-natives having moved into the Minnesota territory, the whiskey trade, and the strategic arming of other tribes close to the Santee Dakota created conflict in the region. Also, due to depleted natural resources, by this time Santee Dakotas were starving. Numerous children, women and the elderly had died due to disease, and others, murdered. Santee Dakota bands had been forced to move out of traditional areas and had signed a series of treaties with the U.S. Government to accommodate the ever-growing encroachment of white settlers. They were put on land that set on both sides of the Minnesota River, which became known as the Upper and Lower Sioux Reservation.

When annuities and food were not delivered, hostilities boiled over into all-out war, known as the U.S.-Dakota War of 1862. Santee Dakota warriors were said to have killed more than 600 white settlers before being subdued. Some 2,000 warriors surrendered, while many others fled west across the U.S. Northern Plains. Many Santee Dakota fled to Canada, where they eventually settled. Over 200 warriors were sentenced to death, with 38 Santee Dakota warriors being hung in public at what still is the largest mass execution in U.S. history.

Santee Dakota people were forever forced out of Minnesota.[8]

~

Hostilities between the Santee Dakota, Sisitunwan and Western Dakota (Yankton and Yanktonai) and the United States continued through 1863 and into 1864. There were two significant encounters.

The first, Whitestone Hill Massacre, happened in September of 1863. The second, the Battle of Killdeer

Mountain, took place in July 1864. Both attacks by the U.S. Army were led by General Alfred Sully and were done in retaliation for the U.S.-Dakota War of 1862.

Whitestone Hill encompasses a roughly fifteen square mile region half-way between the Missouri and Red Rivers in present day North Dakota. It is also close to the James River. All are important migration and travel routes for Native People. It sits on top of a coteau surrounded by the small lakes common to that region.

Before 1863, Native People had gone there for thousands of years. This was a sacred place and spiritual land upon which ceremonies such as "to make relatives," which strengthened bands with one another through and marriages, and other important rituals were conducted. Equally, or perhaps even more, important was the fact that this sacred ground was a traditional spot to "call the buffalo," in order to have a hunt, and to pick wild fruits and vegetables to make and store the all-important food stores for the approaching winter.

The historical record and oral stories state that the people at this gathering were comprised of Yankton, Yanktonai, some Sihasapa (Blackfeet) Lakota, Santee Dakota and possibly some Arikara. When it comes to the Battle of the Little Bighorn, it should be noted that two important individuals had found themselves here. They were Elk Head, the Keeper of the Sacred White Buffalo Calf Pipe and Bundle, as well as Inkpaduta, a Santee Dakota war chief from the Wahpekute Band. Inkpaduta had fought the encroachment of white settlers for many years. Among his own people he had a reputation as a hardened warrior with a keen eye for using terrain to his advantage in warfare. He was leader and a traditionalist regarding the old ways.

As the sun began to set in the midst of their ceremonies and hunting, the encampment at Whitestone Hill was found by Native scouts with the U.S. Army. Some of the chiefs went to negotiate with the soldiers under a white flag that was really a white flour sack. Two of the chiefs were Big Head and Two Bears. Once in negotiations with The U.S. Army, the chiefs realized the seriousness of the situation at hand. The Army was here looking for Santee Dakota People, for revenge for the U.S.-Dakota War of 1862. Now, all they could do was try to buy time for the elderly, women and children to make an escape.

What followed was a massacre that went on for the remainder of that first evening and continued for a least two days. Many were killed while still in ceremonies. The atrocities committed here match in graphic horror any of those already in the historical record. No quarter was given, regardless of age or sex. It is said that after days of killing, the Army made the captured children take bayonets and go throughout the encampment and finish off those who were wounded.

Big Head Pahtanka

The chiefs and those others taken prisoner were forced to march to prisoner of war camps. Many were taken to the prisoner of war camp at Crow Creek in present-day South Dakota. Some survived the imprisonment, but many didn't. It is told that many of the young female prisoners were raped.

Big Head and Two Bears did survive imprisonment and eventually ended up at the Battle of the Little Bighorn. Inkpaduta, too wise to be caught in such a way by the U.S. Army, got away. Elk Head and the Sacred Pipe and Bundle managed to make it out as well. Many of the survivors, like Inkpaduta, headed west and crossed the Missouri River.[9]

After the Whitestone Hill Massacre, the U.S. Army was still not satisfied they had crushed those they suspected had been part of the U.S.-Dakota War of 1862. Now, with the fact that gold had been discovered in Montana Territory, the Army mounted another campaign.

Sully's command found Santee Dakota, Sisitunwan, Yankton, Yanktonai and Lakota people in another traditional hunting and gathering spot, this time in western present-day North Dakota near the Little Missouri River.

The ground was known as Killdeer Mountain and to the Native People as, "The place where they kill deer." It

Two Bears

was here that two Lakota leaders against the white encroachment, Sitting Bull and Gall, found themselves with their people next to Inkpaduta and his followers. In the historical record, sources said the Army destroyed many tipis, food stores and killed 100 warriors or so.

None who shared oral stories with us could recall information related to this battle, other than it was commonly told that Inkpaduta again showed he was a very intelligent war chief. He directed the defensive sites for the Santee Dakota and Lakota here, which bought crucial time for the non-combatants to make their escape. He and his people had been in numerous clashes with the U.S. Army by now, while the Lakota were in the midst of their first since Sicangu Lakota People had been attacked at Ash Hollow, in western Nebraska.[10]

~

The next part of our investigation concerning the Santee Dakota at the Little Bighorn deals with a Cheyenne-Dakota connection: well known Native American writer Dr. Charles Eastman, a young Santee Dakota historian's research, and the War of 1812 between Great Britain and the United States. It should be noted that bits and pieces of the following information are in the historical record and have been available to researchers for many years. It was only when I was made aware of parts to these stories hidden for so long, in part for fear of reprisal, that a clearer picture of events came into focus.

The trail of the Santee Dakota and their connection to the Battle of The Little Bighorn picks back up with a Santee Dakota warrior by the name of Gray Earth Track. The story of Gray Earth Track was shared with me by Ozzie McKay. Ozzie is the great-grandson of Gray Earth Track.

Gray Earth Track was raised by his Dakota people in Minnesota. During U.S.-Dakota War of 1862, in which his father fought in and was never again seen alive by his family, Gray Earth Track's people fled Minnesota for Canada. For centuries, the Dakota People had gone back and forth between what would be Canada and the United States. In early June of 1876, Gray Earth Track and his Santee Dakota people were living west of where the city of Winnipeg, Manitoba, sits when his Cheyenne blood brother came for him. It is not known today from where this Cheyenne man came, or who he was. Nor is it known where this Cheyenne man and Gray Earth Track had crossed paths before.

With his Cheyenne blood brother, Gray Earth Track and some his family embarked on a journey to find the summer ceremonies of the Native People who roamed the U.S. and Canadian Plains. These ceremonies were to take place somewhere in what is present-day southeastern Montana. For two weeks, Gray Earth Track and his Cheyenne blood brother journeyed to find the encampments. We do not know the route they traveled, or how many were in their party. What we do know is that they did catch up with the encampments sometime before the Battle of the Little Bighorn occurred.

Ozzie McKay then told us that his family has history that states Gray Earth Track killed a soldier at the Battle of the Little Bighorn. This soldier used two horses as shields, or it might be that the soldier was attempting to breakout of the fighting. Regardless, Gray Earth Track encountered this soldier as the soldier attempted to fire his revolver from under the neck of one of the horses, but ran out of ammunition. Gray Earth Track was able to charge and shoot the soldier and count coup on him as well.

Gray Earth Track returned to Canada with some of the soldier's personal effects. This included one of the soldier's revolvers, as well as the two horses.

Ozzie McKay's family has guarded this history for many years now. This history, as told to Ozzie from his grandmother, Alice, was that the solider Gray Earth Track killed was General George Custer.[11]

It should be noted here that Gray Earth Track is not the son of the famous Santee Dakota warrior Inkpaduta, who is said to have a son with the same name.

~

I followed the trail Ozzie started me on and continued to look at the Santee Dakota presence in and around Sioux Valley First Nation, Birdtail Sioux First Nation and Pipestone on the Oak Lake Reserve in Manitoba, Canada. From here I met a young Santee Dakota historian by the name of Mitchell BigHunter. Mitchell is a great-great grandson of Gray Earth Track.

Mitchell not only confirmed the story of Gray Earth Track, but told me of the connection Dr. Charles Eastman had with Gray Earth Track. Dr. Eastman was a renowned Native American ethnographer, writer and physician. Mitchell shared with me the fact that Gray Earth Track was in fact Eastman's uncle, who he called Mysterious Medicine. Along with his brother Joseph, Mysterious Medicine was indeed at the Little Bighorn. They had raised Eastman in Manitoba, Canada, after he had ended up there sometime after the U.S.-Dakota War of 1862.[12]

Ozzie McKay stated Gray Earth Track had two families. One family settled and stayed in the area that would become the Sioux Valley First Nation Reserve, the other family, which Dr. Eastman was associated with, settled and lived in the Pipestone area on which the Oak Lake Reserve is now located.[13]

Mitchell BigHunter provided us with a list of Santee Dakota warriors names who had fought at the Little Bighorn. Other names come to us from Dianne Desrosiers, Ozzie McKay, Inkpa Mani and Akisa Peters Manning.[14] See Appendix B.

More help came from veteran writer and researcher James Ritchie. James has been doing research on the Santee Dakota and their history of military engagements for years. His research, like Mitchell's, has led them both to believe those Santee Dakota who were at the Little Bighorn were like no other warriors there. James and Mitchell tracked these warriors and their journeys from and in the Sioux Valley and Birdtail areas of Manitoba, Canada. Their findings are very interesting and should be looked at by students and researchers of the Battle.[15]

It is possible the Santee Dakota warriors who are said to have been at the Little Bighorn are possibly more like a small detachment of soldiers. Many might have been trained in European warfare techniques by their male relatives or fellow warrior society members. These warriors' fathers, grandfathers and uncles would have fought alongside the British in the War of 1812 and, before that, in the American Revolution, and would have been trained in European tactics by the British Army.

This training would include volley fire, coupled with basic infantry techniques and formations. These would be unlike any a Plains warrior would use. It is also more than likely these Santee Dakota warriors were armed with guns and ammunition supplied by Great Britain.[16] Add to this that stories point to the area of Turtle Mountain, in the southern part of the Canadian Province of Manitoba, just across the border with present-day North Dakota, as having been a stronghold for these Santee Dakota warriors. This area afforded them a hideout, a place to trade and buy guns and ammunition, as well as get other supplies for their journeys back and forth across the U.S. and Canadian borders.[17]

Before we summarize our findings on the Santee Dakota, Sisitunwan, Yankton and Yanktonai presence at the Little Bighorn, I wanted to add what was told to me regarding Inkpaduta.

The famous Wahpekute war chief and his follower's whereabouts prior to the Battle has not been looked at in great detail. I was told by multiple people that Inkpaduta and some of his followers were in the Ft. Peck area in present day northeastern Montana prior to coming to the Little Bighorn. After the Whitestone Hill Massacre, it is told that Santee Dakota, Sisitunwan, Yankton and Yanktonai people went to Fort Peck and to the Poplar, Montana, area, which is close to Fort Peck. Many Santee Dakota, Sisitunwan, Yankton and Yanktonai people were married to Nakota (Assiniboine) people in and around the Milk River area. Some Santee Dakota, Sisitunwan and Yanktonai people moved into the Canadian

Provinces of Manitoba and Saskatchewan during and after the U.S.-Dakota War of 1862.[18]

Calvin Bear First, a Native American historian from Fort Peck, Ken Shields, Native American historian and teacher from Poplar, Montana, Jalen Atchico, Native American historian from Poplar, and Tom Shawl, Native American historian from Fort Belknap, Montana, all shared that some Santee Dakota, Sisitunwan, Yankton and Yanktonai warriors came to the Little Bighorn and took part in the Battle. Calvin, Ken and Jalen provided names of some of these Santee Dakota, Yanktonai, Yankton and Cut Head People, who at one time were in the Fort Peck, Saskatchewan and Manitoba provinces and ended up at the Little Bighorn. Calvin Bear First continually advised me to look into the Cut Head People, a sub-band of mixed Sisitunwan and Yanktonai People. He felt these people had had a presence at the Little Bighorn.[19]

Sisitunwan elder and historian Vine Marks told me that he had been told Yankton and Yanktonai People came from the area close to present-day Yankton, South Dakota, prior to their journey west to the Little Bighorn. He had been told these people found Sisitunwan people, he was not sure where, but offered those Sisitunwan who wanted to travel with them the opportunity to do so. Vine added that this group of Sisitunwan, Yankton and Yanktonai people did eventually find the camps of the Native Peoples Coalition somewhere in current day southeast Montana. He had been told that this group camped with Inkpaduta's followers at the Little Bighorn.[20]

Cody Seaboy, a Wahpekute Dakota tribal member, informed me of history pertaining to Santee Dakota and Sisitunwan People at the Little Bighorn. Cody had been told that it was from within the ranks of these Santee Dakota and Sisitunwan people that some of the first warriors to oppose the Reno Battalion in Valley Fight had come. Specifically, Cody stated it was Wahpekute Dakota warriors who helped hold the Reno Battalion, along with elders and many young men, until seasoned warriors could get there.[21]

Doug War Eagle, a Minnikojou Lakota historian, told me that many of the Dakota people who came to the

Little Bighorn were what he called Cut Heads. He and Akisa Peters Manning, a young Sisitunwan educator and historian, said the Cut Heads were a sub-band comprised of a mixed group of Yanktonai and Sisitunwan people. Doug also said that these Dakota people were prodigious warriors and powerful medicine people.[22] See Appendix B. For a list of Santee Dakota, Sisitunwan, Yankton, Yanktonai and Cut Head warriors who fought at the Little Bighorn.

What is in the historical record and how do these stories match up against it?

After the Battle of the Little Bighorn, hundreds, possibly more, Native People and those First Nations People who had come to the ceremonies from Canada did in fact return to Canada. Today, the trail to find these People is long and winding. Sitting Bull and those who followed him eventually settled at what is named Wood Mountain Lakota First Nation Reserve, in the Canadian Province of Saskatchewan. Others melted into the land and did their best to remain quiet about events at the Little Bighorn. We will present a few of these People and their history in later chapters.

There is scant evidence when it comes to accounts of Santee Dakota, Sisitunwan, Yankton, Yanktonai and Cut Head People and their warriors at the Battle of the Little Bighorn.

Our search revealed two pieces of literature from the National Park Service and only nine books on the Battle that gave the Santee Dakota story much credence and research. One of these was from Canadian researcher Gordon Harper, who cited only Minnikojou Lakota oral history given to him by people from The Cheyenne River Reservation. Harper noted Cut Head People among those Dakota and others who had come to present-day Montana for ceremonies.[23]

There are 18 individual accounts that put Santee Dakota people at the Little Bighorn. These accounts come from warriors who were said to have been there. One included is from Dr. Charles Eastman, who placed his two uncles there. There are only nine accounts telling of Yankton and Yanktonai people there.[24]

No accounts tell of these Santee Dakota coming as a unified force supplied with British arms and ammunition. However, I was told by three different Santee Dakota people that these warriors who had come to the Little Bighorn and ended up fighting in it were subsequently buried together some years later after the Battle. These would be the warriors who survived the Battle and they are said to be buried together back in Canada.[25]

As for maps putting Santee Dakota, Yankton, Yanktonai and Cut Head People at the Little Bighorn, our search revealed only three from warriors who were said to have been at the Battle.[26] One came from the National Park Service; the other two from soldiers who interviewed warriors who had been at the Battle and who themselves had been on the Battlefield.[27]

One such map came from Oscar Long, U.S. Army. In the Spring of 1878, Long went to the Little Bighorn Battlefield with three warriors who had fought there. He made a map and an official report based on information shared by those warriors, Hump, a Lakota warrior, and White Bull and Brave Wolf, both Cheyenne.

The report stated, "This Santee (Cut Heads) shot Custer & captured his bald face sorrel horse." It should be noted here that Long put Cut Heads specifically in the report and in parenthesis.[28]

There is one map from Doug War Eagle, Minnikojou Lakota researcher, currently in this writer's possession.[29]

There are two interesting accounts of the story of Gray Earth Track. The first account can be found in the A.B. Welch Dakota Papers, www.welchdakotapapers.com. Welch was an officer in the U.S. Army and served in World War I. After the War, he settled in Mandan, North Dakota, and made it his life's work to interview aged Native American warriors about not only the Battle of the Little Bighorn but other aspects of days long ago on the American Plains.

Welch regularly conversed and exchanged history with Frank Zahn, a local newspaperman, who claimed his father was married to a Native American woman and served as an interpreter for writers and historians coming to the Standing Rock Reservation and surrounding area to interview Native American people.

In 1926, Frank Zahn told Welch he had interviewed a Santee Dakota woman by the name of Mrs. Big Shoulder.

She told Zahn her father was the man who killed Custer. Mrs. Big Shoulder said her father's name is Oyehota, which Zahn translated as Gray Track. She said that her father was Santee Dakota and he came from Wooded Mountain Country, which is now a Dakota Reserve in Canada called Wood Mountain.

She told Zahn she thought her father was related to Inkpaduta. She stated her father came back with a sorrel horse and saddle. She (or Zahn) said the horse and or saddle were identified as belonging to General Custer. In the battle, Gray Track was said to have shot twice at a man wearing buckskin coat and who had a white handed revolver. Gray Track thought that he killed this man.[30] This story has some interesting similarities to the story from Ozzie McKay.

In April of 1929, Frank Zahn, had some of his articles published in an unknown North Dakota newspaper. The following is attributed to him.

"Grey Earth Track (Oye-maka-san) Sioux Indian of Devil's Lake reservation, North Dakota, had the horse (Vic) also field-glasses and watch belonging to Custer. Oye-maka-san does not claim to have killed the man who rode Vic."[31]

In 1936, Frank Zahn interviewed Little Voice, son of the Hunkpapa band chief Crawler. In this interview, Little Voice said, "I heard [that a] Santee [named] Gray Earth Track killed Custer."[32]

In the subsequent footnote to this story, Good Voiced Dog, a Hunkpapa Lakota man, said Gray Earth Track captured a sorrel with white fetlocks and a blaze in the face, along with a military saddle, bridle, and other equipment, including two white-handled pistols. He finished that Gray Earth Track also possessed a watch and papers he had taken from the body of a soldier wearing a fringed buckskin jacket.[33] Again, another story with similarities to the story from Ozzie McKay.

In summary: Santee Dakota, Sisitunwan, Yankton and Yanktonai

Oral history presented to us told of a Santee Dakota presence at the Battle of the Little Bighorn. What is in the historical record to this point is minimal. Nonetheless, the information shared to us during our investigation is interesting.

We were told that Santee Dakota warriors possibly trained by British forces came to the Little Bighorn. These warriors would have been supplied with weapons and ammunition from the British as well.

Did these warriors fight as a unified force, and where did other Santee Dakota warriors fight during the Battle? At this time, answers to these questions are not known. One oral account did say Santee Dakota fought in the Valley Fight against the Reno Battalion.

Were these Santee Dakota warrior-soldiers simply at the Little Bighorn for trading and ceremonies and then got caught up in the Battle? It would stand to reason they would welcome a chance to fight the U.S. Army, after all that had been done to their people before, during and after the U.S.-Dakota War of 1862. One has to wonder, as well, about the significance of the three accounts of these warriors being buried together years after the Battle.

We have presented the names of Santee Dakota warriors shared with us. It is our hope that, upon publication, others with information regarding these warriors will come.

A clearer picture of Inkpaduta and his fighting prowess has been told. Is he connected to the Santee Dakota warrior-soldiers, who are said to have come down from Canada and taken part in the Battle? That has yet to be determined.

Oral stories put Santee Dakota, Sisitunwan, Yankton and Yanktonai people at Fort Peck and in the surrounding area following the U.S.-Dakota War of 1862. Oral history states that some did come to the Battle of the Little Bighorn. So far, only three such sources were found. One from Thunder Bear, a Yanktonai warrior, one from the account from Dr. Charles Eastman, and the three collected by David Humphreys Miller.[34] Seven Native American historians shared with me information seldom talked of when it comes to Santee Dakota, Yanktonai, Yankton, Sisitunwan and Cut Head People not only coming from the Fort Peck area to the Little Bighorn, but from Saskatchewan,

Manitoba, and from what is the current state of South Dakota, as well.[35]

The name of Elk Head, the Sacred Pipe Keeper and Bundle Keeper of the Lakota, has now been mentioned, along with the names of Two Bears and Big Head. All three are said to eventually end up at the Battle of the Little Bighorn. While the stories of Two Bears and Big Head certainly deserve mentioning, students and researchers of the Battle should pay close attention to the story of Elk Head. Elk Head and his role at the Battle has not been told. Not only does his story merit mention, Elk Head's story has many parts to it. As we shall learn, Elk Head's story not only involves Lakota people, but Cheyenne and Arapaho as well.

Once alerted to the story of Elk Head, we attempted to find him in the historical record. Our research produced five accounts mentioning this holy man entrusted with the two most sacred items of the Lakota People, the Sacred White Buffalo Calf Pipe and the Sacred Calf Pipe Bundle, as having had been at the Little Bighorn. The earliest mention comes from Dr. Charles Eastman in 1900.[36]

As for evidence regarding Ozzie McKay's family story that Gray Earth Track was the warrior who killed General Custer at the Battle of the Little Bighorn, there are three interesting accounts that say a Santee Dakota did kill General Custer. All include elements similar to what Ozzie McKay related.

We are eternally grateful for Ozzie McKay, Iris O'Watch, Tommy Christian, Ken Shields, Jalen Atchico, Calvin Bear First, Tom Shawl, Mike Turcotte, Mitchell BigHunter, Dianne Desrosiers, Vine Marks, Doug War Eagle, Akisa Peters-Manning, Inkpa Mani, Cody Seaboy, Bob Saindon, Louis Garcia, Sara Childers and James Ritchie. All believed in us and our project.

Notes

1. Personal communications with Victor Douville-Sicangu Lakota Tribal Historian, Ozzie McKay - Santee Dakota, Jim Red Eagle-Nakota Lakota, Peter Gibbs-Tribal Historian Sicangu Lakota, Mitchell BigHunter-

Santee Dakota, Ben Rhodd-Potawatomi, James Ritchie and Inkpa Mani. See Powers 1977: 17-23; Walker 1982: 14-18; Gibbon 2003: 2-81; Riggs 2004: 1-2, 156-160; Waggoner 2013: 250, 262; Howard 2014: 12.

2. Ibid.

3. Personal communications with Victor Douville-Sicangu Lakota Tribal Historian, Ozzie McKay - Santee Dakota, Harold Salway-Oglala Lakota, Ben Rhodd-Potawatomi, Jim Red Eagle - Nakota/Lakota, Mitchell BigHunter-Santee Dakota, Inkpa Mani, Peter Gibbs-Tribal Historian Sicangu Lakota, Joanne Pompana, Arvol and Paula Looking Horse. See LaPointe 1976: 13-20, 29-34, 51-54, 79-84: Walker 1982: 18; Riggs 2004: 178; Waggoner 2013: 250-252, 262-263; and Goodman 2017: *Lakota Star Knowledge.*

4. Personal communications with Ben Rhodd-Potawatomie, Victor Douville-Sicangu Lakota Tribal Historian, Peter Gibbs-Tribal Historian Sicangu Lakota, Vine Marks-Sisitunwan elder and historian, Akisa Peters Manning-Sisitunwan historian, Calvin Bear First - Yanktonai/Sisitunwan, Dianne Desrosiers-Sisitunwan THPO. For Siouan migrations stories see Mooney 1894; Also see Waggoner 2013: 22-62; 250-252, 262-263.Gibbon 2003: 2-81; Riggs 2004: 168-194; Howard 2014: 31-32. For Sisitunwan and Wahpeton history related to their separate identity from Santee Dakota, see Albers and DeMallie in Handbook Of the North American Indian, 2001 Vol 13, part 2 of 2: 761-820.

5. Ibid. See Gibbon 2003: 23-46.

6. Gibbon 2003: 36-37. Gibbon suggests Nakota (Assiniboine) broke away from Dakota people AD 1300 and that they, 'share more lexical items with Lakota, Yankton and Yanktonai than with Dakota. See Riggs 2004: 160, 180, Riggs states Nakota (Assiniboine) came off the Yanktonai, Specifically, the Pine Shooters Clan. Powers 1977: 23, says Nakoda who are said to be from the Nakota (Assiniboine), came off the Yanktonai; Howard 2013: 3, says Nakota (Assiniboine) and Stoney

from Yanktonai; Warren 2009: 91-92, says Nakota (Assiniboine) came of Yankton.

7. For notes on the societies of the Dakota, see Ella Deloria's notes from her field work *The Dakota and Lakota people at the www.Dakotaindianfoundation.net, Dakota Ethnography,* Box 3, No. 16 and 17; For a snapshot of Santee Dakota history in Canada, see McCrady 1998: 2, 10-31; For Nakoda history see Long 2004: 3. In regards to the Cheyenne and Dakota connection, see Moore 1987, Jablow 1994 and Gibbon 2003, as good references to start with. Personal communications with Victor Douville-Sicangu Lakota Tribal Historian, Rod Alexis - Stoney Nakoda, Vine Marks - Sisitunwan, Akisa Peters - Sisitunwan, Dianne Desrosiers - Sisitunwan THPO.

8. Personal communications with Calvin Bear First-Yanktonai/Sisitunwan. See Meyer 1968:13; McCrady 1998; Howard 2014: 21-29; Gibbon 2003: 108-111.

9. Personal communications with Inkpa Mani, Calvin Bear First-Yanktonai/Santee Dakota, Ozzie McKay-Santee Dakota, Jim Whitted-Sisitunwan and James Ritchie. See Waggoner 2013: 302-303; https: //www.history.nd.gov/historicsites/whitestone/ ; https: //killdeer.com/place-of-interest/killdeer-mountain-battlefield-site/.

10. Personal communication with Sara Childers and Calvin Bear First-Yanktonai/Sisitunwan.

11. Personal communications with Ozzie McKay-Santee Dakota. See Hardorff 2005: 183-184.

12. Personal communications with Mitchell BigHunter-Santee Dakota. See Eastman 1916: *Indian Heroes and Great Chieftains.*

13. Personal communications with Ozzie McKay-Santee Dakota.

14. Personal communications with Mitchell

BigHunter-Santee Dakota, Terry Was'te s'te-Santee Dakota and Dianne Desrosiers-Sisitunwan Dakota.

15. Personal communications with James Ritchie, Mitchell BigHunter-Santee Dakota and Terry Was'te s'te-Santee Dakota. James Ritchie and Mitchell BigHunter have both conducted extensive investigations into the Dakota warriors trained as soldiers. Both have extensive amounts of literature and documents to support this hypothesis. See McCrady 1998: 2-118; and Ritchie 2001.

16. Ibid. Also, see Howard 2014: 32.

17. Personal communications with Luis Garcia, Larus Longie-Chippewa Cree, James Ritchie, Ozzie McKay-Santee Dakota and Mitchell BigHunter-Santee Dakota. See McCrady 1998: 62-100; Ritchie 2001.

18. Personal communications with Sara Childers, Bob Saindon, Tom Shawl-Nakoda, Tommy Christian-Nakota/Dakota/Lakota, Calvin Bear First-Yanktonai/Sisitunwan, Ken Shields - Yankton/Lakota, Jalen Atchico-Yanktonai/Nakota and Mike Turcotte-Nakoda. See Donovan 2008:148, 187- 188. See McCrady 1998: 2-100; See Howard 2014: 35-37.

19. Ibid. Personal communications with Calvin Bear First-Yanktonai/Sisitunwan.

20. Personal communications with Vine Marks-Sisitunwan Dakota.

21. Personal communications with Cody Seaboy-Wahpekute Dakota.

22. Personal communications with Doug War Eagle-Minnikojou Lakota and Akisa Peters Manning-Sisitunwan Dakota.

23. For accounts putting Santee Dakota people at the Battle of the Little Bighorn consult the following: Little Bighorn Battlefield Handbook 1994, No 132; see

Western National Parks Association LBH National Monument 2005; Donahue 2009; See Donovan 2008: 148, 187-188; Donovan cited Marquis, *Wooden Leg,* 182; Vestal 1965: 154; Hardorff 1991: 38, 63, 78; Utley 1993: 133; Miller 1957: 48; In Neihardt 1972: 95, 116; Hammer 1976: 206, 209; Harper 2014: 240, 246, [Ebook] Appendices 3.79. It should be noted here that Harper cited no written sources in regards to the Santee Dakota narrative he put forth. He only cited the oral history given to him from the Miniconjou Lakota people from The Cheyenne River Reservation. In Eastman 1900: "*The Story of the Little Bighorn*"; Miller, "*Echoes on the Little Bighorn*"; Campbell, Box 105, Notebook 5 and p.9.

24. Individual accounts of Dakota at the Little Bighorn. In Welch: See John Grass, and White Cow Walking; In Hardorff 1991: See He Dog 78 and Iron Hawk 63; In Hammer 1976: See He Dog 206 and Flying By 209; In Marquis 1962: See *Wooden Leg* 208; In Eastman 1900: "*The Story of the Little Bighorn*"; In Greene 1994: See Red Horse 33 and Young Two Moon 72; For accounts of Yankton, Yanktonai and Santee Dakota, consult the following: For the Gall accounts see Graham 1953: 87-92; Grinnell 1955: 356: Utley 1993:133; Harper 2014: [Ebook] Appendix 3.79; In Neihardt 1972: See Black Elk 95, 114 and Standing Bear 115-116; In Hardorff 2005: See Iron Thunder 62, Thunder Bear 87 and Gray Whirlwind 131-132; In Miller, "*Echoes of the Little Bighorn,*" see Iron Hail; For maps consult Donahue 2009: See Hardy Horse 239; Red Hawk 169, 173; On Cartwright # 2, 353; On Clark map, 98, 102, 173; On Maguire Maps, 53; In Welch, see John Grass map, 24.

25. Personal communications with Mitchell BigHunter-Santee Dakota, Ozzie McKay - Santee Dakota, Terry Was'te s'te-Santee Dakota and James Ritchie.

26. For the Standing Bear map, see the John G. Neihardt Collection, State Historical Society of Missouri-Columbia, Missouri. See *Black Elk Speaks,* Neihardt 1972: 109, 114, 116-117, for the Black Elk

and Standing Bear accounts. See Donahue 2009: For the Hardy Horse 238-240 and Red Hawk 168-174 maps and accounts.

27. Little Bighorn National Monument Handbook 1994, No. 132, pp. 64-65. See Donahue 2009: For the Maguire map # 7 and its history, see 50-53, the Clark map 98, 102-103 and the Long map 105-112.

28. See Donahue 2009: For the Long map 105-112.

29. Doug War Eagle, a Minnikojou Lakota historian, provided me with a map he annotated on the Battle of the Little Bighorn. This map is based on Doug's years of research and from the oral history shared to him at Cheyenne River Reservation, South Dakota.

30. Welch 2017: 50.

31. Ibid. 61-62. Notice in this article Zahn or the newspaper spelled Gray Earth Track's name as Grey, not Gray.

32. Hardorff 2005: 183-184.

33. Ibid.

34. For the accounts given of Santee Dakota, Yanktonai people and others coming to the Little Bighorn from Fort Peck in Montana, see Hardorff 2005: 87-92; Eastman 1900: 354; Also see McCrady 1998: 63-153; Saindon 2009: 13-14; The David Humphreys Miller collection, "Faces of the Little Bighorn," see https: //davidhumphreysmiller.org/our-collection/.

35. Personal communications with Calvin Bear First-Yanktonai/ Dakota, Tom Shawl- Nakoda, Rod Alexis-Stoney Nakoda, Mike Turcotte-Nakoda, Ken Shields-Yankton/ Lakota, Tommy Christian-Nakota/Dakota/Lakota, Jalen Atchico-Yanktonai/ Nakota, Vine Marks- Sisitunwan Dakota, Akisa Peters Manning-Sisitunwan Dakota, Doug War Eagle-Minnikojou Lakota and Bob Saindon-independent

researcher.

36. For information regarding Elk Head at the Little Bighorn, see Eastman 1900: 354; Hardorff 1997:134; Harper 2014: [Ebook] Appendices 3.79; Humphreys Miller 1985: 57-60, 222; Kammen, Lefthand and Marshall 1992: 47.

4
The Arapaho and a Sicangu Lakota Story

The information that led us to our research on the Arapaho for this chapter comes from the following people: Devin Oldman-Arapaho, Bill Goggles-Arapaho, Cletus Yellow Plume-Arapaho, Henry Goggles Jr.-Arapaho, Martin Blackburn-Arapaho, Fred Mosqueda-Arapaho, Elise Sage-Arapaho, Chester Whiteman-Cheyenne, Gilbert Whitedirt-Cheyenne, Michael Black Wolf-Gros Ventre, Arvol Looking Horse, Garvard Good Plume Jr.-Oglala Lakota, Basil BraveHeart-Oglala Lakota, Rick Two Dogs-Oglala Lakota, Victor Douville-Sicangu Lakota Tribal Historian, Sam High Crane-Sicangu Lakota, Ronnie Cutt-Sicangu Lakota, Phil Two Eagle-Sicangu Lakota, Henry Quick Bear-Sicangu Lakota, Peter Gibbs-Tribal Historian Sicangu Lakota and Jason Pitsch.

When it comes to the Battle of the Little Bighorn, Algonquian speakers are usually not the first tribes thought of as having had played an important part.

The Arapaho people are Algonquian speakers. Arapaho tradition states there were five major divisions among the tribe at one time, each with its own dialect. The first were the Gros Ventre, and they will be the focus of chapter five. The last four divisions consolidated into the Arapaho. It should be noted here that the fourth division is said to resembled the Blackfeet tribe linguistically (see chapter 6 regarding the Blackfeet Tribe), while the fifth had some similarity in dialect to the Cheyenne tribe.[1]

Throughout the countless books and investigations regarding The Battle of the Little Bighorn, no tribe's participation has been more neglected than the Arapaho. When one considers what the Arapaho people had been through -- deadly attacks perpetrated on them by the U.S. Government at Sand Creek in 1864, the Connor's

Massacre and at the Washita in 1868, where their warriors joined the fighting -- it would stand to reason Arapaho people would find their way to the Little Bighorn.

As the writer of these incredible and long-kept pieces of history, I again ask the reader to keep an open mind. Not because I fear you won't believe the stories. Rather, I fear the fact these stories have never been told before and so will not be considered for the historical record will keep researchers, historians and others from learning and understanding. Furthermore, if I had not been lucky enough to not only meet and be taken care of by Cheyenne, Cree, Arapaho, Gros Ventre, Chippewa Cree and Blackfeet people, I doubt this book would include the components it does. I write this to let the reader know that our research has been richly influenced by Algonquin people in many ways. If these trails had not be presented to us, then much of the untold story of what happened that day on the Little Bighorn would still remain a mystery.

The narrative that follows regarding the Arapaho and their participation at the Battle of the Little Bighorn has never before been told from their people and put in written form until now. It warrants attention.

~

The first trail Donovan and myself set on to follow the Arapaho story at the Little Bighorn came from four Lakota men. They were Arvol Looking Horse, Garvard Good Plume Jr., Basil BraveHeart and Rick Two Dogs. All four of these men had relatives at the Battle of the Little Bighorn.

Arvol Looking Horse, whose relative Looking Horse rode with the great Lakota war chief Crazy Horse at the Little Bighorn, was the first person to share information concerning the Arapaho. Arvol related that there was a much bigger story regarding the Arapaho people and their involvement at the Battle.

Arvol, being Keeper of The Sacred White Buffalo Calf Pipe and The Sacred Calf Pipe Bundle of the Lakota, had had many experiences with Arapaho people and other tribes in countless ceremonies and gatherings where oral stories were shared. He remembered a story that stated a group of Arapaho had been camped on the Little Bighorn River at the time of the Battle. These Arapaho people were there with some of their sacred medicine bundles. To which Arvol added that the Lakota people, too, had many of their bundles at the Little Bighorn.

Arvol said, "These bundles were for special ceremonies and were of great importance and needed special care. For these bundles were to be revered as if they were spirits, as within the bundles were great powers."[2]

Garvard Good Plume Jr

The late Garvard Good Plume Jr., whose relatives, Little Killer and White Cow Boy, both fought at the Battle of the Little Bighorn, shared a history he had been told regarding Arapaho people who were at the Little Bighorn. Garvard said the Arapaho had a bigger contingent at the Little Bighorn than is known. He went on to add that one group of Arapaho had come from Fort Robinson in Nebraska.

He said, "They were powerful people." I asked Garvard to clarify what he meant by "powerful people?" Garvard would only say that these people could do things that might today be called, "super natural, but that were not uncommon to some, many years ago."

Garvard went on to state that the Lakota had many sacred bundles there at the Little Bighorn as well. He said that these bundles were key to the keeping of their "medicine lines." Garvard added that it was paramount to protect these bundles at all costs. "If the bundles were destroyed, so too would be the people."[3]

Garvard Good Plume Jr., made his journey to the camp on the other side on September 9, 2021.

Basil BraveHeart and Rick Two Dogs added two interesting pieces to the Arapaho narrative. Basil's relative, Brave Heart, was a warrior at the Little Bighorn, while Rick's great-grandfather, American Horse, was a war chief at the time of the Battle. Rick and Basil both had been told of a bigger Arapaho presence than is commonly accepted.[4]

Rick had been told that one Arapaho warrior had been killed at the Battle. Rick had been told this history by his grandfather, Thomas American Horse, son of American Horse, who was also at the Little Bighorn. Rick had been told that some Arapaho were camped by Lakota people who belonged to the American Horse camp of Oglala people. It was from this group of Arapaho that this warrior had come.[5]

~

Donovan Taylor now went to work. This Cheyenne historian reached out to his Arapaho contacts in hopes we might be able to find more to this story that Arvol, Garvard, Basil and Rick had shared.

Bill Goggles

Bill Goggles was the first person to visit with us in this regard. Bill's relative, Iron Eyes, was an Arapaho warrior at the Battle of the Little Bighorn. Iron Eyes is not one of the five Arapaho warriors always said to be the only Arapaho warriors who were at the Battle.

Bill confirmed the story Arvol and Garvard had told, and he added some more new information to it. Bill informed us that these Arapaho people had possibly been camped at the southern end, and to the east of the main encampment of the Native Peoples coalition on the Little Bighorn River on June 24th, 1876. He had heard about the Arapaho medicine bundles being there, and much more. From all of the oral history he had been told over the years from Arapaho people, Bill believed that there had been close to 100 Arapaho warriors fighting that day at the Little Bighorn, many belonging to their Dog Man military society.

He was not sure if the Arapaho Flat Pipe, their most sacred covenant, was at the Little Bighorn or not. Bill

Black Coal - Arapaho chief

added that if the Flat Pipe was there, it would be there with the Northern Arapaho leader, Black Coal.[6]

~

I was at the ceremonies to commemorate the Battle of the Little Bighorn in June of 2019. There, I was fortunate to hear a talk given by Devin Oldman, a young Arapaho man who was the Tribal Historic Preservation Officer for the Northern Arapaho Tribe at the time. After hearing Devin talk, I made it a priority to visit him regarding the Battle. With the help of Bill Goggles, I was again fortunate enough to be able to hear what this historian could add to the Arapaho narrative.

Devin Oldman is a descendant of Little Ant, an Arapaho warrior who fought at the Battle of the Little Bighorn. Little Ant is another Arapaho not listed as one of the five mentioned Arapaho warriors said to be the only Arapaho at the Battle.

Devin knew exactly what Arvol Looking Horse and Garvard Good Plume's story of the Arapaho at the Little Bighorn referred to. Devin called these people Arapaho holy people. He added that the standard story of Arapaho participation at the Little Bighorn has always been said to be limited to five or six warriors, which was true. However, this handful of warriors were part of a larger group of Arapaho people who had come to the Little Bighorn from Fort Robinson in Nebraska. These Arapaho warriors usually put on the historical record would have been young warriors at this time. They were the protectors to this group, which included the people Devin called Arapaho holy people.[7]

Devin continued to add more significant pieces to the Arapaho narrative. First, he said there were, indeed, Arapaho Dog Soldiers at the Battle, and provided us with some of their names.

Second, Devin expanded on the story that Garvard Good Plume Jr. had shared regarding "powerful" Arapaho people. Devin said, "These Arapaho holy people could heal wounded people and horses who are wounded." He added, "These people could harness the weather and call on the winged and other creatures for help in times of need. And, to do so, these people would have their bundles with them."

Powder Face - Arapaho war chief

Third, Devin told of two Arapaho war chiefs, Sharp Nose and Powder Face, as having had been in the encampment at the Little Bighorn with their followers. He added that Sharp Nose and his band had come from the area around present-day Casper, Wyoming. Devin told me that Sharp Nose was the leader of this Arapaho band's Dog Soldier warrior society. He had also been told that Powder Face and some other Arapaho who fought against the Seventh Cavalry at the Washita in 1868 later fought at the Battle of the Little Bighorn.[8]

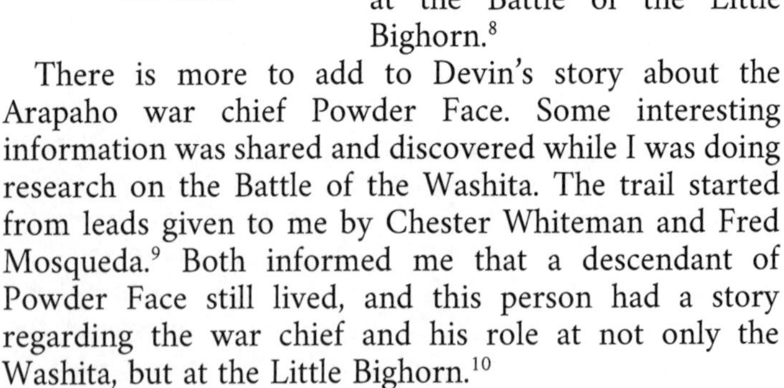

There is more to add to Devin's story about the Arapaho war chief Powder Face. Some interesting information was shared and discovered while I was doing research on the Battle of the Washita. The trail started from leads given to me by Chester Whiteman and Fred Mosqueda.[9] Both informed me that a descendant of Powder Face still lived, and this person had a story regarding the war chief and his role at not only the Washita, but at the Little Bighorn.[10]

~

The Battle of the Washita occurred in 1868 and involved the U.S. Seventh Cavalry. Led by General

George Custer, the Seventh attacked a village of Cheyenne people in current day southwest Oklahoma. The unsuspecting Cheyenne were massacred that morning.

It should be noted that Custer had not had ample opportunity to properly scout the entire area before he launched the attack. Had he been able to so, he would have found that two miles further on down the Washita River lay a large Arapaho camp, with Kiowa people close. More Cheyenne camps were down-river and close, as were Arapaho camps, some camps of Apache and Comanches.[11]

Cheyenne people tried to escape the carnage. They made desperate dashes towards the Arapaho and Kiowa camps. Many were cut down by mounted troopers. One group did manage to make it out and go undetected for some ways before being spotted and pursued. One can only imagine what these Cheyenne people felt, as they knew their very lives were at stake if caught.

The squad of mounted U.S. Seventh Cavalry troopers giving chase were led by Major Joel Elliott. As the Cheyenne escapees were about to be overtaken, help arrived in the form of Arapaho and Kiowa warriors. These warriors burst onto the scene in heroic fashion and quickly went about destroying the pursuing troopers, with Major Elliott. The rescued Cheyenne people told of the destruction happening up-river.

Without hesitation, these warriors, now joined by others, moved to surround the Cheyenne camp in the hope of engaging Custer and his troops.[12]

As General Custer and his force were busy with taking captives and destroying the Cheyenne horse herd, their scouts reported the stark magnitude of the danger they were now in. Outnumbered,[13] Custer put his captives at the front and made as if to move down the river to attack the other camps. His bold strategy, which was a ploy to get the warriors to back off, worked to perfection. The Seventh then halted and abruptly turned around, and before the warriors understood, Custer had gotten out and with over 50 captives.[14]

In an interview with Elise Sage, I was told some very interesting history of her relative, Powder Face. Elise stated Powder Face had been one of the Arapaho warriors who had destroyed the Seventh Cavalry troopers under Major Elliott. She had been told Powder Face eventually made his way north and fought at the Little Bighorn, and with him were other Arapaho who had fought at the Washita.[15]

~

Two Arapaho men, Cletus Yellow Plume and Martin Blackburn, gave Donovan and myself additional information substantiating the Arapaho Holy People story.

Cletus Yellow Plume is a descendant of three Arapaho warriors who fought at the Battle of the Little Bighorn. They are Black Coal, Little Raven, and Waterman. Cletus stated he had been told the Arapaho Flat Pipe was at the Little Bighorn with Black Coal. Only Waterman is said to be one of the five Arapaho warriors to take part in the Battle.[16]

Martin Blackburn is a descendant of Last Bear, another Arapaho warrior not on the list of Arapaho who fought at the Little Bighorn. Both Cletus and Martin said they had heard the stories of Sharp Nose and Arapaho Dog Soldiers being at the Little Bighorn. Cletus corroborated the story of the Arapaho warriors with Powder Face, who had fought at the Washita and then at the Little Bighorn. Both men and Arapaho tribal member Henry Goggles Jr., another descendant of Iron Eyes, gave more names to add to the Arapaho warriors list of their ranks at the Battle of the Little Bighorn. Henry stated that Iron Eyes was a Dog Soldier and that the Arapaho Dog Soldiers were at the Little Bighorn.[17]

The last oral story to introduce here comes from Cheyenne historian Gilbert Whitedirt. This account sheds light on the Arapaho and Cheyenne involvement regarding the Valley Fight with the Reno Battalion.

Gilbert told Donovan Taylor and myself that, "The Arapaho and Cheyennes killed Bloody Knife." When asked, Gilbert could not specifically recall who had told him this information. He recalled only that it, "…has been known among Cheyenne People ever since the Battle."[18] Bloody Knife was an Arikara scout who rode with the Seventh Cavalry to the Little Bighorn and subsequently rode with the Reno Battalion into the Battle. He was killed in the Vally Fight, near the timber, before Major Reno led his Battalion on the retreat movement across the Little Bighorn River.[19]

See Appendix C for the names of Arapaho warriors at the Battle of the Little Bighorn.

What is in the historical record and how do these stories match up against it?

The earliest known record of Arapaho involvement at the Battle of the Little Bighorn came from Edward Maguire. He was an officer and engineer in the U.S. Army. Maguire was in the Little Bighorn campaign and mapped the Little Bighorn Battlefield and the Seventh Cavalry dead two days after the Battle. He produced a series of six maps, and admitted that he didn't cover all the terrain at the Battlefield when doing so.[20]

On the Maguire maps 3, 4, 5 and 6, Maguire noted an area to the south of the Native Peoples coalition encampment on the Little Bighorn. On maps 3 and 4, there are tipis on both sides of the Little Bighorn River. They give the indication of a small camp here. On maps 5 and 6, the majority of the tipis are gone, except for three placed in a rectangle. This area was a clearing of sorts on the West side of the Little Bighorn River. It was near the initial skirmish line and subsequent retreat route for Major Marcus Reno's command. Reno had led the Seventh Cavalry's first attack on the Native Peoples coalition encampment along the valley floor of Little Bighorn River.[21]

The information for this separate camp came to Maguire from one of his subordinates, Sergeant Becker. The Sergeant told surviving Seventh Cavalry officers of this area in July of 1876, one month after the Battle. One officer, Lieutenant Edward Godfrey, noted the information.

"He (Becker) showed me where there had been camped, or supposed, the Arapahos. It was on the three sides of a square the fourth side being filled in by the lodges of the chiefs. It was cut out of the woods and seems was not seen by anyone else and in it were the bodies of three whites."[22]

Maguire never said if he had been to this site or not. It should be noted that this spot was not on any of his previous maps. Maguire stated, "that little space that is marked there is a position where we found evidence of an old camp as of set apart from the main camp for some particular Chief."[23]

Arapaho people are mentioned on what is perhaps one of the earliest known maps on the historical record of the Battle of the Little Bighorn. Bill Goggles had told us the Arapaho were camped to the south of the main encampment. Donovan and I wondered why Maguire mentioned, "for some particular Chief." For theories as to who this might have been, the reader will recall that Garvard Good Plume Jr., stated these Arapaho were, "powerful people." While Devin Oldman had told us the Arapaho here were, "holy people."

Perhaps those who shared information with Maguire and his subordinate Becker about the Arapaho camped in this area on the Little Bighorn had their words misinterpreted or lost in translation? Or, could it be a case of not understanding the context?

We will pick up this discussion as to who and what might have been in the "old camp as of set apart from the main camp for some particular Chief" that was some distance to the south from the main encampment on the Little Bighorn, in more depth in chapters 9 and 12.

Just who were these Arapaho people and how have they remained hidden from the historical record?

I have repeatedly traveled to where the Arapaho site was said to be, looking for answers. Always, my hope is that on one of these occasions some of these questions might finally be answered.

The Gilbert Birdinground family, Crow, own the land. They are direct descendants of one of the six Crow scouts who rode with the Seventh Cavalry, White Swan. Gilbert's Great-Grandmother, Walks To The Hole, was a niece to White Swan.

Gilbert Birdinground could give no answer as to who was camped near his property that June in 1876. No family stories tell of this. He did state the family stories speak of the troopers under Major Reno retreating around and through his property.

Gilbert added, "There was a story I remember being told, but as to who told it, I can't recall. It may have been my father. It was said there was a camp or just horses grazing somewhere near here. It was said to have been seen by Custer's scouts from Reno Creek."

That is all Gilbert could add to the story.[24]

One last note on the area where the Maguire maps and oral history put the Arapaho. Local rancher Jason Pitsch is a student and avid researcher concerning the Battle of the Little Bighorn. He has been gracious with his time over the last year visiting with me regarding this episode in the battle and the possible locations of the Arapaho camps. Pitsch has spent his life exploring the entire river bottom area of the Battlefield and where the Native Peoples coalition encampment stood. He has found Battle artifacts all through these areas.

Pitsch has not found evidence that a camp stood where Maguire put the Arapaho. His conclusion is that the area Maguire had as a possible Arapaho camp on his maps 5 and 6 was in fact on the west side of the Little Bighorn River.

Just across the river, on the east side and a little to the south of the Arapaho camp, he found evidence of another Native People's campsite.[25] This would be the camp that Oscar Long, United States Army, called The Spotted Tail Agency Indians. Long was on the Battlefield in 1878 with Cheyenne and Lakota veterans of the Battle. He made an official report and a sketch map.[26]

We continued to look at the Crow scouts as a possible source for Maguire and Becker. There is nothing in the historical record or countless interviews from the scouts that tell of any Arapaho participation. Nor is there any mention of Arapaho from any of the Arikara, who served as scouts for the U.S. Seventh Cavalry during the Little Bighorn Campaign.[27]

~

The investigation into the Arapaho at the Little Bighorn continued. While looking for clues to the Arapaho story, I found some surprising and interesting pieces from the late Canadian researcher Gordon Harper.

Gordon Harper had lived for a time on the Northern Cheyenne Reservation and had made several trips to the Little Bighorn Battlefield with Cheyenne people. Harper was putting together his life's work, almost 50 years of studying the Battle, into a book when he passed away unexpectedly in 2009. The book was finished in 2014 by some of Harper's associates.[28]

In postings from Harper on the Little Bighorn Association Proboards.com concerning the Battle of the Little Bighorn, he stated (date unknown):

"Actually, there were some lodges on the right bank, within one of the River bends. There might have been another small camp from the Spotted Tail Agency. This is mentioned by many as a dead cert, probably because it appears on the McElfresh map."

"The other one was indeed on the flats down river, just downstream from where the Rees snagged the horses [which probably belonged to this camp], and under Weir Point, depending upon your viewpoint. It is rather hard to say who these people were, with any degree of certainty, but the fact that they were there is beyond doubt. There are some indications there were more Arapahos present that the four usually mentioned."

There is one more intriguing post from Harper to add: Again, I couldn't find the exact date of this post.

"The lodges in the bend were also erected within a timbered setting, which had been used in previous years and had clearings in it. This was a special spot reserved for some special people who did special things in a special way."

Harper asserts that there were lodges, possibly Sicangu people, which are the Lakota band which would be from the Spotted Tail Agency, on the right or east side of the Little Bighorn River. He mentioned the McElfresh Map, which does have the Spotted Tail Indians noted on it and in the above-mentioned location.[29]

Next, in the second post he states there was another group of lodges downstream, which is in the direction of north. He doesn't clarify which side of the river, but does put them under Weir Point. This area is right about where Maguire had tipis on maps 3 and 4. He then noted the Arapaho had their camp on the Maguire maps 5 and 6.[30]

In his third post, he states the lodges were erected within a timbered setting and had clearings in it. This sounds the same as what Becker had told Godfrey.[31] And, just to be fair here, Harper didn't source nor cite where he obtained the stories or sources on the Arapaho or Sicangu Lakota. The standard number of five Arapaho warriors being there is noted in his appendices. There is nothing in it on the Sicangu Lakota. His book contains nothing on either tribe or band. There are no sources listed as cited on the McElfresh Map.[32]

~

There is more to add to the story of the Arapaho and their camp.

The first one comes from the Rising Sun family (Cheyenne).

Their account states, "The Arapaho camp far to the south was plagued by some now unknown disease that kept them from fully participating in the fighting."[33]

The second is from the Hunkpapa Lakota warrior Turning Hawk, who first stated that, "Cheyennes ran Reno from the water." He labeled this with a 7 on a map drawn by another Lakota warrior, One Bull. Turning Hawk went on to say that, "Arapahoes and Cheyennes at 7, and Turning Hawk [was] there."[34]

We found four accounts of Arapaho people telling of their involvement at the Battle of the Little Bighorn. All are from Arapaho warriors who fought there. Three of the accounts come from Arapaho warriors in the historical record as having been at the Little Bighorn. They are Waterman, Well-Knowing One and Lefthand.[35] Two of the three warrior's accounts confirm the story of them coming from Fort Robinson.[36]

The fourth Arapaho account is the most interesting. It is from an Arapaho named Plenty Bear.[37] In it, Plenty Bear said, "The Sioux were great friends of the Arapahos so about twenty-five of the young Arapahos had gone to Sitting Bull's camp on the Greasy Grass. They had quietly left the Arapahos who were down on the Platte around Fort Robinson at that time. They joined the Sioux just to be in one more good fight against the white man." Plenty Bear was with this group as well.[38]

To add to the Plenty Bear story, there is this interesting material from Oscar Long. As stated earlier, Long was an engineering officer in the U.S. Army. He put together an official report and sketch map from interviewing one Lakota warrior, Hump, and two Cheyenne warriors, White Bull and Brave Wolf, in 1878.[39] The Long map does not specifically name or put Arapaho people on it, but in his official report, he does.

"About twenty Arapahos joined Sitting Bull, soon after General Crook's fight with the Indians, and came very near being killed, for the Indians thought they were spies and had been scouting for the soldiers."[40]

In both the Long sketch map and his official report, Long noted and identified a group of what he called, "one small tribe of disaffected Indians from the Spotted Tail Agency. This last numbered about twenty fighting men, who were encamped at the upper end of the village, on the left bank of the Little Bighorn River."

This placement is on the east side of the Little Bighorn River, opposite the side of the Native Peoples coalition encampment.[41] This camp would have been across the river and a little to the south of the location Maguire noted on maps 1,3,4,5,6.[42]

Two Strikes and Crow Dog, Sicangu Lakota war chiefs

The people noted as being from Spotted Tail Agency were indeed Sicangu Lakota, often called The Brule. The story of the Spotted Tail Agency people was told to me years ago by Sicangu elders and historians Victor Douville, the late Sam High Crane, Ronnie Cutt, Henry Quick Bear and Peter Gibbs. These historians said that a good-sized group of Sicangu people led by Two Strike, a war chief, Crow Dog, a renowned medicine man, along with noted Sicangu warriors Swift Hawk, Cloud Man, Quick Bear and Shooting Cat, had gotten to the Little Bighorn River late on the evening of June 24th, 1876. These Sicangu Lakota had captured horses from the Crow, it was told, and had been pursued by the Crow.[43] Remember, Long had one Lakota and two Cheyenne informants who had been in the encampment and in the fight on the Little Bighorn who supplied him with information.[44]

~

There are six Lakota accounts of Arapaho people in the encampment on the Little Bighorn that I found.

The first is a map by White Cow Walking. His map puts Arapaho people at the extreme western edge of the Native Peoples coalition encampment on the Little Bighorn River, June 24 of 1876.[45]

A second account comes from Lone Bear. He stated, "There were a few tepees occupied by some Arapahoes, situated between the Oglalas and Brules."[46] Lone Bear's account can be interpreted as putting Arapaho people in the same general area as did the White Cow Walking map.

The third account comes from Lights. He said, "There were some Arapahoes, [but] their tepees were scattered among the other bands and among the relatives."[47]

A fourth account is a map from White Bull. It simply says, "Cheyenne circle, containing some Arapaho."[48]

The fifth is from Iron Hail, who later in life was known as Dewey Beard and who had the distinction of being the last survivor from the Battle. He said, "Our friends and allies the Cheyenne were there in force, and with them were smaller bands of Arapaho and Gros Ventre."[49]

Lastly, the sixth account came from Gall. The famous Lakota war chief told this story at the tenth anniversary ceremony commemorating the Battle. "We had Ogalallas, Minneconjous, Brules, Teton: Uncpapa Sioux, Cheyennes, Arapahoes, and Gros Ventre."[50]

To add to the evidence of possibly more Arapaho at the Little Bighorn than the historical record states, we have presented Elise Sage's story. She told of her relative, Powder Face, an Arapaho war chief. Elise stated Powder Face was at the Washita and then ended up fighting at the Little Bighorn as well. Devin Oldman and Cletus Yellow Plume both told me that they had heard this as well.[51]

I continued to look at the historical record for pieces regarding Arapaho fighting at the Little Bighorn and at the Washita. I found two interesting pieces.

The first is from Virginia Trenholm in her book, *The Arapahos, Our People*. Trenholm wrote that seven Arapaho braves volunteered to fight with the Sioux at the Little Bighorn. They were cautiously taken in. She then stated, "According to the Southern Arapahos, these were some of their numbers who had stalked Custer since the Battle of the Washita."[52]

The second piece comes from Charles J. Brill's book, *Custer, Black Kettle, and the Fight on The Washita*. Brill interviewed survivors of the Washita for his book. One of those interviewed was Magpie, a young Cheyenne warrior who had been at the Washita. The other was Left Hand, an Arapaho. He too had been a warrior at the Washita and was with the Arapaho party that destroyed Major Elliott's unit. This is not the Left Hand always mentioned as being one of only five Arapaho warriors as having had fought at the Little Bighorn.[53]

Brill stated that after the Washita, one group of Cheyenne from Medicine Arrows' band (Brill said Medicine Arrow was the Keeper of the Cheyenne Sacred Arrows. Other accounts state the Keeper's name as Stone Forehead)[54] went north to be with their people on the northern plains. Magpie was one of the Cheyenne warriors at the Washita and then the Battle of the Little Bighorn.[55]

According to Brill, Powder Face was, indeed, in the fight at the Washita. Brill also said Powder Face was in the party who destroyed Major Elliott's unit. There was no mention by Brill of Powder Face being at the Little Bighorn.[56]

Brill also stated that one group of 100 lodges of Arapaho went to the northern plains and joined their kinsmen the Gros Ventre on the Milk River, in present-day Montana.[57] I was told by Michael Black Wolf, the Gros Ventre and Fort Belknap Indian Community Tribal Historic Preservation Officer, that Powder Face eventually settled with Gros Ventre People at Fort Belknap and became a tribal agency police officer.[58]

Lastly, there is one very, very interesting account in the historical record from Lieutenant William Philo Clark regarding the Arapaho and their medicine people's possession of what might today be called super-natural prowess.

A U.S. Army Officer, by 1877 Clark was stationed at Fort Robinson and served under General Crook. Clark was tasked with interrogating warriors and other Native People coming into the Agency to surrender. Today, Clark's role would be clearly seen as that of an intelligence officer. He became adapt at Plains sign language and became a central figure in surrender of Crazy Horse.[59]

Remember, earlier in this chapter Garvard Good Plume Jr. had said these Arapaho were "powerful." Devin Oldman had said, "These people could harness the weather and call on the winged and other creatures for help in times of need."

Clark not only caught this incredible information from Arapaho People sometime after the Battle of the Little Bighorn, he went on to state that these Arapaho so wanted him to fully understand and comprehend their prowess and capabilities they tried as best they could to make him understand what he was being told. One of Clark's informants was none other than Sharp Nose, who we have been told was not only at the Battle of the Little Bighorn, but was responsible for bringing a contingent of Arapaho there, some of which were Dog Soldiers.[60]

Clark said this regarding the Arapaho and their medicine peoples' powers:

"Some of their medicine-men had the power to produce rain or wind to assist them, and had exercised this power. They could also cause the snow to vanish and rain to come; in fact, could control all these elements through means which they tried to explain, but I could only make out that it was a kind of jugglery."[61]

In Summary: The Arapaho

According to the oral history shared by Arapaho people, the standard story that only one group of Arapaho were at the Little Bighorn is false. We have presented oral accounts from seven Arapaho people that shed light on this and that add names of warriors to the standard list. Five of the Arapaho historians put their Dog Men military society at the Little Bighorn as well.[62] There are four oral Lakota accounts that tell of the Arapaho presence at the Little Bighorn being bigger than in the standard story. These accounts add some interesting information as to who some of these Arapaho people were who had come to the Little Bighorn.[63]

In the historical record, there are two maps made by Maguire that put Arapaho people at the southern end of the Native Peoples coalition encampment on the Little Bighorn River.[64] As early as July of 1876, the U.S. Army claimed Arapaho were at the Battle. There is one account from the Cheyenne on the historical record that states the same and puts them within the same area as does the Maguire maps.[65]

There are two Lakota maps showing Arapaho camped at different locations than the Maguire maps do within the Native Peoples coalition encampment on the Little Bighorn.[66] There are six other Lakota sources that place Arapaho people in the encampment on the Little Bighorn and in the Battle.

The account from Iron Hail, also known as Dewey Beard, stands out. Notice what he says. "Our friends and allies the Cheyenne were there in force, and with them were smaller bands of Arapaho and Gros Ventre." He specifically says smaller bands of Arapaho are at the Little Bighorn. This statement supports what Arapaho People have shared with us.[67]

In his official report, Oscar Long told of the Arapaho coming from Fort Robinson, but with a bigger number than was always said.[68] In the historical record there was one other account that stated such from an Arapaho warrior who was at the Battle, Plenty Bear.[69] Note we have another source confirming what our Arapaho historians have shared with us. Their story, and the Plenty Bear story, both state that more than five Arapaho came to the Little Bighorn from Fort Robinson.

To recap, Long's report told of more Arapaho at the Little Bighorn than is on the historical record and Arapaho historians have corroborated. Second, his report and sketch map place people from the Spotted Tail Agency on the east side of the Little Bighorn River,[70] a fact confirmed by Sicangu Lakota historians. This Sicangu Lakota story of these people on the east side of the Little Bighorn is rarely mentioned.[71]

So, here you have Long in his report telling of twenty Arapahos joining Sitting Bull. Not only that, but these Arapaho were not trusted and were almost killed. It's consistent with what Plenty Bear tells. This is exactly what was told to us by four Arapaho men and four Lakota elders, who said that within this group were the Arapaho holy people, and there were more Arapaho at the Little Bighorn than the standard number of five.[72]

We could find no Cheyenne or Arapaho people who could confirm the Rising Sun family story that told of Arapaho people being sick at the time of the Battle.

The Arapaho narrative from their people and other tribes tells a much different story than the standard narrative put forth in most works on the Battle of the Little Bighorn. There is ample evidence in the historical record, when closely examined, that contradicts the standard narrative and supports what Arapaho People have told us, which is that the Arapaho had more than one contingent at the Little Bighorn and that they were at multiple locations in the Native Peoples coalition encampment on the Little Bighorn River.

We are forever grateful for Bill Goggles, Devin Oldman, Martin Blackburn, Henry Goggles Jr., Cletus Yellow Plume and Elise Sage. These gracious Arapaho People believed in us enough to share these long-kept stories of their tribe's history. The same goes for Victor Douville, Ronnie Cutt, Henry Quick Bear, Phil Two Eagle, Peter Gibbs and the late Sam High Crane, who made his journey to the camp on the other side, on November 17, 2022, for all the help with the Sicangu Lakota story.

Notes

1. See The Arapaho by Loretta Fowler, Handbook of North American Indians, 840 - 846 - Vol 13, Part 2 of 2.

2. Personal communications with Arvol Looking Horse, Keeper of The Sacred White Buffalo Calf Pipe and The Sacred Calf Pipe Bundle and Paula Looking Horse.

3. Personal communications with Garvard Good Plume Jr. - Oglala Lakota.

4. Personal communications with Basil BraveHeart - Oglala Lakota and Rick Two Dogs - Oglala Lakota.

5. Personal communications with Rick Two Dogs - Oglala Lakota.

6. Personal communications with Bill Goggles - Arapaho.

7. Personal communications with Devin Oldman - Arapaho. The standard list of Arapaho warriors at the Little Bighorn are as follows: Left Hand, Waterman, Yellow Eagle, Yellow Fly and Well - Knowing or Green Grass. See Graham 1953: 110 - 111.

8. Ibid.

9. Personal communications with Chester Whiteman - Cheyenne and Fred Mosqueda - Arapaho.

10. Personal communications with Elise Sage - Arapaho.

11. Brill 2001: 132 - 133, 172; See Greene 2004:118, 132 - 133; Hoig 1979: 134.

12. Brill 2001: 162 - 171; Greene 2004: 131 - 134; Hoig 1979: 155 - 160.

13. Brill 2001: 172 - 179; Greene 2004: 134 - 135; Hoig 1979: 134 - 144.

14. Ibid.

15. Personal communications with Elise Sage - Arapaho.

16. Personal communications with Cletus Yellowplume - Arapaho.

17. Ibid. Personal communications with Martin Blackburn - Arapaho and Henry Goggles Jr. - Arapaho.

18. Personal communications with Gilbert Whitedirt - Cheyenne.

19. For accounts of Bloody Knife's death in the Valley Fight, see Donovan 2008: 239 - 240; and Nichols 2010: 30 - 31.

20. Donahue 2009: 26 - 55.

21. Ibid: 39 - 43.

22. Ibid.

23. Ibid: 40.

24. Personal communications with Gilbert Birdinground - Crow.

25. Personal communications with Jason Pitsch. See Donahue 2009: 26 - 55 and 105 - 112; Scott 2013: 80 - 82.

26. Ibid.

27. There is a wealth of information pertaining to the Crow and Arikara scouts and their stories from the Battle of the Little Bighorn. See Hammer 1976; Graham 1953; and Libby 2008.

28. Harper, Gordon. *The Fights on the Little Horn: Unveiling the Mysteries of Custer's Last Stand.* Casemate Publishers, 2014.

29. Little Bighorn Battlefield, Montana Territory, June 1876. (American Battlefields Watercolor Map Series) Map - 1. January 1996. By Earl B. McElfresh (Author).

30. Donahue 2009: See Maps # 3 and # 4, 33 - 38. See Maps # 5 and # 6, 39 - 50.

31. Donahue 2009: 40 - 41.

32. Harper 2014: [Ebook] Appendix 3.79.

33. Viola 1999: 40.

34. Hardorff 2005: Turning Hawk interview, 143 - 146.

35. Graham 1953: 109 - 112.

36. Graham 1953: See Waterman interview, 109 and Left Hand interview 111.

37. Farlow 1998: 132.

38. Ibid.

39. Donahue 2009: 105 - 112.

40. Donahue 2009: 107.

41. Ibid.

42. Donahue 2009: See Maps # 3 and # 4, 33 - 38. See Maps # 5 and # 6, 39 - 50.

43. Personal communications with Victor Douville - Sicangu Lakota Tribal Historian, Sam High Crane - Sicangu Lakota, Ronnie Cutt - Sicangu Lakota, Henry Quick Bear - Sicangu Lakota and Peter Gibbs - Tribal Historian Sicangu Lakota.

44. Donahue 2009: 105 - 112.

45. For the White Cow Walking map see Little Big Horn Survivors Speak of Their Battle: From The Collection of Colonel A. B. Welch, 1874 - 1945. As Told to Colonel A.B.Welch, The First White Man Adopted by the Sioux Nation: 40 - 42. See www.welchdakotapapers.com.

46. For the Lone Bear account see Hardorff 1991: 152 - 162.

47. Lights account see Hardorff 1991: 163 - 174.

48. For the White Bull account see Vestal 1976: 170.

49. Miller, David Humphreys. "*Echoes of the Little Bighorn.*" *American Heritage* 22, no 4 (June 1971).

50. Graham 1953: 89.

51. Personal communications with Elise Sage - Arapaho, Devin Oldman - Arapaho and Cletus Yellowplume - Arapaho.

52. Trenholm 1970: 258.

53. Brill 2001: 5, 161 - 163, 167, 252.

54. Powell 1981: Vol 2, 1329 - 1330.

55. Brill 2001: 5, 161 - 163, 252.

56. Brill 2001: 188 - 189.

57. Brill 2001: 251.

58. Personal communications with Michael Black Wolf - Gros Ventre.

59. Powers, Thomas 2011: 31, 370 - 373; Clark 2015: 1.

60. Personal communications with Devin Oldman - Arapaho, Cletus Yellowplume - Arapaho and Martin Blackburn - Arapaho.

61. Clark 2015: 41.

62. For Arapaho oral stories, we have presented material shared to us from Bill Goggles, Devin Oldman, Elise Sage, Fred Mosqueda, Cletus Yellowplume, Martin

Blackburn and Henry Goggles Jr.

63. For Lakota oral stories pertaining to Arapaho at the Little Bighorn, we have presented information shared to us from Arvol Looking Horse, Garvard Good Plume Jr., Basil BraveHeart and Rick Two Dogs.

64. Donahue 2009: See Maps # 3 and # 4, 33 - 38. See Maps # 5 and # 6, 39 - 50.

65. This is the Rising Sun account, see Viola 1999: 40.

66. For the White Cow Walking map, see Little Big Horn Survivors Speak of Their Battle: From The Collection of Colonel A. B. Welch, 1874 - 1945. As Told to Colonel A.B.Welch, The First White Man Adopted by the Sioux Nation: 40 - 42. See www.welchdakotapapers.com. See Vestal 1976: 170.

67. For the Lone Bear account see Hardorff 1991: 152 - 162; For the Lights account see Hardorff 1991: 163 - 174; For the Gall accounts see Graham 1953: 89 - 91; For the Iron Hail(Dewey Beard) account see Miller, "*Echoes of the Little Bighorn.*" *American Heritage* 22, no 4 (June 1971). For the Turning Hawk account see Hardorff 2005: 143 - 146. For the He Dog account see Hammer 1976: 206.

68. For the Long account see Donahue 2009: 105 - 112.

69. For the Plenty Bear account see Farlow 1998: 132.

70. Donahue 2009: 105 - 112.

71. Personal communications with Victor Douville - Sicangu Lakota Tribal Historian, Sam High Crane - Sicangu Lakota, Ronnie Cutt - Sicangu Lakota, Henry Quick Bear - Sicangu Lakota and Peter Gibbs - Tribal Historian Sicangu Lakota.

72. Personal communications with Bill Goggles - Arapaho, Devin Oldman - Arapaho, Cletus Yellowplume - Arapaho, Martin Blackburn - Arapaho, Arvol Looking Horse, Garvard Good Plume Jr. - Oglala Lakota, Basil BraveHeart - Oglala Lakota and Rick Two Dogs - Oglala Lakota.

5
The Gros Ventre

Gros Ventre warriors - Photo by Edward Curtis

The information that led to this trail on the Gros Ventre comes from the following people: Michael Black Wolf - Gros Ventre, Davey Belgard - Gros Ventre, Leon Eagle Tail - Gros Ventre, Terry Brockie - Gros Ventre, Catcher Cuts the Rope - Gros Ventre, and Devin Oldman - Arapaho.

The Gros Ventre people are seldom mentioned in the historical record as having been present at the Battle of the Little Bighorn. We are proud to present two Gros Ventre stories that have never before appeared in written form.

In the second of these two accounts, the story comes directly from a man whose father was told the oral story from his blood uncle, a participant of the Battle of The Little Bighorn.

Both the Arapaho and Gros Ventre agree that they are related, but as to who broke away from whom and where, that depends on who you ask.[1] One such story states Gros Ventre warriors had discovered the Black Hills while out hunting and raiding. Despite their best efforts to get the tribe to move to this area, tribal leaders refused. The leaders didn't want to leave their present homeland, which at that time was in present-day Montana and the Canadian province of Saskatchewan.

As the story goes, the Gros Ventre leaders preferred to stay where their ancestors' bones had been scattered. Ten years later, the same group who had discovered the Black Hills made the move to break away and set out on their own. It is said that these people became the Arapaho.[2]

For their part, the Arapaho say the Gros Ventre were once one of their original five bands.[3] The Arapaho are noted in countless books, journals and other documents as being in and around the Black Hills, Wyoming, Colorado, Kansas and Nebraska. It is said they and the Gros Ventre were once in Canada, in the Canadian Provinces of Saskatchewan and Alberta.[4]

Cheyenne historian George Bent, who was instrumental in the preservation of not only Cheyenne history, but that of other plains tribes, added history of the Gros Ventre to the historical record. Bent said that in the late 1820s, some Gros Ventre and Blackfeet from Canada had come south to visit the Cheyenne and Arapaho in and around the Black Hills. Their intent was to capture horses. This journey took this Gros Ventre and Blackfeet party south of the Black Hills, clear to the Platte and Arkansas Rivers. The party was successful in capturing a good-sized herd of horses. The Gros Ventre returned to their people; the Blackfeet stayed among the Cheyenne.[5]

There is history of a Blackfeet and Gros Ventre alliance that goes back to the mid-18th century. Also, it is said the Gros Ventre re-united with the Arapaho for a time on the Southern Plains, but separated from them sometime in the early 1800s.[6]

~

Our investigation into the history of the Gros Ventre started with Michael Black Wolf, Fort Belknap Indian

Michael Black Wolf, Fort Belknap Indian Community Tribal Historic Preservation Officer

Community Tribal Historic Preservation Officer. Michael introduced me to Gros Ventre elders Davey Belgard and Leon Eagle Tail.[7]

Davey Belgard told me that there were two groups of Gros Ventre people in the encampment on the Little Bighorn in June of 1876. They had come to find The People, and to take part in the ceremonies. Davey stated these Gros Ventre people may have traveled with some Arapaho people or been camped with them at the Little Bighorn. Davey stated the history he was told by Gros Ventre elders made it clear these Gros Ventre people were there for the ceremonies, and to trade, as well. Davey added that the Gros Ventre had ties and an alliance with the Blackfeet Tribe.[8]

Davey Belgard and Michael Black Wolf, with the Fort Belknap Indian Community Tribal Historic Preservation Office, were gracious enough to provide the names of Gros Ventre warriors that, they had been told, had been at the Little Bighorn.[9]

The next Gros Ventre story came from Leon Eagle Tail regarding his relative, Red Whip. The oral history was shared with Leon sometime in the 1950's by his father, James Bird Tail, as well as from James' brother, George Bird Tail. James Bird Tail was born in 1894, his brother George in 1901. Both had been told the

Leon and Marjean Eagle Tail

story from Red Whip, their blood uncle. Red Whip fought at the Little Bighorn.

Leon Eagle Tail stated that Red Whip and another Gros Ventre man went with a group of Arapaho people to find the camps of Native American and First Nations people said to be gathered in present-day southeast Montana. These people eventually camped with the Native Peoples coalition on the Little Bighorn River. Both Red Whip and the other Gros Ventre man fought in the Battle.[10]

Red Whip (middle), Gros Ventre warrior who fought at the Little Bighorn. -- Photo courtesy of Leon Eagle Tail.

What is interesting about Leon's story is that Red Whip specifically told Leon's father, James, and his brother George, both his blood relatives, that he and other warriors they rode with that day dismounted somewhere near the mouth of a ravine. They left their horses on a flat area near this ravine and then proceeded on foot. They traversed the terrain up and through this ravine to get close to the soldiers near Last Stand Hill.[11]

Leon, who has been to the Battlefield on several occasions and did much research on the Battle himself, felt the area where Red Whip picketed his horse after dismounting was near the Battlefield landmark Deep Ravine, which was used by warriors as a route of infiltration to get close to the Seventh Cavalry Troopers who had taken up positions on and below Last Stand Hill. It was also used by warriors to get close to soldiers on Custer Ridge (Battle Ridge), which today is the National Park Service Road.[12]

Another fascinating piece about Red Whip is that this warrior was mentioned by Davey Belgard as well. Davey said Red Whip was one of the Gros Ventre warriors he had been told was at the Little Bighorn.[13]

The last piece of history that we are honored to present regarding the Gros Ventre participation at the Battle of the Little Bighorn, comes from Catcher Cuts The Rope. This account has never before appeared in print. This history was kept and told to Catcher Cuts The Rope by his grandmother, Matilda White Plume Cuts The Rope and his aunt, Cecilia Cuts The Rope DeCelles.

Eagle Child, Gros Ventre warrior.

Catcher Cuts The Rope had been told that there were approximately 50 Gros Ventre warriors who went to the Little Bighorn to participate in the summer ceremonies, one of which was Catcher Cuts The Rope's great-grandfather, Cuts The Rope. These warriors were in fact according to Catcher Cuts The Rope, the personal protectors to the Gros Ventre Sacred Pipe Keeper, Curly Head. Catcher Cuts The Rope stated that Curly Head and the Sacred Pipe of the Gros Ventre were at the Little Bighorn during the Battle and that these Gros Ventre warriors fought in the Battle. These Gros Ventre warriors who were the Sacred Pipe Keepers personal protectors, had been armed with muzzle loading rifles.

Catcher Cuts The Rope added the names of Curly Head, Red Whip, Eagle Child, Running Fisher, Horse Capture, Flies Alone/Lone Fly and Cuts The Rope, to the list of Gros Ventre warriors at the Little Bighorn. Davey Belgard, Leon Eagle Tail and Michael Black Wolf had previously put forth the names of Curly Head and Red Whip.

Finally, Catcher Cuts the Rope told us that in 1908 the famed photographer and ethnographer, Edward Curtis published photos of his travels to Montana, in which he had spent time among the Gros Ventre. Curtis called the Gros Ventre, the Atsina. According to Catcher Cuts the Rope and Michael Black Wolf, unbeknownst to Curtis, was that in several of his portraits of aged Gros Ventre warriors that he photographed near Hays, Montana, these were in fact the above mentioned Gros Ventre warriors who had fought at the Little Bighorn.[14]

See Appendix D for Gros Ventre names of warriors who were at the Battle of the Little Bighorn.

What is in the historical record and how do these stories match up against it?

We found only three accounts of Gros Ventre participation at the Battle of the Little Bighorn in the historical record. None come from Gros Ventre people, but rather from Lakota people.

The first account of Gros Ventre people at the Little Bighorn comes from David Humphreys Miller. A noted author and painter, David Humphreys Miller interviewed and painted many Native veterans of the Battle of the Little Bighorn. In his book, *Custer's Fall,* Miller stated, "camped with them [The Cheyenne] were several families of Gros Ventres."[15]

The next account regarding the Gros Ventre again comes from David Humphreys Miller. This account was related to Miller from Iron Hail, also known as Dewey Beard.

Iron Hail had the distinction of being the oldest living Battle survivor. His account mentions Gros Ventre people, and some others of note. Iron Hail said, "There were many of our eastern relatives, too - the Yankton and the Santee. And our kinsmen from the north were there - the Yanktonai and the Assiniboine. Our friends and allies the Cheyenne were there in force, and with them were smaller bands of Arapaho and Gros Ventre. It was a great village and we had great leaders."[16]

The only other accounts that mentioned Gros Ventre people at the Little Bighorn came from the noted

Hunkpapa Lakota war chief, Gall. Both are simple statements from 1886. Gall was at the ten-year anniversary ceremonies to remember the Battle. In his first account, he said, "We had Ogalallas, Minneconjous, Brules, Teton: Uncpapa Sioux, Cheyennes, Arapahoes, and Gros Ventre."[17]

In Gall's second account, he said, "Uncpapa, Minneconjou, Ogalalla, Brule, Teton, Santee and Yanktonnais Sioux, Blackfeet, Cheyennes, Arapahoes, and a few Gros Ventres."[18]

Thirteen elders and historians from other tribes and bands shared with us that they had been told of the Gros Ventre participation at the Battle of the Little Bighorn.[19]

In Summary: The Gros Ventre

There are only three accounts that tell of Gros Ventre participation at the Battle of the Little Bighorn. One simply states that Gros Ventre people were camped among the Cheyenne. The other states there were smaller bands of Gros Ventre there. At this time, no maps have been found that put Gros Ventre people on the Little Bighorn in June of 1876.

It was only because of the willingness and effort of Michael Black Wolf, Fort Belknap Indian Community Tribal Historic Preservation Officer, that I was able to meet their two elders. It is our hope that after this work is published other Gros Ventre people may come forward and add to their peoples' history at the Battle of The Little Bighorn. Our hope is that this work opens the door for future dialogue between the tribe and researchers, and that the Gros Ventre are included when studying or writing about the Battle of the Little Bighorn.

We are eternally grateful to Gros Ventre elders, Davey Belgard and Leon Eagle Tail; both for their belief in us and our project and for graciously sharing their stories of the Gros Ventre participation at the Battle of the Little Bighorn.

Notes

1. See The Arapaho by Loretta Fowler, Handbook of North American Indians 2001: 840-846, Vol 13, Part 2 of 2 and The Gros Ventre by Loretta Fowler and Regina Flannery, Handbook of North American Indians 2001: 677, Vol 13, Part 2 of 2.

2. Personal communications with Terry Brockie-Gros Ventre.

3. Trenholm 1970: 8-11; Also see Fowler 2001: 840-849; Kroeber 1908: 145.

4. Personal communications with Michael Black Wolf-Gros Ventre. See Kroeber 1908: 146; Also see Scott 1907 and Fowler 2001: 677; Trenholm 1970: 10-11.

5. Hyde 1968: 31-40.

6. Scott 1907: 547, 560; Also see Ewers 1958; Hyde 1968: 32-33; Trenholm 1970: 10-11.

7. Personal communications with Michael Black Wolf-Gros Ventre.

8. Personal communications with Davey Belgard-Gros Ventre.

9. Ibid. Personal communications with Michael Black Wolf-Gros Ventre.

10. Personal communications with Leon Eagle Tail-Gros Ventre.

11. Ibid.

12. Ibid.

13. Personal communications with Davey Belgard-Gros Ventre.

14. Personal communications with Michael Black Wolf-Gros Ventre and Catcher Cuts The Rope - Gros Ventre. Edward S. Curtis, The North American Indian, Volume V., Mandan, Arikara, Atsina.

15. Miller 1985: 47.

16. For the Iron Hail (Dewey Beard) account see Miller: "*Echoes of the Little Bighorn.*" *American Heritage* 22, no 4 (June 1971).

17. For the Gall accounts see Graham 1953: 87-92.

18. Ibid.

19. Elders and historians that had been told of the Gros Ventre as having had been at the Battle of the Little Bighorn were: Garvard Good Plume Jr.-Oglala Lakota, Harold Salway-Oglala Lakota, Rick Two Dogs-Oglala Lakota, Victor Douville-Sicangu Lakota Tribal Historian, John Eagle Shield-Hunkpapa Lakota, Devin Oldman-Arapaho, Henry Goggles Jr.-Arapaho, Donovan Taylor-Cheyenne, Wallace Bearchum-Cheyenne, Keith Spotted Wolf-Cheyenne, Chester Whiteman-Cheyenne, Tom Shawl-Nakoda and Ernie Heavy Runner-Blackfeet.

6
The Blackfeet

The trail we followed on the Blackfeet for this chapter comes from the following people: Ernie Heavy Runner - Blackfeet, Jimmy Stgoddard - Blackfeet, Devin Oldman - Arapaho, Tim Mentz - Hunkpapa Lakota, Jim Red Eagle - Nakota/Lakota, Victor Douville - Sicangu Lakota Tribal Historian, Tom Shawl - Nakoda, Kenny Shields - Yankton/Lakota, Chester Whiteman - Cheyenne.

Now the oral stories lead us to the trail of another Algonquian speaking people, the Blackfeet. Their involvement at the Little Bighorn has been kept quiet and out of the historical record until now.

Based on linguistics, the Blackfeet are so distinct from those Algonquin speakers who resided in the east-central and northeastern woodlands of the United States that they could not have been a recent offshoot.[1] This would seem to lend credence to the "Ancient Occupancy Theory," which would put the Algonquian speaking peoples' migration to the Northern Plains at a much earlier time than is noted, and so remote in the past that it is not in the historical records.[2]

As for the Blackfeet, their current oral stories remain the same as those to reported by acclaimed ethnologist John Ewers many years ago. The Blackfeet say they have always been on the land they inhabit now, this being northern Montana and in the Canadian Provinces of Alberta and Saskatchewan.[3] George Bird Grinnell, another acclaimed ethnographer, first put the Blackfeet in present-day Alberta, Canada. From his interviews with the elders, Grinnell had the Blackfeet north of Edmonton, Alberta, and he was told they were at times allies with Cree bands.[4]

The Blackfeet are comprised of three sub-tribes: The Siksika or Blackfeet proper, the Blood, and the Piegan. The Blackfeet and Gros Ventre alliance goes back to the mid-18th century. And, the Gros Ventre, it is said, reunited with the Arapaho for a time on the Southern Plains, but again separated from them sometime in the early 1800s.[5] There is also a shared story among the Cheyenne and their Suhtai or Sutaio allies (the Suhtai or Sutaio were an Algonquian Tribe that joined and merged with the Cheyenne)[6] which resembles one to which the Blackfeet adhere to as well. Both the Cheyenne and Blackfeet tell of their tribes having parts of their people separated at a great river crossing when the ice broke as the tribe was crossing. The two groups were never able to reconnect afterwards and were lost to history. As to where both say this happened, that depends on which elders or historians you speak to.[7]

There is this fascinating piece from George Bent to add to this Algonquian speakers' narrative. I add the following story to open the reader's eyes in regards to this Algonquian union and to show their interwoven histories on the Northern Plains.

Bent's mother was the daughter of The Cheyenne Tribe's Medicine Arrows Keeper. His father had the trading post, Bent's Fort, in present-day southeast Colorado. Bent himself rode with Cheyenne warriors after the Sand Creek Massacre. He was consulted by historians and writers on the Cheyenne and other aspects of Native American Plains peoples' history while he lived out his later years in Oklahoma.

Bent told a story that when the Cheyenne and Arapaho still lived near the Black Hills, the Arapaho were visited by their Gros Ventre kinsmen from Canada in 1825 or 1826. With these Gros Ventre came, "eighteen or twenty young Blackfeet." Bent continued on with the story and told that these young Blackfeet warriors had come on this journey to capture horses.

These young Gros Ventre and Blackfeet warriors continued on their journey and went south to find the horses they had come so far in search of. They were successful in finding the massive herds, and captured and then ran off with a large herd from the Kiowas and Comanche. Once they returned with the horses and told of the countless others further south between the Arkansas and Platte Rivers, Cheyenne and Arapaho bands took notice. There were no large herds of horses like this near the Black Hills.

A short time later, a Cheyenne band started the movement to live south of the Platte River. Some Arapaho moved as well and according again to Bent, this caused the division of not only the Cheyenne but the Arapaho. From this point on in the historical record there was Southern Cheyenne and Southern Arapahos, while north of the Platte there remained the Northern Cheyenne and Northern Arapahos.

Eventually the Gros Ventre went back to Canada but, Bent finished the story, "the Blackfeet never went back. Most of them married into the Cheyenne and Arapaho tribes."[8]

~

The Blackfeet story pertaining to their participation at the Little Bighorn started with three historians.

Devin Oldman, an Arapaho historian and who is mentioned in chapter 4, told me to look into the Blackfeet having had people at the Little Bighorn.[9]

The second historian is Yankton / Lakota educator Ken Shields, mentioned in chapter 3. He has been teaching Nakota history for years. His relative, Feather Earring, fought at the Battle of the Little Bighorn. Ken was gracious enough to refer me to Ernie Heavy Runner.[10]

Ernie Heavy Runner is a Blackfeet elder and historian who has some interesting pieces of the story of Blackfeet involvement with the Battle of the Little Bighorn. Ernie told of Sitting Bull sending trusted advisors to the Blackfeet, sometime around 1869 or 1870, in order to form an alliance against the United States Government. Ernie also stated that Sitting Bull

Ernie Heavy Runner - Blackfeet elder and historian.

himself came to the Blackfeet. This was somewhere in the Sweet Grass Hills, in present-day north central Montana.

As to what year this happened, Ernie could not recall. But what he did remember is that the Blackfeet refused to join Sitting Bull and the alliance he was seeking.[11] Despite the refusal, Sitting Bull gave the Blackfeet an honor song, which is still in use today by the tribe in ceremonies. Jim Red Eagle, a Nakota/Lakota historian, said that Sitting Bull gave a headdress to the Blackfeet. Sitting Bull named his son Crowfoot, after the Blackfeet Chief of the same name.[12]

Ernie stated that some young Blackfeet warriors then either accompanied Sitting Bull back to his people, or they simply went on their own accord at a later date. These young Blackfeet warriors then found themselves at the Little Bighorn. Ernie could not provide any names of these young Blackfeet warriors, or details of what they did in the Battle.[13]

There are three more interesting pieces to the Blackfeet story. The first again comes from Ernie Heavy Runner. He was told that Gros Ventre warriors brought the Lakota to see the Blackfeet.[14]

Tim Mentz, a Hunkpapa Lakota historian, shared a very interesting story with me regarding the Blackfeet. Tim stated that after the Battle of the Little Bighorn there was a big ceremony in the Cypress Hills, located in the Canadian Provinces of Saskatchewan and Alberta. Here, young Lakota women who had been at the Battle of the Little Bighorn and who had participated in the Battle in some capacity, were then married to Blackfeet men. The exact location of this ceremony is not known. Tim stated Sitting Bull was there.[15] The very first time I spoke to Ernie Heavy Runner, he told me of the same story.[16]

The third Blackfeet story was shared with me by three different people, Ben Rhodd, Marcus Dewey and Alden Bigman Jr., in essentially the same form. It told that a large group of Blackfeet people were on their way to find the Native Peoples coalition encampment on the Little Bighorn River. As this group neared the Valley of the Little Bighorn, they encountered scouts from the encampment who informed them the Battle was over and the U.S. Army had been destroyed. The Blackfeet turned around and went back home. All three had received the story from Blackfeet historian Curly Bear Wagner.[17]

The last piece of Blackfeet history pertaining to their involvement in the Battle of the Little Bighorn comes from Sicangu Lakota Tribal Historian Victor Douville. Victor's grandmother, Moves Camp Woman, was a young girl in the Native Peoples coalition encampment on the Little Bighorn in 1876. Victor stated that sometime after the Battle, a Blackfeet Chief by the name of White Quill brought some of his band to live among the Sicangu Lakota people in present-day South Dakota. Victor had been told that White Quill's band had been at the Little Bighorn and that many of the warriors in this band fought in the Battle. Over the next few years, many of the Blackfeet from White Quill's band married into the Sicangu Lakota people.[18]

Blackfeet elder and historian Jimmy Stgoddard had been told the same Blackfeet history. However, Jimmy informed me he was told the name of this Blackfeet Chief was White Quiver.[19]

~

Jimmy Stgoddard - Blackfeet elder and historian.

Jimmy Stgoddard shared two more pieces of history regarding the Blackfeet. The first being that the Blackfeet tribe have a much closer relationship to the Lakota People than is known and that is in the historical record. Jimmy stated that oral history of the Blackfeet Tribe claims that as Lakota bands pushed west across the Plains, they encountered bands of the Blackfeet tribe.[20] Victor Douville knew the same story and both he and Jimmy were told this happened in what is now South Dakota.[21]

Victor Douville and Jimmy Stgoddard both told me that oral history among the Lakota and Blackfeet put the Blackfeet in and around the Black Hills at a much earlier time than is in the historical record. The Blackfeet also had horses at this time and gave horses to the Lakota, and a trading network came about between the Lakota and Blackfeet that lasted until the reservation period.[22] Victor and Jimmy also related that a Lakota band settled in what is now South Dakota near a Blackfeet band. Eventually, these two bands assimilated into one, today recognized as the Sihasapa Blackfeet, part of the Teton Lakota Tribe.[23]

The last story Jimmy shared was of a party of Blackfeet warriors possibly being at the Battle of the Little Bighorn. Jimmy said that he had been told these warriors had ties to Chief Heavy Runner's band. He didn't know any names or how many went to the Little Bighorn. Heavy Runner was killed in 1870 by U.S. Army troops at what is sometimes called the Heavy Runner Massacre, or Baker Massacre.[24]

What is in the historical record and how do these stories match up against it?

There is, possibly, one mention of the Blackfeet Tribe's participation at the Battle of the Little Bighorn. This is from Gall, noted Hunkpapa Lakota war chief. He said, "Uncpapa, Minneconjou, Ogalalla, Brule, Teton, Santee and Yanktonnais Sioux, Blackfeet, Cheyennes, Arapahoes, and a few Gros Ventres."[25]

This is an interesting piece. It can't be ascertained for certain if Gall has mentioned the Blackfeet Tribe or the Sihasapa Blackfeet Lakota band. However, we now know from Victor Douville and Jimmy Stgoddard that if Gall did not specifically mention the Blackfeet Tribe here, then we at least know the Sihasapa Lakota band had Blackfeet Tribe people within it.[26]

We found eight maps that put Blackfeet people on the Little Bighorn River during the Battle of the Little Bighorn. There are two accounts that do as well.[27] It is clear from the accounts that accompany the maps that they are referring to the Sihasapa Blackfeet Lakota band.[28]

In Summary: The Blackfeet

While the Blackfeet stories do not add a great deal of significance to the Battle itself, they include some very intriguing parts. Ernie Heavy Runner and Tim Mentz told of Blackfeet warriors and Lakota people together in ceremonies in Canada after the Battle. It is interesting to consider the story of Lakota young women who were said to have participated in some way in the Battle of the Little Bighorn and marrying Blackfeet men.

Lastly, we have the story from Victor Douville and Jimmy Stgoddard telling of Blackfeet People belonging to White Quill or White Quiver's band, who are said to have been at the Battle of the Little Bighorn. These people are said to have come to live among the Sicangu Lakota and eventually married into the Sicangu and, presumably, other Lakota bands. Jimmy Stgoddard added the history of a Blackfeet Tribe band and the Sihasapa Lakota connection that is not in the historical records.

We are forever grateful to Blackfeet elders and historians, Ernie Heavy Runner, who made his journey to the camp on the other side, on June 12th, 2023, and Jimmy Stgoddard. A note of thanks to Victor Douville, Sicangu Lakota Tribal historian, as well. All shared long kept history of their people in hopes that future generations could someday learn and grow from it.

Notes

1. Michelson 1906-1907: 221-90. Also see Trenholm 1970: 3-32.

2. Scott 1907 and Trenholm 1970. Also see Ewers 1958: 6-7.

3. Personal communications with Ernie Heavy Runner-Blackfeet. See Ewers 1958: 6-7.

4. Grinnell 1892: 161-162, 164; Grinnell 1961: 84

5. Scott 1907: 547, 560; Also see Ewers 1958;

Hyde 1968: 32-33; Trenholm 1970: 10-11.

6. Michelson 1910: 9-11; 1913: 11; Grinnell and Fitzgerald 2008: 11. Personal communications with Rufus Spear-Cheyenne, Leroy Whiteman-Cheyenne, Donovan Taylor-Cheyenne and Keith Spotted Wolf-Cheyenne.

7. Grinnell 1892: 162-164; Dusenberry 1956; 26-33. Personal communications with Rufus Spear-Cheyenne, Leroy White Man-Cheyenne, Donovan Taylor-Cheyenne and Keith Spotted Wolf-Cheyenne.

8. Hyde 1968: 31-40.

9. Persoanl communications with Devin Oldman-Arapaho.

10. Personal communications with Ken Shields-Yankton/Lakota.

11. Personal communications with Ernie Heavy Runner-Blackfeet.

12. Ibid. Personal communications Jim Red Eagle-Nakota/Lakota.

13. Personal communications with Ernie Heavy Runner-Blackfeet.

14. Ibid.

15. Personal communications with Tim Mentz-Hunkpapa Lakota.

16. Personal communications with Ernie Heavy Runner-Blackfeet.

17. Personal communications with Ben Rhodd - Potawatomi, Marcus Dewey - Arapaho and Alden Bigman Jr.-Crow.

18. Personal communications with Victor Douville-Sicangu Lakota Tribal Historian.

19. Personal communications with Jimmy Stgoddard-Blackfeet.

20. Ibid.

21. Personal communications with Victor Douville-Sicangu Lakota Tribal Historian and Jimmy Stgoddard-Blackfeet.

22. Ibid.

23. Ibid.

24. Personal communications with Jimmy Stgoddard-Blackfeet. See Ewers 1958: 248-250.

25. For the Gall accounts see Graham 1953: 87-92.

26. Personal communications with Victor Douville-Sicangu Lakota Tribal Historian and Jimmy Stgoddard-Blackfeet.

27. Donahue 2009: 401.

28. Ibid.

7
The Nakota, Nakoda and Cree

The information that led to the trail we followed for this chapter comes from the following people: Garvard Good Plume Jr. - Oglala Lakota, Dr. Leo J. Omani - Santee Dakota, Tom Shawl - Nakoda, Ira McArthur - Nakota, Tommy Christian-Nakota / Dakota / Lakota, Ken Helgeson - Nakoda, Rod Alexis-Stoney Nakoda, Francis Alexis - Stoney Nakoda, Dennis Paul - Stoney Nakoda, Jaelin Rask - Stoney Nakoda, Iris O'Watch - Nakota / Dakota, James Desjarlais – Nakota / Cree, Joanne Lethbridge Pompana - Hunkpapa Lakota / Seneca / Iroquois, Michael Black Wolf - Gros Ventre, Ernie Heavy Runner - Blackfeet, Hughie Chalifoux - Saulteaux, Floyd Favel - Cree, Murray Ironchild - Cree, Danita Strawberry - Cree, Don Myers-Chippewa / Cree, Alvin Windy Boy – Chippewa / Cree, Elaine Blyan Cross - Cree, Jim Red Eagle-Nakota / Lakota, Rick Two Dogs - Oglala Lakota, Richard Iron Cloud - Oglala Lakota and Bob Saindon, independent researcher.

The following narrative is not meant to be a complete and all-encompassing piece regarding the people of the Nakota, Nakoda and Cree. Rather, it is simply meant to give the reader a better understanding of these groups and their history as it pertains to their participation at the Battle of the Little Bighorn.

~

I was first made aware of a possible Nakoda presence at the Battle of the Little Bighorn while talking to the late Garvard Good Plume Jr. It is a touching and endearing story that speaks to the humanity of the Native American and First Nations people. Joe Pop, a Lakota and Cree man, told Garvard the story. He did not know where Joe Pop had come by the information.

Garvard said Joe Pop told him these Stoney Nakoda who came to the Battle were with Nakota people and others of mixed Santee Dakota heritage. He further added that after the Battle, the chief of these Nakoda and some of his followers went around to all the bands of Lakota, Dakota, and Nakota, and offered to take any and as many of their orphans who wanted to go with his band the opportunity to do so. Many did go back with these Nakoda to what is now the current day Canadian Province of Alberta, Canada.[1]

Following the story's trail, I was introduced to Francis Alexis and his nephew, Rod Alexis, by Dr. Leo J. Omani.[2] Francis and Rod Alexis informed me that their people, the Stoney Nakoda, who reside in parts near Edmonton, in the Canadian Province of Alberta, had oral stories of their people pertaining to the Battle of the Little Bighorn, and what happened to them after the Battle.

Rod Alexis - Stoney Nakoda.

This band of Nakoda, had been led to the Little Bighorn by a chief named Aran Inazhi and his brother, Mazaa Pa. Francis and Rod are descendants of the chief. They have been investigating their relative's participation and story of their people at the Little Bighorn for over 50 years.[3]

No one, including their present-day relatives or historians, knows how Aran Inazhi and his band got word to come to the Little Bighorn and where they were before. At this time, despite the best efforts of Stoney Nakoda historians Dennis Paul and Jaelin Rask, all we can add to this story is the name of one warrior, Yellowhead, as having possibly been with Aran Inazhi's band at the Little Bighorn.[4]

So, who are these Nakoda people? The standard answer is they come from the Nakota. Yankton and Yanktonai people are part of the Western Dakota and called Nakota. As we saw in chapter 3, Yankton and Yanktonai people broke away from the Santee Dakota. Before this, band(s) had left a Siouan alliance on the northern plains of Canada and in present-day northern Minnesota, then made their way to the north and west. Some had found their way to the regions in and around Lake Winipeg, as well as the Saskatchewan and Assiniboine Rivers. These people were called Nakota (Assiniboine). Some sources say the Nakota (Assiniboine) broke off from the Yankton near the Red River, in parts of what is now northern Minnesota and Manitoba, Canada. They joined Cree people there, eventually to be joined by Ojibwe people as well.[5] The name Assiniboine is said to have been given to them because they were, "those who cooked with stones."[6]

The Nakoda, also called the Stoney Nakoda, are said to have been bands of Nakota out in front of their migration from the Santee Dakota. It is thought that they broke off from the Nakota somewhere in present-day North Dakota and made their way to the Rocky Mountains. Some groups moved further northwest into what is today northwestern North Dakota and into eastern present-day Montana. Others moved to the present-day Canadian Province of Alberta and allied themselves with the Cree tribe. Nakoda elders long ago told their people that they had moved in migrations from the southern regions of America and into the Midwest Plains. These elders said the Nakoda were the northern most vanguard of these migrations.[7]

Other stories of the Nakoda tell of the devastating waves of smallpox that swept over the northern plains and killed thousands of these Native People. In some cases, the only survivors of bands were the children and elders. It is said that, at times, these orphans were found by Nakoda parties and taken in.[8] Other bands of orphans continued to move west to get away from the deadly disease that had taken so many of their people in and around the areas near Fort Buford and Fort Union, both in present-day North Dakota, as well as Fort Belknap in present-day Montana.[9] Over time, with the countless numbers of Nakoda orphans on the Plains, these groups' grasp of their language lapsed so much so that the Nakoda language changed drastically and became even more distinct from the tongue of their Nakota kinsmen, a point not lost on their sometime allies and sometime enemy, the Cree. The Cree had contempt and little regard for these youngsters and said they were weak and helpless.[10]

~

The Cree are an Algonquian-speaking people. They were first encountered by French and British fur traders in northeastern Canada with their Nakota (Assiniboine) allies.[11] Because of the influx of white settlers in eastern Canada, many Cree people moved for the Canadian Plains of Saskatchewan and Alberta by the late 1600's.[12] The Cree were in an ever-changing landscape on the plains that saw them allied with the Nakota (Assiniboine) and Ojibwe. These three formed what was known as the Iron Confederacy.[13]

Prior to the Battle of the Little Bighorn, groups of Native American people, as well as First Nations People from what is now Canada, had come for many, many years, to what is now the state of Montana. They came to hunt, trade, and be part of ceremonies, since all were, at one time, The People, as we presented in chapter 2.

Northern plains bands did not necessarily align with others of the same linguistic stock.[14] In fact, there are numerous instances of a band noted in the historical record as being from a certain tribe, when actually they were at one time part of a different tribe. Much of this history has been glossed over, a fact reiterated to me countless times by many, many different people from different tribes and bands. Evidence of such history and stories can be found in the historical record. We presented an example of this, between Blackfeet people and Lakota bands, in a previous chapter.[15]

Ira McArthur shared another example of this type of an alliance. Ira stated that he had picked up bits and pieces of this story over the years from elders on the First Nation Reserves in Saskatchewan. He said that a large group of Nakota and Dakota people comprising close to 300 tipis, eventually ended up at the Little Bighorn. Ira then told me that this group ended up in the Cypress Hills of Saskatchewan after the Battle. This was the home of these Nakota people.[16]

This is not the first time we have heard of people who are said to have been at the Battle of the Little Bighorn ending up in the Cypress Hills. In the previous chapter, Ernie Heavy Runner and Tim Mentz told of people from the Battle ending up there as well.

~

We stayed on this trail from the Little Bighorn to the Cypress Hills. Donovan Taylor went to work exploring the Cree connection to these events, and was told by one source from Rocky Boy Reservation that two chiefs with Nakota (Assiniboine), Cree, and Ojibwe heritage, known as Poundmaker and Big Bear, were both at the Battle of the Little Bighorn.[17]

While on the research trail of the Cree I was able meet Don Meyers, Chippewa Cree historian. He informed me he had been told there was 10 to 20 Cree warriors in the Battle. He also said that not only were Poundmaker and Big Bear both at the Little Bighorn, another Cree / Nakota (Assiniboine) Chief by the name of Piapot was there as well.[18] He did not know if these people and their bands had traveled together or simply ended up at the Little Bighorn like other Cree men who might have been there because they were married into other tribes.

Rick Two Dogs, Oglala Lakota elder and historian, informed me of one such instance. Rick knew of stories that told of at least two Cree men at the Little Bighorn because they were married to Lakota women.[19]

James Desjarlais, a Nakota/Cree historian and descendant of Piapot and Big Bear, shared with me that he had been told Piapot and some of his people were at the Little Bighorn. James claimed, based on information from his uncle, that some of Piapot's warriors fought in the Battle as well.[20]

Elaine Blyan Cross, a Cree historian and descendent of Big Bear, shared this war chief and holy person, a spiritual leader to a large contingent of Nakota and Cree people, was indeed at the Battle of the Little Bighorn. Big Bear not only led his contingent of people, but was instrumental in getting Poundmaker, a noted Cree chief, and Pheasant Rump, a noted Nakota chief, to go to the

Little Bighorn. Combined, these three chiefs had over 350 lodges in this group.[21] This sounds very much like the information Ira McArthur had been told.

At this part of our investigation, I contacted Alvin WindyBoy Sr., Chippewa Cree and Rocky Boy Reservation historian, as well as Floyd Favel, Cree historian and curator of the Chief Poundmaker Museum. I reached out to them for help following up on Poundmaker, Big Bear, Piapot, and any other Cree people possibly being at the Little Bighorn. Despite Alvin's and Floyd's immense knowledge, contacts, and willingness to help, neither could find corroborating accounts or sources confirming Poundmaker, Big Bear or Piapot were ever at the Battle.

Despite coming up empty, Alvin did add an interesting piece. He had been told by his family that it had been common knowledge among Chippewa Cree People in and around the Rocky Boy Reservation in north central Montana that Cree people had in fact, been at the Battle of the Little Bighorn.[22]

~

Still on the trail of the Cree, we were lucky enough to meet more historians and descendants of those said to have been at the Battle of the Little Bighorn. The name of Wandering Spirit was mentioned to me as someone possibly at the Little Bighorn as well. I was lucky enough to meet Hughie Chalifoux, a Plains Ojibwe (Saulteaux) man, who told me Wandering Spirit was Big Bear's war chief. Hughie informed me that Iamsees, sometimes called Little Bear, a son of Big Bear, was at the Little Bighorn as well. Hughie is a descendant of Iamsees.[23]

There are two more stories to add to Nakota, Nakoda and Cree participation at the Battle of the Little Bighorn. The first came to me and Donovan with help, again, from Floyd Favel. Floyd introduced us to Danita Strawberry, a descendant of Big Bear, who told a very interesting story:

"When I was around 8 or 9, my uncle had a great uncle from his other side of his family who lived with him. This man was named Yelloweye, at the time he was 103 years old, when he used to tell us stories. He told us he remembered when yellow hair (that's what he called

Custer in Cree) came to war with the Indigenous people. He said many blue coats were coming (I didn't know what a blue coat was, I had to ask my mom later and she told me that's how they described U.S. soldiers. Anyway, Yelloweye's camp was given the option to go to war or leave. His family chose to leave, as a group they left but many Crees joined the war to help Sitting Bull. He was just a young boy of around 6 years old but he remembered walking all night (2 nights in a row) and sneaking through the prairies during the day to get to the Canadian line to seek safety. Him and his family never returned to Montana. Yelloweye later became a band member in Sunchild, he lived to be around 113 or 115 years old and didn't speak a word of English. He told us many stories but this one stood out for me."[24]

Before moving on to the next story, we feel it is necessary to add some more pieces to the question of Cree participation.

In chapter 6, Blackfeet historian Ernie Heavy Runner told of Sitting Bull and his emissaries working on a union with the Blackfeet. Some of these meetings, Ernie said, took place in the Sweet Grass Hills of present-day northern Montana.[25] I was told that the Sweet Grass Hills are sacred to the Cree people and to many other tribes and their bands... many not on most lists of Native American tribes said to have been in this area of Montana. This comes by way of Chippewa Cree historian Alvin WindyBoy Sr.[26]

Alvin also stated that there had been some bands of Cree people on the U.S. Northern Plains possibly as far back as the 1400s. He had been told some of this information from Native American and First Nations historians and elders, as well as having had done extensive research himself when he was the Tribal Historic Preservation Officer for the Rocky Boy Chippewa Cree Tribe.

The bands were the Plains or Rocky Cree (Mountain Cree), Woodland, Swampy, Moose Cree and Eastern Cree. Incidentally, Alvin added that the Woodland Cree were closely tied to the Nakoda of Chief Aran Inazhi's band and his brother Mazaa Pa, who are both said to have been at the Little Bighorn.[27] The same bit of information regarding the Woodland Cree and their ties to the Nakoda of Chief Aran Inazhi's band and Mazaa Pa was told to me by Stoney Nakoda historian Dennis Paul, from Paul First Nation, and Rod Alexis-Stoney Nakoda, from Alexis Nakota Sioux Nation.[28]

So, if Sitting Bull and his people were in the Sweet Grass Hills, the Cree people there knew it and would have had to have given their approval. I had been told of ceremonial exchanges between the Cree and Lakota that had to do with the Horse Ceremony and the Sun Dance. The Horse ceremony story came from Arvol and Paula Looking Horse, and the Sun Dance ceremony story came from Jim Red Eagle, Nakota / Lakota.[29]

Our last story pertaining to the Nakoda and their involvement at the Battle of the Little Bighorn comes again from Rod Alexis. Parts of it were also told to me by Joanne Lethbridge Pompana.

As we saw earlier, Rod Alexis told me of a Nakoda Chief named Aran Inazhi and his people possibly being at the Battle of the Little Bighorn. The last part of the story, having to do with what happened after Sitting Bull and his people had crossed into Canada, has never been written.

We have been told they were in the Cypress Hills and there were ceremonies that possibly not only involved Nakota people, but also Blackfeet and maybe even Cree.[30] Jim Red Eagle added that Sitting Bull had been invited to ceremonies there in the Cypress

Big Darkness / Shows Himself Big At Night, Nakota War Chief, said to have been at the Little Bighorn. Photo courtesy of Jim Red Eagle, descendant of Big Darkness / Shows Himself Big At Night.

Hills by his relative, a Nakota Chief, who was known as Big Darkness or Shows Himself Big At Night. Big Darkness had been at the Battle of the Little Bighorn as well, according to Jim Red Eagle.[31]

Rod Alexis and Joanne Lethbridge Pompana both conveyed that Sitting Bull first made his way west to the Canadian Province of Alberta, to what is now Paul First Nation (where the Nakoda people under Mazza Pa / Iron Head settled). From there, he went to what is now called Alexis Nakota Sioux Nation, where the Nakoda People under Aran Inazhi (later called Alexis), settled. Perhaps he had come to check on all the orphans who had come with Aran Inazhi and Mazza Pa? Rod Alexis was told that Sitting Bull sought out Aran Inazhi and Mazza Pa and their people. At a ceremony, near a holy sacred lake now known as Mirror Lake, Sitting Bull instructed these men to keep the stories of their people and their involvement at the Little Bighorn quiet. Sitting Bull's words were, "leave the past behind."[32]

What is in the historical record and how do these stories match up against it?

Aran Inazhi and his band of Stoney Nakoda are nowhere to be found in the historical record as far as their possible participation at the Battle of the Little Bighorn. There are three Stoney Nakoda warriors accounts, all from the same source.[33]

We found only one specific account mentioning Nakota (Assiniboine) people; it came from Gordon Harper. Nothing in it pertains to any trails to and from the Cypress Hills.[34] There are five accounts that mention Nakota (Assiniboine) people as having had been at the Little Bighorn.[35]

At this time, only one map, from Doug War Eagle, Minnikojou Lakota and now in this writer's possession, could be found that put Nakota or Nakoda at the Little Bighorn during the Battle.[36]

As for the Cree trail, there are two pieces we found, and one oral. The first comes from Gordon Harper, who told the Cree were at the Battle of the Little Bighorn. Haper simply told that the Cree had promised the Lakota they would be there for them in time of need. The oral story shared with us from Danita Strawberry tells of the same.[37] No maps have been found putting Cree people on the Little Bighorn River.

The last source for a Cree narrative is very interesting, to say the least. It comes from the Thomas E. Mail's book *Fools Crow*.

In the book, *Fools Crow* says his grandfather, Knife Chief, was at the Battle of the Little Bighorn. Knife Chief was said to be the camp crier for Sitting Bull.[38] According to Battle veteran Austin Red Hawk, Knife Chief was said to be at the forefront of organizing the Native resistance against the Seventh Cavalry at the Little Bighorn. Red Hawk even went so far as to say Knife Chief was a leading chief that day, along with Gall and Crazy Horse.[39] Knife Chief was wounded in his arm during the Valley Fight with the Reno Battalion. He was treated by a medicine man by the name of Crutch, who was thought to be Cree.[40]

Rick Two Dogs told me the same story. Rick's story came from his grandfather Thomas, who was in the encampment at the Little Bighorn as a young boy. Rick had been told the Cree Medicine Man Fools Crow calls Crutch was named Jatela.[41]

I interviewed Richard Iron Cloud, a descendant of Fools Crow. The family knew the story of Knife Chief being wounded at the Battle. The only new piece they could add to it was that after the Battle, Knife Chief was called Broken Arm.[42]

To date, no further information has been found on Nakoda or Nakota people said to be at the Little Bighorn. There is nothing in the historical record on Big Darkness, the Nakota chief who invited Sitting Bull to a sun dance in the Cypress Hills of Saskatchewan and who himself was said to have fought at the Little Bighorn.

In Summary: Nakota, Nakoda and Cree

Stories pertaining to the Nakota narrative of their participation at the Little Bighorn tell the following:

Number one, they tell of some of these people coming to the Little Bighorn from the Fort Peck area and from the Canadian province of Saskatchewan.[43]

Second, the accounts tell of a series of ceremonies and / or meetings between Nakota people who are said to have been at the Little Bighorn and Lakota people, which include Sitting Bull's people and the Blackfeet Tribe people. It is believed these encounters happened in the Cypress Hills of Saskatchewan.[44] Prior to this, there were other ceremonies and meetings between Sitting Bull and the Nakoda which took place in Alberta, Canada.[45]

As researchers, we should ask ourselves why Sitting Bull would venture that far to Alberta, Canada, and address the Nakoda about their involvement in Battle if they had not been there?

Regarding the Cree and their participation at the Battle of the Little Bighorn, there is not much to present at this time. However, when the stories are looked at, the Cree narrative does not warrant dismissal. And, we must remember that the Cree and the Nakota were in an alliance, part of what was known as the Iron Confederacy.

Canadian researcher Gordon Harper mentioned the Cree being at the Little Bighorn and suggested it was because they were in some type of alliance with the Lakota. Harper gave no source for this information.[46] From interviews I have conducted with many Lakota people, this alliance seems common knowledge,[47] and we have been told by one Cree historian and one Nakoda historian that the Woodland Cree and Nakoda were extremely close.[48] Coupled with stories shared with Donovan and myself regarding Cheyenne people and their ties to the Cree, together with what we know of the Cheyenne and Lakota alliance, the Cree narrative continues to intrigue.[49]

Despite our best efforts and with many, many people helping us, we are not able at this time to add more information regarding Pound Maker, Big Bear, Piapot and Wondering Medicine. These prominent warriors and chiefs mentioned earlier in this chapter have remained hidden from the historical record when it comes to their suggested participation at the Battle of the Little Bighorn.

The Nakota, Nakoda and Cree story of their participation at the Battle of the Little Bighorn deserves attention. At this time, Donovan Taylor and myself could not add information to specific parts of the Battle regarding these people. The Nakota, Nakoda and Cree narrative is worthy of more research, as it might just possibly add information to the Battle at a later time.

We are eternally grateful to Alvin WindyBoy Sr., Floyd Favel, Ira McArthur, Danita Strawberry, Rod Alexis, Joanne Lethbridge Pompana, Ernie Heavy Runner, Don Meyers, Jim Red Eagle and Dennis Paul, who all thought enough of us and this project to share with us these bits and pieces of history.

Notes

1. Personal communications with Garvard Good Plume Jr. - Oglala Lakota.

2. Personal communications with Dr. Leo J. Omani - Santee Dakota.

3. Personal communications with Rod Alexis - Stoney Nakoda and Francis Alexis - Stoney Nakoda.

4. Personal communications with Dennis Paul - Stoney Nakoda and Jaelin Rask - Stoney Nakoda.

5. Gibbon 2003: 36 - 37. Gibbon suggests Nakota (Assiniboin) broke away from Dakota people AD 1300 and that they, "share more lexical items with Lakota and Yankton - Yanktonai than with Dakota. See Riggs 2004: 160. Edward Curtis, the noted photographer/ ethnographer, published Vol Three The North American Indian: The Teton Sioux, Yanktonai and Assiniboine in 1908, said Nakota and Nakoda (Assiniboin) broke off Yanktonai, pp 127 - 128. Riggs states Nakota (Assiniboin) came off the Yanktonai, specifically, the Pine Shooters Clan. See Long 2004: 3. Warren 2009: 90 - 92, says Nakota (Assiniboin) came of Yankton near the Red River in parts of what is now northern Minnesota and Manitoba, Canada, then joined Cree people there. Eventually to be joined by the Ojibwe as well. Howard 2013: 3, says Nakota (Assiniboin) and Stoney from Yanktonai.

6. Personal communications with Tom Shawl - Nakoda and Peter McArthur - Nakota.

7. Personal communications with Ben Rhodd - Potawatomi, Tom Shawl - Nakoda and Rod Alexis - Stoney Nakoda. See James Long (First Boy) 2004: 3 - 4.

8. Personal communications with Tom Shawl - Nakoda, Ken Helgeson - Nakoda and Peter McArthur - Nakota. https: //www.thecanadianencyclopedia.ca/en/article/stoneynakoda.

9. Personal communications with Ken Helgeson - Nakoda.

10. Personal communications with Tom Shawl - Nakoda.

11. Mandelbaum 1940: 171.

12. Milloy 1988: 159; Mandelbaum 1940: 165; Warren 2009: 90 - 92.

13. Ibid.

14. Personal communications with Alvin Windyboy Sr. - Chippewa Cree, Tom Shawl - Nakoda, Ken Helgeson - Nakoda, Douglas Bonaise - Cree/Saulteaux, Rod Alexis - Stoney Nakoda, Rufus Spear - Cheyenne, Victor Douville - Sicangu Lakota Tribal Historian, Peter Gibbs - Tribal Historian Sicangu Lakota, James Ritchie and Bob Saindon. See Grinnell 1892 and 1961; Moore 1987; Albers 1996; McCrady 1998; Ritchie 2001; Vroom 2014.

15. Personal communications with Tom Shawl - Nakoda, Tommy Christian - Nakota/Dakota/Lakota, Calvin Bear First - Dakota/Yanktonai, Rod Alexis - Stoney Nakoda, Dennis Paul - Stoney Nakoda, Alvin Windyboy Sr. - Chippewa Cree, Ken Shields - Yankton/Lakota, Jalen Atchico - Yanktonai/Nakota, Mike Turcotte - Nakoda, Hughie Chalifoux - Saulteaux,

Floyd Favel - Cree, Donita Strawberry - Cree, Don Myers - Chippewa Cree and Victor Douville - Sicangu Lakota Tribal Historian. See Grinnell 1892 and 1961; Moore 1987; Albers 1996; McCrady 1998; Ritchie 2001; Vroom 2014.

16. Personal communications with Ira McArthur - Nakota.

17. Personal communications with Donovan Taylor - Cheyenne. Donovan's source for this story has asked to remain anonymous.

18. Personal communications with Don Myers - Chippewa Cree.

19. Personal communications with Rick Two Dogs - Oglala Lakota.

20. Personal communications with James Desjarlais - Nakota/Cree.

21. Personal communications with Elain Blyan Cross - Cree.

22. Personal communications with Alvin WindyBoy Sr. - Chippewa Cree and Floyd Favel - Cree.

23. Personal communications with Hughie Chalifoux - Saulteaux.

24. Personal communications with Floyd Favel - Cree and Donita Strawberry - Cree.

25. Pesonal communications with Ernie Heavy Runner - Blackfeet.

26. Alvin Windy Boy Sr. - Chippewa Cree. One tribe mentioned by Alvin as having ties to the Sweet Grass Hills was the Pawnee.

27. Personal communications with Alvin WindyBoy Sr. - Chippewa Cree, Rod Alexis - Stoney Nakoda and Dennis Paul - Stoney Nakoda.

28. Personal communications with Dennis Paul - Stoney Nakoda and Rod Alexis - Stoney Nakoda.

29. Personal communications with Arvol and Paula Looking Horse and Jim Red Eagle - Nakota/Lakota.

30. Personal communications with Ernie Heavy Runner - Blackfeet and Tim Mentz - Hunkpapa Lakota.

31. Personal communications with Jim Red Eagle - Nakota/Lakota.

32. Pesonal communications with Rod Alexis - Stoney Nakoda and Joanne Lethbridge Pompana - Hunkpapa Lakota/Iroquois/Seneca.

33. See The David Humphreys Miller collection, "Faces of the Little Bighorn," see https: //davidhumphreysmiller.org/our- The three warriors mentioned here are Bobtail Bear, Crazy Bull and Red Feather.

34. Harper 2014: [Ebook] Appendices 3.79.

35. Marquis 2003: 208; and 1967: 83; Miller 1985: 48; Harper 2014: 240; Donovan 2008: 85, 187.

36. Personal communications with Doug War Eagle - Minnikojou Lakota.

37. Harper 2014: 243. Personal communications with Danita Strawberry - Cree.

38. For the account of Knife Chief being wounded see Hardorff 2005: 146.

39. See Hardorff 1997: 42 - 48.

40. Ibid. Hardorff 2005: 146; Mails 1979: 37 - 38.

41. Personal communications with Rick Two Dogs - Oglala Lakota.

42. Personal communications with Richard Iron

Cloud - Oglala Lakota.

43. Personal communications with Sara Childers, Tom Shawl - Nakoda, Tommy Christian - Nakota / Dakota / Lakota, Calvin Bear First - Yanktonai / Sisitunwan, Ira McArthur - Nakota. Also see the David Humphreys Miller collection, "Faces of the Little Bighorn," see https: //davidhumphreysmiller.org/our- collection/, see faces of the Little Bighorn collection. The three warriors mentioned here are Bobtail Bear, Crazy Bull and Red Feather.

44. Personal communications with Ira McArthur - Nakota, Tom Shawl - Nakoda, Jim Red Eagle - Nakota/Lakota, Ken Helgeson - Nakoda, Ernie Heavy Runner - Blackfeet and Tim Mentz - Hunkpapa Lakota.

45. Personal communications with Rod Alexis - Stoney Nakoda and Joanne Lethbridge Pompana - Hunkpapa Lakota/Iroquois/Seneca.

46. Harper 2014: 243.

47. Personal communications with Arvol and Paula Looking Horse, Jim Red Eagle - Nakota/Lakota, Rick Two Dogs - Oglala Lakota, Ira McArthur - Nakota, Victor Douville - Sicangu Lakota Tribal Historian, Garvard Good Plume Jr. - Oglala Lakota, Alvin WindyBoy Sr. - Chippewa Cree, Dennis Paul - Stoney Nakoda and Peter Gibbs - Tribal Historian Sicangu Lakota.

48. Personal communications with Alvin WindyBoy Sr. - Chippewa Cree and Dennis Paul - Stoney Nakoda.

49. Personal communications with Donovan Taylor - Cheyenne, Keith Spotted Wolf - Cheyenne, Wallace Bearchum - Cheyenne, Vernon Sooktis - Cheyenne, Dwight Bull Coming - Cheyenne, Chester Whiteman - Cheyenne, John Eagle Shield - Hunkpapa Lakota and Victor Douville - Sicangu Lakota Tribal Historian.

8
Some Cheyenne and Lakota History Within an Encampment of Special Camps

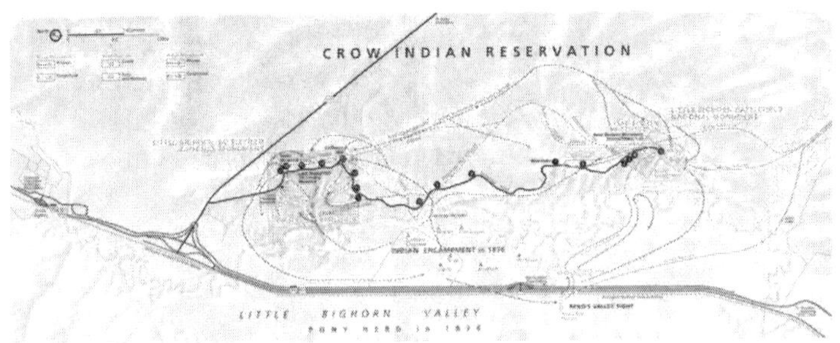

Map courtesy of the National Park Service.

The information that led to this trail we followed for this chapter came from the following people: Arvol Looking Horse, Victor Douville - Sicangu Lakota Tribal Historian, Garvard Good Plume Jr. - Oglala Lakota, Rick Two Dogs - Oglala Lakota, Basil BraveHeart - Oglala Lakota, Chico Her Many Horses - Oglala Lakota, Rhonda Funmaker - Ho-Chunk, Rod Alexis - Stoney Nakoda, Dennis Paul - Stoney Nakoda, Ozzie McKay - Santee Dakota, Doug War Eagle - Minnikojou Lakota, Jim Red Eagle – Nakota / Lakota, Alvin WindyBoy Sr. - Chippewa Cree, Jimmy Stgoddard - Blackfeet, Ernie Heavy Runner - Blackfeet, Michael Black Wolf - Gros Ventre, Chester Whiteman - Cheyenne, Dwight Bull Coming - Cheyenne, Donovan Taylor - Cheyenne, Vernon Sooktis - Cheyenne, Florence Whiteman - Cheyenne, Keith Spotted Wolf - Cheyenne, Gilbert Whitedirt - Cheyenne, Eddie Whitedirt - Cheyenne, Roger Red Hat - Cheyenne, Scott Doser, Al Joe Strange Owl - Cheyenne, Rufus Spear - Cheyenne, Linwood Tall

Bull - Cheyenne, Harold Salway - Oglala Lakota, Ronnie Cutt - Sicangu Lakota, Devin Oldman - Arapaho, Bill Goggles - Arapaho, Ben Rhodd – Potawatomie, Iris O'Watch – Dakota / Nakota, Joanne Pompana - Hunkpapa Lakota / Iroquois / Seneca and Peter Gibbs - Tribal Historian Sicangu Lakota.

We have discussed and presented oral history regarding tribes and bands that are said to have been at the Battle of the Little Bighorn. We have also presented historical evidence that we found that adds to these stories. We now shift our focus and look at the encampment and the camps within it on the Little Bighorn. In doing so, we take you the reader, back to a time that has hardly been discussed when accurately depicting the Native American and First Nations People who were at the Little Bighorn.

The information in this chapter and those that follow gives a glimpse of just who The People were, and what they were capable of as individuals. The veil of ignorance and intolerance to the capabilities of The People and their powers connected to this planet are falling to the wayside. Their world was made up of a life force with spiritual potency and its higher powers of consciousness. It was a place in which they prospered and lived in harmony. This life force or power protected the very earth, and was visible to the People at times in varying ways, shapes and forms. It was, for all intents and purposes, what still makes up the North American Continent.

The Americas and its inhabitants, Bernard Bailyn writes, were "densely populated by active, sentient, and sensitive spirits with consciences, memories, and purposes that surrounded them, instructed them, impinged on their lives at every turn." Only now are we, as human beings, able to look at this concept in an open frame of mind scrutinized under the scientific lens and in the mainstream media. It was this world and its full powers that the U.S. Army came into contact with. The date was June 25th, 1876.[1]

Based on oral history shared with us, this gathering of Native American and First Nations People, while a coalition of sorts, has its roots in long-ago oral history that clearly states The People had been going to an area encompassing current-day northeast Wyoming and southeastern Montana for centuries for ceremonial purposes and the renewing of sacred covenants. They did not fear the U.S. Army, for as Devin Oldman informed me, "This was a fight for their right to pray where they needed to be able to do so." Add to this plenty of evidence in oral history shared and kept among tribes today of how at one time they all banded together many, many centuries ago.[2]

What we present is simply the oral stories and history shared with us, plus some finer points and hidden pieces our research came up with from these stories. These stories reveal some interesting information that has been kept from history regarding some special people and their camps scattered on and about the Little Bighorn River, on June 24th and June 25th of 1876.

~

By the late afternoon of June 24th, 1876, the Native Peoples coalition encampment along the banks of the Little Bighorn River had begun to take shape. What does the oral history tell us about the camps?

This was a moving encampment comprised of groups of camps. The coalition had been led to the area by the Cheynne People, who by 1876 were in constant conflict with the Crow Tribe for control of the Little Bighorn valley. The need for resources was always great, especially food. Buffalo had been spotted west of the Rosebud River and then large herds of antelope had been sighted. There was always a need for meat, skins to make clothing and hides for tipis. This was a catalyst for the bands to move over to the Valley of the Little Bighorn River.

Access to water, sheltering timber and grazing for horses was paramount. This determined how the tipis were distributed at various points along the Little Bighorn river. Sanitation and clean water were also considerations for how and where bands settled. Contrary to what has been written before and said time and time again, there were no ceremonial circles other than those of the warrior societies.[3] This is not to say that members of the same band or tribe did not camp within proximity of one another.

Now that we have put forth that this encampment had its roots in an ancient time, let us turn our attention to some other intricate parts of the camps. There was far more to the People who had gathered, now classified by the U.S. government as tribes and bands. The coalition was filled with special people taught and learned in the old ways of a culture that was totally spiritual without religion. Spirituality was key to life for the Native American and First Nations People, not just in ceremony, but in everything they lived and believed in.

Within the camps were people who "walked with the stars." These men followed the movements of the celestial bodies. This was an important part of the People's world, not only for navigating the continent, but for spiritual purposes, as well. These knowledge keepers of the celestial movements and planets, stars, moon and sun, noted and recorded events and were keenly aware of events such as meteor showers, comets, lunar and solar eclipses.[4]

This encampment had areas set aside on the periphery for ceremonial people, men and women alike. They had received sacred knowledge, songs and rituals in dreams or visions. Thus, they could mediate between the spirit beings and powers, as well as the common people. These people were called wakan (wicasa wakan, "man sacred"' or holy Man; and winyan wakan or wiyan wakon, "woman sacred, or holy Woman) by the Lakota.[5]

The Cheyenne holy men, called Ma'heónėhetane, and their holy women, called Maheone' ne' e, received instructions and help from sacred powers / spiritual beings called the Ma heono, or Maiyu. They might appear to them in dreams or visions in the forms of a living creature, birds, animals, or mysterious men and women, painted with sacred colors. These holy men and women were scattered throughout the Cheyenne camps as well.

Power was a sacred life force from the universe and present in all things. Spiritual beings, which have souls, were powerful and existed in things which too had a soul, such as animals, winged creatures such as birds and insects, places such as the stars, the moon, the sun, mountains and rocks. If these spirits conferred power to humans through a vision quest, dreams or visions, they became an individuals' guardian spirits or dream spirits. Mastering several spirits was necessary to be an effective holy person. These people sometimes called upon their spirit helper or ally, also called the sicun, or used power through medicine bundles.[6]

There were medicine men and medicine women (pejuta wicasa- "medicine men" and pejuta winyan, "medicine woman" for the Lakota), who administered aid in the form of grass and herbs in rituals accompanied with songs that summoned spirit helpers into rattles, which held the healing powers.[7]

These holy people were also credited with the power of spirit flight, in which the free soul or spirit could manifest outside the body in sleep or unconsciousness to visit far-away places, as well as access the sacred, who, through the use of spirit helpers, or their animal spirit helper, or direct flight into the spiritual realm, receive important information.

A holy person may be called upon to rescue a lost soul. This is where the free soul or spirit of the sick or wounded person has left, leaving behind their bodily soul. Some free souls stay close for a few days, while others begin their journey on the spirit road across the Milky Way. They are in route to Seana, which is the place of the dead for the Cheyenne. For the Lakota, it was to the land of the shades in the northern skies. The holy man or holy woman, bestowed with the gifts for just such an undertaking, now went into a trance-like state and their own free soul or spirit would seek after their "patient's" soul with the intent to bring it back![8]

These holy people, medicine men and medicine women from all tribes and bands, were tasked with a monumental undertaking that appears to be ignored when discussing this Battle. They had to care for and heal the wounded and dying warriors and horses from the Battle of the Rosebud fought just seven days before the Battle of the Little Bighorn.[9]

~

The oral history opened our eyes to another important aspect to the Battle: the role the sacred covenants of the Lakota and Cheyenne played that day.[10]

It starts with Elk Head, the Sans Arc Lakota Holy Man. He was responsible for the Sacred White Buffalo Calf Pipe and the Sacred Calf Pipe Bundle, the two most sacred covenants of the Lakota People. Oral history shared with me clearly states Elk Head was at the Little Bighorn by June 24th.[11] This was emphasized by stories told by Rick Two Dogs, Garvard Good Plume Jr., Basil BraveHeart, Arvol and Paula Looking Horse, and, in subsequent interviews, Harold Salway, Victor Douville and Doug War Eagle that made Elk Head's role at the Battle of the Little Bighorn clear, as well as after the Battle of the Rosebud. These Lakota elders knew this holy man had played an integral part that had been kept quiet.[12]

Donovan Taylor received intriguing information regarding the sacred covenants of the Cheyenne at the encampment on the Little Bighorn. Very little has been said or written regarding the Medicine Arrows, one of the two sacred covenants in the possession of the Cheyenne people.

Cheyenne Sacred Buffalo Hat Tipi said by Cheyenne historians to have been at the Little Bighorn in June of 1876. -- *Source: Stanley J Morrow*

In the early 1990's, while attending Chief Dull Knife Community College at Lame Deer, Montana, Donovan had the privilege to take Florence Whiteman's class on the Cheyenne language.

Florence Whiteman was raised by her maternal grandparents. Her maternal grandfather, Louis Dog, whose Cheyenne name was Dog, was a Cheyenne warrior and veteran of the Battle of the Little Bighorn. Florence was herself a member of the Cheyenne military society, the Elkhorn Scrapers. She was the last warrior woman among the Northern Cheyenne.[13]

Florence knew of Donovan's passion for his peoples' history and his interest in the Battle of the Little Bighorn. Florence decided to share with Donovan some vital information regarding the Medicine Arrows. She told Donovan that not only was the sacred Buffalo Hat of the Cheyenne at the Little Bighorn at the time of the battle, but so too were the Medicine Arrows! Florence could not add where exactly the Medicine Arrows were at the time of the Battle, or who might have been entrusted in caring for them there.[14]

Florence Whiteman made her journey to the camp on the other side on April 22, 2001.

~

Growing up on the Cheyenne Tribal Reservation in Busby, Montana, Donovan Taylor had known the respected historian and elder Gilbert Whitedirt his entire life. Gilbert shared pieces of Cheyenne history with Donovan when Donovan visited Gilbert's home on Muddy Creek. Donovan would take tobacco and food, as was customary when asking for such history.

Gilbert Whitedirt, Cheyenne elder and historian. Gilbert's relative Crazy Head fought at the Little Bighorn.

In 2018, Donovan went to visit Gilbert

regarding the Battle of the Little Bighorn. Gilbert Whitedirt was a member of the Elkhorn Scraper warrior society and a descendant of the noted Cheyenne war chief, Elkhorn Scraper Society member and Little Bighorn veteran Crazy Head. Gilbert was told this story by his father, Charlie Whitedirt, who was also an Elkhorn Scraper member.

Gilbert told Donovan that both the Buffalo Hat and Medicine Arrows were both at the Little Bighorn during the Battle. Gilbert added that the Medicine Arrows resulted in the demise of Custer and his men. Gilbert added that the Cheyenne People used the Medicine Arrows in an impromptu ceremony. This ceremony, which Gilbert told Donovan, "was a blinding ceremony," was done, Gilbert said, to stop the Custer men as they moved for the area where the non-combatants had gathered to, presumably, try to capture women and children. Gilbert said he thought this happened somewhere north and down the river from the Cheyenne camps. Gilbert was not certain, nor could he remember, who had done this ceremony at the Battle. He reasoned it might have been an Arrow Priest.[15]

In June of 2019, Donovan Taylor and I went to see Gilbert and his son Eddie Whitedirt at their home on Muddy Creek on the Cheyenne Reservation. Although weak from failing health, Gilbert visited with us most of an afternoon.

Gilbert was adamant that not only were the Medicine Arrows there at the Little Bighorn, they were responsible for helping the Cheyenne be victorious that day. Gilbert went on to state that the Medicine Arrows and the Buffalo Hat, the other sacred covenant of the Cheyenne, had been there at the same time in the Cheyenne camps on the Little Bighorn. Gilbert stressed that this story, especially of the blinding ceremony, needed to be finally told, and that the Cheyenne people needed to know the truth, once and for all.[16]

Gilbert Whitedirt made his journey to the camp on the other side, on March 12th, 2021.

One year after Gilbert's death, I met Scott Doser, who had been adopted by Gilbert Whitedirt's family. Scott told me that he, too, had been told the Buffalo Hat and the Medicine Arrows were both at the Little Bighorn. He added that he had been told the Medicine Arrows were moved down the Little Bighorn River, and of the impromptu blinding ceremony done with them against the soldiers. Scott said he had been told this history by Gilbert's father, Charlie Whitedirt.[17]

~

Three Cheyenne tribal members, Vernon Sooktis, Chester Whiteman, who is the Coordinator of the Culture Program of the Cheyenne and Arapaho Tribes, and Rufus Spear, all told me they had been told that the Medicine Arrows were at the Little Bighorn. All three men had ancestors at the Little Bighorn as well.

Rufus Spear shared information that historians need to pay close attention to when studying the Battle of the Little Bighorn. "Both the Cheyenne Sacred Arrows and the Sacred Hat Covenants were in the Cheyenne camp. The 'war medicine' of the Cheyenne Covenants is to blind and confuse the enemy."[18]

Rufus's story is similar to Florence Whiteman's, Gilbert Whitedirt's and Scott Doser's. All three put the two sacred covenants of the Cheyenne at the Battle of the Little Bighorn. However, Gilbert Whitedirt and Scott Doser specifically said the Medicine Arrows were used against the Custer Battalion during the Battle in some type of impromptu blinding ceremony.[19]

Two Lakota historians, Rick Two Dogs and the late Garvard Good Plume Jr., both shared what they had been told regarding the Medicine Arrows of the Cheyenne being at the Little Bighorn. Both are descendants of people who were at the Little Bighorn.

Rick's grandfather, Thomas American Horse, his great-grandfather American Horse, and great-uncles Samuel and Ben were all at the Little Bighorn. However, it was from Charlie Whitedirt, Gilbert Whitedirts's father, that Rick was told the Cheyenne Medicine Arrows were at the Little Bighorn. Rick had no idea as to where the Medicine Arrows were during the Battle, or how they were used.[20]

Garvard's relatives, Little Killer and White Cow Bull, who both fought at the Battle, told their people that there was a, "Cheyenne Arrow Camp," at the Little Bighorn. As to where this camp was, Garvard was not told. Nor could he ever ascertain where exactly it was located throughout the course of his own research and interviews.[21]

What makes these stories regarding the Medicine Arrows even more intriguing is that the Sacred Buffalo Hat has been said to be at the Little Bighorn as well.[22] Now, add to this the story told throughout Cheyenne history of what General Custer had been told would happen should he attack the Cheyenne People again. The part of the Cheyenne in the Battle that day are overlooked in the historical record of battles and massacres perpetrated by the United States on Native American people. To deny this and ignore the Cheyenne narrative is a common mistake of historians and researchers studying or writing on the subject.[23]

Custer and his Seventh Cavalry attacked and massacred Cheyenne people at the Washita River, in 1868, in present day Oklahoma. Some months after this attack, in early 1869, Custer met the Keeper of the Medicine Arrows, Stone Forehead.

According to Father Peter Powell, in his work, *People of the Sacred Mountain, Vol* 2, Stone Forehead prayed with Custer under the Medicine Arrows and "even implored the Arrows to use their divine power to touch Custer's heart." Powell added that Stone Forehead said, "if this soldier chief (General Custer) broke his promise and harmed the People again, then he, their Keeper, begged the Arrows to bless the People as they avenged all the wrongs the white man had done to them." Stone Forehead, it is told, offered a pipe to Custer, which he smoked.

From Powell again:

"Stone Forehead spoke to him (Custer) quietly, saying in Cheyenne if you are acting treacherously towards us, sometime you and your whole command will be killed." When Custer was finished, Stone Forehead emptied the pipe's ashes onto Custer's boots and said, 'thus will the Arrows destroy the soldier chief if he ever walks contrary to the peace pipe again.'"[24]

~

In chapter 4, we presented information regarding the

Arapaho presence in the encampment on the Little Bighorn. Two Arapaho men, Bill Goggles and Devin Oldman, had both been told the stories of their Arapaho people and their bundles being at the Little Bighorn. Devin added to this history by sharing about their holy people and their abilities.[25] There was one Arapaho historian, Cletus Yellow Plume, who thought the Arapaho Flat Pipe was in fact at the Little Bighorn.[26] Two Lakota elders, Arvol Looking Horse and Garvard Good Plume Jr., specifically mentioned the Arapahos as being at the Little Bighorn. Arvol Looking Horse, Keeper of The Sacred White Buffalo Calf Pipe and The Sacred Calf Pipe Bundle of the Lakota, specifically recalled he had been told bits and pieces of stories regarding the Arapaho and their medicine bundles.[27]

The medicine bundles and how they relate to the people in the Little Bighorn encampment was a common topic discussed on the research trail. Many Native American and First Nations elders and historians felt this topic was never discussed because it was to be kept quiet for fear the U.S. and Canadian Governments would learn what the medicine bundles were capable of.[28]

I was told a bundle is like a spirit and should be treated as such, with care and respect. These were carried in soft pouches of tanned animal hides, or the skin of an animal or bird, which were ornamented and fringed. Others were carried in a parfleche, made of stiff rawhide. The medicine bundles were sacred. Native People believe spirits are everywhere in nature. In order to obtain power from nature, which was seen as a mystery, and much stronger than any human power, every boy and in some cases, girls, would go alone to secluded place. It was thought these places were special, with an unseen lifeforce permeating. It was thought that four days were the sacred number in order to dream and seek visions in securing the aid of a powerful spirit, which was the desired outcome. If the spirit came to the candidate, it was usually the spirit of animal in human form. If obtained, this protection and gift might enable a person to become a healer, hunter or warrior. Power was also given by spirits of inanimate objects.[29]

There were tribal medicine bundles, as well as

medicine bundles for war. A warrior's bundle for his war medicine contained what his spirit helper, bird or animal helper showed him to need for protection. And, how to heal himself, for when he went on the warpath. When warriors set out on the war path, the spirits from the medicine bundles for war were summoned. These ancient spirits not only acted as guides and scouts for a war party, they kept watch over the camps while the warriors were away. Once the enemy was found, the spirits helped the warriors in a variety of ways.

Tribal medicine bundles were for sacred rituals for the entire band or group. They were said to be alive with powers from spirits, other non-human persons and tribal cultural heroes. Some tribal medicine bundles were of utmost importance to a tribe's history and continuance. These bundles were the key to continued spirituality among the bands and tribes. Not only could they cure, but it could bring one back who had started their journey to the land of the dead. Not all people of the tribe or band were privy to these.[30]

They are paramount because by 1876 the reservation system was in place and the buffalo herds had been decimated. Spirituality was one of the last key pieces to the old ways holding the People together.[31]

Lakota elder and historian Basil BraveHeart instructed me about this encampment and the bundles and the holy people, the medicine men and medicine women.

"They [the Army], had no worldly idea just how powerful an encampment they were attacking. That is, this encampment was sacred and protected. It was from these bundles and the medicine people, that an intrinsic shield of divine protection was believed to be in place that covered the people. The camps were covered with a sense of invincibility."[32]

At this point on the research trail, we now know from Native American and First Nations historians and elders that after the Battle of the Little Bighorn there was a concentrated effort to get these bundles out of the area. Specifically, small bands, or even a tiospaye, which was an extended family unit of relatives, took the bundles and dispersed, not only across and throughout the American and Canadian Plains, but in some cases, to much farther destinations than anyone to this day has any idea of.

These people, bands and tiospayes, were followed and hunted without mercy.[33]

Who hunted these bands and the bundles is not clearly known at this time. It is thought by the elders and historians who shared this information with me that the pursuers were possibly other Native American and First Nations People. Most likely, they accompanied, tracked, or scouted for bounty hunters associated with United States and Canadian military forces. Clearly, the medicine bundles were coveted.[34]

Why did the United States and Canadian Governments want these bundles so badly? According to elders and historians, the governments had learned just what the bundles were made up of and capable of, and that if the medicine bundles could be destroyed if not taken, then the people's spirituality could be wiped out, leaving them with no ties to the old ways, their ancestors, star knowledge, countless medicinal remedies and so many other invaluable spiritual elements of everyday.

If this had happened, the collapse of Native American and First Nations Plains Peoples' culture would have been even more catastrophic than it was.

Knowledge of the medicine bundles would have had to come from Native People that either had been taken as prisoners or had been turned against the people. Another possible source might be from mixed-blood people who married into the bands and tribes. Many of the mixed-blood people had trading posts scattered across the plains of the American West and in the Canadian territories.[35]

No one could say for certain what was told to the United States and Canadian Governments regarding the bundles, but the elders and historians felt confident it included the following:

- Harnessing the weather, which might also be means to control lightning.
- Plants and medicinal information.
- Telepathic communication and means to communicate with animals.
- Spirit flight and remote viewing.

If those do not get your attention, then these last ones should:

It was thought by the elders and historians that the

United States and Canadian Governments had been told the medicine bundles could not only heal people and horses, but bring a person back from death. Lastly, it was thought they might have been told the bundles could enable a person to physically fly and change forms... in other words, shape shift.

Therefore, the medicine bundles could be said to hold the secrets to opportunities the United States and Canadian Governments could use against an enemy.

As to where some of these bundles were taken, I was told of a few places of interest. Many went to Canada, some to Yellowstone National Park and others to the surrounding area adjacent to Mato Tipila / Grey Horn Butte, as it is known to Siouan speakers, Bear's Lodge or Bear's Tipi, to Algonquian speakers. To Americans, it is called Devil's Tower.[36]

What is in the historical record and how do these stories match up against it?

Regarding the history of The People, the Ancient Alliance, and sacred medicine bundles, there is nothing in the historical record. This history has been kept quiet and is only now being brought out for the sake of future generations. It is important to tell this history now and the elders have instructed it to be put forth in order to start future conversations regarding the fact that, the People have always been here on this continent. This is their history, as they had history long before the coming of the white man. The bundles tied the People to one another and to this continent. Only now are the U.S. and Canadian Governments starting to acknowledge this.

Elk Head, the Lakota holy man and Keeper of the Sacred Buffalo Calf Pipe and Bundle of the Lakota, was first discussed in chapter 3.[37] Now, we add his involvement at both the Battle of the Rosebud and the Little Bighorn, along with the holy people, medicine men and medicine women there.

There is only one mention in historical record regarding Elk Head and the holy people playing any significant role at Little Bighorn. It comes from Gordon Harper and is only cited in his appendices.[38]

In chapter 9, we will discuss in more detail where some of these people were, who they were made up of, and what they were doing prior to and during the Battle.

The story of the Cheyenne Sacred Covenants being at the Little Bighorn can be found sparingly in the historical record. It was, again, the Canadian researcher and historian Gordon Harper who revealed that the Cheyenne conducted their Sacred Arrow Ceremony and that it was held near the junction of (what is now) U.S. Highways 212 and 39 two miles north of Lame Deer, before the Battle of the Rosebud. Harper said he got this information from the Minnikojou Lakota People of the Cheyenne River Reservation.[39]

There are a few accounts placing the Buffalo Hat of the Cheyenne Tribe at the Little Bighorn, notably from Dr. Marquis, Father Powell,[40] and Wooden Leg, who put the Cheyenne Tribal Medicine Lodge there as well.[41]

Garvard Good Plume Jr. was told there was a, "Cheyenne Arrow Camp," at the Little Bighorn. He was never able to ascertain where this camp was. Nothing in the historical record was found to support this camp site at the Little Bighorn.

The are two accounts that put the Medicine Arrows at the Little Bighorn. The oldest is from Young Two Moons. He fought at both the Battle of the Rosebud and at the Little Bighorn. The date of his interview with veteran historian Walter Campbell is 1929 and took place at Custer Battlefield, now called Little Bighorn Battlefield National Monument. All that was recorded by Campbell is that the Medicine Arrows and [Sacred] Hat were in the Custer Fight.[42]

The only other account found that puts the Medicine Arrows at the Battle of the Little Bighorn comes from noted Cheyenne historian John Stands In Timber. He first told anthropologist Margot Liberty that the Arrows had come north after the Battle of the Washita in 1868. When asked by Liberty if the Medicine Arrows were at the Custer Battle, Stands in Timber simply said, "I think they were there too."[43]

Stands In Timber and Father Powell told another story regarding the Medicine Arrows. In November of 1876, a large contingent of Cheyenne people who had been at the Little Bighorn were attacked by the U.S. Army on the

Powder River, near Kaycee, Wyoming. This is sometimes called the Dull Knife Fight. According to Father Powell and John Stands in Timber, the Medicine Arrows were there, in the possession of Stone Forehead's son, Black Hairy Dog. The Medicine Arrows were said to be used by Black Hairy Dog to defend the Cheyenne People against the attack.[44]

There is one more example from John Stands In Timber. He said there was a group of Cheyenne families who refused to surrender to the U.S. Army in 1877. These people were in the areas adjacent to the Little Bighorn Valley and other areas where fights took place between the Cheyenne and the Army following the Battle of the Little Bighorn. What's interesting is that Stands In Timber said this group took the Medicine Arrows with them and headed south.[45]

To be fair, we want to make sure we present the other side to the history told to us, if there was something found that contradicts it or simply can't be ignored. Father Powell followed the Medicine Arrows trail based on the work of George Grinnell and George Bent. Both said that Stone Forehead died in late 1875, or in early 1876 in the Powder River Country, which runs through the states of Montana and Wyoming. Both stated that Stone Forehead had not named his successor and, according to Grinnell, therefore didn't perform the customary duties through intricate rites and ceremonies to pass the Medicine Arrows to another.[46]

It is said Stone Forehead's wife took possession of the Medicine Arrows until his son could take over responsibilities as the Keeper. Black Hairy Dog, Stone Forehead's son, was in the south and not close to the Little Bighorn. Powell stated Stone Forehead's wife was at the White River Agency, which at the time of the Battle was in northwest Nebraska, near Fort Robinson. Therefore, the Medicine Arrows were not at the Little Bighorn. Wooden Leg said the Medicine Arrows were not at the Little Bighorn as well.[47]

As for the spiritual belief in the bundles and the role this played in the outcome of the Battle, there are glimpses of it in the historical record.

The first is from Alberta American Horse, a Northern

Cheyenne woman, who has since made her journey. Alberta visited with Donovan Taylor on several occasions regarding the Battle. She related a story from her father about the Battle of the Little Bighorn that was recorded by Dr. Herman Viola.

Alberta said, "Whatever the spirits revealed to the Cheyenne People, they did very faithfully. The Cheyennes knew beforehand that an incident was going to take place, and they were warned not to stray from their ceremonies and spirits. After the Custer battle, one of the elderly ceremonial chiefs told everyone that this was the incident that they had been warned about."[48]

The renowned Cheyenne historian John Stands In Timber mentioned an interesting piece regarding the venerated Cheyenne holy man, Ice. Stands In Timber said he was told Ice was conducting ceremonies to heal a wounded Cheyenne (presumably from the Battle of the Rosebud), "when spirits called from Bear Butte predicted the coming victory."[49] This same story was told to researcher Verne Dusenberry by Cheyenne Tribal member and historian William Hollow Breast. Dusenberry was taken to the Cheyenne Reservation, specifically to Busby, Montana, where today a monument stands for Ice, and where Dusenbery was told the story.[50]

There is one more interesting piece in the historical record providing a glimpse into the spirit world and how sacred and powerful the people's spirituality was the day of the Battle. It comes from the noted Hunkpapa Lakota War Chief, Gall, in an interview a mere ten years after the Battle in the St. Paul Pioneer Press, 18 July, 1886.

"Gall asserts with gravity that the Great Spirit was present riding over the field, mounted on a coal black pony and urging the braves on."[51]

Gall's narrative has now been put forth for consideration. John Stands In Timber related Ice's story and Alberta American Horse shared what she had been told. All pull back the veil on the component of spirituality that is perhaps hard to accept, since it might be from another dimension, reality or a different world. We hope this type of information as it pertains to the Battle will be looked at in closer examination by other researchers.

In Summary:

Based on the history shared with us and the trail we followed in the historical record, it does appear that the Buffalo Hat and the Medicine Arrows of the Cheyenne Tribe were in the vicinity of the Little Bighorn Valley, both before the Battle and after it. Oral history from Cheyenne tribal people and their historians, Florence Whiteman, Gilbert Whitedirt, Scott Doser and Rufus Spear, tell that the two most sacred covenants of the Cheyenne, the Medicine Arrows and Sacred Buffalo Hat, were both at the Little Bighorn that June of 1876. This is in agreement with two noted Cheyenne accounts, one from John Stands In Timber and the other from Little Bighorn veteran Young Two Moons, who both told the same account. Gilbert Whitedirt and Scott Doser both said that the Medicine Arrows of the Cheyenne were used against the Custer Battalion in an impromptu blinding ceremony of some sorts during the Battle.

The Lakota Sacred Pipe and Sacred Bundle, as well as the Arapaho Flat Pipe, are said to be at the Little Bighorn. It is thought that other medicine bundles from the Lakota and Arapaho, maybe the Cheyenne and other tribes, are said to be at the Little Bighorn as well.

To our knowledge and to the elders and historians who shared regarding the subject of their tribes sacred covenants for this chapter, this may be the first time in recorded history that these sacred covenants of the Lakota, Cheyenne and possibly Arapaho are being discussed as all being in the same encampment. Whether or not this might have happened with, the People of the Ancient Alliance and ceremonies associated with it centuries before, we do not know at this time. And yes, we are told that the People who had gathered on the Little Bighorn, are militant in defiance of the U.S. Government because they wanted to adhere to the old ways. That is undeniable. However, based on the history shared with us, the People who had gathered on the Little Bighorn that late June in 1876 did so with the intent to renew their covenants, bundles, and strengthen the bond of an ancient alliance of the People who were much, much more, than the historical record has led the world to believe.

If not for the initial assistance of Gilbert Whitedirt, Florence Whiteman and of course, Donovan Taylor, parts of this chapter would simply not have been investigated. The same goes for Arvol and Paula Looking Horse, Bill Goggles, Devin Oldman, Doug War Eagle, Rhonda Funmaker, Victor Douville, Peter Gibbs, Basil BraveHeart, Rick Two Dogs, the late Garvard Good Plume Jr., with a special note of thanks to Rufus Spear and Scott Doser.

Notes

1. Personal communications with Arvol Looking Horse, Victor Douville-Sicangu Lakota Tribal Historian, Garvard Good Plume Jr.-Oglala Lakota, Rick Two Dogs-Oglala Lakota, Basil BraveHeart-Oglala Lakota, Chico Her Many Horses-Oglala Lakota, Rod Alexis-Stoney Nakoda, Dennis Paul-Stoney Nakoda, Ozzy McKay-Santee Dakota, Jim Red Eagle-Nakota/Lakota, Alvin WindyBoy Sr.-Chippewa Cree, Jimmy Stgoddard-Blackfeet, Ernie Heavy Runner-Blackfeet, Michael Black Wolf-Gros Ventre, Chester Whiteman-Cheyenne, Dwight Bull Coming-Cheyenne, Donovan Taylor-Cheyenne, Vernon Sooktis-Cheyenne, Keith Spotted Wolf-Cheyenne, Gilbert Whitedirt-Cheyenne, Harold Salway-Oglala Lakota, Devin Oldman-Arapaho, Bill Goggles-Arapaho, Ben Rhodd - Potawatomie, Iris O'Watch-Dakota/Nakota, Joanne Pompana-Hunkpapa Lakota/Iroquois/Seneca, Ken Shields-Yankton/Lakota, Frenchy Dillon- Crow, Dennis Limberhand-Cheyenne, Doug War Eagle-Minnikojou Lakota, Peter Gibbs-Tribal Historian Sicangu Lakota and Chris Dixon. See Bailyn 2012: 3-5.

2. Ibid. See chapter 2, The Ancient Alliance.

3. Personal communications with Rufus Spear-Cheyenne, Linwood Tall Bull-Cheyenne and Chris Dixon.

4. Personal communications with Victor Douville-Sicangu Lakota Tribal Historian, Peter Gibbs-Tribal

Historian Sicangu Lakota, Harold Salway-Oglala Lakota, Rick Two Dogs-Oglala Lakota, Basil BraveHeart-Oglala Lakota, Garvard Good Plume Jr.-Oglala Lakota, Arvol and Paul Looking Horse and Doug War Eagle-Minnikojou Lakota. See LaPointe 1976: 29-30; Bailyn 2012: 6; Goodman 2017; Kracht 2017: 61-63.

5. Personal communications with Victor Douville-Sicangu Lakota Tribal Historian, Peter Gibbs-Tribal Historian Sicangu Lakota, Harold Salway-Oglala Lakota, Rick Two Dogs-Oglala Lakota, Basil BraveHeart-Oglala Lakota, Garvard Good Plume Jr.-Oglala Lakota, Arvol and Paul Looking Horse and Doug War Eagle-Minnikojou Lakota. See Powers 1977: 56-61; Powers 1986: 126; Hultkrantz 1992: 32-35; St. Pierre and Long Soldier 1995: 24-32. Dooling 2000:129; Deloria 2006: 52-54, 116-117.

6. Personal communications with Chester Whiteman-Cheyenne, Leroy Whiteman-Cheyenne, Rufus Spear-Cheyenne, Donovan Taylor-Cheyenne, Vernon Sooktis-Cheyenne and Keith Spotted Wolf-Cheyenne. See Powell 1981, vol. 1, xxxvii; Grinnell and Fitzgerald 2008: 203.

7. Personal communications with Victor Douville-Sicangu Lakota Tribal Historian, Peter Gibbs-Tribal Historian Sicangu Lakota, Garvard Good Plume Jr.-Oglala Lakota, Keith Spotted Wolf-Cheyenne, Chester Whiteman-Cheyenne, Vernon Sooktis-Cheyenne, Ernie Heavy Runner-Blackfeet, Devin Oldman-Arapaho and Doug War Eagle-Minnikojou Lakota. See LaPointe 1976: 17-19; Walker 1991: 118-128; St. Pierre and Long Soldier 1995: 96-121; V. Deloria 2006: 9, 43-44, 52-54; Bailyn 2012: 3-8; Howard 2014: 11; Kracht 2017: 32-33, 58-61.

8. Personal communications with Victor Douville-Sicangu Lakota Tribal Historian, Peter Gibbs-Tribal Historian Sicangu Lakota, Harold Salway-Oglala Lakota, Rick Two Dogs- Oglala Lakota, Basil BraveHeart-Oglala Lakota, Garvard Good Plume Jr.-Oglala Lakota, Arvol and Paul Looking Horse and Doug War Eagle-

Minnikojou Lakota. See Powell 1981, Vol. 1: xxxviii; Walker 1991: 91-128; Hultkrantz 1992: 34; St. Pierre and Long Soldier 1995: 96-121; Deloria 2006: 9, 43-44, 52-54, 116-117; Densmore 2016: 86-106; Kracht 2017: 32-33, 58-61.

9. Personal communications with Victor Douville-Sicangu Lakota Tribal Historian, Harold Salway-Oglala Lakota, Rick Two Dogs-Oglala Lakota, Basil BraveHeart-Oglala Lakota, Garvard Good Plume Jr.-Oglala Lakota, Arvol and Paul Looking Horse, Doug War Eagle-Minnikojou Lakota, Chester Whiteman-Cheyenne, Leroy Whiteman-Cheyenne, Keith Spotted Wolf-Cheyenne, Wallace Bearchum-Cheyenne and Donovan Taylor-Cheyenne. Peter Gibbs-Tribal Historian Sicangu Lakota and Chris Dixon.

10. Ibid.

11. Personal communications with Victor Douville-Sicangu Lakota Tribal Historian, Harold Salway-Oglala Lakota, Rick Two Dogs-Oglala Lakota, Basil BraveHeart-Oglala Lakota, Garvard Good Plume Jr.-Oglala Lakota, Arvol and Paul Looking Horse, Doug War Eagle-Minnikojou Lakota. Peter Gibbs-Tribal Historian Sicangu Lakota and Chris Dixon. For information regarding Elk Head at the Little Bighorn, see David Humphreys Miller 1985: 57-60; Kammen, Lefthand and Marshall 1992: 47; Hardorff 1997: 134.

12. Ibid.

13. Regarding Florence Whiteman, personal communications with Donovan Taylor-Cheyenne, Gilbert Whitedirt-Cheyenne, Eddie Whitedirt-Cheyenne, Roger Red Hat-Cheyenne, Scott Doser-Cheyenne, Keith Spotted Wolf-Cheyenne, Dennis Limberhand-Cheyenne, Wallace Bearchum-Cheyenne, Leroy Whiteman-Cheyenne, Al Joe Strange Owl-Cheyenne, Vernon Sooktis-Cheyenne, Dwight Bull Coming and Linwood Tall Bull-Cheyenne. For Florence Whiteman's story on her relative Dog, See Viola 1999: 46-49.

14. Ibid.

15. Personal communications with Gilbert Whitedirt-Cheyenne, Eddie Whitedirt-Cheyenne, Donovan Taylor-Cheyenne.

16. Ibid.

17. Personal communications with Scott Doser.

18. Personal communications with Vernon Sooktis-Cheyenne, Chester Whiteman-Cheyenne and Rufus Spear-Cheyenne.

19. Personal communications with Rufus Spear-Cheyenne, Gilbert Whitedirt-Cheyenne and Scott Doser.

20. Personal communications with Rick Two Dogs-Oglala Lakota

21. Personal communications with Garvard Good Plume Jr.-Oglala Lakota.

22. Powell 1981, Vol 2: 1004-1005; Miller 1985: 65; Marquis 2003: 209-210.

23. See Liberty and Wood 2011, "Cheyenne Primacy: New Perspectives on a Great Plains Tribe."

24. Powell 1981, Vol 2: 706-711.

25. Personal communications with Bill Goggles-Arapaho and Devin Oldman-Arapaho.

26. Ibid. Personal communications with Martin Blackburn-Arapaho and Cletus Yellow Plume-Arapaho.

27. Personal communications with Arvol Looking Horse and Garvard Good Plume Jr.-Oglala Lakota.

28. Personal communications with Garvard Good Plume Jr.-Oglala Lakota, Basil BraveHeart-Oglala Lakota, Ernie Heavy Runner-Blackfeet, Jimmy Stgoddard-Blackfeet, Rhonda Funmaker-Ho-Chunk, Chester

Whiteman-Cheyenne, Keith Spotted Wolf-Cheyenne, Donovan Taylor-Cheyenne, Arvol Looking Horse, Victor Douville-Sicangu Lakota Tribal Historian, Doug War Eagle- Minnikojou Lakota, Rick Two Dogs-Oglala Lakota, Harold Salway-Oglala Lakota, Peter Gibbs-Tribal Historian Sicangu Lakota, Alvin WindyBoy Sr.-Chippewa Cree, Ozzie McKay-Santee Dakota, Bill Goggles-Arapaho, Devin Oldman-Arapaho, Rod Alexis-Stoney Nakoda and Dennis Paul-Stoney Nakoda.

29. Ibid. See Powers 1977:146; Powell 1981: vol 1, xxxvii; Clark, Ella. 1988: 17-19; St. Pierre and Long Soldier 1995: 126-128; James Long (First Boy) 2004: 56; Grinnell and Fitzgerald 2008: 203; Howard 2014: 47; Densmore 2016: 75-224; Kracht 2017: 137-142.

30. Ibid.

31. Ibid.

32. Personal communications with Basil BraveHeart-Oglala Lakota.

33. Personal communications with Garvard Good Plume Jr.-Oglala Lakota, Basil BraveHeart-Oglala Lakota, Ernie Heavy Runner-Blackfeet, Jimmy Stgoddard-Blackfeet, Rhonda Funmaker-Ho-Chunk, Chester Whiteman-Cheyenne, Dwight Bull Coming-Cheyenne, Keith Spotted Wolf-Cheyenne, Donovan Taylor-Cheyenne, Arvol Looking Horse, Victor Douville-Sicangu Lakota Tribal Historian, Doug War Eagle-Minnikojou Lakota, Rick Two Dogs-Oglala Lakota, Harold Salway-Oglala Lakota, Peter Gibbs-Tribal Historian Sicangu Lakota, Alvin WindyBoy Sr.-Chippewa Cree, Iris O'Watch-Nakota/Dakota, Ozzie McKay-Santee Dakota, Bill Goggles-Arapaho, Devin Oldman-Arapaho, Rod Alexis-Stoney Nakoda and Dennis Paul-Stoney Nakoda.

34. Ibid.

35. Ibid.

36. Ibid.

37. For information regarding Elk Head at the Little Bighorn, see David Humphreys Miller 1985: 57-60; Kammen, Lefthand and Marshall 1992: 47; Hardorff 1997: 134.

38. Harper 2014: [Ebook] Appendices 3.79.

39. Ibid.

40. Maquis 2003: 209-210.

41. Powell 1981, Vol. 2: 1004-1005.

42. Hardorff 1998: 161. See the Walter Stanley Campbell Collection, Box 105, Notebook 15, University of Oklahoma Libraries, pages 1-42.

43. Stands In Timber and Liberty, Margot 2013: 318-319.

44. Stands In Timber and Liberty, Margot 1967: 217; Powell 1981, Vol. 2: 1056-1071.

45. Stands In Timber and Liberty, Margot 2013: 318-319.

46. Powell 1981, Vol. 2: 936, Endnote 1, 1361; 1005, Endnote 1,1355. See Grinnell, George Bird. "The Great Mysteries of the Cheyenne." American Anthropologist, Vol. 12, No. 4 (Oct. - Dec., 1910), pp. 542-575.

47. Powell 1981, Vol. 2: 1004-1005, Endnote 8, 1367; Marquis 2003: 209-210.

48. Viola 1999: 38.

49. Stands In Timber and Liberty 1967: 106, footnote 19.

50. Dusenberry 1962: 167.

51. Graham 1953: 91.

9
Sacred Healers, Camps for the Wounded and Warrior-Only Camps

The information that led to this trail we followed came from: Rick Two Dogs - Oglala Lakota, Garvard Good Plume Jr. - Oglala Lakota, Basil BraveHeart - Oglala Lakota, Harold Salway - Oglala Lakota, Victor Douville - Sicangu Lakota Tribal Historian, Doug War Eagle - Minnikojou Lakota, Arvol and Paula Looking Horse, Ernie Heavy Runner - Blackfeet, Bill Goggles - Arapaho, Devin Oldman - Arapaho, Donovan Taylor - Cheyenne, Vernon Sooktis - Cheyenne, Dwight Bull Coming - Cheyenne, Chester Whiteman - Cheyenne and Frederick Lefthand - Crow. Independent researchers: Chris Dixon and Jason Pitsch.

In the previous chapter we put forth information from Lakota, Cheyenne and Arapaho elders and historians regarding holy people, medicine men and medicine women. According to those who shared with us, these people and their role at the Little Bighorn has been overlooked. It is time to look more closely at these people and the role they played at the Battle.

By the evening of June 24th, Elk Head and the other holy people, medicine men and medicine women from the Santee Dakota, Sisitunwan Dakota, Lakota, Nakota, Cheyenne, Arapaho, Cree and maybe even others from the other tribes, were now set up on the Little Bighorn. These holy people and medicine people worked through a series of rituals only they could do that could not be rushed even though time was of essence: healing the wounded warriors and wounded horses from the Battle of the Rosebud.

None of the Dakota, Lakota, Cheyenne, Arapaho, or other elders and historians consulted could give an approximate number to the wounded and number of wounded horses from the Battle of the Rosebud. However, there are four accounts in the historical record that stand out.

The first came from Kill Eagle, a Sihasapa (Blackfeet) Lakota Chief. He said that, "It was impossible to say how many were wounded, there were so many - nearly 400." He then added, "One hundred and eighty Indian horses were killed."[1] Kill Eagle was in the Native Peoples coalition encampment from which the warriors left for the Battle of the Rosebud, and he was there when they returned. He was also in the encampment on the Little Bighorn when it was attacked on June 25th, 1876.

The second account we found came from Robert Utley, veteran historian and writer on the Battle of the Little Bighorn. He wrote, "The Cheyennes bore away several badly wounded men, one mortally."[2] Utley gave no sources as to where he got this information in his endnotes.

The last two are from Young Two Moon, a Cheyenne warrior, and Feather Earring, a Miniconjou Lakota warrior. Young Two Moon fought in both the Battle of the Rosebud and at the Battle of the Little Bighorn. In his account of the Battle of the Rosebud, Young Two Moon said, "Many men were wounded and many horses killed and wounded so that many Indians were on foot." Feather Earring's account is similar. He was asked how many Indians were killed in Crook's fight (the Battle of The Rosebud). Feather Earring said, "Four. Many were Wounded."[3]

~

Who were some of these holy people, medicine men and medicine women, entrusted with the all-important task of healing the warriors and horses? Only one Lakota elder, Harold Salway, and two Cheyenne elders, Vernon Sooktis and Chester Whiteman, could provide any information.

Harold Salway told me of Left Heron, also known as Makula and of Horn Chips. A Lakota medicine man and a relative to Elk Head, Makula, was said to have been with Elk Head and the other healers at the Little Bighorn.

Horn Chips was Lakota and a spiritual adviser to Crazy Horse. He was noted for his ability to secure help from the spirits to make war medicine.[4] Vernon Sooktis related that from Cheyenne people he was told the names of two Cheyenne holy people that were at the Little Bighorn and took care of these wounded warriors and horses. They were Ice, later known as White Bull, and Black Horse.[5] Chester Whiteman added the name of Lame Bull, as another holy person from the Cheyenne.[6]

Donovan Taylor added to the list of Cheyenne holy men and medicine men the names Crazy Mule, Bridge, and Sleeping Rabbit. Donovan had heard the names of these men pertaining to the Little Bighorn from Cheyenne elders. Donovan had not heard any stories specific to these men performing healing ceremonies to take care of the wounded warriors and the horses of the Cheyenne from the Battle of The Rosebud. He did recall how it was said Crazy Mule was a powerful medicine man who could kill an enemy with his powers by just looking at them.[7]

~

Where were Elk Head and these other holy people and medicine people in relation to the camps on the Little Bighorn? I was told these groups would have to be away from the main encampment and others. They had to be. Theirs was a work only a few could do. This was so the ceremonies could be done accordingly and that all the necessary precautions would be adhered to. For example, these ceremonies and rituals could not be performed near women who were pregnant or on their menstrual cycle.[8]

The following information first came from Lakota elders, Rick Two Dogs, Doug War Eagle and Garvard Good Plume Jr. They had been told how Elk Head and the holy and medicine people were set up in relation to the camps on the Little Bighorn.

All three elders put Elk Head's camp(s) of healers and others somewhere south, west and east of the Native Peoples coalition encampment, and close to the Little Bighorn River. This would be in close proximity and a little way to the east of where the current Garry Owen Museum / gas station sits.[9]

To administer to so many wounded warriors and horses, the holy people and medicine people required a great deal of assistance and protection from elders and young men respectively. Many of these young men had yet to even go through ceremonies to begin preparations to be warriors, let alone go on and participate in any raids where honors could be obtained. At this same time, the elders were said to be giving these youngsters instructions, teachings and spiritual guidance through ceremonies to protect them, should they be called upon to defend these camp(s) of healers.[10]

Many of these elders and youngsters set up wickiups, a form of crude brush shelter, mixed with an occasionally tipi or two. I was told some of these wickiups were near the Little Bighorn River, as well as to the west. Some were set away from the others, while some stretched to the land which is across from the current U.S. Interstate 90. Those in this area were close to a warrior-only camp. There were other small groups set even further apart, some of which were much further away from the main camps than is told.[11]

As to why some of the camps were so spread out, Basil BraveHeart shared knowledge he had known for many years. Basil told me the story of, "making the horses sacred," after the Battle of the Rosebud. Basil said that it was imperative to get the horses ready and healed up for the upcoming fight that most in the encampment reasoned was still yet to come. Sitting Bull's vision of soldiers falling into the camp had not yet happened. Basil was told that those doing the ceremonies needed a quiet and secluded spot so songs could be sung and paints and medicines applied.[12]

Basil then told me that as a young man, he was taken by his grandparents to a very remote area on the Pine Ridge Reservation in South Dakota. It was there, in 1939, that he got to witness the very same ceremonies that had been done at the Little Bighorn. They were still being done to commemorate the Battle and the role the sacred holy horses played that day for the Lakota people.[13]

Basil recounted one ceremony, called the "early morning charge." He remembered how the horses were sung to and painted in the ceremonies and then seemed to, "come alive, and it was as if they were running on air. It would be hard to hit a horse like that and you would not have to worry about your horse stumbling or stepping into a hole while in battle. A warrior was being carried by something special."[14]

Basil added one more very interesting piece about the ceremonies at the Little Bighorn. He was told there were many other ceremonies performed just prior to the Battle, and that these ceremonies were very, very ancient and that they were sacred. To which he added, "These rituals and ceremonies that the people did, covered the camp in a divine and sacred shield of sorts. But the ceremonies died there!" Basil said they were never done again. He didn't know what caused these ceremonies to be stopped or why.[15]

~

More information was shared with me from Doug War Eagle by way of a map he had made based on years of research. Some of the information on the map came from the countless number of oral stories shared with him. Doug was gracious enough to share some vital information regarding this area and what was going on before the Battle began.

Doug puts a warrior-only camp almost directly west of the current Garry Owen Museum / gas station. His map does not specify if it went across U.S. Interstate 90. Doug added that this camp was west of the Hunkpapa camp. He stated this was a good-sized camp of warriors and within it were holy people, the medicine men, and medicine women. Doug called these people healers. This camp or camps would have been directly to the north and possibly west of the U.S. Seventh Cavalry's initial skirmish line that Major Reno had deployed at the outset of the Valley Fight.[16] Doug also put designations for wickiups and tipis directly to the east of the current Gary Owen Museum / gas station and near the Little Bighorn River.[17]

Doug War Eagle presented two more items worth mentioning. The first pertains to Elk Head and just how busy he and the rest of the holy people, Medicine Men, and Medicine Women were that day. Doug was told there were at least 12 tipis set up along and close to the Little Bighorn River for the healing ceremonies.[18]

The last piece from Doug has to do with what bands were here and helping with the healing ceremonies. Doug stated it was the Miniconjou, Sihasapa (Blackfeet), Itazipcho (Sans Arcs) and Oohenunpa (Two Kettles).[19]

~

Jason Pitsch is a local rancher who has lived his entire life in the Little Bighorn Valley of Montana. Jason has metal detected the entire Little Bighorn River Valley area for a number of years and has meticulously catalogued his findings. He has compared his findings to warrior accounts, as well as to those of other researchers work and books on the Battle. Jason was gracious enough to share a very interesting map of his findings.

He places a camp of sorts west of U.S. Interstate 90, almost directly across from the current Garry Owen Museum / gas station. This would be in the general vicinity of where Doug War Eagle stated a camp of youngsters, holy people and medicine people were as well.[20] Additionally, his map shows indications where he found areas of where he thought wickiups or some type of shelters could of possibly have been erected. Jason stated he found debris and material from the time period of the Battle in these areas. This is just east of the current Garry Owen Museum / gas station, close to the Little Bighorn River and identical to Doug War Eagle's placements.[21]

~

On several occasions I had the fortunate pleasure to visit with Frederick Lefthand, Crow elder and historian, regarding the Battle of the Little Bighorn. Fred, as he preferred to be called, was gracious with his time and knew so much history pertaining to this Battle. Fred had been taught the history of this Battle by Jack Little Nest, Crow. Little Nest's grandfather was the father-in-law of the scout Mitch Bouyer, who rode with Custer and the Seventh Cavalry.[22] Bouyer was killed at the Battle of the Little Bighorn. It was told to me by Fred and by one other Crow historian, Frenchy Dillon, that Bouyer's wife, Magpie Outside, had actually been in the encampment on the Little Bighorn, on June 24th, 1876. She subsequently made it out of the encampment before the Battle.[23]

The last map we examined regarding camps comprised of young warriors comes from the book, *Soldiers Falling Into Camp: The Battles At The Rosebud and the Little Bighorn*. Frederick Lefthand wrote this book as part of a collaboration with Robert Kammen and Joe Marshall, Sicangu Lakota. There is one map in this book of interest. The map places brush shelters at the Little Bighorn on June 25, 1876 south of the main encampment in an area west of the Hunkpapa Lakota camps that today would be near U.S. Interstate 90. It also places brush shelters just north and a little east of where the current Garry Owen Museum / gas station sits. Some are very close to the Little Bighorn River.[24]

By the time I had found Fred and was able to get to know him, this great historian's health had deteriorated. Despite his health issues, Fred loved to visit about Crow history and many other aspects of Plains life before the Buffalo disappeared. When asked if he could remember much regarding who made the map or from what stories and sources he and the other writers pulled the information to make it, Fred could simply not recall. He could only relate that he and Joe Marshall knew oral stories from the Battle.[25]

Frederick Lefthand made his journey to the camp on the other side, in March of 2022.

What is in the historical record and how do these stories match up against it?

There are five references in the historical record mentioning some of the information we have been told regarding Elk Head, the holy people, medicine men and medicine women. These stories pertain to the wounded warrior camps and to doctoring wounded warriors and horses from the Battle of the Rosebud.

The first account comes from Gordon Harper's book, *The Fights on the Little Horn*. In his appendices, Harper told of a warrior-only camp west of all the other camps in the encampment scattered along the Little Bighorn River. Harper said it was 300 tipis strong and within it was the tipi of Elk Head, with the Sacred Pipe and Sacred Bundle. He went on to state Elk Head was surrounded by sweat lodges along the Little Bighorn River.[26] Harper put this camp somewhere to the west of the main encampment on the Little Bighorn. The information on Elk Head and the camps of healers was, strangely, omitted from the book and can be read only in the online appendices.[27]

The next account is from Black Elk. At the time of the Battle, this famous Lakota Holy Man was only 14 years of age. He told of taking part in the ceremonies to heal a wounded warrior from the Battle of the Rosebud. It is an interesting account and is the only one of its kind. Black Elk does not mention Elk Head. The only name of any Lakota medicine man at the Little Bighorn he told of was that of Hairy Chin. Black Elk said, "There were five other boys there, and he needed us for bears in the curing ceremony, because he had his power from a dream of the Bear. He painted my body yellow, and my face too, and put a black stripe on either side of my nose from the eyes down. Then he tied my hair up to look like bear's ears, and put some eagle feathers on my head. The other boys were painted all red and had real bear's ears on their head. Hairy Chin, who wore a real bear skin with the head on it."[28]

What Black Elk told of was a ceremony from the Bear Society. These medicine men and medicine women had dreamed of the Bear and were known for curing wounds. The medicine men paint their bodies red and may wear the entire skin of a bear. In battle, they were known to grunt and growl like a bear in order to frighten their enemy.[29]

The third account came from Two Moons, a noted Cheyenne war chief. Two Moons simply said, "Elk Head's band were down on the river."[30]

Fourth, we have another Cheyenne account. This comes from the noted Cheyenne historian John Stands In Timber. We mentioned it in the previous chapter. The story is only a footnote stating, "Fred Last Bull said that a few days before the Custer Battle, Ice officiated at a similar affair. During ceremonies conducted to heal a wounded Cheyenne, spirits called from Bear Butte predicted the coming victory."[31]

Lastly, there is this piece from Sitting Bull's step-son, Little Soldier, who said, "There were other Indian camps up the river who did not know of the battle."[32]

This is interesting, to say the least, especially, when you consider what we have been told in regards to the need for these wounded men and horses to be away from others so ceremonies could be performed correctly. Little Soldier also made a map of the encampment on the Little Bighorn showing the different camps. His map does not show any satellite camps, nor any tipis near the river or to the west. Up the river would be in southerly direction.[33]

~

Next, in an effort to see if any stories told of coming upon a camp, or camps far away from others, I looked at accounts from U.S. Seventh Calvary soldiers, and then from warriors who fought in this part of the Battle, which is sometimes called the Valley Fight. The accounts of the Arikara scouts and the two Crow scouts who fought in this part of the Battle were examined as well.

I found two accounts in the historical record from James Wilber and Little Hawk that might be possible clues as to where some of the wickiups or a tipi were, and if they were set apart from the main encampment. These might have been used for healing ceremonies or been part of a warrior only camp

James Wilber, who was a private in M Company, U.S. Seventh Calvary, said, "Sergeant O'Hara was killed near the tepees and was the first man killed in the battle."[34] Sergeant Miles O'Hara's place of death has been marked as being on the extreme left of Major Reno's first skirmish line in the Valley Fight. This spot would be very close to the current U.S. Interstate 90,[35] just south of both placements by Doug War Eagle and Jason Pitsch's findings of a possible warrior only camp and of a camp(s) of healers.[36]

There is this account from Little Hawk. This Cheyenne warrior told of how warriors got behind the Reno Battalion after the three companies under Major Reno had redeployed from their initial skirmish line across the Little Bighorn Valley floor. Now, Reno's men were with their backs and horses to the Little Bighorn River and surrounding timber.

Little Hawk said, "At the center of the stand of timber there was a small clearing, where the lone tipi of a Lakota Holy Man had been erected earlier. The soldiers pulled back to this clear spot, where they began to mount their horses."[37]

This area would be just to the south of where, in chapter 4, we presented information on the Arapaho; in particular, maps and testimony from not only U.S. Army personnel but from Cheyenne and Lakota as well.[38] These pieces put Arapaho people within the same general area as where the wounded warrior camps were said to be by Lakota historians and elders. Gordon Harper's research stated the same.[39]

Lastly, there is the Sicangu Lakota story that needs to be remembered here. This story was noted in chapter 4. Oscar Long noted these Sicangu warriors on his map and sketch in 1878 as the group of Spotted Tail Agency Indians. These people camped on the east side of the Little Bighorn River and within close proximity of where Elk Head and the camp(s) of healers are said to be.[40]

In Summary: Sacred Healers and Camps for the Wounded

We were fortunate to meet Lakota elders that shared the incredible story of not only Elk Head, but of the groups of holy people, medicine men and medicine women. These healers, camped to the south of the main encampment on the Little Bighorn River, on June 24th, 1876, tended to the wounded warriors, camps and horses.

We have one map from a Lakota elder that goes into some detail about Elk Head and the camps of healers.[41] Also, we have told of the work of Jason Pitsch, local historian and researcher, who provided me with a map of his findings. Pitsch's findings are unique, and add to what we were told.

First, Pitsch found material that led him to believe a

good-sized camp was at one time on the east side of the Little Bighorn River. This is in the same area as a camp of Sicangu Lakota, who got to the Little Bighorn late on June 24th, 1876. Second, he found material that could indicate where a small shelter or groups of them might have been, scattered and close to the Little Bighorn River. The area of these findings is east of the current Gary Owen Museum / gas station, which is the same area where Doug War Eagle put tipis as well. Lastly, Pitsch found material to the west of U.S. Interstate 90 that seems to fit the story that there was a warrior-only camp in this vicinity. Again, same as what Doug War Eagle told, as well as Gordon Harper.[42]

In chapter 4, we presented information on a group of Arapaho, who had come from Fort Robinson. These were called "the Arapaho holy people" by the Arapaho historians who shared with us. Two Arapaho historians, Bill Goggles and Devin Oldman, shared that their people had camped somewhere to the south of the main encampment on the Little Bighorn and that they could heal wounded men, horses and harness the weather. Plus, these Arapaho possibly had some of their sacred medicine bundles with them, including their tribe's sacred covenant, their Flat Pipe.[43] We also have U.S. Army maps by Maguire putting Arapaho people somewhere to the south of the main encampments. There is also information putting Arapaho people south of encampment on the Little Bighorn from Gordon Harper and Cheyenne people.[44]

The last piece to consider in this chapter has to do with the Sicangu Lakota, coupled with the Arapaho holy people and their bundles and sacred covenant. Is it a coincidence that this group of Sicangu Lakota, with a war chief who had a record of many exploits and was a respected medicine man, camped close to the Sacred Pipe Keeper and the Arapaho, who possibly had their sacred covenant, the Flat Pipe, in this area as well? This is noted by U.S. Army personnel on a map, just two years after the Battle.[45]

There is ample evidence in oral stories, U.S. military maps, a map from a Lakota historian, and research from a local historian and researcher to introduce the subject of Elk Head, as well as that of camps for wounded warriors, wounded horses and a warrior-only camp, and that they were located and in the vicinity to the south and west of the Native Peoples coalitions encampment on the Little Bighorn River, on June 24th, 1876. This evidence should be considered when discussing the Battle of the Little Bighorn.

If not for assistance from Garvard Good Plume Jr., Basil BraveHeart, Harold Salway, Rick Two Dogs, Arvol and Paula Looking Horse, Victor Douville, Sam High Crane, Doug War Eagle, Bill Goggles, Devin Oldman, Chris Dixon and Jason Pitsch, this story of wounded warriors, horses and camps, would still remain hidden from history and the actions of these people still largely unknown at this time.

Notes

1. For the Kill Eagle account, see Graham 1953: 52.

2. Utley 1993:141.

3. Young Two Moon in Greene 1994: 30; Feather Earring in Graham 1953: 97-98.

4. Personal communications with Harold Salway-Oglala Lakota.

5. Personal communications with Vernon Sooktis-Cheyenne.

6. Personal communications with Chester Whiteman-Cheyenne.

7. Personal communications with Donovan Taylor-Cheyenne. See Powell 1981: Vol 1, 461; Chapman 2004: 102, 109.

8. Personal communications with Rick Two Dogs-Oglala Lakota, Garvard Good Plume Jr.- Oglala Lakota, Basil BraveHeart-Oglala Lakota, Harold Salway-Oglala Lakota, Arvol and Paula Looking Horse, Victor Douville-Sicangu Lakota Tribal Historian, Doug War Eagle-

Minnikojou Lakota, Peter Gibbs-Tribal Historian Sicangu Lakota and Chris Dixon.

9. Personal communications with Rick Two Dogs-Oglala Lakota, Garvard Good Plume Jr.- Oglala Lakota, Basil BraveHeart-Oglala Lakota and Doug War Eagle-Minnikojou Lakota.

10. Ibid.

11. Ibid. Personal communications with local rancher and historian Jason Pitsch and Chris Dixon.

12. Personal communications with Basil BraveHeart-Oglala Lakota.

13. Ibid.

14. Ibid.

15. Ibid.

16. Personal communications with Doug War Eagle-Minnikojou Lakota.

17. Ibid.

18. Ibid.

19. Ibid.

20. Personal communications with Jason Pitsch.

21. Ibid.

22. Personal communications with Frederick Lefthand-Crow.

23. Personal communications with Frederick Lefthand-Crow and Frenchy Dillon-Crow. Frenchy is a descendant of Mitch Bouyer, as well as a descendant of Tom LeForge, who was a scout for General Alfred Terry. LeForge eventually took in Bouyer's wife Magpie Outside.

24. Kammen, Robert and Lefthand, Frederick and Marshall, Joe 1992: 225.

25. Personal communications with Frederick Lefthand-Crow. I tried on repeated occasions to make contact with Joe Marshall, but to no avail.

26. Harper 2014: [Ebook] Appendices 3.79.

27. Ibid.

28. Neihardt 1972: 106-108.

29. Wissler 1916: 88-90; St. Pierre and Long Soldier 1995: 24-29, 95-99, 109-110; V. Deloria 2006: 52-54.

30. Hardorff 1991: 134.

31. Stands In Timber and Liberty 1967: 106.

32. Hardorff 2005: 176.

33. Ibid.

34. Hammer 1976: 148.

35. Hardorff 1999: 92,114-116; Hardorff 2002: 124-125, 141-142.

36. Personal communications with Doug War Eagle-Minnikojou Lakota and Jason Pitsch.

37. Powell 1981: Vol 2., 1014.

38. Viola 1999: 40; Donahue 2009: 30-55, 105-112.

39. Harper 2014: [Ebook] Appendices 3.79.

40. Personal communications with Victor Douville-Sicangu Lakota Tribal Historian, Sam High Crane-Sicangu Lakota, Phil Two Eagle-Sicangu Lakota, Ronnie Cutt-Sicangu Lakota Henry Quick Bear-Sicangu Lakota and Peter Gibbs-Tribal Historian Sicangu Lakota.

Donahue 2009: 105-112.

41. Personal communications with Doug War Eagle-Minnikojou Lakota.

42. Personal communications with Jason Pitsch.

43. Personal communications with Bill Goggles-Arapaho, Devin Oldman-Arapaho and Cletus Yellow Plume-Arapaho.

44. Donahue 2009: See Maps # 3 and # 4, 33-38. See Maps # 5 and # 6, 39-50; Harper 2014: [Ebook] Appendices 3.79; See Chapter 3 of this book. Viola 1999: 40.

45. Personal communications with Victor Douville Sicangu Lakota Tribal Historian, Sam High Crane-Sicangu Lakota, Phil Two Eagle-Sicangu Lakota, Ronnie Cutt-Sicangu Lakota, Henry Quick Bear-Sicangu Lakota and Peter Gibbs-Tribal Historian Sicangu Lakota, Cletus Yellow Plume-Arapaho, Bill Goggles-Arapaho and Devin Oldman-Arapaho. See Donahue 2009: 105-112.

10
Crazy Horse and his Last Born Child Society

The following information that led to this trail came from: Chris Dixon - Independent researcher, Arvol and Paula Looking Horse, Garvard Good Plume Jr. - Oglala Lakota, Rick Two Dogs - Oglala Lakota, Rufus Spear - Cheyenne, Keith Spotted Wolf - Cheyenne, Donovan Taylor - Cheyenne, Linwood Tall Bull - Cheyenne and Wallace Bearchum - Cheyenne.

Crazy Horse, the Lakota war chief, is perhaps the most well-known warrior to have taken part in the Battle of the Little Bighorn. His life and the part he played in the Battle have been written about in length.[1] It is our intention here to focus on the society of young men he assembled to follow him and, if need be, go to war with him. Many of these young warriors did just this on June 25th, 1876, at the Little Bighorn.[2]

Eagle Elk.

Who were these young men Crazy Horse chose? According to Eagle Elk, who was himself a chosen member, "They were all very brave warriors and always went out with him and fought with him. He picks the last child in the family. If they did great deeds or something very brave, then they would have greater honor than the first child. They were always making themselves greater."[3]

Chris Dixon, an independent researcher and scholar, has spent a great deal of time studying the life of Crazy Horse. Chris has generously given me valuable insight over the years, not only with regard to Crazy Horse's exploits on the field of battle, but on some little-known aspects of his Last Born Child Society. Much of what Chris Dixon has shared with me has come while we walked the Little Bighorn Battlefield on many occasions, and time spent at the Fetterman Fight Battlefield.

Dixon said, "This was a short-lived and highly unusual warrior society in Lakota terms. The society had no office bearers, no regalia and no ritual feasts. It only operated from about 1872 to 1877." He finished with, "The members chosen for the Last Born Child Society were from Lakota families that were intermarried with Cheyenne families." Dixon then guided me to look into Crazy Horse's time among the Cheyenne people.[4]

Crazy Horse had come to the attention of the Cheyenne war chiefs, and others, at what is called the Fetterman Fight. This was in December of 1866 near what is the present-day town of Sheridan, Wyoming. This fight is known among the Cheyenne People as The Hundred-Soldiers-Killed-Fight or The-Battle-of-One-Hundred-in-the-Hands.[5] It was here that Crazy Horse's fighting prowess and spirited determination caught the eye of a Cheyenne Chief, Little Wolf.[6]

A noted warrior, Little Wolf was the headsman of the Elkhorn Scraper Warrior Society. Little Wolf was later bestowed with the title of Old Man Chief. He held this position, of which there are only four members at one time, while he was still the headsman of the Elkhorn Scraper Warrior Society.[7]

~

There are more interesting pieces about Crazy Horse and his close association with the Cheyenne. The first comes from Serle Chapman in his book, *Promise,* which is comprised of oral history shared with Chapman from Cheyenne, Lakota and Crow people, including the Fetterman Fight, and twice asserts Crazy Horse was a member of the Elkhorn Scraper Warrior society.[8] Chapman was told Crazy Horse was close to three prominent Cheyenne men, Little Wolf, White Bull (also known as Ice, the famous medicine man and holy man), as well as the famous Cheyenne warrior, Roman Nose.[9] Little Wolf, Ice and Roman Nose were, or were at one time, Elkhorn Scraper Society members.

Chapman also cited White Bull, a noted Minnikojou Lakota warrior and nephew of Sitting Bull. White Bull said of Crazy Horse's close ties to the Cheyenne, "Little Wolf, White Bull (Ice) and Roman Nose had taken him into the Elkhorn Scrapers and given him powerful medicine." This same information was told to me by Cheyenne tribal members as well.[10]

There is more history to examine regarding the link between Crazy Horse and the Cheyenne from Chris Dixon. At the 32nd Annual Symposium by the Custer Battlefield Historical Museum Association in 2018, Dixon presented *Crazy Horse and The Cheyenne.*[11] Dixon included two intriguing pieces in his 2018 presentation.

Dixon cited White Bull, the same prominent Minnikojou Lakota warrior mentioned earlier, who had many war deeds, some from his fighting at the Little Bighorn. White Bull is credited with seven coups at the Little Bighorn and the warriors he led that day, fought in the same area as Crazy Horse and the warriors he led in the Battle.[12] White Bull said Crazy Horse was, "a Cheyenne war chief."[13]

Second, Dixon cited a letter from Aaron McGaffey Beede to Walter S. Campbell, who wrote under the name Stanley Vestal. Beede told, "While Crazy Horse was an Oglala Sioux, he was sometimes talked of among Sioux as a Cheyenne Chief, because he frequently or generally had many extremely brave Cheyenne with him in battle."[14]

Chris Dixon added this last piece of history from his field research and trip to the Fetterman Fight Battlefield and the Little Bighorn Battlefield with Cheyenne historian Tim Lame Woman Sr. An Elkhorn Scraper society member himself, Tim Lame Woman Sr. told Dixon that Crazy Horse was, "actually a member of it (the Elkhorn Scrapers military society.)[15]

Then there is this intriguing piece of hidden history shared with me by an individual who has asked to remain anonymous. My source claims that Crazy Horse at times wore a cape said to be from a colt, a horsehide cape of sorts. The significance of this cape is in the fact that it was dyed and / or painted blue, a signifier of belonging to the Cheyenne military society, the Elkhorn Scrapers.[16]

One last thought on Crazy Horse and the important role he played at this time. Largely ignored by historians, is the fact that Crazy Horse was in command of Lakota forces at the Battle of the Rosebud.[17] Not only that, but he was also in the thick of the fighting there that day. His exploits that day were noticed and added to his reputation as a fearless man and esteemed warrior.[18]

~

Kicking Bear.

Short Bull.

Flying Hawk.

Stinking Bear.

It is only fitting that we finish this chapter with the names of the known warriors that were chosen by Crazy Horse to join his warrior society, the Last Born Child Society. We hope by presenting these names that they and Crazy Horse will never be forgotten.

The Last Born Child Society Members: Eagle Elk, Flying By, Flying Hawk, Good Weasel, Iron Plume, Kicking Bear, Little Killer, Looking Horse, Low Dog, Shell Boy, Short Bull and Rock.[19]

A warrior by the name of Stinking Bear, might have been a member as well.[20]

The late Garvard Good Plume Jr. is a descendant of Little Killer. Arvol Looking Horse, the Sacred White Buffalo Calf Pipe and the Sacred Calf Pipe Bundle Keeper, is a descendant of Looking Horse. Rick Two Dogs is a descendant of Rock.

What is in the historical record and how do these stories match up against it?

We have no oral stories to present regarding Crazy Horse and his society fighting together at the Battle of the Little Bighorn. The only accounts of the Last Born Child Society fighting together at the Battle of the Little Bighorn come from Chris Dixon[21] and from members themselves claiming they fought beside Crazy Horse in the Battle. They were from Flying Hawk, Kicking Bear, Eagle Elk and Short Bull.[22]

As for accounts that show Crazy Horse and his close association to the Cheyenne, only one such source was found, this being Serle Chapman's book, *Promise*. Chapman cited oral history shared to him from Lakota and Cheyenne People, as well as the Minnikojou Lakota warrior, White Bull. Chris Dixon cited White Bull earlier in this chapter, as well.[23]

There are two absolutely intriguing pieces hidden in the historical record regarding the information shared with me from an anonymous source regarding Crazy and the cape he wore. The cape was said to be dyed and / or painted blue for his affiliation with the Cheyenne Elkhorn Scraper military warrior society. The first, a drawing by a relative of Black Elk, Standing Bear, who

Standing Bear.

was himself at the Little Bighorn. In the drawing he depicts warriors thought to be Standing Bear, Black Elk and Crazy Horse, with a cape over his shoulders. All are shown besieging the Reno and Benteen Battalions. This was drawn long after the Custer Battalion had been destroyed to the last soldier and the Reno and Benteen's Battalions had taken up defensive positions on Reno-Benteen Hill.[24]

The next account regarding Crazy Horse and the cape he was said to wear at times comes from Thomas Powers' book *The Killing of Crazy Horse*. The author states, "from his shoulders he sometimes hung the hide of a colt."[25] Powers' assessment of information told by the Crow Tribe, enemies of the Lakota, was the basis

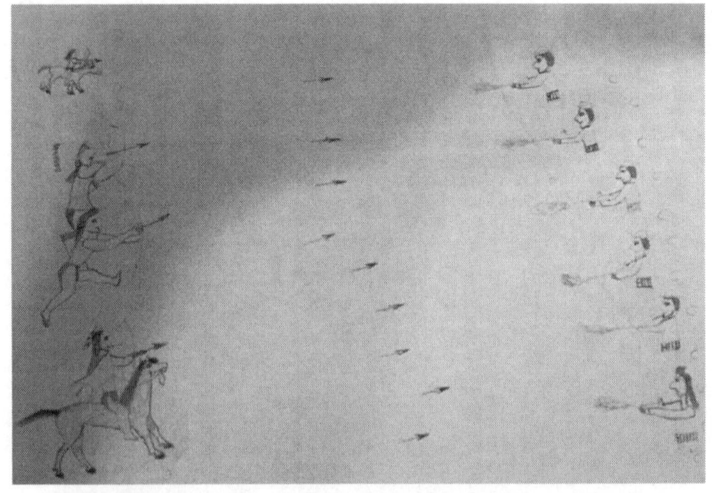
Standing Bear drew this drawing of Crazy Horse wearing a cape while fighting at the Little Big Horn (*Northwestern University Libraries' Digital Collections*).

for this statement. He added, "The Crow said they recognized Crazy Horse in battle by this horsehide cape."[26]

There is one more interesting piece from the wife of Spotted Horn Bull, a Hunkpapa warrior. His wife was known as Mrs. Spotted Horn Bull. When interviewed, she claimed she was a cousin to Sitting Bull. She said, "I saw Crazy Horse lead the Cheyennes into the water and up the ravine; Crow King and the Hunkpapa went after them; and then Gall, who had led his young men and killed the soldiers he had been fighting further up the river, rode along the bench by the river to where Long Hair had stopped with his men."[27]

In Summary: Crazy Horse and his Last Born Child Society

We have presented information regarding Crazy Horse and his Last Born Child Society to let future generations know these warriors fought at the Battle of the Little Bighorn. It is hoped that those who might have names and additional information regarding these warriors and this society might bring the stories forward and share.

Lastly, as for Crazy Horse and his association with the Cheyenne, we have presented one piece from historian and scholar Chris Dixon. There is also history told to Dixon from a then-current Elkhorn Scraper society member, Tim Lame Woman Sr., regarding Crazy Horse and the Elkhorn Scrapers. This history from Tim Lame Woman Sr., said Crazy Horse was a member of the Cheyenne military society, the Elkhorn Scrapers.

Information that supports Crazy Horse being a member of the Cheyenne Elkhorn Scraper society was told to author Serle Chapman, which he presented in his book, *Promise*. We have presented that it is still known today among Cheyenne and Lakota people that Crazy Horse was close to the Cheyenne people. We will look at this connection between Crazy Horse and the Cheyenne at the Battle of the Little Bighorn continually in future oral history shared throughout the remainder of this work.

Notes

1. Kadlecek and Kadlecek 1981; Greene, Jerome A. 1994; Michno 1997; Hardorff 1998; Bray 2006; Powers, Thomas 2011; Amos Bad Heart Bull 2017: 212-272.

2. See Short Bull, Flying By, Kicking Bear and Flying Hawk in Michno 1997 and in Hardorff 1997; Bray 2006: 215-231; Powers, Thomas 2011: 308-320; Amos Bad Heart Bull 2017: 212-272.

3. Hardorff 2001: 151-153; Bray 2006: 177-178.

4. Personal communications with Chris Dixon. See Dixon, 2018: *Crazy Horse and the Cheyenne.*

5. Personal communications with Chris Dixon. Powell 1981: Vol. 1, 451-461; Chapman 2004: 85-110; Monnett 2008.

6. Ibid.

7. Powell 1969: Vol. I, 197.

8. Chapman 2004: 71-72, 86, 167.

9. Ibid.

10. Ibid. Personal communications with Dennis Limberhand-Cheyenne, Leroy Whiteman - Cheyenne, Donovan Taylor-Cheyenne, Keith Spotted Wolf-Cheyenne, Rufus Spear - Cheyenne, Wallace Bearchum-Cheyenne and Linwood Tall Bull-Cheyenne. See Powell 1981 Vol 1: 747-757, 774-776.

11. Dixon 2018: 54-62.

12. Ibid 56; Vestal 1984: 191-205; Chapman 2004: 85-110; Donahue 2008: 224-233.

13. Ibid 56; Walter Stanley Campbell Collection, University of Oklahoma, Box 107, Folder 3.

14. Aaron McGaffey Beede To Walter Stanley Campbell, January 19, 1930. Walter Stanley Campbell Collection, University of Oklahoma, Box 107, Folder 3,

26/66.

15. Personal communications with Chris Dixon. See Dixon 2018: 56-57.

16. The source who provided me this information has always asked to remain anonymous and shall.

17. Vestal 1976: 153; Bray 2006: 206-211; Powers 2010: 175. Personal communications with Chris Dixon, Garvard Good Plume Jr.-Oglala Lakota, Arvol Looking Horse and Doug War Eagle-Minnikojou Lakota.

18. Ibid. Dixon 2018: 57; Kamm, Lefthand and Marshall 1992: 3-13; Utley 1993: 140.

19. Personal communications with Chris Dixon. See Dixon 2018: 54-62. Hardorff 2001: 135, 152-153. Bray 2006: 177-178.

20. Personal communications with Chris Dixon.

21. Ibid. Dixon 2018: 56-57.

22. See Michno 1997; Hardorff 2001: 152-153; Bray 2006: 215-231; Powers, Thomas 2011: 308-320; Amos Bad Heart Bull 2017: 212-272.

23. Chapman 2004: 71-72, 86, 167; Dixon 2018: 54-62.

24. Personal communications with anonymous source regarding the Standing Bear drawing. This anonymous source pointed out to me this drawing by Standing Bear, which depicts Crazy Horse in the book, *Black Elk Speaks*. See *Black Elk Speaks*: The Complete Edition. University of Nebraska Press: Lincoln, 2014, 13. Custer's Battle: Siege of Reno's Troops.

25. Thomas Powers 2011: 400; and see Kadlecek, Edward and Mabell 1981: 121.

26. Ibid.

27. Graham 1953: 87; McLaughlin 174.

11
The Oglala Sacred Bow Society and the Cheyenne Contrary and Thunder Bow

The following information that led to this trail we followed for the Sacred Bow Society of the Oglala Lakota comes from the following people: Independent researchers Mike Cowdrey and Chris Dixon. Rick Two Dogs - Oglala Lakota, Garvard Good Plume Jr. - Oglala Lakota, Basil BraveHeart - Oglala Lakota, Richard Iron Cloud - Oglala Lakota, and Donovan Taylor - Cheyenne.

The historical background to this society was first presented by anthropologist Helen Blish in 1934, and then brought back to the forefront of Native American Plains Indian ledger art by historian and writer Mike Cowdrey in 2015. I am greatly indebted to Mike Cowdrey for his unwavering support and for teaching me Plains ledger art and history.

The following information is taken from Blish's work, "*The Ceremony of the Sacred Bow of the Oglala Dakota*" and from Cowdrey, as it appeared in his report, "The Wilkins Ledger, An Oglala Lakota Record of the 1870s."

Thunder Bull carried the Sacred Bow at the Little Big Horn.

~

The Sacred Bow was originated in

response to a vision that Black Road, an Oglala Lakota man had. Black Road had been driven out into the wilderness by a medicine man of the band he belonged to because he had smallpox. Black Road dreamed, As he languished in his pain and suffering, Black Road dreamed of Thunder Beings instructing him about the Sacred Bow. Black Road returned to his people and, with his dream of the Sacred Bow, organized the society. Those who would be chosen to the carry the Sacred Bow would only be chosen by Black Road.

The Sacred Bow Society among the Oglala Lakota was just as honored and revered as others that existed at the time. There were ten officers. Four bow carriers and four hanger-carriers, with two club bearers. The leaders were the bow carriers.

The four bow carriers were chosen because of their bravery, integrity and generosity. Same went for the four hanger-carriers. All were governed by and adhered to strenuous rules and obligations, one of which was to always lead in battle. They were expected to always be brave and without a doubt, the most difficult obligation was for the bow carriers to strike at least one enemy with the bow in every encounter!

The Sacred Bows were about four and half feet long. Double-curved and unstrung, a long spearpoint of flint was on one end. A rattlesnake skin was suspended from the banner near the bow. Society members stood out because of a headband they wore, a rawhide band cut in the shape of a snake.

Painted red in times of war and peace, the bow carriers had one more obligation. In times of war, if they carried the Sacred Bow upright, then they didn't have to adhere to what might be a certain death sentence: a no-retreat vow. If they pointed the spear end of the Sacred Bow at the enemy, then the bow carrier could not retreat, no matter the odds or dangers.

The four hanger-carriers were painted yellow. The hangers they carried were sticks of ash or cherry, about six feet long. They were not under the no-retreat. All eight men were under severe stress to carry the positions and all the obligations during peace time, let alone in war. A member could hold the position until death found them in an admirable way during war, or simply resign after so many years of defying and courting death. After so many years of proving themselves, the members honorably returned either their Sacred Bow or the hanger.[1]

Black Road's uncle was Standing Elk, a noted Dog Soldier War Chief of the Cheyenne Tribe.[2] Mike Cowdrey has theorized that Black Road would have surely been exposed to the Cheyenne Contrary warriors from time spent with his uncle and the Cheyenne people.[3]

Oglala Lakota elder and historian Basil BraveHeart is a descendant of a warrior who fought at the Battle of the Little Bighorn, Charging A Fight. Basil informed me that Black Road came under the tutelage and learned the, "Holy ways of a medicine man, by White Lance. He (White Lance) was a very powerful medicine man."[4]

~

A Cheyenne Contrary carried a Thunder Bow. This was a sacred bow lance. It was shaped like a bow and strung with two strings. It had a lance head on one end and was about five feet in length. A Cheyenne Contrary was possessed by an overwhelming fear of thunder, as he had dreamed of the thunder and its awesome powers. Each Contrary wore a cap of owl feathers, the beard of a buffalo bull was attached to the heel of each moccasin. Around each warrior's neck hung a whistle.[5]

A Cheyenne Contrary lived a life of hardships and obligations. They had to live away from the rest of the camp and did things backwards. They did exactly the opposite of which behavior was expected, or did things the reverse of what is said. It was a lonely existence. They were warriors but not a society. The Cheyenne Contrary warriors were extremely brave warriors and carried the Thunder Bow to protect themselves. The Thunder Bow was said to influence lighting.[6]

A Cheyenne Contrary painted himself red when they carried their Thunder Bow. Their lodges and their clothing were painted red as well. When the Contrary went to war, he carried his Thunder Bow into a fight in the hollow of his left arm. He might advance and retreat, so long as he held the Thunder Bow in his left hand. If he was to switch the Thunder Bow to his right hand and then blew his whistle, he must charge the enemy and never retreat, no matter the odds. He had to advance until the enemy was met. If when the Contrary passed the Thunder Bow to his right hand as he charged upon the enemy and blew his whistle, then cried like an owl, the bows of his enemy were said to break.[7]

~

In November, 2020, I was alerted to the names of two Oglala Lakota Sacred Bow Society warriors through the Oglala Lakota historian, elder and spiritual leader, Rick Two Dogs. As a young man, Rick had been in a sweat ceremony with a respected Oglala Lakota elder, historian and spiritual leader, by the name of Matthew Zack Bearshield. Matthew informed Rick that his grandfather, Bear Shield, had been a member of the Oglala Sacred Bow Society and he had carried the Sacred Bow at the Battle of the Little Bighorn.[8]

After all these years, the stories of the Sacred Bow were still there. The name of Bear Shield and what he did at the Battle of the Little Bighorn had been kept alive by his descendants. And, as if that was not enough, Rick then informed me of another Sacred Bow Society warrior named Thunder Bull.[9]

Rick's father, Asay Two Dogs, had witnessed a ceremony at Kyle, South Dakota, in which Thunder Bull danced. It was told to Rick that Thunder Bull actually danced in that ceremony with the very Sacred Bow that he had carried at the Battle of the Little Bighorn![10]

~

Donovan Taylor and I made it a priority in our research and interviews with Cheyenne people to look for and ask about any information related to the Cheyenne Contrary and if any of these men were at the Little Bighorn. Despite many, many great Cheyenne people helping us, constantly researching and asking on our behalf, no names had come up until Chris Dixon informed me of a Cheyenne warrior by the name of Little

Horse.[11]

Chris Dixon had been told by Tim Lame Woman Sr. that a Cheyenne Contrary by the name of Little Horse had led the resistance efforts against the U.S. Seventh Cavalry at the Battle of the Little Horn. Tim Lame Woman Sr. said Little Horse led this resistance effort, which amounted to stopping the Seventh Cavalry from getting to the non-combatants, in an area that today is called Ford D, below the Little Bighorn Battlefield Monument National Cemetery. It runs parallel with U.S. Interstate 90. The Little Bighorn River meanders through this area, moving in a northwesterly direction.[12]

What is in the historical record and how do these stories match up against it?

Bear Shield carried the Sacred Bow at the Little Big Horn.

There is nothing in the historical record that mentions the Oglala Sacred Bow Society warriors fighting at the Battle of the Little Bighorn in 1876 besides the Cowdrey piece. What is extremely interesting about Cowdrey's piece and his research is what he put forth regarding drawings done by Red Horse, a Miniconjou Lakota.

Red Horse had been at the Battle of the Little Bighorn and did a series of forty large drawings[13] depicting warriors who had been killed fighting at the Battle of the Little Bighorn. Each warrior lay in their distinctive war clothes and headgear. In one drawing, there appears to be a forked stick of sorts.[14]

Is this a hanger for the Sacred Bow? Is the Red Horse drawing depicting a Sacred Bow Hanger Carrier?

Black Road, the Oglala Lakota Medicine Man, is mentioned by Black Elk as a Medicine Man in *Black Elk Speaks*. Black Elk makes no mention of the Sacred Bow

Society or the members.[15] One interesting side note concerning the Sacred Bow and Black Elk pertains to what Black Elk said when he described himself fighting at the Wounded Knee Massacre in 1890. He recounted, "I had no gun, and when we were charging, I just held the sacred bow out in front of me with my right hand. The bullets did not hit us at all."[16]

The two Oglala Lakota warriors named by Rick Two Dogs said to have carried the Sacred Bow at the Battle of the Little Bighorn, Bear Shield and Thunder Bull, are not on any lists or in the historical record as having had fought there.

The only name mentioned in the historical record of a Cheyenne Contrary fighting at the Battle of the Little Bighorn is Brave Wolf. This Thunder Bow carrier is mentioned in many, many accounts related to his participation at not only the Battle of the Little Bighorn, but at the Battle of the Rosebud.[17] In all the accounts regarding Brave Wolf, there is not one mention of him carrying his Thunder Bow, nor of what he was painted like at the Little Bighorn. According to Father Powell and John Stands in Timber, Brave Wolf lost his Thunder Bow at the Dull Knife Fight, near Kaycee, Wyoming, in November of 1876.[18]

As for Little Horse, the Cheyenne Contrary, there is much to present and sort out. Noted Cheyenne historians George Grinnell and Father Peter Powell both told of this Cheyenne Contrary leading the Cheyenne at the Fetterman Fight. Neither mentioned Little Horse having led the Cheyenne resistance in the Ford D fight or of fighting at the Battle of the Little Bighorn.[19] Father Powell does mention a Little Horse as a Kit Fox Society war chief and of being at the Little Bighorn.[20]

Author Serle Chapman first pointed out that Little Horse was no stranger to fighting and was a noted warrior by 1865. Chapman had been told that Little Horse led the Elkhorn Scrapers military society charge against the U.S. Army at the Platte Bridge Fight in 1865.[21] Now, at The Hundred-Soldiers-Killed-Fight (Fetterman Fight), he is said to be a Contrary.[22] Little Horse was given the esteemed honor of not only leading the Cheyenne charge on the U.S. Soldiers from Fort Phil Kearney, but he wore the Cheyenne Tribe's Sacred

Buffalo Hat. This Contrary warrior, with the aid of his Thunder Bow and the Sacred Buffalo Hat, got within 20 to 40 feet of the U.S. Soldiers before he began to engage them.[23]

Is the Little Horse who is a Contrary and fought at the Fetterman Fight the same man Tim Lame Woman Sr. says fought at the Little Bighorn? Tim Lame Woman Sr. had accompanied Chris Dixon and the author Serle Chapman to the Fetterman Fight site and to the Little Bighorn Battlefield, when he told both of a Little Horse, who was a Contrary, leading the resistance in the Ford D area. Chris Dixon stated Tim Lame Woman Sr., made no mention that this man had been an Elkhorn Scraper society man, nor was he the same man who fought at the Fetterman Fight, a fact Tim Lame Woman Sr., would have indicated, since he himself was an Elkhorn Scraper society member.[24]

At this point in this work, the historical record gives us no indications that the Cheyenne Contrary by the name of Little Horse, who fought at the Platte Bridge Fight and the Fetterman Fight, is the same man who fought at the Battle of the Little Bighorn.

We will discuss Little Horse much more in-depth in chapter 16 of this book and take a closer examination of his role in the Ford D fight.

In Summary: The Oglala Sacred Bow Society and the Cheyenne Contrary and Thunder Bow

The names of Bear Shield and Thunder Bull are now known as two warriors who carried the Sacred Bow of the Oglala Sacred Bow Society at the Battle of the Little Bighorn. We hope they will be included as being two warriors of the Oglala Sacred Bow Society by not only future historians and researchers, but by their people. At this time, this is all we can add to this story. Maybe some future researcher or family members will come forth with more information.

Donovan Taylor and myself felt extremely lucky to have been guided to Rick Two Dogs. We are forever grateful that this Oglala Lakota historian thought enough of us and our work to share with us the names of Bear Shield and Thunder Bull.

Notes

1. Blish, Helen, H. "*The Ceremony of the Sacred Bow of the Oglala Dakota.*" American Anthropology N.S., 36, (1934); Cowdrey, Mike. "The Wilkins Ledger- An Oglala Lakota Record of the 1870's." (2015). Plainsledgerart.org./essay files/Blackroadwilkinsledger.

2. Personal communications with Donovan Taylor-Cheyenne. Donovan Taylor interviewed Alec Sandcrane-Cheyenne, in regards to Standing Elk. Alec is a descendant of Standing Elk. Alec stated Standing Elk was a Dog Soldier War Chief and fought at the Battle of the Little Bighorn.

3. Cowdrey 2015. Personal communications with Mike Cowdrey.

4. Personal communications with Basil BraveHeart-Oglala Lakota.

5. Grinnell 1923: Vol 1., 79-83; Powell 1981: Vol 1., xxxviii.

6. Ibid.

7. Ibid.

8. Personal communications with Rick Two Dogs-Oglala Lakota.

9. Ibid.

10. Ibid.

11. Personal communications with Chris Dixon.

12. Ibid.

13. Cowdrey 2015.

14. Ibid. Tenth annual report of the Bureau of Ethnology to the Secretary of the Smithsonian Institution, 1888-89, by J. W. Powell, Director. Plate XLV, Battle of the Little Bighorn. The Dead Sioux.

15. Neihardt 1972: 165-166.

16. Ibid: 260-265.

17. Grinnell 1955: 352; Hardorff 1995: 32-36; Hardorff 2005: 43-51; Michno 1997; Stands In Timber and Liberty 2013.

18. Powell 1981: Vol. 2., 1057-1058, see endnote 16, 1377.

19. Grinnell 1955: 241-244. Powell 1981, Vol 1: 457-459; Vol 2: 1005; Marquis 2003: 211.

20. Ibid.

21. Chapman 2004: 71-72, 92, 95, 100, 104.

22. Again, see Chapman 2004: 166. This account states Little Horse who was the Contrary at the Fetterman Fight was not an Elkhorn Scraper military society man. It does state this Little Horse led the Cheyenne at the Platte Bridge Fight in 1865.

23. Chapman 2004: 92, 95, 104-109, 166.

24. Personal communications with Chris Dixon.

12
Additional Pieces to the Valley Fight: The First Defenders, Calling on the Winged Creatures and Animals for Help

Citation: LITTLE BIG HORN: A map included in James E. Dean Jr.'s "Western North Carolina Man Fought with Custer Against Sioux," illustrates the layout of the battle.

The following information that led to this trail we followed came from: Rick Two Dogs - Oglala Lakota, Garvard Good Plume Jr. - Oglala Lakota, Basil BraveHeart - Oglala Lakota, Harold Salway - Oglala Lakota, Victor Douville - Sicangu Lakota Tribal Historian, Doug War Eagle - Minnikojou Lakota, Phil Two Eagle - Sicangu Lakota, Arvol and Paula Looking Horse, James Desjarlais - Nakota/Cree, Ernie Heavy Runner - Blackfeet. Independent researchers: Chris Dixon and Jason Pitsch.

The historical record says that on June 25th, 1876, Major Marcus Reno, U.S. Seventh Cavalry, led companies A, G and M, of the Seventh Cavalry and crossed the Little Bighorn River. On the west side of the Little Bighorn River, Major Reno's command was still well south of the camps that made up the Native Peoples coalition encampment. Major Reno and his command, augmented with Arikara and civilian scouts, formed up and proceeded down (north) the Valley of the Little Bighorn. Altogether, Reno had approximately 170 men.[1]

General George Custer, companies C, E, F, I and L, of the U.S. Seventh Cavalry and the Headquarters unit, both under his direct command, remained on the east side of the Little Bighorn at this time. After Major Reno and his command had moved out of sight, General Custer and his command resumed moving down the Valley of the Little Bighorn while the slow-moving pack train, which consisted of mules with one company of the Seventh as escort, continued to fall further behind the trail Major Reno and General Custer had left.[2]

Earlier, General Custer had ordered Captain Frederick Benteen, with companies B, D and H, to move to the south. Benteen was to reconnoiter the valley to ascertain if Native People were fleeing the encampment on the Little Bighorn. If he was to find any of these people, Benteen and his three companies were to drive them back towards the encampment.[3]

~

In chapter 9 we discussed camps for wounded warriors and horses to the south, east and west of the Native Peoples coalition encampment on the Little Bighorn River. Scattered around the peripheral edges, they consisted of clusters of wickiups, a form of a crude brush shelter, mixed with an occasionally tipi or two. These camps were attended to by holy people, medicine men and medicine women. Assistance came from elders and young men, who also served as protection should these camps be attacked. We also discussed stories that put forth the notion that to the west of the encampment on the Little Bighorn there was a warrior-only camp.

Now, we continue with stories shared with us from Native American and First Nations historians that describe the first defenders of the encampment on the

American Horse, Oglala Lakota war chief whose sons Samuel, Charles, Ben and Thomas all rode into the Valley Fight against the Reno Battalion.

Little Bighorn. This is the Valley Fight that involved Major Reno's command. It was from within these clusters of shelters and scattered tipis that the first defenders -- young men, young women and elders[4] -- of the Native Peoples coalition encampment along the Little Bighorn River emerged.[5]

~

I was first told stories of who the Native People were who fought in the Valley Fight by seven Lakota tribal members and one Cheyenne tribal member. They were Rick Two Dogs, Garvard Good Plume Jr., Victor Douville, Sam High Crane, Phil Two Eagle, Doug War Eagle, Wayne Goodwill and Gilbert Whitedirt.[6]

The American Horse family are Rick Two Dogs' ancestors. American Horse was a prominent Oglala war chief at the Battle of the Little Bighorn. His wife was a daughter of Chief Red Cloud, one of the best known Native American resistance leaders against white encroachment.

Camped within the encampment of the Native Peoples coalition that June on the Little Bighorn, American Horse was there with his four sons, Charlie, Samuel, age 13, Ben, age 12, and Thomas age 10.[7]

These young men of American Horse were scattered throughout the camps of holy people, Medicine Men and Medicine Women. These healers were somewhere to the south of the Native Peoples Coalition encampment on the Little Bighorn. When the Valley Fight commenced, Samuel, Ben, and Thomas took off with the other youngsters and young women, many of whom had come to ride with their brothers and cousins.[8]

Many of these young men had not even accompanied a war party yet. Most did not own, let alone have firearms. Bows and quivers full of arrows were all they had. A sheath carried a knife for most; some had a war club.

Protection, it was told to me by Doug War Eagle, was quickly administered to them by the elders and holy people in a ceremony . These young men had yet to go through the Hanblecheya (crying for a vision) ceremony / ritual[9] in which the candidate sought a vision that might assign some type of spirit helper or animal spirit helper, which in turn the warrior would carry or wear for protection in battle and life.[10] Regardless, they fearlessly moved forward among the deadly hail of bullets fired by the Reno Battalion. Most were on foot and were led by elders.

According to Rick Two Dogs, American Horse rode from his camp to find his boys. In the fighting that ensued, Rick's great-uncle, Ben American Horse, was wounded fighting the U.S. Seventh Cavalry.

Susie Shot In The Eye, Lakota, who as a young woman rode into the Valley Fight and fought the Reno Battalion.

Rick had another family member in the Valley Fight as well, his great-grandmother, Susie Shot-In-The- Eye. As the Valley Fight went on, Susie had been told that her cousin, White Eagle, had been killed. She and a couple of female cousins went on horseback to find his body. Susie was armed with a revolver. Rick went on to say that as the Reno Battalion broke out of the timber and made their dash for the river, Susie got caught in the movement of warriors who gave pursuit. She found herself riding next to a trooper and shot him from his horse before he could do the same to her. A little way further on and now closer to the Little Bighorn River, Susie was able to get her horse out of the mad rush of warriors plunging into the river after the Reno Battalion. It was here on the banks of the river that she noticed a wounded trooper crawling next to the river. She calmly raised her revolver and fired. Then, she dismounted and scalped the trooper.[11]

No other stories were shared with us regarding specifics of young men, young women and elders fighting the Reno Battalion of the U. S. Seventh Cavalry. More stories of youngsters and elders fighting the Custer Battalion in later stages of the Battle will be discussed later in this work.

~

The late Garvard Good Plume Jr., told me an interesting story that coincided with the Valley Fight. It bears mentioning that this story is yet another example of the spiritual components and their potency that were on display at the Battle that day. It incorporates the concept of animism.

Animism encompasses beliefs that animals, birds, places and objects possess spiritual essence. To Native American and First Nations People, all things have a soul, spirit or capacity for sentience.[12] Before moving forward, again, you the reader are asked to throw away preconceived notions. Do not dismiss the information shared by these elders and historians simply because it doesn't match our notions of what we have been taught of reality.

Blackfeet elder and historian Ernie Heavy Runner shared with me what he had been taught about the world of spirituality and how animals and birds were an integral part of it.

"Some people through dreams or visions could predict or change the weather, while others through dreams and visions had been lucky enough to have an animal spirit helper find them. When this was the case, the dreamer or the one who was given the vision had an obligation to uphold for just such a gift of power from the animal guardians. For they now had acquired an ally who bestowed to them powers only their kind possessed. All animals were believed to have souls and their own ancestral spirits. It is believed that animals could communicate and help humans while the animals were alive." Ernie added this intriguing piece to help me understand this world of animal spirit helpers. "Our ancestors were fascinated by animals. The animals didn't mistreat one another, they were honest. They had spiritual powers because they were so honest. The animals could predict the weather or a disaster. The animals were watched and studied closely."[13]

Perhaps though, there was much, much more to this than those of us alive today can comprehend? Native American ethnographer Ella Deloria, herself from Yankton People and who had been raised among Lakota People, put forth long-held history pertaining to where the societies of the Dakota had originated.

Ella Deloria had been educated at prestigious Columbia University under the tutelage of acclaimed anthropologist Franz Boas. She was the aunt of acclaimed writer and activist Vine Deloria Jr. Ella Deloria recorded that six animal spirits, the bull (buffalo), the prairie-chicken, the rabbit, the skunk, the badger, and the owl, organized the first societies among the Dakota. Each had a guardian spirit.

From these societies came leaders of the people, the Itaca or Chiefs, which were the bull (buffalo). Camp police, or soldiers, came from the prairie-chicken, also called the stout-hearts, as well as from the kit fox and badger. The owl, called the Miwatani, provided wisdom and council.[14]

Nakota/Cree historian James Desjarlais, shared with me this long-held history from First Nations People in Canada concerning the powers of the animals. "The animals were spiritual. They had been blessed by the Creator with spiritual powers and knowledge. They, being the bear, wolf, eagle and others, could change form and become humans."[15]

Santee Dakota history pertaining to their prowess as medicine and holy people had been told to researchers and historians for centuries but ignored.[16] James H. Howard, the renowned Native American and First

Nations ethnographer and writer, caught glimpses of this when he traveled in Canada to visit the Dakota reserves. Howard recorded this information from Dakota elders and historians who were not afraid, nor bashful about telling of their kinsmen's exploits. Howard captured this information in the 1970's, when it was rare to hear the like. It would have even been more rare to be told to put it in print, since the Dakota were in a constant state of fighting against the Canadian Government regarding treaties, human and social rights, and policy reform. Howard put forth the following, which ties into what Ernie and James told and to what Garvard will expand on.

"The Santees were and still are considered by other Sioux to be great magicians and shamans, with power to change themselves into birds and fly through the air, to walk on hot coals, and to compound lethal medicines to kill enemies."[17]

Regarding the Valley Fight with the Reno Battalion, Garvard said that when the battalion had finally been repulsed and driven up the steep bluffs overlooking the Little Bighorn River, only then did Native People and warriors scattered throughout the encampment and over the valley catch a glimpse of the demonstration they heard over the roar of the Battle. Garvard explained that those in the encampment witnessed a demonstration of sorts, high above the bluffs that rose some 300 feet in the air above the river. Those in the camps witnessed a massive flock of winged creatures, which was compromised of many species, such as hawks, eagles, crows, magpies, meadowlarks, ravens and others, swooping and making their distinctive calls.

Diving and pitching through the air, silhouetted against a cloudless sky, these winged sentinels told those in the encampment that more soldiers were present. Not only that, they signaled the alarm that their women, children and elderly, who had earlier fled the camps at the outset of the Valley Fight, were now in grave danger. The birds continued to doggedly track the soldier's movements, even dividing from the flock and hovering above the very ground that groups of soldiers were positioning themselves to fight on. The message was now plainly clear to those in the encampment: the soldiers were going after the woman and children!

Garvard added that the birds, as well as animals, had been called for assistance by the holy people. These holy people were somewhere to the south of the main encampment of the Native Peoples coalition encampment on the Little Bighorn River. Garvard did not state what animals were called, and if any in fact had responded in some way.[18]

The same Arapaho elders and historians who put Arapaho somewhere to the south of the main encampment on the Little Bighorn and which we have discussed in chapters 4, 8 and 9 told Devin Oldman the same story Garvard related. Devin had been told these Arapaho holy people were able to heal wounded people and horses, as well as communicate with animals and birds.[19]

Doug War Eagle had been told the same story Garvard told me, to which he added that the majority of medicine men and holy people in the camps south of the main encampment, healing the wounded warriors and horses, as well as calling on the winged creatures for help, were from the Sans Arc Lakota. Doug called these people No Bow Healers. The Sans Arc were at times called Those Who Hunt Without Bows, and are a subgroup of the Teton Lakota.[20]

There is one more fascinating piece from Doug War Eagle's story. Doug stated that in the camps of healers, as he called them, there was one specifically made up of unmarried medicine men. These medicine men, Doug said, "had the gift to protect the people. They had the power to shoot their medicine at enemies and did this against the soldiers of the Reno Battalion in the Valley Fight." He added, "Some could change into wolves, deer or buffalo. They lived on the highest points of hills and valleys, and communicated with birds and animals to protect camps." Doug was told that there was a society for these men at one time, long ago. He could not recall its name.[21]

The last oral story to introduce comes from Cheyenne historian Gilbert Whitedirt. We first introduced Gilbert and this story in chapter 4, when discussing the Arapaho and their involvement at the Little Bighorn, specifically the Valley Fight with the Reno Battalion.

Gilbert told us that, "The Arapaho and Cheyennes killed Bloody Knife." Gilbert could not specifically recall who had told him this information, only that it, "has been known among Cheyenne People ever since the Battle."[22]

Bloody Knife was an Arikara scout who rode with the U. S. Seventh Cavalry to the Little Bighorn and subsequently rode with the Reno Battalion into the Battle. He was killed in the Vally Fight, near the timber, before Major Reno led his battalion on the retreat movement across the Little Bighorn River.[23]

What is in the historical record and how do these stories match up against it?

In regards to accounts that tell of youngsters and elders as either the first group of resistance, and / or those that engaged the Reno Battalion in the Valley fight, we found some interesting pieces, presented here in the order they were recorded.

The first comes from Dr. Charles Eastman in 1900 in his article *The Story of the Little Bighorn*. Remember, Eastman's two uncles who raised him were at the Little Bighorn, and he was an agency physician at Wounded Knee, South Dakota, when the Wounded Knee Massacre took place in December, 1890. The U.S. Seventh Cavalry was the Army unit directly responsible for the horrific event.

In this account, Eastman related that, "there were hundreds of young men and boys upon the flats, playing games and horse-racing. Anyone who knows at all about the natural life of the Sioux upon the plains, would know that these young men were armed as far as they had weapons." A little farther on in the article he wrote, "The young men who had been playing upon the flats were the first to meet Major Reno." Eastman recorded the youngsters were instructed to use caution and not go charging into the soldiers, and to hold the Reno troopers until the warriors could get mounted.[24]

In 1905, Eastman interviewed the famous Hunkpapa Lakota warrior Rain In The Face. Eastman found the aged warrior who fought at the Little Bighorn in poor health on the Standing Rock Reservation. In regards to youngsters fighting in the Valley Fight, Rain In The Face said the following.

"I ran to my teepee and seized my gun, a bow, and a quiver full of arrows. I already had my stone war club, for you know we usually carry those by way of ornament. Just as I was about to set out to meet Reno, a body of soldiers appeared nearly opposite us, at the edge of a long line of cliffs across the river. All of us who were mounted and ready immediately started down the stream toward the ford. There were Ogallalas, Minneconjous, Cheyennes, and some Unkpapas, and those around me seemed to be nearly all very young men." He then said, "When the troops were surrounded on two sides, with the river on the third, the order came to charge! There were many very young men, some of whom had only a war staff, or a stone war club in hand, who plunged into the column, knocking the men over and stampeding their horses."[25]

This third account comes from Mrs. Spotted Horn Bull. She was a Hunkpapa Lakota woman in the encampment on the Little Bighorn in 1876, and her husband fought in the Battle. Her account was first taken in 1883. This account comes from 1910.

"But when they (the Reno Battalion) began to run away they ran very fast, and dropped their guns and ammunition. Our braves were not surprised by this time, and killed a good many when they crossed the plain to the river, while they were fording and on the hill beyond. I saw boys pull men from their horses and kill them on the ground."[26]

The fourth account is from Red Feather, in 1919. He was an Oglala Lakota warrior who participated in the Battle of the Little Bighorn. This is what he told regarding the Valley fight with the Reno Battalion.

"When the soldiers got to their horses, they retreated. There was a deep place in the timber that was a good place for defense, but instead they took to the open country which made it easier for the Indians to catch them. The Indians in the lead were the younger men, [who] didn't have enough experience and were reckless. The older ones held off for safety. The younger men were killed mostly, and they [the young men] took most of the guns."[27]

The fifth account is from White Cow Walking, in 1929. He was in Sitting Bull's Band at the Little Bighorn. He said, "Sitting Bull and some women fought Reno [and] then Custer. It was foretold [about the battle], but [it was] not known whether Sitting Bull's [vision was correct] or not. [We were] not prepared or camped to fight."[28]

The sixth account dates to 1936 and comes from a Minnikojou warrior, One Bull, who was at the Little Bighorn. He was a nephew of Sitting Bull and brother to the renowned warrior, White Bull. One Bull stated, "Many warriors [were only] 13 to 18 years [old]."[29]

The last account comes from Little Soldier in 1936. He was a stepson to Sitting Bull and was himself at the Little Bighorn. He said, "[The] women took [the] children. [The] older warriors were out hunting buffalo, [and] for that reason [only] boys [from] 13 to 18 [years old] did the fighting. Old men sang death songs for [the] warriors."[30]

~

As we continued to look into the historical record for information regarding these first defenders in the Valley Fight, we found these seldom discussed accounts. There are some other noteworthy pieces of information here.

The first account can be found in the A.B. Welch Dakota Papers. Welch was an officer in the U.S. Army and served in World War I. After the War, he settled in Mandan, North Dakota, and made it his life's work to interview aged Native American warriors about not only the Battle of the Little Bighorn but other aspects of days long ago on the American Plains. Welch regularly conversed and exchanged history with a local newspaperman by the name of Frank Zahn. Zahn claimed his father was married to a Native American woman by the name of Pretty Woman, who happened to be the daughter of Chief John Grass. A Shihasapa (Blackfeet) Lakota, John Grass said he had been at the Battle of the Little Bighorn.

Zahn served as an interpreter for writers and historians who came to the Standing Rock Reservation and surrounding area to interview Native American people. In April of 1929, Zahn published an article on the Battle of the Little Bighorn. He does not list who he interviewed for this story. In this story he wrote, "Most of the Indians who participated in this battle were boys, their ages ranging from 14 to 20 years."[31]

The second comes from the Hunkpapa Lakota warrior Turning Hawk. We discussed this account in chapter 4, and it bears mentioning here again for how it pertains to the Valley Fight. In this account, Turning Hawk first said that, "Cheyennes ran Reno from the water." He labeled this with the numeral 7 on a map drawn by another Lakota warrior, One Bull. Turning Hawk went on to say that, "Arapahoes and Cheyennes at 7, and Turning Hawk [was] there."[32]

Turning Hawk's account has elements that corroborate what Gilbert Whitedirt shared with us. Gilbert said the Arapaho and Cheyenne were the ones who killed Bloody Knife.[33]

These two accounts become even more substantial because of another hidden gem buried in, of all places, Reno Court of Inquiry documents. It comes from Frederic Girard, a frontiersman civilian scout and interpreter who rode with the Seventh Cavalry. Girard was in the Reno Battalion and participated in the Valley Fight. On the seventh day of the court of inquiry for Major Marcus Reno, Reno asked Girard whether he knew if Bloody Knife had been killed. Girard responded, "I heard he was killed. I understood he was killed by the Cheyenne Indians."[34]

One has to wonder where Girard got this information. The historical record states Girard was fluent in the Siouan, Algonquian and Caddoan languages. He was also an experienced trader and trapper in the fur industry who had worked on the northwest plains among many Native tribes and people for a number of years.[35] The possibilities are endless.

Feather Earring, a Minneconjou warrior who fought at the Little Bighorn and had a brother killed in the fight there, told this: "Reno was driven across the river into the hills and began to dig in the ground. He was fought by the Cheyennes and Ogalallas."[36]

Father Peter Powell had discussed in his research the fact that the Cheyenne were in the Valley Fight and that they had suffered some casualties there.[37] Cheyenne elder and historian John Stands In Timber told of Cheyenne participation as well.[38] Wooden Leg told the same to Dr. Marquis.[39]

Another fascinating hidden account in the historical record that intrigued Donovan and me comes from Kill Eagle, a Sihasapa (Blackfeet) Lakota Chief. We mentioned him in chapter 9. Regarding the Valley Fight, he said that Sitting Bull himself told him that Reno attacked on the right near Sitting Bull's tipi and was immediately engaged by the famous dog soldiers.[40] To be clear, we do not know if means the famous Cheyenne Dog Soldiers, who were a prominent warrior society among the Cheyenne tribe, or is he referring to the Dog Soldier Band, which was at one time a band among the Cheyenne tribe comprised of not only Cheyenne people, but of Lakota People as well.[41]

There is one more account regarding fighting youngsters. While it did not take place at the Battle of the Little Bighorn, it did happen at the Battle of the Rosebud. This account was given to George Grinnell and recorded in his book *The Fighting Cheyennes*.

Grinnell had been told that, "a little Sioux boy," rode with the contingent of warriors from the Native Peoples Coalition encampment to fight the U.S. Army at what would become known as the Battle of the Rosebud. Grinnell wrote that this, "little Sioux boy," twelve or thirteen years old, followed the noted Cheyenne warrior, Chief Comes in Sight, in a charge against the soldiers. This young Sioux boy was overtaken by either Crow or Shoshoni warriors who fought for the U.S. Army and was killed.[42]

In Summary:

We have presented eight accounts in the historical record that tell of youngsters and elders engaging the Reno Battalion in the Valley Fight. Three Lakota elders shared oral history that tells of these youngsters and elders fighting in the Valley Fight, and of women and even young women participating in the Valley Fight as well.

In researching the Valley Fight, we found six accounts that told of Cheyenne and two of Arapaho participation. We found one account that specifically mentioned dog soldiers. At this time, we do not know if this story is mentioning the Cheyenne Dog Soldiers from their military society, or the Dog Soldier tribal band. There is one oral story that the Arapaho and Cheyennes killed the Arikara scout Bloody Knife, who rode with the Reno Battalion and fought in the Valley Fight. The historical record, which in this case is the Reno Court of Inquiry, has recorded another story of the Cheyenne being the ones who killed Bloody Knife.

Based on oral history that can seemingly be corroborated in the historical record, it is worth adding the story of young women, young men, and elders added to the Valley Fight narrative, and that these people were the first to oppose the Reno Battalion. Based on information we presented in chapter 4 and in this chapter as well regarding the Arapaho and Cheyenne in the Valley Fight, both tribes, at the very least, should be looked at as playing a bigger role here than the historical record tells.

A special note of thanks to Rick Two Dogs, Doug War Eagle, Devon Oldman, Garvard Good Plume Jr., Gilbert Whitedirt and James Desjarlais, for believing in us enough to share these pieces of history.

See Appendix G for a list of the names of youngsters who fought at the Battle of the Little Bighorn.

Notes

1. Gray 1988: 295; Liddic 2004: 61.

2. Donahue 2018: 151-158. Liddic 2004: 61-69.

3. Ibid.

4. Personal communications with Steve Vance-Minnikojou Lakota, Rick Two Dogs-Oglala Lakota, Garvard Good Plume Jr.-Oglala Lakota, Doug War Eagle-Minnikojou Lakota, Victor Douville-Sicangu Lakota Tribal Historian, Sam High Crane-Sicangu Lakota, Wayne Goodwill - Santee Dakota and Hunkpapa Lakota, Phil Two Eagle-Sicangu Lakota, Gilbert Whitedirt - Cheyenne and Chris Dixon.

5. Ibid.

6. Ibid.

7. Personal communications with Rick Two Dogs-Oglala Lakota.

8. Ibid.

9. Personal communications with Doug War Eagle-Minnikojou Lakota.

10. Ibid. See St. Pierre and Long Soldier 1995: 96-121; Kracht 2017: 85-135.

11. Personal communications with Rick Two Dogs-Oglala Lakota.

12. Personal communications with Garvard Good Plume Jr.-Oglala Lakota.

13. Personal communications with Ernie Heavy Runner-Blackfeet.

14. For the Ella Deloria's vast research and ethnographic notes on the Dakota societies, see www.dakotaindianfoundation.org. Dakota ethnography: Box 3-Origin of the Dakota Societies: A Legend. 309-321.

15. Personal communications with James Desjarlais-Nakota/Cree.

16. See William K. Powers 1977: 53-55; Walker 1991: 93-96; Riggs 2004: 214-218.

17. Howard 2014: 11.

18. Personal communications with Garvard Good Plume Jr.-Oglala Lakota.

19. Personal communications with Devin Oldman-Arapaho.

20. Personal communications with Doug War Eagle-Minnikijou Lakota.

21. Ibid.

22. Personal communications with Gilbert Whitedirt-Cheyenne and Donovan Taylor-Cheyenne.

23. For accounts of Bloody Knifes death in the Valley Fight, see Donovan 2008: 239-240; and Nichols 2010: 30-31.

24. Eastman, "*The Story of The Little Bighorn,*" 356.

25. See Eastman 1918, *Indian Heroes and Great Chieftains*.

26. Graham 1953: 84.

27. Hardorff 1991: 85-86.

28. Hardorff 2005: 134.

29. Ibid: 179.

30. Ibid: 175.

31. Welch 2017: 63. www.welchdakotapapers.com.

32. Hardorff 2005: 143-146.

33. Personal communications with Gilbert Whitedirt-Cheyenne and Donovan Taylor-Cheyenne.

34. Nichols 2007: 124.

35. Nichols 2010: 141-143.

36. Graham 1953: 97.

37. Powell 1981, Vol 2: 1009-1017.

38. Stands In Timber and Liberty 2013: 369-370, 380-382.

39. Marquis 2003: 217-226.

40. Milligan 1976: 74.

41. Moore 1987: 197-203.

42. Grinnell 1955: 339.

13
The Story of Deeds: He Wanted to Die Like a Warrior

The following information on the history of Deeds came from John Eagle Shield Sr.

Moving Robe Woman / Mary Crawler, veteran of the Little Bighorn and sister of Deeds.

Much has been written about the story of Deeds. There is a common thread repeated time and time again: Deeds and his father (some stories place another young Lakota with them as well) were out bringing in horses, they encountered U.S. Seventh Cavalry troopers or Arikara scouts from the Seventh Calvary, and Deeds was killed.[1]

The following is history told to me by John Eagle Shield Sr. John is a direct descendant of the Crawler family. This history will contradict most of what the historical record has recorded regarding Deeds and his death at the Little Bighorn on June 25th, 1876.[2]

The story of Deeds must first begin with his physical stature. From his earliest days, it was known that Deeds had been inflicted with some form of illness which rendered him a cripple. John Eagle Shield Sr. told me that the stories handed down throughout generations of his family consistently include this otherwise overlooked and important piece of information.[3]

Additionally, Deed's story deals with the fact that, for reasons unknown to John, Deeds was continually cared for by the family of the Hunkpapa band chief Crawler.

Mary Crawler, also known as Moving Robe Woman, was Crawler's daughter. She fought at the Battle of the Little Bighorn, where, according to John Eagle Shield Sr., she rescued a wounded Lakota warrior by pulling him off the battlefield. Because of her heroic acts of valor during the Battle, she earned two names, They Shoot at Her in the Midst and Brings Him Back.[4]

Mary Crawler had a brother, a young warrior by the name of One Hawk. According to Mary Crawler, as well as John Eagle Shield Sr., One Hawk was killed at the Battle of the Rosebud.[5]

John Eagle Shield Sr., had been told that Deeds physical condition made it virtually impossible for him to ride a horse. He was routinely carted around by a horse or dog travois. Much of the time his care fell to the sisters of Crawler.[6]

When Deed's learned of One Hawk's death, he was overcome by grief. One Hawk and Mary had taken him in and treated him with kindness, as if he was their very own brother. It was at this time that Deeds decided he wanted to die like a brave warrior and have songs sung in his honor. He did not want to be remembered as a cripple.[7]

After the Battle of the Rosebud there was much elation among the Native Peoples coalition for driving the U.S. Army unit to the south out of the field. However, this joy was tempered because many warriors and horses had been killed and wounded in the Battle, and, Sitting Bull's vision of soldiers falling into the camp upside down had still not happened. Somewhere in the time after the Battle of the Rosebud and before the Battle of the Little Bighorn, Deeds and those who took care of him reasoned his opportunity to fulfill his wish to die like a warrior was now at hand.

John Eagle Shield Sr., said that at the outset of the Valley Fight with the Reno Battalion, two female relatives took Deeds on a travois far south of the Hunkpapa camp. Where, exactly, John does not know. All John was told over the years is that the female relatives got Deeds to somewhere in the vicinity of where the troopers of the U.S. Seventh Cavalry under Major Reno were either approaching or were already close to.

Then, they simply left this young boy to die like a warrior, which is precisely what happened. Because of this youngster's bravery in meeting his death, songs were sung for him over the years and his story is still being told to this day.[8]

What is in the historical record and how do these stories match up against it?

I found the following when comparing the historical record to the story of Deeds as told by John Eagle Shield Sr.

First, Frank Zahn, who we mentioned in the previous chapter as a newspaperman and interpreter, interviewed Mary Crawler (Moving Robe Woman) in 1931. She is said to be the daughter of Crawler, a band chief of the Hunkpapa Lakota, just as John Eagle Shield Sr. told me. In this interview, she stated she did have a brother by the name of One Hawk and that he had been killed.[9] She did not say where or at what battle, but again, this matches what John Eagle Shield Sr., told us.[10]

In his 1900 article on the Battle of the Little Bighorn, Dr. Charles Eastman is said to confirm the fact that Mary's brother was killed at the Battle of the Rosebud. However, I could find no such mention of this fact in the Eastman article.[11] However, in Eastman's book *Indian Heroes and Great Chieftains,* published in 1918, he interviewed the noted Hunkpapa Lakota warrior Rain-In-The-Face, who told him that Mary Crawler (Moving Robe Woman) carried her brother's war staff. According to Rain-In-The-Face, her brother had been killed in the Battle of the Rosebud.[12] This makes three parts of the John Eagle Shield Sr., story now corroborated in the historical record.

In 1936 Frank Zahn interviewed Little Voice, a Hunkpapa Lakota. Zahn said Little Voice was born in 1864 and was the son of the Hunkpapa band chief Crawler. What is strange is that Little Voice was, according to One Bull, the noted Minnikojou warrior, a brother to Deeds.[13] Little Voice was said to be with Deeds when the boy was killed, but never mentioned to Zahn that he was a brother to Mary Crawler, nor that he was with Deeds when the boy was killed.[14]

Frank Zahn interviewed Mary Crawler (Moving Robe Woman) in 1936, as well. This is what he recorded, and it should be noted this is not a direct quotation.

Mary Crawler, [an] Indian woman who fought Custer, was [the]daughter of Crawler and [the] sister of Deeds (boy 10 yrs old [and] first [one] killed), and when [she] heard that her brother was killed she rushed into [the] battle.[15]

There are two more accounts in the historical record that should be noted regarding the story of Deeds. The first is found in the Welch Dakota papers. The account was taken by Welch in 1933, with Bear Heart, a Hunkpapa Lakota man, who had fought at the Little Bighorn in 1876. Here is what Bear Heart said.

"I was 17 years old then. I did not have any gun. I had bow and arrows. Lots of the young men did not have guns. There were many fireplaces there (meaning tribes and bands). They were on the west side of the Greasy Grass (Little Big Horn). Some soldiers crossed the water and rode in on the south end of the camps. I was half way in the camp (north and south). Some more soldiers rode toward the ford there. They found a boy there and shot him. There were some women there, too, but they hid and did not get killed."[16]

One has to wonder if Bear Heart is in fact mentioning Deeds and the female relatives of Crawler here? John Eagle Shield Sr. did not know exactly where Deeds was taken and he didn't mention the female relatives being caught up in the action.[17]

Here is the last piece to the story of Deeds. Again, it comes from the Welch Dakota Papers and it is noteworthy. This story was found in assorted notes and papers among 4,000 pages of uncatalogued material Colonel Welch had collected. The story was told to Welch by Eva Little Chief and was titled, *Story of the Crippled Boy Who Died "Bravely."*[18]

"Mrs. Crawler (Sun Flower Face) was sick one time. I went to see her that time. She was very sick. She told me that one time she had a nephew, the son of her brother, who was a cripple."

Eva continued on with the story. "She took care of him. He had a bad backbone. She carried him around with a dog travois. She placed him on those poles. The dog then dragged him around that way. She got awful tired of looking out for him. She told him he never would walk; that it would be better if he were dead. He said, 'Yes.'"

"They got to the Little Greasy Grass (Big Horn). The soldiers were going to fight them that time. She said to the crippled boy, 'If you died someplace, you would just be dead. If you are killed by the enemy you would be brave. Then I could sing for you.' He said, 'Yes.'"

"So when the soldiers came she placed him upon the dog travois. She put him out there in the middle where the soldiers would kill him. She hit him with a stone club. By and by the soldiers did kill the boy."

"That made him a brave man. She often would sing a song for him and call out his name among the people."[19]

In Summary: The Story of Deeds

Based on findings in the historical record, the story of Deeds, told to me by John Eagle Shield Sr., has been corroborated.

The corroborating elements include:

Mary Crawler (Moving Robe Woman) was the daughter of the Hunkpapa Lakota band chief Crawler. She did have a brother by the name of One Hawk who was killed at the Battle of the Rosebud. The noted Hunkpapa warrior Rain-In-The-Face verified the One Hawk story as well. Mary Crawler also confirmed that she was the sister of Deeds, who was killed at the outset of the Battle of the Little Bighorn.[20]

The last account from Eva Little Chief seemingly verifies John Eagle Shield Sr.'s family history as well.[21] The Bear Heart account does nothing to diminish the John Eagle Shield Sr. story. If anything, it only adds to the distinct possibility that he is in fact telling of Deeds being taken to die bravely.

A big thank you to my friend John Eagle Shield Sr., for sharing this long-kept family history of how Deeds died bravely. Hopefully, this story will encourage other people to share their stories before they are forgotten and gone.

Notes

1. Hardorff 1999, *Hokahey: A Good Day to Die*! 17-30.

2. Personal communications with John Eagle Shield Sr.-Hunkpapa Lakota.

3. Ibid.

4. Ibid.

5. Ibid. Hardorff 1991: 93.

6. Ibid.

7. Ibid.

8. Ibid.

9. Hardorff 1991: 93; Hardorff 1999: 21-22; Hardorff 2005: 185-186; Welch 2017: 57, 63.

10. Personal communications with John Eagle Shield Sr.-Hunkpapa Lakota.

11. Eastman 1900.

12. Eastman 1918.

13. Hardorff 2005: 183-186; Hardorff 1999: 20.

14. Ibid.

15. Hardorff 2005: 185-186.

16. Welch 2017: 57-59.

17. Personal communications with John Eagle Shield Sr.-Hunkpapa Lakota.

18. Welch 2017: 57-59.

19. Ibid.

20. Hardorff 1991: 93; Hardorff 1999: 21-22; Hardorff 2005: 185-186; Welch 2017: 57, 63.

21. Welch 2017: 57-59.

14
A Cheyenne Hunting Party

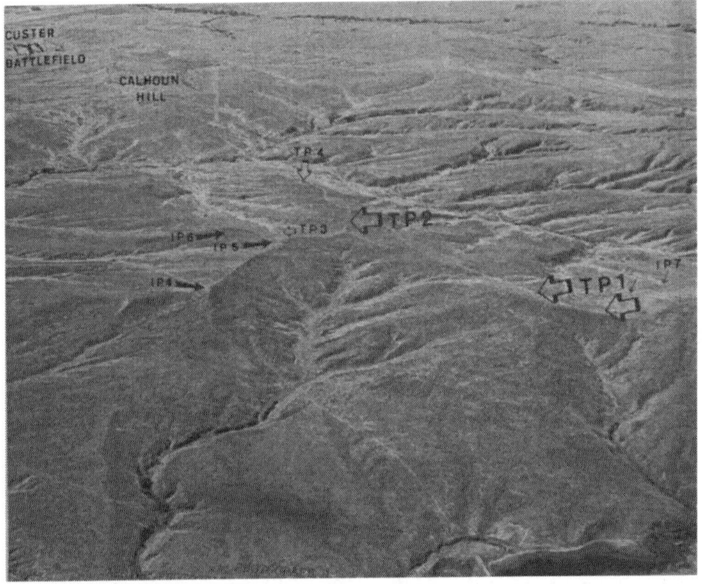

From *Custer, Cases and Cartridges: The Weibert Collection Analyzed* by Don Weibert. Luce / Blummer / Nye / Cartwright Ridge Complex Fight.TP = U.S. Seventh Cavalry Troop positions. IP = Native American positions.

Information that led to this trail came from independent researcher Chris Dixon. Help with navigating the terrain, getting to this area, and with interpreting data from years of archeological findings came to us from veteran researchers Faron Iron - Crow, Steve Andrews, Bob Snelson and Will Hutchison.

Up to this point in the book we have told stories shared with us focused on identifying the bands, tribes and people within the camps of the Native Peoples Coalition at the Little Bighorn River in 1876. We have presented stories that tell of the participation of more than just Lakota, Cheyenne and Arapaho people, as well as of some of the first defenders of the encampment on the Little Bighorn.

The following oral story has never before appeared in print. It could be said that this segment of the battle had a significant role in the outcome of what happened that day to General George Custer, the five companies, C, E, F, I, L, and the headquarters unit of the U.S. Seventh Cavalry, he commanded. Together, this group is called the Custer Battalion. There were no survivors from the Custer Battalion.

I was first told this oral history in June of 2014 while on the Little Bighorn Battlefield with veteran researcher Chris Dixon, by way of people from the Minnikojou Lakota of the Cheyenne River Reservation, which is home to the four bands of the "Titunwan" People of the Plains: The "Mnicoujou" Planters By The Water, "Oohenumpa" Two Kettle, "Itazipco" Without Bows, and "Siha Sapa" Black Foot.

For those of you who have never been to the Battlefield, there are many areas where you can simply pull over and get off the National Park Service Road. At some of these areas there are wayside exhibits that tell what happened during the Battle at that spot. At one of these areas, you can look southeast into what is called Medicine Tail Coulee. Above it, Luce Ridge runs parallel, then intersects with Blummer / Nye / Cartwright Ridge. It is within these environs that this oral history is set.

To feed the people within the camps that comprised the Native Peoples Coalition encampment on the Little

The Luce / Blummer / Nye / Cartwright ridge complex.

Bighorn River, there were many groups of hunters routinely going out and coming back. As we told earlier in chapter 8, large herds of antelope had been spotted in the Little Bighorn Valley. Our oral history centers on one Cheyenne hunting party.

Leaving the camps on the Little Bighorn, they crossed the river and went south and east. Eventually, they followed an old buffalo trail that hunters had used and the People had followed for who knows how long. Remember, the People had frequented this area for many, many years, possibly for centuries, before this time. This buffalo trail became what is today U.S. Highway 212. Following it will take you through the Northern Cheyenne Reservation, with stops at Busby and Lame Deer, Montana.

Looking from Nye-Cartwright Ridge down towards the Little Bighorn River. The Native Peoples coalition encampment would have stretched to the area behind the trees and to the surrounding area.

On the afternoon of June 25th, 1876, this Cheyenne hunting party had begun to make its way back to the encampment on the Little Bighorn, following the same old buffalo trail when they caught glimpses of movement against the terrain.Perhaps, they were alerted to this possible enemy force when they saw the massive flock of birds, an ominous sign these seasoned hunters and warriors certainly would have been keen to.

Their approach slowed and they became cautious, for they now found themselves in a precarious situation. These hunters, who were warriors as well, now hunted a new quarry. This Cheyenne hunting party had spotted the Custer Battalion amid the endless prairie scrub, pockets of sage, hillocks and tall grass.

Some 200 cavalry troopers of the U.S. Seventh Cavalry, clad in different shades of blue and grey, mounted on horseback, easily stood out. The Custer Battalion maneuvered to get into position for a better look at the Little Bighorn River. Should the Custer Battalion attempt to maneuver through Medicine Tail Coulee and attempt to cross the river, this path would put them within close proximity to the Cheyenne camps.

Grossly outnumbered, the Cheyenne hunting party moved ahead without hesitation. These proud and brave warriors were not going to stay put and let the Custer Battalion move unimpeded towards their people. The Cheyenne hunting party still had the element of surprise on their side, as they had yet to be seen by the Custer Battalion. The Cheyenne hunters had another advantage: they knew the dangerous and foreboding terrain the Custer Battalion was about to navigate!

The Cheyenne hunters pressed ever closer to the unsuspecting Custer Battalion. These hunters used the ravines and coulees for cover, then, like wolves, ran just below the top of the ridges. These hunters were careful not expose themselves, they always moved with the terrain at their backs, cautious never to be noticed against the sky's blue horizon. They had to get between the Custer Battalion and the Little Bighorn River, for the Cheyenne hunting party was all that stood in the way of their people being attacked. Some of the Cheyenne hunters, who had dismounted by this time, left their horses with young boys who had accompanied them on the hunt. The hunters now fired!

To the soldiers of the Custer Battalion, it must have been as if the Cheyenne hunters appeared to have sprung from the very earth! Hidden behind pockets of scrub and sage brush, they fired one or two shots, then dropped back into the tall prairie grass and moved along, undetected.

General Custer deployed his Custer Battalion. The cavalry troopers were eager to get into the action ever since they had witnessed the Reno Battalion thunder through the valley towards the camps on the Little Bighorn. General Custer deployed one, maybe two of the companies to cover the Battalion, as the remaining companies moved on the Cheyenne hunting party.

The landscape can be deceiving in this lethal terrain. One minute you can see for great distances, then in the blink of an eye, it is broken and conceals an enemy within it. A series of skirmishes broke out as the troopers tried to drive the Cheyenne hunters away. The sound of the firing not only alerted those in the camps along the Little Bighorn River, but it brought some Cheyenne and Lakota fighters from the north.

The oral history shared with me concludes with the members of the Cheyenne hunting party who had scattered on foot to positions between the river to their west and the Custer Battalion on the east being picked up by this new group of mounted Cheyenne and Lakota warriors. Both of these groups, some riding double, continued to follow the old buffalo trail. Whether this was done in an effort to lead the Custer Battalion away from the encampment, or simply because the old buffalo trail presented the best possible means of escape for these brave hunters and warriors, remains to be seen.[1]

~

The Cheyenne hunting party who attacked the Custer Battalion in and about the confines of the Luce / Blummer / Nye / Cartwright Ridge complex and continued fighting into the Medicine Tail Coulee area are not part of the historical record. The established oral history primarily comes from noted Cheyenne historian John Stands In Timber.[2]

John Stands In Timber said that Cheyenne and some Sioux (Lakota) warriors, which included his relative Wolf Tooth and another Cheyenne warrior, Big Foot, came to the fighting on the Luce / Blummer / Nye / Cartwright Ridge complex from a creek north of Highway 8. Today, Highway 8 is U.S. Highway 212 (the old buffalo trail). These warriors joined in on the attack of the Custer Battalion, as some of the Battalions companies were thought to have moved for the Little Bighorn River, or had returned from scouting the river's banks.[3]

The Cheyenne hunting party's story as told to me through oral history from the Minnikojou Lakota People emphatically stated that the party was returning to the encampment on the Little Bighorn River. The Cheyenne hunting party spotted the Custer Battalion from the old buffalo trail and then attacked and engaged the Battalion above from the east and in the ridge complex before the Wolf Tooth and Big Foot party arrived.

I am not sure if any of the Cheyenne hunting party or the other Cheyenne and Lakota with the Wolf Tooth and Big Foot party were killed. I am also not sure if any soldiers from the Custer Battalion were killed in this fighting, either. I was told some troopers followed the Cheyenne hunters and the other Cheyenne and Lakota clear past Calhoun Hill. The chase continued through the Keogh Sector and then behind and past the Last Stand Hill area. Soldiers of the Custer Battalion followed the Cheyenne hunters and warriors all the way to the Little Bighorn River to what is today called the Ford D area, which is below the current Little Bighorn National Monument Cemetery and also encompasses the area where U.S. Interstate 90 and U.S. Highway 212 intersect.[4]

~

I have been on the Luce / Blummer / Nye / Cartwright Ridge complex on several occasions. We know there was fighting in this area. It's not that something did or didn't happen here, but rather, it's time to determine who the people the Custer Battalion fought here were.

It is not easy getting to the ridge complex. One has to first get off U.S. Highway 212 and traverse the terrain.

You had better be in the company of someone who knows the area and has a rugged all-terrain vehicle. Up on these ridges, it is quiet and serene. The wind blows hot and dry up here, and it's as if history swirls around you. The ground is still pristine, just like it was that day in June of 1876.

On the ridges, there is something that makes a researcher and seeker like myself feel as if a person has stepped back in time. At times, you feel what the action might have been like that day. If you are lucky, sometimes you will encounter horses, running free and fast. They are from the local Crow families who own land adjacent to this area. Sometimes the horses will stop if they see you. They look in wonderment at who might be up here, in their domain. They give you a snort and then bolt away. The longer you watch them run away, the more it looks as if they are truly running on air.

From this vantage point, you can see Weir Point, a significant landmark when one studies the Battle of the Little Bighorn, for history tells us that the Custer Battalion rode near and even across Weir Point prior to moving to Luce Ridge. The fastest way to traverse the terrain between Weir Point and the Luce / Blummer / Nye / Cartwright Ridge complex is to travel through what is called the North Fork of Medicine Tail Coulee. Medicine Tail Coulee runs almost parallel to the ridge complex, then turns to run towards the Little Bighorn River.

In the years that followed being told this story of the Cheyenne hunters, I searched desperately for any signs or clues to it in all the literature ever written on the Battle of the Little Bighorn. Donovan Taylor and I always made it a point to ask about this part of the battle and this story when interviewing Cheyenne, Lakota, Dakota, Nakota, Arapaho and other people. No Native American historians or elders, even those from the Cheyenne Tribe or those from Cheyenne River Reservation, had ever heard of such a story.

There is archeological evidence, as well as pieces of information in the historical record telling of this encounter in the Battle of the Little Bighorn. There is a great deal of information to take in with this story. While the story itself is relatively straightforward, it is what is left in its aftermath that must be looked at now that the story has been told.

As we go through these accounts, keep in mind the oral story we shared. Remember, those researchers and historians who came before us and put together what they found and had shared with them did not know of this Cheyenne hunting party's story.

What is in the historical record and how do these stories match up against it?

There are many pieces of sound research to discuss here. I am going to summarize these researchers, their findings and other pieces. Please see the endnotes to further your own journey of learning and research.

The first piece of evidence to attest to the fighting in this area came about in the 1920s. A local rancher, Joseph Blummer, began finding expended army cartridges on the ridgetops that would later be called Blummer / Nye / Cartwright Ridge.[5]

It was in the 1940s that Elwood Nye and Ralph Cartwright, close friends to then Little Bighorn National Monument Park Superintendent Edward Luce, began to find cartridges as well. So many, in fact, that Cartwright noted the empty cases were in groups of three.[6] He surmised that the troopers from the Custer Battalion were engaged here on the ridge and that they had been halted long enough for each trooper to fire three times. Cartwright added that 103 cases had been found here. He went on to produce a series of maps showing and telling of his findings in this area.[7]

Superintendent Luce, not to be outdone, did his own fieldwork on the area south of the ridge. He focused on a spur that runs to the ridge complex and that comprised part of the area of the north rim that overlooks Medicine Tail Coulee. This area would be later called Luce Ridge. Luce stated he found expended carbine cartridge shells here. He surmised this is the route the Custer Battalion had traveled in order to engage the warriors out in this area. He gave no indications that he had any idea as to who the warriors were. Luce felt the troopers were mounted as they fired at these warriors.[8]

Because of Luce's field work, he plotted his findings on a 1908 edition of the U.S.G.S. map. According to Mike Donahue, in his 2009 book, *Drawing Battle Lines*, Luce produced the map with the intention of future finds being added to it.

Donahue included the map in his book.[9] There are four interesting elements to it, starting in the south and working their way north.[10] In his findings, Luce surmised that at the outset of this fight, the Custer Battalion, or at least parts, remained mounted while firing on the warriors who had surprised them. As the fight progressed, Luce noted the Custer Battalion was at times dismounted at later stages.[11]

Continuing with more data in the way of archeological evidence brings us to the massive work of Jerome A. Greene, as well as Don and Henry Weibert.

Greene, a noted historian and author of several books on the American West, worked as a seasonal historian at Custer Battlefield National Monument in the summers of 1968, 1970 and 1971. It was at this time Greene was given the task of correlating all the known battle relic finds across the Little Bighorn Battlefield. He produced a detailed map that clearly shows the intensity of the action on and in the Luce / Blummer / Nye / Cartwright Ridge complex through Medicine Tail Coulee.[12] Some interesting pieces to note from his gathering of findings in this area, specifically the north fork of Medicine Tail Coulee and south side of Luce Ridge, are three horse skeletons, plus additional horse bones.[13] Lastly, to the east of Luce / Blummer / Nye / Cartwright Ridge, one fragment of human phalanx was found.[14]

Henry Weibert and his son, Don Weibert, were ranchers who resided in the Valley of the Little Bighorn for many years. Henry started roaming the Battlefield in the mid-1920s. For the next 40 plus years, Henry, with help of a metal detector and family members, went about exploring and finding relics on land adjacent to the Little Bighorn Battlefield. He and his family amassed a massive collection.

Henry Weibert was intrigued by the Luce / Blummer / Nye / Cartwright Ridge fight. He spent a great deal of time in this area, and in fact, had aerial photos taken. Because of his familiarity with the difference between

Indian and soldier's cases and cartridges, Weibert was able to use the aerial images to deduce where the warriors and troops from the Custer Battalion were. We added the photo from their book, *Custer, Cases & Cartridges.*[15]

Weibert clearly noted in the book that the warriors held a ridge to the west, while the Custer Battalion had troops on the eastern opposing ridge.[16] There was no mention from Weibert as to who he thought the warriors were, nor did he mention that he was ever told where they had come from.

One of the many trips to the Battlefield with other researchers stands out with regard to this part of the Battle. On this day, myself, Chris Dixon and two other veteran researchers, Steve Andrews and Faron Iron, were atop of Weir Point. Earlier in the day, we had been on the Luce / Blummer / Nye / Cartwright Ridge complex. Chris Dixon has always maintained that while the Custer Battalion was on and or near Weir Point, this was where the Cheyenne hunting party had first spotted them.[17] Dixon had also felt that the Hunkpapa Lakota war chief Gall had then seen the Custer Battalion on what is called East Ridge, which is the ridge to the south of Luce Ridge. The Custer Battalion would have presumably at this time be moving for Luce and the Blummer / Nye / Cartwright Ridge complex. Dixon had been told that at this time Gall had taken up a position at the shoulder of Sharpshooter Ridge.[18]

Steve Andrews and Faron Iron have explored this area of the Battlefield countless times, using previous researchers maps and findings. Steve's conclusion is that the Custer Battalion had only one possible direction in which they could fire, even if mounted, and that is into the north fork of Medicine Tail Coulee.[19]

Veteran researcher Gordon Harper, who we have mentioned in previous chapters, also weighed in on the Luce / Blummer / Nye / Cartwright Ridge fight in a thread on the Little Bighorn Proboard, back in January of 2009. He said, "There is no doubt that there was firing from Blummer Ridge, and at least one volley directed at a few warriors who were toward the river-at least that what the evidence, taken as a whole suggest. There was also firing at a larger group of warriors who were coming from the east, commencing at Luce."[20]

Harper never said who these warriors from the east were. And, remember, Harper was said to have lived on the Northern Cheyenne reservation in the early 1960s. He also told other historians and researchers that he had actually been taken to the Battlefield in the early 1960s by Cheyenne elders and historians. In this correspondence he made no mention of the fighting at the Luce / Blummer / Nye / Cartwright Ridge complex, nor of the Cheyenne hunters.[21]

In 1935, Dr. Charles Kuhlman began his quest to find out what happened at the Little Bighorn. Dr. Kuhlman had at one time been a professor of history at the University of Nebraska. He was forced into early retirement because of going deaf. For the next 16 years, he was routinely driven from Billings, Montana, to the Battlefield, by a relative. Kuhlman would be dropped off with his satchel of writing and recording supplies, plus a backpack of food and water. Left on his own, Kuhlman wandered the Battlefield.[22]

In 1940, Dr. Kuhlman wrote the first of his two publications dealing with the Battle. In *Custer and the Gall Saga,* Kuhlman tells of the Custer Battalion maneuvering across the landscape after leaving Weir Point. "When Custer struck the coulee, he turned east and followed it to where it flattens and branches to the south, then cut across northeastward to the ridge and was seen by the warriors who dashed up to exchange shots with him. These warriors must have been in the rough ground north of the coulee and did not see him until he mounted the ridge. If they had seen him from the camps, it does not seem reasonable to suppose that so few of them would have gone."[23]

To be clear here, Kuhlman stated previously in his work that the Custer Battalion had traversed the ridges to get to Medicine Tail Coulee. It is thought he based this off of a map from Dr. Thomas Marquis. And, Kuhlman didn't say it was Cheyenne warriors.[24]

Dr. Marquis was at one time the agency physician for the Northern Cheyenne Tribe. He passed away in 1935, while he lived in Hardin, Montana. He interviewed countless Cheyenne warriors who had fought at the Little Bighorn and had accompanied many to the Battlefield, as well.[25]

In Kuhlman's second publication that came out in 1951, *Legend into History*, he theorized that warriors who had been seen by elements of the Custer Battalion on the bluffs overlooking the Little Bighorn River were in fact Cheyenne. Some researchers and historians suspect these warriors were the reason that General Custer took his Battalion to the bluffs, instead of following Major Reno's command into the Valley Fight. Kuhlman added this:

"The warriors he had flushed here were not part of the village. They were the warriors of a small band of Cheyennes on their way to their tribesmen in the camps and did not flee to the village directly. The fled down the trail for only a short distance and then turned northward to rejoin their non-combatants.[26]

In his endnotes, Kuhlman thought these Cheyenne were in fact, scouts from the noted Cheyenne war chief Little Wolf. This renowned Cheyenne leader, who was also one of four Old Man Chiefs among the Cheyenne tribe, was desperately trying to get his small group of Cheyennes into the safety of the camps on the Little Bighorn.[27]

Regardless of who Kuhlman thinks these Cheyenne are, it's what he said about them, "and then turned northward to rejoin their noncombatants," that stands out. I had been told this same scenario from Chris Dixon.

Dixon has always made it a point to remind me that the Cheyenne hunting party and then the warriors who came later, as told from John Stands In Timber, after skirmishing with the Custer Battalion, continued on the old Buffalo trail that is today Highway 212. They followed it in a northerly direction and then it swung west, towards the river and to the Ford D area. Parts of the Custer Battalion did eventually give pursuit to the Ford D area and this area was in fact, full of non-combatants who had fled the camps within the encampment on the Little Bighorn at the outset of the Valley Fight.[28]

In 1956, The noted Cheyenne historian John Stands In Timber, shed some light on this part of Battle. Stands In Timber was interviewed and then accompanied across the Battlefield by Little Bighorn Battlefield National

Monument Historian Don Rickey. Stands In Timber stated that a group of 40 or 50 warriors, which included his grandfather, Wolf Tooth, and Sioux (Lakota) warriors, had snuck out the night before the Battle. They wanted first honor to engage the enemy and so they hid out hoping to accomplish this task. These warriors were alerted by Lakota scouts that soldiers were getting ready to attack the village from the direction of southeast.[29]

Stands In Timber told Rickey the following information and I have put it here word for word.

"Beginning of the battle: A band of forty or fifty warriors, returning to the village, met the Custer soldiers on a high ridge east of the Battlefield." Stands In Timber pointed out this area to Rickey as above and east of the Luce / Blummer / Nye / Cartwright Ridge area. There is no mention in the Rickey notes that Stands In Timber ever mentioned his relative Wolf Tooth or Big Foot with this group. This should give us reason as researchers to note and pause. A search of Rickey's notes shows no mention of Wolf Tooth of Big Foot and their group in this segment, which Rickey noted as, "Beginning of the Battle," from Stands In Timber.[30]

Stands In Timber at no time in the Rickey interviews, nor in subsequent interviews with Margot Liberty, does Stands In Timber ever mention the Cheyenne hunting party story.

It is interesting to remember that in the oral history shared with me from Minnkiojou Lakota People from Cheyenne River Reservation, it was told that the Cheyenne hunting party's fight had brought another group of warriors to the fight. This other group of warriors were said to have picked up members of the hunters, who had dismounted and left their horses.[31]

At this time in our investigation of this oral history, I can present only two names of Cheyenne warriors as possible members of this Cheyenne hunting party. They are Plenty of Meat and Long Sioux. Long Sioux also went by the name of Tall Sioux or Turtle Road. These names come from George Bent in a letter to noted historian George Hyde.[32] I have put it in its original form so the reader can read for themselves and see some interesting pieces that seem to coincide with the Cheyenne hunter's oral history and the information we subsequently found.

Bent also spoke to another veteran warrior, Long Sioux, also known as Tall Sioux, or Turtle Road, whom he described as "one of the two Cheyennes that Custer chased to the Village."

Long Sioux is not mentioned at all in *Life of George Bent* and I have been unable to find out much about his life, other than that he seems to have acted as a source for James Mooney when he carried out research among the Southern Cheyennes in the early twentieth century.

He may be the Tall Sioux who was in the sweat lodge with Lame White Man when the Battle of the Little Bighorn began. He was a member of the Elk society and helped to defend Dull Knife's village in November 1876.

Earlier, he had been a Dog Soldier and appears to have also survived the Battle of Summit Springs in 1869.

According to this account, "They were out looking for Buffalo when they seen Custer following the trail from [the]Rosebud."

Part of this information seems to have been general knowledge among the Southern Cheyennes, as Bent went on to add that "from what I hear from other Indians, Long Sioux or Turtle Road says their horses were giving out when they ran into [a] herd of Cheyenne ponies and got on fresh ponies. Custer was getting close to them."

He clearly took his research seriously, as he went on to say that "If I do not see Long Sioux. I will get all [the] information from

Brave Bear and Yellow Nose and will give you [a] long account of the whole fight." (Bent to Hyde 2 September 1905.)

He promised to give Hyde a full account of the whole battle, including Benteen and Custer's fights, but that account –if it was ever provided – seems to have been lost.

Nevertheless, just over a week later, he wrote again to provide additional details supplied by Brave Bear and Long Sioux.

He went on to say that he had "not had [a] talk with Yellow Nose, as he is blind and can not get around."

He then expanded upon Long Sioux's experiences: Long Sioux and Plent[y] of Meat were out hunting buffalo when they seen Custer and his Men riding very fast towards the big village. They were obside [outside?]

of Custer['s troops], about one mile [away], when they seen him.

They first seen dust rising way up in the air and could not tell what made it, until they came up on [a] hill where they seen [a] long line of soldiers making for the village. So they rode back for the camp, [as] fast as they could, to give the alarm.

But Custer [had] seen them, so he to went [sic] faster with his men. Long Sioux says Custer must have knew right where the village was, as he made straight for it. He says that Custer did not follow them.

They ran along side of Custer all away. He says [that] if Custer [had] wanted to, he could have overtaken him and Plenty of Meat and cut them off, as their horses were playing out on them.

He says Custer paid no attention to him and Plenty of Meat. [It was] the village what he was after. He says Custer got to the bluffs of [the] Little Big Horn [at the] same time as they did. He says [that a] good many Indians seen Custer with his command before he got there.[33]

In Summary: A Cheyenne Hunting Party

We have presented the oral history of the Cheyenne hunting party, which came to us from the Minnikojou Lakota People of the Cheyenne River Reservation. It appears that this is the first time that not only has this story appeared in print, but that it has even been discussed when the Battle of the Little Bighorn is studied.

While the archeological evidence of fighting and the positions of the Custer Battalion compared to that of the warriors who engaged them at the Luce / Blummer / Nye / Cartwright Ridge complex is undeniable, the question as to who these warriors were still remains a mystery. Researcher and writer Charles Kuhlman put Cheyenne warriors in this area of the fighting, but gave no inclination they were from a Cheynne hunting party returning to the encampment on the Little Bighorn River. Gordon Harper implied the Custer Battalion fired on warriors coming from Luce Ridge. However, Harper did not say whether or not this action involved Cheyenne hunters or even Cheyenne warriors.

Cheyenne historian John Stands In Timber told of fighting in the area of the Luce / Blummer / Nye / Cartwright Ridge complex. He stated the fighting was started here by a band of forty or fifty warriors. Stands In Timber does not mention his relative Wolf Tooth or any Lakota as being in this group.

Minnikojou Lakota oral history shared with me states that a Cheyenne hunting party, returning to the encampment on the Little Bighorn, were the first to engage the Custer Battalion above and to the east of the Luce / Blummer / Nye / Cartwright Ridge complex. This fight then brought the other group of warriors described by Stands In Timber. Stands in Timber said that these Cheyenne had in fact come from north of the encampment on the Little Bighorn and that these warriors had Lakota with them as well. This group also included Stands In Timber's relative, Wolf Tooth.

Last is George Bent's information. Bent's story tells of Cheyenne hunters coming back to the camps on the Little Bighorn and encountering the Custer Battalion. It does not, however, tell of any fighting between these Cheyenne hunters and the Custer Battalion.

The Cheyenne hunting party's history has now been introduced to the historical record. It had seemingly been swept into the Stands In Timber account from 1956. Stands In Timber told of two groups of Cheyenne but his detailed account was not given much thought.

It is evident that more research will need to be conducted if any light might be shed on this account. Open communication and dialogue with and among the many bands and tribes who fought at the Battle of the Little Bighorn regarding their history of events is long overdue. Our hope is that when this story appears in print, maybe some Cheyenne families or possibly people from Cheyenne River Reservation will be able to add to it.

A special note of thanks to Chris Dixon and Bob Snelson, for their unwavering support, friendship and help over the years in studying this aspect of the Battle. And, to Faron Iron, Steve Andrews and Will Hutchison, three of the best old United States Marines you could ever hope to run around southeast Montana with.

Notes

1. Personal communications with Chris Dixon.

2. Ibid. Hardorff 1998, *Cheyenne Memories of the Custer Fight*: 166-173; Donahue 2009: 241- 247, iv; Stands In Timber and Liberty 2013: 364-366, 382-383, 440-441, and Maps Commentary by Michael Donahue I, Ii, Iii. Iiii, Iiv, Iv, Ivi.

3. Ibid.

4. Personal communications with Chris Dixon.

5. Greene, J. 2008: 195; Donahue 2009: 337-341, 349-360.

6. Ibid.

7. Ibid.

8. Ibid.

9. Donahue 2009: 337-341, xxiv.

10. Ibid.

11. Ibid.

12. Greene 1979: 26-33, 59.

13. Ibid. Human skeletal remains are marked on Greene map at 20D, 21D and 22D. Horse skeletal remains are marked at 11D, 20D and 21D.

14. Ibid. Human skeletal remains are marked as 26D.

15. Weibert 1989: 45-52. Personal communications with Steve Andrews.

16. Ibid

17. Personal communications with Chris Dixon.

18. Ibid. See the Bonafede 1999 Map, Little Bighorn Battlefield Map: Archeological Finds and Historical Locations, as a source for East Ridge.

19. Personal communications with Steve Andrews and Faron Iron. See Donahue 2009: 337-341, xxiv; 347-360.

20. Gordon Harper email on The Little Bighorn Proboard website, Jan of 2009.

21. Personal communications with Gordon Richards.

22. Donaue 2009: 342-346.

23. Kuhlman 1940: 30.

24. Ibid and Donahue 2009: 332-336.

25. Ibid. For Marquis, see *Custer on the Little Bighorn, Wooden Leg: A Warrior who Fought Custer* and *The Cheyennes of Montana.*

26. Kuhlman 1951:152-154; See endnote 54, 228-229.

27. Ibid.

28. Personal communications with Chris Dixon.

29. Hardorff 1998, *Cheyenne Memories of the Custer Fight*: 166-173; Stands In Timber and Liberty 2013: 364-366, 382-383, 440-441.

30. Ibid.

31. Personal communications with Chris Dixon.

32. Bent to Hyde: 11 August 1905.

33. Ibid.

15
Dog Men and Dog Soldiers at the Little Bighorn

The information that led to this trail we followed for this chapter came from the following people: Linwood Tall Bull - Cheyenne, Alec Sandcrane - Cheyenne, Steve Littlebird - Cheyenne, Dwight Bull Coming - Cheyenne, Tim Lame Woman Sr. - Cheyenne, Roger Red Hat - Cheyenne, Wallace Bearchum - Cheyenne, Keith Spotted Wolf - Cheyenne, Chico Her Many Horses - Oglala Lakota, Rick Two Dogs - Oglala Lakota, Basil BraveHeart - Oglala Lakota, Victor Douville - Sicangu Lakota Tribal Historian, Bill Goggles - Arapaho, Devin Oldman - Arapaho, Martin Blackburn - Arapaho, Cletus Yellow Plume - Arapaho, Henry Goggles Jr. - Arapaho, independent researcher and writer Randy Tucker and Chris Dixon.

In 2016, Linwood Tall Bull, a noted Cheyenne educator and historian, gave me some valuable advice. I was trying to ascertain who the Cheyenne people who had fought at the Little Bighorn were. Linwood's simple suggestion during one our many conversations stands out. He told me to look at the Dog Soldiers. Linwood felt these famous warriors, who come from the Cheyenne military society, the Dog Men, and who so freely sacrificed themselves fighting the U.S. Army for the Cheyenne people, had simply not been studied with regard to the Battle of The Little Bighorn.

Linwood, who is a member of the Cheyenne Dog Men society himself, theorized that there were reasons why certain warriors fought when and where they did. He felt some of these Cheyenne warriors had obligations, maybe, for some, as a result of being in a military society. These obligations ultimately led to these warriors getting into the Battle of the Little Bighorn at a certain interval or place. He stated that at the time of the Battle, each

Cheyenne military society was camped separately, within the Cheyenne camps. These military society men would have had their families camped with them as well.

Linwood then told me that the Cheyenne Dog Men had guarded the Sacred Buffalo Hat of the Cheyenne Tribe during the Battle of the Little Bighorn. Linwood said this was why some Dog Soldiers fought and charged Last Stand Hill at the end of the Battle. One of these warriors was his relative Tall Bull, who had his horse shot out from under him.[1]

Donovan Taylor is a member of the Cheyenne Dog Men. He had been following these warriors' trails to, and at, the Little Bighorn for many years. In countless talks and interviews with Cheyenne elders, he has recorded a great deal of information on Cheyenne warriors said to have fought at the Battle of the Little Bighorn. Donovan had always wanted to do some type of project on what societies these Cheyenne warriors were in, if any.

As luck would have it, Linwood provided us with a document compiled by the Northern Cheyenne Tribe that is a list of Cheyenne warriors who fought at the Little Bighorn. This document also names the warriors society they belonged to, if any.[2]

See Appendix F for the list of Cheyenne warriors said to have fought at the Battle of the Little Bighorn and for the list of Cheyenne Dog Men who fought at the Little Bighorn.

In 2018, it was then that Donovan came across an interesting story from veteran historian and writer Randy Tucker.

Randy resides in Wyoming and has for many years been researching the American West and all related. Randy is a close friend to Chico Her Many Horses, an Oglala Lakota man from Pine Ridge Reservation in South Dakota. The story Randy told had come to him from Chico.[3]

In his story, Randy said that the legendary Cheynne Dog Soldiers were in action at the Little Bighorn. Randy's story told that the Seventh Cavalry, presumably those in the Custer Battalion, ran into these Dog Soldiers at some episode in the Battle. Not only that, but there were 12 Cheyenne Dog Soldiers that were picketed! The story concluded with some of the Dog Soldiers being wounded, while others were killed in the fighting that day.[4]

In my subsequent interviews with Chico Her Many Horses over the years, Chico informed me that his family's home on the Pine Ridge Reservation was a gathering spot for Oglala Lakota families. Chico said that it was not uncommon for wagon loads of Lakota families to come to his family's place, and camp for a week or so. It was during this time that many oral stories pertaining to Lakota history were preserved. When specifically asked as to who shared the Dog Soldier story with his family, Chico could not recall. Chico had not heard where exactly these Dog Soldiers fought at in the Battle, nor did he hear any of their names. Chico did feel that the Dog Soldiers in this oral history, were, in fact, more of a mixed group. He thought they might have been from the Dog Soldier Band of the Cheyenne, rather than from the Cheyenne military society.[5]

~

The Cheyenne Dog Soldiers are Dog Men, one of the four original Cheyenne military societies. The other three are Red Shields, also called Bull Soldiers, Elkhorn Scrapers, also called the Crooked Lances, and Kit Foxes. Over time, the Dog Men military society evolved into a band of its own within the Cheyenne Tribe. As the fighting of white encroachment on the western plains grew, so did the Dog Soldiers band. Closely associated with the Oglala Lakota, Sicangu Lakota and Arapaho, along with other Cheyenne warriors (some of whom may have been in another military society), joined the Dog Soldier Band. These Dog Soldiers, some of whom were part Cheyenne and part Lakota, did not follow customary Cheyenne ways when they married. Instead of going to live with their wife's people, they instead brought their wives to live with their band.[6]

Many Dog Men wore the distinctive headdress of a cap, with a narrow-beaded band along the front edge. The crown would be covered with either eagle, magpie or raven feathers, with the sides covered with hawk and crow feathers.[7] Known for their tenacious fighting abilities, the Dog Men military society warriors were noted for their bravery and, to an extent, the fact that they proudly adhered to strict discipline.[8]

When in the midst of battle, it was not uncommon for one of the Dog Men's four bravest warriors of their society, known as Dog Rope Men, to take a no-retreat stance in front of the enemy. The Dog Rope Men wore a sash over their left shoulder and under the right arm. Others were attached to the owner's belt by a string. The sash was a tanned strip of buffalo hide. Some were eight feet long, decorated with feathers from an eagle and adorned with porcupine quills. These Dog Ropes had a red-painted, sharp pointed wooden pin that had a picket pin at the end of it.[9]

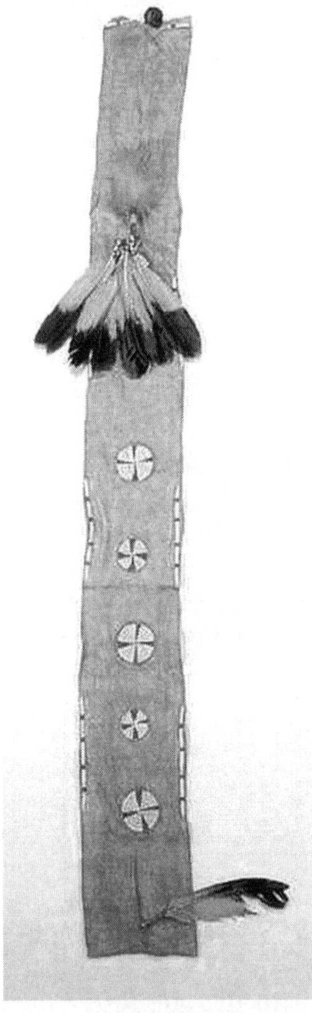

Arapaho Dog Lodge sash - *Manuscript* 2811, *National Anthropological Archives, Smithsonian Institution*

The Dog Men staked themselves to the ground with the picket pin at the end of the Dog Rope. And so, these Dog Men could only be released from this incredible act of bravado and obligation of fighting until death if a fellow warrior pulled the picket pin and then drove them away by hitting them with a quirt.

There were only four dog ropes at a given time among the Dog Men.[10]

This display of bravery and the use of a sash with the picket pin was not uncommon among other Plains tribes' warriors. Nor was the Dog Men military society exclusive among the Cheyenne. The Arapaho were one tribe who had a Dog Men warrior society.[11]

As Donovan and I continued on the trail of the Dog Men and Dog Soldiers, five Arapaho historians shared with us more never-before-told information regarding the Arapaho at the Battle of the Little Bighorn. Bill Goggles, Devin Oldman, Martin Blackburn, Cletus Yellow Plume and Henry Goggles Jr. told us that within the three groups of Arapaho who were at the Little Bighorn, there were Dog Soldiers from the Arapaho Dog Men warrior society.

Some Dog Soldiers in the Arapaho group came from Fort Robinson in Nebraska, while others were with the Arapaho war chief, Sharp Nose. Devin Oldman told me that Sharp Nose was in fact the headsman for the Dog Men at this time. There was no mention of these Dog Men being picketed, or where they specifically fought at during the Battle.

We were very fortunate to be given the known names of these Dog Men: Little Soldier, Crazy Hair, Yellow Bear, Runs Behind Enemy, Falls Off His Horse, Iron Eyes and their leader, Sharp Nose. See Appendix C.[12]

It was Basil BraveHeart and Rick Two Dogs, Oglala Lakota elders and historians, who both shared this story of Dog Soldiers fighting at the Battle of the Little Bighorn. This history comes from the Oglala Lakota People at Pine Ridge Reservation in South Dakota. The story even said that some of these Dog Soldiers picketed themselves during the Battle. No names were given for these warriors, nor was it known where exactly these Dog Soldiers fought. It was not known if any of these Dog Soldiers died in the Battle.[13]

Sicangu Lakota Tribal Historian Victor Douville informed me that he had been told that the Minnikojou Lakota Chief, Lame Deer, had led Dog Soldiers at the Little Bighorn. Victor added that he was told this action took place somewhere in the Medicine Tail Ford area. Victor was told these Dog Soldiers were in fact part of the Dog Soldier Band, which was made up of Cheyenne, Lakota and Arapaho.[14]

Based on oral history shared with us at this part of in our investigation, we had three Oglala Lakota historians and one Sicangu Lakota tribal historian putting Dog

Soldiers at the Little Bighorn. All three Oglala Lakota historians said that in the stories they were told, some of these Dog Soldiers were in fact picketed. In our interviews with Chico, Basil and Rick, none knew exactly where these Dog Soldiers fought and no one had any names of these warriors. Chico does believe these Dog Soldiers were of mixed Cheyenne, Lakota and Arapaho heritage.[15] Victor Douville's story told of Dog Soldiers from the Dog Soldier Band and who fought in the Medicine Tail Ford engagement.[16] We also had five Arapaho historians tell us that their military warrior society, the Dog Men, were also at the Little Bighorn.[17]

~

What about the Cheyenne Dog Soldiers and their possible involvement at the Battle of the Little Bighorn? Donovan, as I mentioned earlier, had been on the Dog Soldiers trail for a number of years. In an interview he conducted with Alec Sandcrane, a Northern Cheyenne Tribal Member, some astounding information was revealed.

Alec informed Donovan that his relative, Standing Elk, was a member of the Dog Men and that Standing Elk was indeed at the Little Bighorn. Alec said Standing Elk was instrumental in getting the Dog Soldiers into some type of concentrated resistance effort. Namely, he was imploring others to help these warriors get horses. Alec stated this took place in and around the area that is known on the Battlefield as Medicine Tail Ford.

Standing Elk was mentioned in chapter 11. He is the uncle of Black Road, the Oglala Lakota man who started the Sacred Bow society among the Oglala Lakota.[18]

In April of 2019, Donovan Taylor interviewed Steve Littlebird, a Cheyenne tribal member. Steve is an Elkhorn Scraper military society man who informed Donovan that he had been told the names of two Dog Soldiers who fought at the Little Bighorn, Tangle Hair and Broken Rope, but not precisely where they fought.[19]

Tangle Hair is in the historical record as belonging to the Dog Men, and was their headsman at this time. No stranger to fighting, this Dog Man had fought at Summit Springs in 1869. Afterwards, he had brought some of the surviving Dog Soldiers to the north country. He was also the brother of American Horse, the Cheyenne war chief. Perhaps Tangle Hair, being the Dog Men headsman, had his Dog Soldiers guarding the sacred Buffalo Hat, as Linwood Tall Bull had said?[20]

I followed the trail of Broken Rope and found his relative, Vine Brokenrope. The family thought Brokenrope was half Lakota and half Cheyenne. Vine knew of no one in the family who could add anything more about Brokenrope's participation in the Battle.[21]

Dwight Bull Coming, a Cheyenne tribal member, shared information related to the Cheyenne Dog Men

Standing Elk, Cheyenne Dog Soldier War Chief, middle right, in headdress. Cheyenne oral history puts this Dog Soldier at the Little Bighorn and leading resistance near Medicine Tail Coulee.

with me in April of 2021. Dwight said that the Cheyenne Dog Men, who might have had Lakota with them, fought at the Little Bighorn in the northern fight, which is a reference to the Ford D fight. This would be the area below Last Stand Hill and the current Little Bighorn Battlefield National Cemetery, as well as near the Little Bighorn River and U.S. Interstate 90.

Dwight added that he had been told Porcupine and Tangle Hair, both Dog Men, were in the northern fight, and that some of these Dog Soldiers are buried in the same cemetery in King Fisher, Oklahoma. Two other Dog Soldiers buried there are Whirlwind Soldier and Three Fingers.[22]

Tim Lame Woman Sr., a noted Cheyenne historian, told me the name Buffalo Bull Hump , another Cheyenne Dog Man he was told was in the Ford D fight. The son of one of the four Cheyenne Old Man Chiefs, Morning Star (sometimes called Dull Knife), Buffalo Bull Hump was said to be a leading Chief among the Cheyenne at the Little Bighorn. Tim did not know where exactly Buffalo Bull Hump fought in the Ford D area.[23]

Northern Cheyenne tribal member Roger Red Hat told us that he had been told that Dog Soldiers rode with the Cheyenne war chief Lame White Man, Roger's great-great grandfather, at the Battle of the Little Bighorn. Lame White Man was an Elkhorn Scraper society war chief who was killed in the fighting. We asked Roger specifically if these Dog Soldiers were Cheyenne, Lakota or the Arapaho contingent of Dog Men. Roger did not know.[24]

~

The last story we present on Dog Soldiers fighting at the Little Bighorn has to do with the famous Cheyenne warrior, Yellow Nose.

The story originates with George Bent, who, after the Sand Creek Massacre, rode with the Dog Soldiers Band in retaliatory raids against civilians and the U.S. Army. George Bent was the grandson of Stone Forehead, who was at one time the Keeper of the Cheyenne Medicine Arrows. Bent himself was an Elkhorn Scraper military society man.[25]

Yellow Nose's exploits during the Battle of the Little Bighorn, in particular his capture of a guidon from one of the Custer Battalion companies, have been documented and discussed at length in many publications and books.[26]

Veteran researcher Chris Dixon told me he was taken to the Real Bird family property on one of his many trips to the Little Bighorn Battlefield. The Real Bird family are

Crow and own land along the Little Bighorn River. On the west side of the Little Bighorn River, the Real Birds have bleachers set up to accommodate spectators for the re-enactments of the Battle every June. Dixon stated to me that the story came to him from a woman who lived in Busby, Montana.

This woman's grandmother had witnessed Yellow Nose get the guidon from somewhere down river of the Real Bird re-enactment site. This would mean that the witness would have been looking across the Little Bighorn River at what could be any one of several areas, including Medicine Tail Coulee, Medicine Tail Ford, or, more intriguingly, Deep Coulee.[27]

There's more oral history from Chris Dixon that pertains to this part of the Battle in the area of Deep Coulee and Medicine Tail Coulee. This story has to do with a soldier being shot off his horse somewhere there.

Dixon and I were at Medicine Tail Coulee Ford the day he told me this story. It is just a stones' throw across the Little Bighorn River from where we stood to parts of where Cheyenne camps were and where a handful of warriors had gathered to protect their people.

To Dixon, what specifically stood out about this story was the incredible feat of the fellow soldier's horse, who had stopped to rescue the wounded and horseless soldier. After the wounded soldier was helped onto the horse, that both soldiers now rode, this incredible horse somehow miraculously climbed a very steep bluff. A feat so heroic it did not go unnoticed by warriors and others in the camps across the Little Bighorn River, and is still kept alive to this day in oral history

This bluff the horse climbed overlooks not only Deep Coulee but Medicine Tail Coulee, Medicine Tail Ford, the Little Bighorn River and the Real Bird property where the reenactments are held.[28]

Chris Dixon believed that the wounded soldier in this story he was told of was Captain Myles W. Keogh, I. Company, U.S. Seventh Cavalry. Dixon said that the soldier who rescued him was Sergeant Edwin Bobo, C. Company, U.S. Seventh Cavalry.[29] The historical record states that Sergeant Bobo was not found among the dead of his C. Company, but rather among the dead troopers of I Company. Bobo was with a group of I Company

Troopers who had surrounded Captain Keogh and subsequently perished with him in the Keogh Sector on the Battlefield.[30]

Based on the information told to Chris Dixon regarding the soldier's movements back towards the Deep Coulee and Medicine Tail Coulee/Ford areas, Dixon told me that he believed that Captain Keogh had led a charge of sorts. Dixon thought that Captain Keogh's objective here was to bring the warriors out and away from the encampment, into a field of fire. This way, the Seventh Cavalry's Troopers could dismount and with their powerful single shot Springfield carbine (rifles), possibly drive warriors away and open a corridor. This would have been done for either a retrograde maneuver, in the direction of the Reno and Benteen Battalions, or to clear the way for the Reno and Benteen's Battalions to link up with Custer Battalion.[31]

This retrograde maneuver might have been undertaken after elements of the Custer Battalion were repulsed in the Ford D area. Captain Keogh, as Dixon theorized, perhaps had C Company in the lead of this maneuver. Once Captain Keogh was hit, C Company was then thrust into action to cover the movement out of and away from Deep Coulee and Medicine Tail/Ford.

Soon after this, C Company was engulfed by warriors at what is today called Finley-Finckle Ridge, where most of the company perished. This ridge bears the names of two other sergeants from C Company, Jeremiah Finley and August Finckle, who both died with the troopers of C Company trying to hold this area.[32]

What is in the historical record and how do these stories match up against it?

Only one account was found in the historical record that told specifically of Dog Soldiers fighting at the Little Bighorn. We told this story from Kill Eagle, a Sihasapa (Blackfeet) Lakota Chief, in chapter 13.

Regarding the Valley Fight, Kill Eagle said that Sitting Bull himself told him this information, which stated Reno attacked on the right near Sitting Bull's tipi and was immediately engaged by the famous dog soldiers. To be clear here, we do not know if he is stating the Cheyenne

Dog Men military society, or is he referring to warriors from the Dog Soldier Band, which was at one time a band among the Cheyenne tribe. It was comprised of not only Cheyenne people, but of Lakota and Arapaho People as well.[33]

As for accounts of known Dog Men fighting at the Little Bighorn in the historical record, there are a few. One of the most noted Cheyenne warriors at the Little Bighorn was Brave Bear, who was a Dog Man society member. It was George Bent who reported that Brave Bear survived the fighting at Summit Springs, fought at the Rosebud, and then took part in the Valley Fight against the Reno Battalion. Brave Bear also fought against the Custer Battalion at or near Calhoun Hill and in the Keogh Sector.[34]

Another Dog Soldier in the historical record who fought at the Little Bighorn was Mad Wolf. This Cheyenne warrior is also known as Mad Hearted Wolf and Wolf That Has No Sense. In the historical record, Mad Wolf is said to be with the first group of Cheyenne warriors to engage the Custer Battalion. Where this happened on the Battlefield remains the subject of much speculation.[35]

At the beginning of this chapter, I wrote of Tall Bull, a noted Cheyenne warrior. In the historical record, Tall Bull said that his horse died underneath of him from seven gunshot wounds sustained fighting at the Little Bighorn. Specifically, Tall Bull's horse died as it carried him in a charge for the area that today is known as Last Stand Hill. The monument for the U.S. Seventh Cavalry dead stands here.[36]

No accounts were found in the historical record that told of Cheyenne Dog Men, namely of Tangle Hair, Porcupine or Buffalo Bull Hump, fighting in the Ford D area. However, Buffalo Bull Hump is listed as being at the Little Bighorn and as one of the Cheyenne Tribes' leading Chiefs there.[37]

We could find no accounts in the historical record of the Cheyenne Dog Men military society being tasked with guarding the Sacred Buffalo Hat of the Cheyenne Tribe at the Little Bighorn. No accounts were found that tell of the fighting in the Medicine Tail Coulee and Medicine Tail Ford areas that also mention Dog Soldiers specifically. No accounts were found that told of Dog

Soldiers picketing themselves at any time or place during the Battle of the Little Bighorn.

Based on information Roger Red Hat told us regarding Dog Soldiers riding with Lame White Man, we then turned our attention to what the historical record tells of Lame White Man's actions at the Little Bighorn. From oral history told to us by Cheyenne historians and Victor Douville and Chris Dixon, we can confidently assert that Lame White Man and those who followed him into the Battle that day did so through Deep Ravine,[38] a noted landmark on the Little Bighorn battlefield and a significant component to that story.

No Arapaho historians can put their Dog Men at this part of the Battlefield or in this part of the Battle.[39] More on the Deep Ravine fight and Lame White Man story will be told in chapter 18.

In Summary: Dog Men and Dog Soldiers

There is only one account in the historical record that tells of Dog Soldiers fighting in the Valley Fight against the Reno Battalion, that of Cheyenne Dog Soldier Brave Bear. As of yet, no oral stories have been found to support this.

We presented two oral stories, one from a Cheyenne tribal member and other from a Sicangu Lakota Tribal Historian, that put Dog Soldiers fighting in and around the Medicine Tail Ford area. Nothing can be found in the historical record that corroborates these stories without a doubt, nor are there other oral histories to present at this time to do so. There are two noted Cheyenne Dog Soldiers, Yellow Nose and Mad Wolf, that may have participated in this part of the Battle, but this cannot be determined without a doubt. We will discuss Yellow Nose and his exploits more in depth in chapter 18.

Nothing can be found in the historical record that tells of the Cheyenne Dog Men military society being entrusted with the all-important task of guarding their Sacred Buffalo Hat at the Little Bighorn. We have one oral history that makes this claim, but nothing to corroborate this.

Lastly, two Cheyenne tribal members put Cheyenne

Dog Men fighting in and around the Ford D area. To which another Cheyenne tribal member corroborated one of the names of these Dog Men fighting in and around the Ford D area. This is the Cheyenne Dog Man Headsman, Tangle Hair. Another Cheyenne tribal member puts Dog Soldiers with the Cheyenne war chief Lame White Man, who fought and died near Deep Ravine. So far, no accounts in the historical record attest to this and no other oral histories have been shared with us that can corroborate this as well.

We have presented 15 accounts, five from Arapaho historians, six from Cheyenne, three from Oglala Lakota historians, and one from a Sicangu Lakota historian, that tell of Dog Soldiers fighting at the Battle of the Little Bighorn. However, we cannot, as of this writing, distinguish if all of these accounts are telling of Cheyenne Dog Men from a military society within both the Arapaho and Cheyenne tribes, or from the Dog Soldier Band, a band among the Cheyenne Tribe, comprised of Cheyenne, Lakota and Arapaho people without a doubt.

The historical record only notes one account of Dog Soldiers fighting at the Little Bighorn. If stories were shared to historians and writers in the late 1800s and early 1900s of Dog Soldiers fighting at the Little Bighorn, it would stand to reason they would have been recorded, as such accounts would have been deemed remarkable.

So, were stories that told of not only Dog Soldiers fighting and possibly picketed, but fighting as a unified force, brushed aside and (or) dismissed simply because it was thought Native warriors were incapable of fighting in an organized group?

It will be up to you, the reader, to decide whether or not these warrior societies were acting in unison and as a cohesive fighting force.

We will examine and present more stories regarding Cheyenne military societies fighting at the Little Bighorn in chapter 18.

A heartfelt thanks to Linwood Tall Bull, Alec Sandcrane, Roger Red Hat, Steve Littlebird, Dwight Bull Coming, Tim Lame Woman Sr., Chico Her Many Horses, Rick Two Dogs, Basil BraveHeart, Victor Douville, Devin Oldman, Bill Goggles, Cletus Yellow Plume, Martin

Blackburn and Henry Goggles Jr., for their assistance with these stories regarding the Dog Soldiers.

Notes

1. Personal communications with Linwood Tall Bull-Northern Cheyenne.

2. Ibid.

3. Personal communications with Randy Tucker and Chico Her Many Horses-Oglala Lakota.

4. Ibid.

5. Ibid.

6. Grinnell 1955: 151; Hyde 1968: 113; Powell 1981: Vol. 2, pp 1429; Moore, J. 1987: 197-203; Afton, Halass and Masich 1997: 364-365.

7. Dorsey 1905: 21; Afton, Halass and Masich 1997; 364-365; Grinnell 2008:165-167.

8. Ibid. Personal communications with Donovan Taylor-Cheyenne.

9. Ibid.

10. Ibid.

11. Trenholm 1970: 79; Mails 1973: 382-384; Fowler 2001: 844-846, in Handbook of North American Indian, Vol 13, Part 2 of 2. Personal communications with Bill Goggles, Devin Oldman, Martin Blackburn, Cletus Yellow Plume and Henry Goggles Jr. See chapter 4.

12. Ibid.

13. Personal communications with Rick Two Dogs-Oglala Lakota and Basil BraveHeart-Oglala Lakota.

14. Personal communications with Victor Douville-Sicangu Lakota Tribal Historian.

15. Personal communications with Rick Two Dogs-Oglala Lakota, Basil BraveHeart-Oglala Lakota and Chico Her Many Horses-Oglala Lakota.

16. Personal communications with Victor Douville-Sicangu Lakota Tribal Historian.

17. Personal communications with Bill Goggles-Arapaho, Devin Oldman-Arapaho, Martin Blackburn-Arapaho, Cletus Yellow Plume-Arapaho and Henry Goggles Jr.-Arapaho.

18. Donovan Taylor personal communications with Alec Sandcrane-Northern Cheyenne and with Lance Dorrel.

19. Donovan Taylor personal communications with Steve Littlebird - Northern Cheyenne and Lance Dorrel.

20. See Powell 1981: Vol 2, Regarding Tangle Hair, 793-795, 810, 1420; Personal communications with Linwood Tall Bull-Northern Cheyenne.

21. Personal communications with Vine Brokenrope-Oglala Lakota/Yakama.

22. Personal communications with Dwight Bull Coming-Cheyenne and Dee Cordry - independent researcher.

23. Personal communications with Tim Lame Woman Sr.-Cheyenne. Regarding Buffalo Bull Hump, see Powell, P. 1981: Vol 2, 1004.

24. Donovan Taylor and Lance Dorrel personal communications with Roger Red Hat-Northern Cheyenne.

25. See Hyde 1968: *Life of George Bent*: 201; Bent said he belonged to the Crooked Lances, which are the Elkhorn Scrapers as well. Also see Afton, Halass and

Masich 1997: 98-101.

26. For Yellow Nose see Bent to Hyde, 10 April 1905. See Powell 1981: Vol 2, 1023; Hardorff 1998: 53-54, 62-63. Hardorff 2005: 85.

27. Personal communications with Chris Dixon.

28. Ibid.

29. Ibid.

30. Ibid. For Keogh and Bobo see Michno 1997: 182-183; See Burst, Pohanka and Barnard 2005: 102-110; Donovan 2008: 268-272.

31. Ibid.

32. Ibid. For the Finley-Finckle Ridge fight, See Burst, Pohanka and Barnard 2005: 90-94; Donovan 2008: 268-273; Donahue 2009: 162-167, 270-280.

33. For the Kill Eagle account see Milligan 1976: 74.

34. For Brave Bear see Bent to Hyde, 11 August 1905. Also see Afton, Halass and Masich 1997; 160, 174, 244, 320; Hardorff 2005: 81-86.

35. For the Mad Wolf account see Grinnell 1955: 350-351; Hardorff 1998: 50-53.

36. Personal communications with Linwood Tall Bull-Cheyenne. For Tall Bull's account, see Hardorff 1998: 46-47.

37. Powell, P. 1981: Vol 2, 1004.

38. Personal communications with Keith Spotted Wolf-Northern Cheyenne, Linwood Tall Bull - Northern Cheyenne, Dennis Limberhand-Northern Cheyenne, Wallace Bearchum-Northern Cheyenne, Rufus Spear-Northern Cheyenne, Gilbert Whitedirt-Northern Cheyenne, Eddie Whitedirt-Northern Cheyenne, Roger Red Hat-Northern Cheyenne, Steve Littlebird -

Northern Cheyenne, Cleve Littlebear-Northern Cheyenne, Dwight Bull Coming-Northern Cheyenne, Chester Whiteman-Cheyenne, Roy Dean Bull Coming-Cheyenne, Vernon Sooktis - Cheyenne, Scott Doser-Cheyenne, Leroy Whiteman-Northern Cheyenne, Victor Douville - Sicangu Lakota Tribal Historian and Chris Dixon.

39. Personal communications with Bill Goggles-Arapaho, Devin Oldman-Arapaho, Martin Blackburn-Arapaho, Henry Goggles Jr.-Arapaho, Cletus Yellow Plume-Arapaho and Elise Sage-Arapaho.

16
Ford D

Looking toward the area known as Ford D.

The information that led to the trail we followed for this chapter came from the following people: Tim Lame Woman Sr. - Cheyenne, Dennis Limberhand -Cheyenne, Florence Whiteman - Cheyenne, Linwood Tall Bull - Cheyenne, Leroy Whiteman - Cheyenne, Rufus Spear - Cheyenne, Gilbert Whitedirt - Cheyenne, Scott Doser, Alberta American Horse - Cheyenne, Steve Littlebird - Cheyenne, Dwight Bull Coming - Cheyenne, Vine Brokenrope - Oglala Lakota/Yakama, Victor Douville - Sicangu Lakota Tribal Historian, Wayne Goodwill - Dakota/Lakota, Sam High Crane - Sicangu Lakota, Doug War Eagle - Minnikojou Lakota, Frenchy Dillon- Crow, Faron Iron -Crow and independent researchers Mike Donahue, Chris Dixon, Steve Andrews, James "Putt" Thompson and Jason Pitsch.

One comes to the Little Bighorn Battlefield National Monument via U.S. Highway 212, which we have described in chapter 14 as the old buffalo trail, or by U.S. Interstate 90. These are good reference points for the history of Ford D and the area it encompasses.

Understanding the lay of the land is vital to the study of the history of the Battle.

The designation of this area as "Ford D" stems from one of the earliest maps produced from eyewitness Battle participants such as the unknown warrior who gave an account to Lieutenant William Philo Clark in 1877. Assigned as an aide to General Crook after the Battle of the Little Bighorn, Clark was then at Fort Robinson and interviewed surrendered warriors said to have fought at the Little Bighorn.

Clark noted soldier movements on his map with blue dots; warrior movements in red. At a ford, which is simply a place to cross a river, he was shown where soldiers were prevented from crossing the Little Bighorn River. On his map, he had already used the letters A, B and C, so the ford north of the Cheyenne camps (the most northward of the Native Peoples' coalition encampments) was assigned the letter D.

Soldiers from the Custer Battalion were shown on the map to have gotten within close proximity to this ford, which was dangerously near an area where many non-combatants had congregated after fleeing the Native Peoples coalition encampment.[1]

Ford D sits below the Little Bighorn Battlefield National Monument Cemetery and runs parallel with U.S. Interstate 90. The Little Bighorn River meanders through this area, flowing in a northwesterly direction. The river's course has changed since 1876, as a loop in the river has since dried up. Farther to the northwest of Clark's Ford, another ford of the Little Bighorn River was said to exist.

These fords were noted by Dr. Richard Fox, who labeled them Ford D 1 and Ford D 2 and were included in his book, *Archaeology, History and Custer's Last Battle*. Fox gathered information based on Cheyenne historian John Stands In Timber's history in order to bring awareness of these two fords and possible fighting in the Ford D area to then Little Bighorn Battlefield National Monument Historian Don Rickey, in 1956. Fox noted the ford known as Ford D 1 to be near where U.S. Interstate 90 crosses the Little Bighorn River. Ford D 2 exists in the historical record due to information and the map supplied by Lieutenant William Philo Clark.[2]

The fords are key points to remember moving forward with this part of the Battle.

Possibly a thousand or more non-combatants had congregated on the west side of the Little Bighorn close to the two fords after fleeing the Reno Battalion's attack in the Valley Fight. As other non-combatants moved down river and followed it to the northwest, they found themselves in the midst of the Cheyenne horse herd. We are not sure how far to the west / northwest some of these people went.

Today, the Little Bighorn River still runs towards Crow Agency, past where U.S. Highway 212 and U.S. Interstate 90 intersect. Exiting off U.S. Interstate 90 onto Highway 212, if you go in a northeasterly direction you will come to the original Little Bighorn Battlefield National Monument entrance road. Taking this old park entrance road will run you back to the dried up riverbed loop.

One of the original souvenir stores that sat near the Little Bighorn River and Burlington Railroad track. It is believed this store sat near the ford Philo Clark labeled "D" on his 1877 map. -- *Photo courtesy of James "Putt" Thompson*

Once back on Highway 212, to your left, which is north, sits Crow Agency, the tribal seat of the Crow

People. Journey a little further up U.S. Highway 212 and you run into the Custer Battlefield Trading Post. Just across from this famous tourist destination, which I mention here as a reference for stories presented in this chapter, is the current Little Bighorn Battlefield National Monument entrance.

~

In chapter 14, oral history shared with us said a party of Cheyenne hunters engaged the Custer Battalion, or parts of it, in the area of the Luce / Blummer / Nye / Cartwright Ridge complex. This fight, it was said, brought other Cheyenne and some Lakota warriors. Some Cheyenne hunters who had left their horses to fight on foot were then picked up by the new arrivals. It was told that some of the Cheyenne hunters, and possibly the others who came later, then followed the old buffalo trail, which is U.S. Highway 212 in a northeasterly direction, which puts these warriors paralleling the modern National Park Service road of the Little Bighorn Battlefield, but well east of it. This road runs along what is today called Custer Ridge or Battle Ridge.

The backside of the ridge dips, and the hunters and warriors passed where today stands the Last Stand Hill Monument. This is the show piece to the Battlefield, the very hill of Custer's Last Stand. At the top of the hill sits the monument, which commemorates the U.S. Seventh Cavalry dead. Just to the right of it, as one looks in the direction of north, sits the Indian Memorial, which names some of the warriors and tribes who fought here. The hunters and warriors raced past this area, across what is called the Custer Ridge Extension, as the old buffalo trail had turned to the west. It now took them towards the Little Bighorn River.

A short distance farther, some of the hunters and warriors crossed the current National Park Service entrance road to the Battlefield. Others split off and went towards the northwest, past the Custer Battlefield Trading Post, to what is now Crow Agency. Some of the other warriors and hunters may have continued moving through a ravine at one time called Crazy Horse Ravine, and toward the Little Bighorn River. Where these hunters and warriors went or did after this, has been lost to history at this point. Perhaps after publication, someone or some families will come forth and add names and details to who these men were and what they did.

For now, we at least know some companies of the U.S. Seventh Cavalry, thought to be E and F Companies, as well as Seventh Cavalry's headquarters unit, all attached to the Custer Battalion, eventually gave pursuit.

Oral history long kept by Cheyenne People confirms this. Cheyenne historian John Stands In Timber was the first historian to make this known and part of his focus, all of which he shared with the National Park Service by the 1950s. Prior to this, there were three accounts, from 1886, 1909, and 1913, and a map from the famous Cheyenne war chief and veteran of the Little Bighorn, Two Moons.

The first two accounts came from him while he was at the Battlefield. Two Moons said in 1909, "Custer marched up from behind the ridge on which his monument now stands, and deployed his soldiers along the entire line of the ridge. They rode over beyond where the monument stands [and] down into the valley until we could not see them." Before this, in 1886, he stated, "He [Custer] turned down the ridge at Custer Hill where the Monument is and followed the deep ravine thence to the River, supposing that he could make a crossing there."[3]

Returning to the soldiers and their journey to the Ford D environs: Some traversed the terrain through Crazy Horse Ravine, while others split off earlier and rode across Last Stand Hill, where the current monument stands. Again, both Stands In Timber and Two Moons supported this. Once near the Little Bighorn River, the two companies split up. One company possibly probed the area near Ford D 1, which again is the ford put forth by John Stands in Timber. The other company moved south, along the flats, which are above and to the east of the Little Bighorn River. They moved towards Ford D 2; the ford put forth on Lieutenant Clark's map.[4]

Had these hunters and warriors made a mistake and inadvertently brought the U.S. Army to where the non-combatants were said to congregate? Or, had General Custer and his command seen the mass exodus of the camps from within the encampment on the Little

Bighorn at an earlier time and deduced a plan to come to this area all along? Only history knows this for sure.

We now pick back up with oral history pertaining to the Ford D fight. Our intention here is to add the history shared with us. Consider to what is told and use this information in conjunction with what is in the historical record. Some pieces we are sharing may give clarity to events that were said to have happened in this area. Names of warriors fighting in this area shared with us will perhaps help future researchers and their efforts to understand parts of this Battle as well.

~

The first story we present comes from veteran researcher Chris Dixon. It was in 2015, in the parking lot of the Custer Battlefield Trading Post, that Chris Dixon told me this story. Dixon and I faced west, towards Crow Agency. Dixon shared a story with me about soldiers from the Seventh Cavalry, presumably those from the Custer Battalion. These soldiers had been in the Ford D area and were now moving through what would become the parking lot where we stood.

Tim Lame Woman Sr. - - Cheyenne.

Chris Dixon said he had been told this story by Tim Lame Woman Sr., a Cheyenne tribal member, historian, and member of the Elkhorn Scraper military society[5], at the Little Bighorn Battlefield some years ago. Serle Chapman, author of the book, *Promise,* who we featured in chapters 10 and 11, was along as well.

During this trip to the Battlefield, Tim Lame Woman Sr. told Dixon that soldiers tried to cross the Little Bighorn River to get to the non-combatants. Chris Dixon told me that he understood from Tim that this attempted crossing by the soldiers of the Little Bighorn River was to the northwest of the current railroad bridge, which sits just to the west of, and runs parallel to, U.S. Interstate 90. This bridge sits near a ford where U.S. Interstate 90 crosses the Little Bighorn River, at what is called Willy Bend's Crossing. Willy Bend was a Crow tribal member who owned the land at one time where this crossing and ford sit. This crossing would be Ford D 1 on the Dr. Fox map, first put forth by John Stands In Timber.[6]

Tim Lame Woman Sr., told Dixon that when the soldiers were stopped from getting the non-combatants, they had to put a, "soldier chief," back on his horse. The "soldier chief," had been hit by gunfire from warriors concealed in the brush along the river. The soldiers tied the "soldier chief's" hands around the pommel of his saddle. The soldiers pulled the "soldier chief's" horse as they retreated through the area where the parking lot of what is now the Custer Battlefield Trading Post sits. It was here the soldiers were attacked again, and the "soldier chief" was shot again.[7]

Tim also told Chris Dixon that a Cheyenne warrior by the name of Little Horse was responsible for organizing the resistance efforts in and around the area where the two fords labeled Ford D are located. Tim told Dixon that Little Horse was a Cheyenne Contrary.[8]

Chief Little Horse, Cheyenne. Oral history from Cheyenne historian Tim Lame Woman Sr. says Little Horse led resistance in the area of Ford D.

Thanks to Chris Dixon and Donovan Taylor, I was fortunate enough to interview Tim Lame Woman Sr., twice. With regard to the fighting in the Ford D area, Tim said, "Some fighting took place below the cemetery. The soldiers tried to cross the river down from the old railroad bridge. Some soldiers might have gone over close to some place over there, by U.S. Interstate 90 and 212. The Cheyennes were the ones to stop Custer's men." He added, "some of the soldiers pulled another one, 'a soldier chief,' along and they went through Putt's (Thompson) place."[9]

Regarding Little Horse, Tim could only say that previous to the Battle of the Little Bighorn, Little Horse had been in several Cheyenne camps when they had been attacked by the U.S. Army. He was not sure which fights Little Horse participated in. What he did say was that Little Horse had dreamed or had some premonition of this Battle. He went on to say that this warrior was full of resolve and determined that the next time the Cheyenne were attacked, he would do all he could in his power to protect the people.

I asked Tim if Little Horse was the same Cheyenne warrior who not only fought at the Fetterman Fight, also called, The Hundred-Soldiers-Killed-Fight or One-Hundred-White-Men-Killed, in 1866? Plus, had been chosen to wear the Sacred Buffalo Hat of the Cheyenne Tribe there?

Tim did not know. Tim was also not sure if this Little Horse is the warrior listed as a Kit Fox war chief at the Battle of the Little Bighorn, as well.[10]

Before I recap the Tim Lame Woman Sr. information, I must add the names, provided by Tim and Chris Dixon, of three more Cheyenne warriors who fought in the area of where the two fords are located, plus something Tim got from the family of the Cheyenne war chief, Two Moons.

Tim Lame Woman Sr., told me that Bobtail Horse, a noted Cheyenne warrior, fought at some point in the Battle in the area of the two fords labeled Ford D. Tim did not know where Bobtail Horse fought anywhere else prior. Tim said Bobtail Horse was a member of the Cheyenne Elkhorn Scraper military society and that he had his horse shot out from underneath him in this fighting. Tim then identified Buffalo Bull Hump as a warrior who fought in the area of the fords We mentioned this warrior in the previous chapter on Dog Soldiers. Buffalo Bull Hump was the son of one of the four Cheyenne Old Man Chiefs, Morning Star, sometimes called Dull Knife. Tim did not know where exactly Buffalo Bull Hump fought in the area of the two fords, but said he was a member of the Cheyenne Dog Men military society.[11]

Lastly, Tim shared a story he had been told by Austin Two Moons and Matthew Two Moons, both Cheyenne tribal members. This oral history the family had kept regarding Two Moons fighting at the Little Bighorn had been told by the famous warrior himself. Two Moons said he witnessed some of the soldiers losing their horses below the current Little Bighorn Battlefield National Monument Cemetery and near the Little Bighorn River. I asked Tim if he had ever accompanied the Two Moons family to or across the Battlefield, to which he told he had not.[12]

Tim Lame Woman Sr., shared four pieces of information to consider when studying the Ford D fight with Chris Dixon and then with me.

One, the name of Little Horse. Tim stated this Cheyenne warrior led the resistance in the Ford D fighting.

Two, Tim said the Cheyenne warriors Bobtail Horse and Buffalo Bull Hump both fought in the Ford D fight. Again, like Little Horse, he did not know exactly where these warriors fought.

Third, Tim said that a "soldier chief," was wounded in the Ford D fighting. He did not know where specifically or who this, "soldier chief," was, but did tell this, "soldier chief," was put back on his horse and taken through the area which is now the parking lot of the Custer Battlefield Trading Post.

Interestingly, the Custer Battlefield Trading Post sits just across Highway 212, but some distance from the fords that the two companies are thought to have attempted to cross the Little Bighorn River to get to the non-combatants. Tim put one such attempt at crossing the Little Bighorn River northwest of the current railroad bridge and within the area of the ford at what is Willy Bend's Crossing. Tim did say that he had heard that some soldiers may have gone further down river, to the northwest and close to the area where U.S. Interstate 90 and U.S. Highway 212 intersect. An exit for the Little Bighorn Battlefield sits in this area, as well as an abandoned and dilapidated hotel. The Little Bighorn River still flows behind this area today.[13]

Could the soldiers retreated through the area that today is the Custer Battlefield Trading Post parking lot, according to Tim, be because they had already traversed this terrain on their way to attempt a crossing of the Little Bighorn River? If so, it would make sound tactical sense that they would retreat through an area already reconnoitered and found suitable to maneuver.

Tim's information from the Two Moons family says that some soldiers, presumably some of those from the Custer Battalion, lost their horses somewhere near the Little Bighorn River during the Ford D fight. Were these soldiers trying to cross the river to get the non-combatants, or were they in some type of retreat, having been repulsed? Could they have even been dismounted and fighting on foot, in an effort to hold back warriors from advancing on their positions?[14]

Tim Lame Woman Sr., made his journey through the Milky Way, to the camp on the other side, on October 25, 2018.

~

More information came to Donovan Taylor and me from Cheyenne people that told of fighting in the area of the fords. These stories seemingly corroborated what Tim Lame Woman Sr. had said.

Gilbert Whitedirt, historian and Cheyenne tribal member, along with Scott Doser, who had been adopted by the Whitedirt family, both Elkhorn Scraper military society men as well, told us in chapter 8 that the Cheyenne Medicine Arrows and Buffalo Hat were at the Little Bighorn. In that same chapter we wrote of Florence Whiteman telling Donovan Taylor that the Medicine Arrows and Buffalo Hat were at the Little Bighorn. Vernon Sooktis and Chester Whiteman, two Cheyenne tribal members, told me the Medicine Arrows were at the Little Bighorn as well. Gilbert Whitedirt and Scott Doser both added that the Medicine Arrows were used against soldiers in an impromptu blinding ceremony of some sort, presumably those of the Custer Battalion. The Medicine Arrows had been, or were in the process of being, moved down the Little Bighorn River. Both Gilbert and Scott stated the soldiers got attacked in the

Ford D area. Neither Gilbert, nor Scott, knew exactly where this happened.[15]

One last thing to add here from Scott Doser, who told me that in the early 1980's, he had been told by Austin Two Moons, that Two Moons, the Cheyenne war chief, had said that some of the soldiers had lost their horses in the Ford D area. This is the Two Moons family's oral history. Scott told me that he was, in fact, at and on the Battlefield with Cheyenne Tribal members when this was discussed and the area of the fords was pointed out to him.[16]

To recap, both Gilbert Whitedirt and Scott Doser put the Cheyenne Medicine Arrows and Buffalo Hat at the Little Bighorn during the Battle. Gilbert and Scott said the Medicine Arrows were used against the soldiers. Scott Doser confirmed the Two Moons' story of soldiers losing horses in the Ford D area. Not only that, he also confirmed what Tim Lame Woman Sr., told, in that the story was kept by the Two Moons family. This history was told to them by the noted Cheyenne war chief and veteran of the Battle of the Little Bighorn, Two Moons.[17]

~

So far regarding the Ford D fighting, we have been told that something happened to a "soldier chief," and he had to be put back on his horse and pulled along. Then, this "soldier chief," is hit again in the area where today the Custer Battlefield Trading Post parking lot is located. We have been told that some of the soldiers lost their horses in the Ford D fighting, and we were told that a Cheyenne warrior by the name of Little Horse organized the resistance efforts somewhere in the area of the fords. Lastly, the sacred Medicine Arrows of the Cheyenne, we were told, were being moved down the Little Bighorn River in direction of the fords.

There is more oral history regarding the Ford D fight. Three Cheyenne historians shared information regarding what they had been told and found in their own research efforts.

In 2017, I accompanied Linwood Tall Bull to the Little Bighorn Battlefield. As we wrote in the previous chapter, Linwood is a Cheyenne elder and belongs to the

Cheyenne Dog Men military society. He is a noted educator and historian, as well. Linwood and I were below the National Park Service administration buildings and living quarters for park staff when I asked what he had been told of the fighting said to have taken place below this area. He simply pointed out to the area that sits between U.S. Interstate 90 and Highway 212. It was in this area, Linwood said, that some fighting had gone on. He could add no names of warriors who fought in this area, nor could he tell what exactly happened here.[18]

Linwood shared more information with me regarding the Cheyenne camps on the Little Bighorn River, that June 25th, 1876. He stated the Cheyenne camps were further down river, to the north. He put the camps close to the mouth of Deep Ravine and to the west, near U.S. Interstate 90. As we wrote in the previous chapter, Linwood had said that the Cheyenne Dog Men military society was responsible for guarding the Sacred Buffalo Hat at the Little Bighorn. He also said that the Cheyenne military societies were camped within the Cheyenne camps on the Little Bighorn.[19]

Cheyenne tribal member Rufus Spear was gracious enough to share information with me concerning Cheyenne history at the Little Bighorn in chapter 9. Rufus had told me that the Cheyenne Medicine Arrows were at the Little Bighorn, on June 25th, 1876.[20]

Rufus informed me of protocols that the Cheyenne had to adhere to regarding, "specific rules of conduct surrounding both the Sacred Arrows and the Sacred Hat Covenants, which is one of the reasons that they Cheyenne camped so far away from the Sioux encampments. The other reason was an environmental issue, the Cheyenne being downstream of the Sioux encampments." Rufus has always maintained that Cheyenne oral history and interviews with Cheyenne veterans of the Battle state the Cheyenne were camped a couple of miles north of the Sioux encampments. Rufus put the Cheyenne camps just south and west of the Battlefield landmark Deep Ravine. These camps were all on the west side of the Little Bighorn River.[21]

In 2018, Dennis Limberhand, a Cheyenne tribal member, accompanied me to the Battlefield. In the same area where Linwood Tall Bull and I had been a year earlier, Dennis showed me two interesting pieces of the Ford D fighting.

First, Dennis pointed to the old railroad bridge that sits next to and just west of U.S. Interstate 90 in the area of Willy Bend's Crossing. Remember the crossing would have been where U.S. Interstate 90 crosses the Little Bighorn River today. Dennis had been told that the Cheyenne prevented soldiers from crossing the Little Bighorn River in this area. He added some soldiers had gone even further to the northwest. Why, he didn't know, but surmised that possibly the soldiers were looking for another crossing. Or, perhaps they were chasing non-combatants. Dennis then said he had been told of fighting in the area below the Custer Battlefield Trading Post, which is in Crow Agency.[22]

When asked about the Medicine Arrows of the Cheyenne being at the Little Bighorn, Dennis stated he didn't know. Dennis did add that the Cheyenne camps were further down the river and were closer to the area of where Ford D 2 is located, than is put forth in the historical record. Dennis told me that there were Lakota people and their warriors fighting in area of the fords as well. Lastly, Dennis mentioned the name of Bobtail Horse as a Cheyenne warrior who fought in the Ford D area.[23]

A quick recap of the information shared with me by Cheyenne historians so far:

First, Dennis Limberhand puts the Cheyenne camps further north, down river and close to the area of where Ford D 2 located. Second, soldiers tried to cross the Little Bighorn River and get to the non-combatants in the area of Willy Bend's Crossing. Some soldiers may have gone even further down river to the northwest, looking for a crossing as well. Both scenarios are similar to what Tim Lame Woman Sr. had said. Dennis Limberhand also told of fighting across U.S. Highway 212 and near the Custer Battlefield Trading Post. Again, just like Tim Lame Woman Sr., said.[24]

Linwood Tall Bull and Rufus Spear both said that the Cheyenne camps locations are much closer to the area of where Ford D 2 is located, than is noted in the historical record. Same as Dennis Limberhand. Rufus told me the Cheyenne Medicine Arrows were indeed at the Little

Bighorn in June of 1876.[25] This corroborates stories regarding the Medicine Arrows told to us from Gilbert Whitedirt and Scott Doser, in which Gilbert and Scott both said they were used in an impromptu blinding ceremony of some sort against soldiers.[26] Florence Whiteman, Vernon Sooktis and Chester Whiteman, all said the Medicine Arrows of the Cheyenne were at the Little Bighorn, during the Battle in 1876.[27]

~

As told in chapter 15, Donovan Taylor interviewed Steve Littlebird, a Cheyenne tribal member. Steve is an Elkhorn Scraper military society man. When discussing the Battle of the Little Bighorn with Donovan, Steve added some interesting names to the growing list of Cheyenne warriors we are told fought in the area of the fords. Steve said that Bobtail Horse was in the fighting at the fords.[28] This now makes three Cheyenne historians putting this Cheyenne warrior in this area of the Battle. Steve also added the names of two Cheyenne warriors, Tangle Hair and Broken Rope.[29]

In the previous chapter, I wrote of my interview with Dwight Bull Coming, a Cheyenne tribal member. Dwight shared with me in April of 2021 that Cheyenne Dog Men, who might have had Lakota with them, were indeed in the northern fight, which is a reference to the fighting in the area of the two Ford D's . Dwight and I viewed what he called the northern fight area, from the Custer Battlefield Trading Post parking lot, in April of 2021. The area he pointed to and referenced was to the south and is well within the area of the two fords. Dwight then added that he had been told Porcupine and Tangle Hair, both Dog Men, were in the northern fight.[30]

Alberta American Horse - - Cheyenne

Donovan Taylor interviewed Alberta American Horse, a Cheyenne tribal member and elder, in April and May of 2019. We briefly mentioned Alberta in chapter 8, regarding her relative, American Horse. A Cheyenne war chief, American Horse fought in the Battle of the Little Bighorn.

Alberta American Horse told Donovan that as American Horse returned to the Cheyenne camps on the Little Bighorn, he came upon the Battle in progress. Alberta stated American Horse had come from the direction of Hardin, Montana, which would be northwest of the Little Bighorn Battlefield. The family story told that he rode through the area of where the current Crow Agency now stands. It was somewhere in this area, Alberta told Donovan, that the oral history of her family said American Horse fought soldiers. Alberta had never been told any names of other warriors who might have been riding with American Horse.[31]

Could American Horse, possibly accompanied, have fought soldiers from the Custer Battalion, who we have been told, attempted a crossing of the Little Bighorn River in the area of where the two Ford D's are? Perhaps this is the same fighting which was related by Tim Lame Woman Sr. and Dennis Limberhand. These soldiers were said to have been attacked somewhere in Crow Agency and in the area where the Custer Battlefield Trading Post sits. American Horse would have swung to the east in order to hit the Custer Battalion as the soldiers retreated out of the area of the Ford D's and towards the area of where the Custer Battlefield Trading Post sits today.

Alberta American Horse made her journey through the Milky Way and to the camp on the other side, on July 14, 2021.

~

In December of 2019, I interviewed Leroy Whiteman, a Cheyenne tribal member, elder and member of the Kit Fox military society who had helped me since 2016. Leroy told me the same story Alberta American Horse had shared with Donovan and added some more information to it.

Leroy told me that he had been told that American

Horse and some warriors fought soldiers near the ground where the Custer Battlefield Trading Post now sits. Leroy said American Horse and the warriors with him saw the fighting in the northern fords area and swung to the east. Leroy said these warriors were on the north side of U.S. Highway 212 when they engaged what we suspect were soldiers from E and / or F Companies of the Custer Battalion. He said the fighting was a running skirmish of sorts that spilled to the east, over Highway 212, and went south for one mile or so. Leroy had been told that some of the soldiers fled and scattered in several directions, only to be pursued and killed. He had been told on several occasions by Cheyenne tribal members of one soldier tombstone set approximately 200 yards northwest of the Little Bighorn Battlefield National Monument which rests on Last Stand Hill. He had been also told by Cheyenne People that some tombstones set southeast of where James "Putt" Thompson's place, now the Custer Battlefield Trading Post, sits.[32]

When I asked what he knew of where the Cheyenne camps were on the Little Bighorn and if the Medicine Arrows were there, Leroy answered that he was not sure. He did state that he was told there was a warrior-only camp of sorts somewhere down river (north) from the Cheyenne camps. Leroy said he didn't know if the camp was comprised of only Cheyenne, or were others there as well.[33]

Leroy wanted me to know who the elders were who shared this history with him: Willie Whitehorse, Red Bird, and Black Bear. Leroy said Willie Whitehorse's grandfather fought at the Little Bighorn, as did Black Bear's father, who was Leroy's grandfather. Red Bird was Leroy's great-grandfather.[34]

A short time after our last phone call, which was in December of 2019, Leroy made his journey across the Milky Way to the camp on the other side, on February 23rd of 2020.

~

Doug War Eagle, Minnikojou Lakota Tribal member and historian, who we have presented information from in chapters 2, 8, 9 and 12, told me an interesting story pertaining to soldiers retreating from the area where the two Ford D's are located..

Doug said a Cheyenne hunting party that had come from the northwest then swung to the east and stopped the soldiers from going back the way they came from. On a map Doug annotated and gave to me, the soldiers had tried going back in a northerly and then easterly direction. This would put the soldiers presumably trying to move back in the direction of the trail that had brought them to the area of the fords. Doug said the Cheyenne hunting party had some casualties. He added that some Minnikojou Lakota and Sans Arc Lakota warriors hit these retreating soldiers as well. They too had casualties and were led by a war chief by the name of Eagle Hat. Doug said Eagle Hat was killed at the Battle of The Little Bighorn.

These Lakota warriors may in fact have come from a warrior-only camp somewhere north of the Cheyenne camps on the Little Bighorn. This camp is annotated by Doug on the map he gave me as well. Could this warrior-only camp be the same one that Leroy Whiteman mentioned?[35]

One now has to wonder if this Cheyenne hunting party that had initially come from the direction of the northwest, and who then hit the Custer Battalion from out of the east, is possibly the very same party told to us by Alberta American Horse, Leroy Whiteman and Doug War Eagle. Alberta and Leroy both said that this Cheyenne party was led by the Cheyenne war chief American Horse.[36]

~

In May of 2019, Donovan interviewed Frenchy Dillon. Frenchy, who is a Crow tribal member, also has bloodlines to Oglala Lakota People. This is only half of his family lineage. Frenchy is not only a descendant of Mitch Bouyer, the scout who rode with the Custer Battalion, he is also the great-grandson of Thomas Leforge, as well. Leforge was a civilian scout and frontiersman who rode with General Alfred Terry and General Gibbon, the U.S. Army unit that was moving towards the Little Bighorn River from the west. General

Terry and Gibbon were to reunite with General Custer and the Seventh Cavalry somewhere near the mouth of the Little Bighorn River by the 26th of June. Terry and Gibbon's unit would be the blocking force for General Custer and the Seventh Cavalry.

Frenchy told Donovan that Thomas Leforge had taken in Mitch Bouyer's wife, Magpie Outside, a Crow woman, after Bouyer was killed at the Battle of the Little Bighorn. Leforge and Bouyer were good friends. Frenchy's grandfather was John Dillon, who married Thomas Leforge and Magpie Outside's daughter, Rose Leforge. They had a son by the name of Charles Dillon, born in 1916, who is Frenchy's father.[37]

Frenchy shared with Donovan what Thomas Leforge had told his grandson regarding the Battle. Leforge said he was tired of riding in the wagon, as he had injured his collar bone earlier in the campaign. He either had a horse or got one and subsequently moved ahead of the Gibbon and Terry unit. Eventually, Leforge came to the outskirts of what is the current Crow Agency. It was here that he first heard and then found himself approaching the Battle as it played out. Leforge told that as he moved west of the Little Bighorn River, he made for the bluffs that sit some distance further to the west. It was from somewhere either on or below these bluffs, that Leforge told his grandson, that he witnessed fighting near the Little Bighorn River. Leforge said he had field glasses and with these he said he witnessed soldiers getting close to the river.[38]

In late April of 2021, I and veteran Little Bighorn Battle researcher Steve Andrews had the fortunate pleasure to spend an afternoon with Frenchy Dillon. It was a cold, dark and blustery day when I, Steve and Frenchy, braved the elements and wandered parts of area where the two Ford D's are located. The three of us were eager to make sense of Frenchy's family story. Not only that, but we hoped that by being in the Ford D's area, we might make sense of what Leforge had seen and then told of, from his vantage point.

Our first stop was the Custer Battlefield Trading Post, which offers a commanding view of Ford D and the surrounding area. It also happens to be the area Tim Lame Woman Sr., said some of the Custer Battalion retreated through, all the while pulling a "soldier chief," atop his horse. From the parking lot you look west, right into Crow Agency. We then crossed U.S. Highway 212 and moved for the old Little Bighorn Battlefield entrance road. From here, we walked south as Frenchy filled in more of the story Leforge had told his grandfather.

Pointing towards the area where a tombstone was said to be placed for Mark Kellog, the sole reporter who accompanied, and died with, the Seventh Cavalry, Frenchy said his father showed him this area, just a few yards to the northeast of the dried up riverbed loop, way back in the early 1960's. From here, you can see the old railroad bridge near the Willy Bend's Crossing, which is again, Ford D 1. Frenchy said Leforge told, "The soldiers were close to a bend in the river. Some went closer to the river, but they stopped. Then, they tried to get away." That was all he was ever told.

Next, we looked at the bluffs to the west, across the Little Bighorn River. It was here Leforge told his family he was positioned when he witnessed this episode in the Battle. You quickly realize that is a considerable distance from the are of where the two Ford D's are located.. Unless one is at the exact spot Leforge was at when he witnessed the fighting, it's really hard to tell what he could have seen. Having field glasses surely would have helped. Perhaps Leforge had told more and it had been forgotten? Frenchy didn't know.

At that moment we felt like we were so close, but still left with many questions. Sometimes this happens when chasing history at the Little Bighorn. It's at times like you are back there in June of 1876 and in the very moment. You are sure you are just about to uncover something, or add to some part of the Battle, long forgotten. Then, in a blink of an eye, that window in time just closes on you.

Frenchy did add that, at one time, in the area next to where the dried-up riverbed loop sits, a Crow rancher by the name of John Hill had lived. I have since wondered many times, what tales John Hill might have been told by the locals or discovered himself?[39]

~

The last collection of oral stories we want to share tell the brave deeds of some of the non-combatants at the Little Bighorn. The elders who shared these stories only knew that they happened on the west side of the Little Bighorn River and to the north, down the river from the Native Peoples Coalition encampment.

Sicangu Lakota tribal historian Victor Douville shared with me the story of his grandmother, Moves Camp Woman, a Minnikojou Lakota. She was just a young child at the time of the Battle.

She told Victor that when the Valley Fight with the Reno Battalion began, she just remembered how it seemed all the women, children and elderly took off down the river. She then said that when these people got some distance from the camps, a great many began to make makeshift barricades of some sorts. Moves Camp Woman said that some of the people were grabbing and pulling up tall grass, while others were piling up brush. She went on to say that they placed these crude barriers somewhere along the river. The last part she added was that she had been told by her family later in her life, that the intent was to light these on fire, if needed, to thwart the soldiers from crossing the Little Bighorn River.

Victor, who has been to the Little Bighorn Battlefield on numerous trips to study this story and many, many others shared with him in his capacity as tribal historian, believes at this time, his grandmother's story took place somewhere west of the mouth of Deep Ravine. He also feels this action was directly related to the Custer Battalion getting close to the non-combatants in the area of where Ford D 2 is located.[40]

Victor shared a remarkable story that had to do with a Sicangu Lakota woman who, at the time of the Battle, was known as Center Woman. Her actions at the Little Bighorn solidified her place in her tribe's history. Victor stated she was the wife of renowned Sicangu Lakota war chief and Little Bighorn veteran Iron Shell. Center Woman was thought to be a medicine woman. Victor had been told that Center Woman rescued and then cared for many wounded warriors and people during and after the Battle. Because of her selfless acts of heroism and her curing capabilities, she was then bestowed the name She Cherishes Her Nation.[41]

Sam High Crane, a Sicangu Lakota elder and historian, told me the story of his great-grandmother, Laura Hollow Horn Bear, who told Sam this story in 1951. As an eight-year-old little girl in the Native People's Coalition encampment on the Little Bighorn, Laura fled down river with her family at the outset of the Valley Fight. She said that all the women, grade school children and elderly stopped their flight at some point in this mass exodus and confusion. These non-combatants, Laura said, all began to make preparations to fight. She reasoned those up ahead had seen soldiers coming towards them. Laura told Sam that those with weapons now brandished them, while others began looking for any type of clubs and rocks they could get their hands on. Sam was never sure where this action took place.[42]

Sam High Crane made his journey to the Camp on the other side, on November 17th, 2022.

Dakota / Lakota elder and historian Wayne Goodwill shared the story of his great-grandmother Katherine with me. Wayne said at the outset of the Valley Fight, hundreds of youngsters immediately fled the camps on the Little Bighorn. Many were led by older siblings and cousins. Some of these youngsters went down river and then hid in the brush along the Little Bighorn River. In one such group of these youngsters, soldiers nearing the Little Bighorn River were dangerously close to them. Wayne does not know where exactly this took place, or if these soldiers saw these youngsters.

What he does know is that Katherine, who was only seven years old herself, took it upon herself to do everything she could to protect this group. Sensing the soldiers were making for this group, she jumped on a horse she had brought along to carry the younger kids. Katherine set out from the river's edge and rode away from the other children to draw the soldiers' attention away from where they were concealed. Her incredible act of bravery worked. This group of children were not captured. The same goes for Katherine on that day.[43]

What is in the historical record and how do these stories match up against it?

There is a significant amount of material in the historical record on activity in and around the location of the two fords, labeled Ford D 1 and Ford D 2. The following are just a few to present related to the oral history shared with Donovan and I.

The first account we address was brought to my attention by Cheyenne tribal member Rufus Spear from a Cheyenne Dog Soldier warrior by the name of White Eagle. The account was taken by ethnographer Dr. Truman Michelson in 1910 and is in the Bureau of American Ethnology Catalogue of Manuscripts, National Museum of Natural History.[44]

First, White Eagle told Michelson, "Custer came right down where his grave is." Second, "The soldiers all got together again." Third, "The horses acted just as if flies were biting them as the Indians shot them." Fourth, "Below Custer Battlefield there bodies of troops." Fifth, "There right in the midst of the Indians all the horses ran away. The Indians killed all the soldiers. The horses ran above Crow Agency." Sixth, "There were infantry soldiers. The Indians didn't see them. They began to fire. The Indians scalped and killed all." Seventh, "Below Crow Agency - about 6 Cheyenne fell."[45]

White Eagle told of soldiers losing horses below Custer Battlefield. We have been told this by Tim Lame Woman Sr., and Scott Doser, who both got the story from the Two Moons family. Then White Eagle says the Indians killed all the soldiers. There are no tombstones for soldiers in the area of the two fords, but at one time there was one for Mark Kellogg, the lone reporter who rode with the Custer Battalion. It set near the road of the original park entrance road.[46]

It has also been told that, at one time, there were tombstones for soldiers killed in the Battle over in Crow Agency. Mike Donahue, a seasonal interpreter and historian for over 35 years at the Little Bighorn Battlefield National Monument, has written extensively on the Battle, and in particular, this part. In his 2003 article, "Beyond Custer Hill," Donahue told of Crow oral history that stated there were soldier tombstones north of the Battlefield at one time. Donahue said he was told that at one time two soldier tombstones were near Highway 212, about one mile northwest of the Battlefield gate. Don't forget what Leroy Whiteman had been told as well, that there was one soldier tombstone 200 yards northwest of Last Stand Hill and some tombstones southeast of where "Putt" Thompson's Custer Battlefield Trading Post sits.[47]

White Eagle goes on to say horses ran above Crow Agency and in the very next sentence he says there were infantry soldiers that were not seen. Does he mean these are soldiers who lost their horses and now fought on foot? He finishes with saying these soldiers were all killed, and again he mentions Crow Agency as an area where 6 Cheyenne fell. We were told of fighting in this area by Tim Lame Woman Sr., Dennis Limberhand and Alberta American Horse. Leroy Whiteman said fighting took place to the north of Highway 212, then went east and then south. Leroy mentioned soldiers were scattered during this fighting. No history shared with us from Cheyenne tribal members mentioned Cheyenne casualties in this area of the fighting.[48]

Doug War Eagle spoke of a Cheyenne hunting party that had come from the northwest. He told of fighting that was farther to the east, back near the old buffalo trail that the soldiers had followed to get to the Ford D area. Doug said there were Cheyenne and Lakota fighting in this area; both suffered casualties.[49]

There are two maps to be examined in light of the oral history presented to us regarding fighting in and around Crow Agency.

The first comes from Russell White Bear, a Crow historian. According to Mike Donahue, White Bear lived on the Crow reservation and spent a great deal of time researching the Battle of the Little Bighorn. White Bear interviewed Cheyenne and Lakota people about the Battle and was an interpreter used by Battle researchers. He was also the official guide at the Battlefield in 1930 and 1931.White Bear produced a map from his years of research and stories from the Crow scouts who were veterans of the Battle of the Little Bighorn.[50]

Of note are two things White Bear related in 1929.

"Cheyennes came in northern ravine—Custer Creek to head Custer off."[51] Custer Creek is in Crow Agency and runs behind the Custer Battlefield Trading Post. Is this referring to American Horse and his party, who we were told went through Crow Agency and fought here? Or, is this possibly the history told to us from Doug War Eagle of the Cheyenne hunting party from the northwest?[52] Might this be the same Cheyenne group Cheyenne historian John Stands in Timber mentioned, which included his grandfather, Wolf Tooth? Stands In Timber first told this story to Battlefield historian Don Rickey in 1956 and again to anthropologist Margot Liberty, who published it in 1967.[53]

The second piece from White Bear is his map. He drew the Native Peoples Coalition encampment and camps as being all the way to the area of where both Ford D 1 and Ford D 2 are located similar as what Cheyenne tribal members Dennis Limberhand, Rufus Spear and Linwood Tall Bull told us.[54]

We now turn our attention to Michael Reynolds and his research based on his interactions with the Crow scouts who rode with the Seventh Cavalry to the Little Bighorn. Reynolds was brought to the forefront of research on the Battle by author Jack Pennington in his book, *Custer, Curley, Curtis*. Mike Donahue then picked up the trail of Reynolds a few years later and published Reynolds' map.[55]

According to Pennington and Donahue, Reynold's father was a government agent at Crow Agency. At an early age, Reynolds started going to the Little Bighorn Battlefield with the Crow scouts who were at the Little Bighorn, and U.S. Army Little Bighorn Battle survivors. In fact, according to Pennington, Reynolds rode over the Battlefield when he was just seven years old, with the Crow scouts and his father. Pennington said Reynolds was, "present when his father interviewed Two Moons and other members of the Cheyenne Tribe and American Horse and numerous other members of the Sioux Tribes." At this time, I am not sure if this is the Cheyenne war chief American Horse, or the Lakota American Horse. Reynolds was interviewed by National Park Service Little Bighorn Battlefield historians by audio tape. He told these historians where the skeletal remains were said to be of for soldiers and Native participants who fought in the Battle. These sites were marked on a 1967 U.S.G.S. map.[56]

What stands out the most on the Reynolds map is a 1908 story from the Sioux. They told of a site that is said to be where the Sioux chased down and killed an (officer). This spot is near Custer Creek, which is behind the Custer Battlefield Trading Post and said to be almost one-half mile to the north. Donahue pointed out that tombstones for soldiers were at one time said to be in this area, so this might be a separate one.[57] Could this soldier have been chased from the fighting in the Ford D area? Perhaps this was in reference to the fighting told to us by Leroy Whiteman, which was said to be north of U.S. Highway 212 and where soldiers were scattered and chased.[58] Might this soldier be from the fighting north and east of the area where the fords are, told to us by Doug War Eagle? [59] And, what about Tim Lame Woman Sr., Dennis Limberhand and Alberta American Horse's stories? All told of fighting in around Crow Agency and the Custer Battlefield Trading Post.

Alberta American Horse and her history regarding American Horse, the Cheyenne war chief, now becomes very interesting, considering Reynolds may in fact have been present when his father interviewed American Horse, and then perhaps was told of where a soldier was killed, somewhere north of where the Custer Battlefield Trading Post sits today.[60] We will look at more of Reynolds research in chapter 18 as well.

~

The next information from the historical record comes from the Cheyenne historian, John Stands In Timber. In 1956, Stands In Timber took then Little Bighorn Battlefield Historian Don Rickey, to the Ford D fight area. Here is what Rickey wrote based on his interview with Stands In Timber:

"Custer came toward the village from the high ridges to the east. The Custer men tried to cross the river at a ford west of the present railroad tracks, on what is now the Willy Bend's place (behind Sage Motel). Cheyennes hidden in the brush on the south side of the ford drove the soldiers back and killed a couple of them in the brush by the river. Then the Custer men retreated to the flats below where the superintendents house is now located." Stands in Timber then added, "The first fighting in the Battlefield vicinity was at the ford on the west side of the valley. Lame White Man and most of the Cheyennes crossed here after the troops were driven back."[61]

What is notable here is that Stands in Timber said the Custer men attempted a crossing at Willy Bend's place. They were repelled, with some casualties. This is the same crossing Tim Lame Woman Sr., and Dennis Limberhand told us about, which Dr. Fox noted as For D 1. Stands In Timber said Willy Bend's place is behind the Sage Motel. It just so happens that today there rests the remains of a dilapidated and abandoned hotel, close to the U.S. Interstate 90 and U.S. Highway 212 intersection. This area is to the northwest of Willy Bend's crossing and where Tim Lame Woman Sr., said he had heard some soldiers may have actually gone that far to the northwest as well.[62]

Of extreme interest now is the route of the Custer Battalion drawn by Little Bighorn Battlefield Historian Don Rickey over a pamphlet of the Battlefield from his interview with Stands In Timber in 1956. Rickey drew the soldiers route terminating above, which is to the northwest of, Ford D 1, which is the Willy Bends Crossing at U.S. Interstate 90. It should be noted here that Stands In Timber told of the soldiers retreating, and

Railroad bridge next to U.S. Interstate 90 where a ford was located at Willy Bend's crossing. It is believed elements from the Custer Battalion got to this area before being repulsed. -- *Photo courtesy of Faron Iron.*

he puts the soldiers now near the current Little Bighorn Battlefield National Monument Cemetery adjacent to the superintendent's house.

John Stands In Timber was interviewed by anthropologist Margot Liberty in the late 1950's. Together they produced *Cheyenne Memories,* which came out in 1967. Here is what Liberty recorded:

"The soldiers crossed the south end of the ridge where the monument (Last Stand Hill) now stands. The soldiers followed the ridge down to the present cemetery site. Then this bunch of forty of fifty Indians came out by the monument and started shooting at them again. But they were moving on down toward the river, across from the Cheyenne camp. Some of the warriors there had come across, and they began firing at the soldiers from the brush in the river bottom. This made the soldiers turn north, but they went back in the direction they had come from, and stopped when they got to the cemetery site."[63]

Notable here is that Stands In Timber tells of some soldiers, riding over the very ground they will later defend and where the monument on Last Stand Hill now stands. Next, he claimed the soldiers went toward the Cheyenne camp. Is this the camp(s) told to us by Cheyenne tribal members they said are further north, down the Little Bighorn River, closer to the Ford D area? Or, is it the warrior-only camp?[64] Lastly, in the subsequent retreat, the soldiers stop in the cemetery.

In 2013, Margot Liberty put forth more material from her countless hours of interviews with Stands In Timber. Here is one interesting piece related to the Ford D fight:

"About that time the Cheyennes were camped below they crossed the river, and there was a number of trees there. They succeeded in crossing and they started shooting behind those trees and almost came to where the railroad crossing is. That made the soldiers turn back straight north towards the souvenir store; they were about halfway to that place when they started retreating back to where they came from." Stands in Timber in the 1967 book, *Cheyenne Memories,* had added the name of a warrior to this fighting. "Hanging Wolf was one of the warriors who crossed the river and shot from the brush when Custer came down to the bottom. He said they hit one horse down there, and it bucked off a soldier, but the rest took him along when they retreated north."[65]

Stands in Timber again mentioned the railroad crossing, which is near Willy Bend's place. What stands out in this account and should be looked at by researchers is, "That made the soldiers turn back straight north towards the souvenir store; they were about halfway to that place when they started retreating back to where they came from."

Add to this the mention of a soldier's horse hit, with the soldier bucked off but still able to be brought along. Might this be what Tim Lame Woman Sr. had been told, which had to do with a, "soldier chief," being hit and brought along atop his horse?[66]

Stands in Timber drew a map that may depict this souvenir store. This map was shown by Mike Donahue in his 2009 book, *Drawing Battle Lines: The Map Testimony of Custer's Last Fight*.[67] On the map, just across what is labeled HWY 8, which is today Highway 212, are three shapes that are in the vicinity of where a souvenir store sat.[68]

Tim Lame Woman Sr., and Dennis Limberhand both told of fighting in Crow Agency and below, around and through the area where today sits the parking lot of the Custer Battlefield Trading Post. However, this establishment was not yet built when Stands In Timber related this history.[69]

According to James "Putt" Thompson, owner of the Custer Battlefield Trading Post, there were, in fact, two souvenir stores, with one in close proximity to Ford D 2.The exact dates these were in existence are not precisely known at this time. However, their locations are known.[70]

James "Putt" Thompson said one souvenir store was on the Little Bighorn River. This store sat on the allotment of John Wesley and was a railroad stop at one time. It would have been somewhere near the area of where the non-combatants gathered after fleeing the camps at the outset of the Valley Fight. Squaw Creek, an important area for this part of the Battle, is within this area.[71]

The map put forth by Dr. Richard Fox, which shows two fords, Ford D 1 and Ford D 2, is significant here. According to Putt Thompson, the souvenir store set in the area of Ford D 2, which Fox noted from the William

Philo Clark map.[72] This land came to be eventually owned by a Crow family, the Stops.[73]

The last souvenir store to mention was run by Mary Jane Williams. It was located on the north side of U.S. Highway 212 where, today, the exit from U.S. Highway 212 to Billings, MT, is located. This may in fact be the store Stands In Timber told of and depicted with three shapes. He put the shapes across Highway 8, which is today Highway 212. These shapes would appear to be in the proximity of the area where the Mary Jane Williams store sat. One other map from Bruce R. Liddic's book, *Vanishing Victory*, shows these same shapes and labeled them as Sally's Last Stand.[74]

~

The next piece of information comes from the late Canadian researcher, Gordon Harper. Let's first examine what Harper said about his time living on the Northern Cheyenne Reservation and his trip to the area of where the Ford D's are located with Cheyenne elders. Harper posted this on the LittleBighorn History Alliance Board under the Custerania heading, page 20.

"I was taken to Ford D [near the railroad bridge] in 1960, while I was living at Busby on the Rez, by five Cheyenne men, one of whom was very old, two of whom were probably in their 60s and two who were a bit older than I was. I was 21 and was in my second year of interest in the Custer Fight. That visit was part of summer-long trips to the battlefield and environs."

"The trip to Ford D [for which they had no special name] was part of their teaching me some of the history of the battle. Being one of the smartest guys in the world at the time, and not thinking of posterity, I took very few notes."

"According to the very old man, [through translation mostly. He did speak some English, but was most comfortable in his own language-sometimes he just nodded his head when one of the sixty-year olds was speaking], this was where Custer came down to the river. There were some Cheyenne [mostly] and Sioux on the Indian side of the river who saw him coming from about where the Cemetery is located, and there was also a party of Cheyenne hunters coming back from a hunt to the east, who were on the high ground about where the monument is located and who were following the soldiers. Both groups of warriors were involved in shooting at the troops.

Custer never really attempted a crossing, but swung around and retraced his steps, driving away the Cheyenne party on the higher ground, and very shortly being followed by growing numbers of fighters coming over the river."

"The old man, who supposedly was a young boy at the time of the battle, about five or six, was told of this by his father, who was apparently at that very spot fighting, and who took him there many times over the years, recounting the story. It was the highlight of the father's life, and he took a great deal of pride in his part in the fight. Somewhere, I have a Camp-like piece of notebook paper with the names of some of the Cheyenne men written down. It's probably stuck inside a box someplace, slid into a book or record jacket for safekeeping-somewhere where I knew I wouldn't lose it, but where I now have no idea about. Like I said - 21."[75]

As Gordon Harper continued his research on the Battle of the Little Bighorn, he managed to secure information from the Minnikojou Lakota people pertaining to a Cheyenne hunting party. The source who obtained this piece of Harper's research and then passed it on to me has asked to remain anonymous. Here is what they claimed Harper said:

'Coming down from the northwest, there was a hunting party of about 20 Cheyenne and they set up a skirmish line north of Last Stand Hill. It kept Custer's men from retreating in that direction. This party lost 4 elder members of the hunting party.'[76]

We have Gordon Harper first stating that while he was with Cheyenne elders in the area of the two fords, they told him a Cheyenne hunting party from the east had followed the Custer Battalion to the Ford D environs. This would seem to be corroboration regarding the oral history shared with us from the Cheyenne River Reservation in chapter 14. Some years later, Harper stated he was told that apparently another Cheyenne hunting party had come on the scene. This time, these

Cheyenne had come from the northwest and set up a skirmish line of sorts north of Last Stand Hill. This hunting party lost some of the elders, which might mean they were killed. He said that he got this information from the Minnikojou Lakota People, some of whom are in fact from the Cheyenne River Reservation.[77]

Was this information given to Harper the same as as what Doug War Eagle shared with me? As stated earlier in this chapter, Doug specifically mentioned a Cheyenne hunting party that had come from the northwest and stopped the soldiers from going back the way they came. Doug had annotated a map he gave to me that showed soldiers going back in the direction from which they came after being repulsed in the area of the Ford D fight. These soldiers followed the old buffalo trail. This was the trail that brought them to the area of the fords. Doug said the Cheyenne hunting party had some casualties.

He added that some Minnikojou Lakota and Sans Arc Lakota warriors hit these retreating soldiers as well. These Lakota warriors may have come from a warrior-only camp somewhere north of the Cheyenne camps on the Little Bighorn. This camp is annotated by Doug on the map he gave me as well. These Lakota had casualties and were led by a war chief by the name of Eagle Hat. Doug said Eagle Hat was killed at the Little Bighorn.[78]

The historical record does list Eagle Hat as a Sans Arc Lakota warrior and that he was killed in the Battle of the Little Bighorn. However, the lone source for this states Eagle Hat was a young warrior and was killed later in the Battle, at Reno Hill.[79] There appears to be a discrepancy between this source and the information Doug War Eagle has.

What about the story Alberta American Horse shared with Donovan regarding American Horse? She had told that American Horse had come back to the Little Bighorn from the northwest.[80] Are the Gordon Harper, Doug War Eagle and Alberta American Horse stories all talking about the same Cheyenne party?

~

Two Moons was a Cheyenne war chief and a member of the Kit Fox military society at the time of The Battle of the Little Bighorn. A map drawn by Willis T. Rowland, who was the interpreter, is based on information Two Moons told for the interviewer, Eli Ricker. Mike Donahue is again responsible for bringing not only this map to light, but the interview and answers that came from it.[81]

The Two Moons map showed that soldiers went past the famous Last Stand Hill and to the northwest, outside of the Little Bighorn Battlefield boundary and near the area that is close to the fords. It not only showed soldiers losing horses in this area, it shows where, "a man in buckskin was shot at 4 & staggered to 5 and fell." Remember too, as far back as 1886 and again in 1909, Two Moons had said the soldiers had come past Last Stand Hill and marched past it, down into the valley.[82]

Soldiers losing horses was a story long kept by the Two Moons family and shared to Tim Lame Woman Sr., and Scott Doser. Scott even recalled when this map and story was discussed among Cheyenne people who were at the Little Bighorn Battlefield.[83] According to Donahue, this map is the only map in the historical record to show soldiers horses captured near the river in the area of the fords.[84]

More pieces to add to the Two Moons story and map include this account from Mary Crawler, also known as Moving Robe Woman. We told of her in chapter 13. What should be noted here at this time is Mary Crawler's (Moving Robe Woman's) story of soldiers losing their horses, at what is thought by scholars to be in and or near the area of the fords.

Again, it was Donahue who brought this significant event out. In his book, *Where the Rivers Ran Red,* he went into great detail on Mary Crawler's testimony. Based on what Scott Doser and Tim Lame Woman said, it bears worth repeating a part of it here.

"One soldier was holding the reins of eight or 10 horses. An Indian waved his blanket and scared all the horses. They got away from the men [troopers]. On a ridge just north of us, I saw blue clad men running up a ravine, firing as they ran."[85]

Let's also consider a map presented by Mike Donahue from James Bell. In his endnotes, Donahue wrote, "The Bell map reinforces (Mary Crawler) Moving Robe

Woman's narrative and shows a wooded area near the river where 'horses left in woods. Stampeded by squaws with blankets.' Two Moons noted 'horses captured' bear the same vicinity in his sketch."[86]

As for who the "man in buckskin was shot at 4 & staggered to 5 and fell" might be, this is an intriguing piece. In his assessment of this map, Donahue felt that 4 was outside the boundary of the Little Bighorn Battlefield. The soldier then made it to 5, which is below Custer Hill, and fell. Donahue stated he made his assessment based on Eli Ricker's notations.

Could this, again, be from the fighting mentioned by Alberta American Horse, Leroy Whiteman, or Doug War Eagle? Or, is it the soldier John Stands In Timber was told of and which Tim Lame Woman Sr. mentioned as the "soldier chief?"[87]

Lastly, regarding Two Moons, is this piece from Frederick Server.

At the ten-year anniversary of the Battle of the Little Bighorn, Server interviewed Two Moons and Gall. Frederick Server was a Sergeant with the U.S. 2nd Cavalry and rode with the Terry and Gibbon unit to the Little Bighorn. Server had a hotel in Crow Agency some years after the Battle. He served as an interpreter for researchers and for the warriors who were veterans of the Battle they interviewed.

Here is what Server told Little Bighorn researcher Eli Ricker, from Two Moons.

"Custer was moving down the river to cross. He had not yet tried to cross. Instead of going on down past where the buildings now are and following where the road leads down the canyon towards the Crow Agency on to the flat and reaching the river by that route, he turned down from the ridge at Custer Hill where the Monument is and followed the deep ravine thence to the River, supposing that he could make a crossing there. When he reached the outlet of the ravine, he found that it was several feet to the water and his horses could not get down." He then finished with, "Two Moons with a strong party came up the river from the north at the same time, an unfortunate conjuncture for Custer. Here 12 of Custer's men suddenly killed, not having had time to fire a shot themselves."[88]

Here is Server saying that Two Moons told him he came up the river from the north. Two Moons then said he hit presumably what are elements of the Custer Battalion, after they had attempted to cross the Little Bighorn River. Where this happened is open to debate and speculation. If it is not Deep Ravine, perhaps, it is the Crazy Horse Ravine?

Two Moons finished with, "12 of Custer's men died here!" Are these the same soldiers who Two Moons told of and were noted on his map that lost their horses in the area close to the fords? This is similar to what both Mary Crawler (Moving Robe Woman) and the Bell map showed.[89]

~

The next story to investigate in the Ford D episode is regarding the Cheyenne warrior, Little Horse. I had been told, first by Chris Dixon and then by Tim Lame Woman Sr., that this Cheyenne warrior was responsible for organizing some of the resistance efforts in the Ford D area. [90]

Little Horse first appears in the historical record in 1900 and was written about by Dr Charles Eastman. In the Eastman piece, Eastman said his uncle was at the Little Bighorn. We discussed this in chapter 3, as I had been told that it was two of his uncles that fought at the Little Bighorn.[91] Remember, too, that Eastman was an agency physician at Pine Ridge Reservation in 1890 and administered to the Lakota people wounded at the Wounded Knee Massacre. Many of these Lakota people at Pine Ridge at this time would have either been at the Little Bighorn, or had had family there.

Eastman simply stated the Northern Cheyennes at the Little Bighorn were under Little Horse. Eastman stated Little Horse led the Cheyennes earlier as well, at the Rosebud Battle on June 17th, 1876. Eastman added two more names of leaders of the Cheyenne at the Little Bighorn, Two Moons and White Bull, also known as Ice. Eastman added the names Spotted Eagle and Elk Head, as leaders of the Sans Arcs Lakota. Eastman made no mention of Little Horse or any other Cheyennes fighting or stopping the Custer Battalion at any area near a ford or by the Little Bighorn River.[92]

Two Moons being mentioned in the Eastman account along with Little Horse and Ice (White Bull), is rather intriguing. We have previously discussed Two Moons' map, which had soldiers losing horses and captured in the area near the fords.[93] Is this just a coincidence that Eastman mentioned Two Moons and Little Horse together in his writing on the Battle? Two Moons told of the fighting in the area of the fords while Little Horse is said to be leading the resistance there. Two Moons never mentioned a Little Horse in any of his accounts.

This mentioning of Ice (White Bull) leading the Cheyenne by Eastman in 1900 is one of the first in the historical record. George Bird Grinnell had interviewed Ice in 1895 regarding his participation in the Battle and Walter Camp interviewed him in 1910.[94] So, could Eastman have read it somewhere else? Yes, he could have. We will talk more of Ice in chapter 18 as well.

Eastman told of nothing more regarding Little Horse. Did he get the Little Horse story from his uncles, or was it from someone during his tenure at Pine Ridge? Maybe he got the Little Horse story from another Battle participant he interviewed? At this time, we simply do not know.

Little Horse's name turned up a few years later, in 1909, in the book *The Conquest of the Missouri* by Joseph Mills Hanson. The book is on the life of Grant Marsh, the famous steamboat captain who piloted the steamer carrying wounded Seventh Cavalry Troopers after the Battle of the Little Bighorn. In record time, Marsh's navigation skills brought the wounded back to Fort Lincoln, just outside Bismarck, North Dakota.[95]

The author, Joseph Hanson, simply states Little Horse, White Bull, who we believe is, Ice, and Two Moons as all being at the Little Bighorn and leading the Cheyenne. He also says Spotted Eagle lead the Sans Arcs.[96] Is this a case of the author simply putting forth what he might have found from the Eastman article which came out in 1900?

Sometime in the 1930s, Little Horse's name came to Dr. Marquis from Wooden Leg. The name Little Horse is listed as a little chief for the Cheyenne Kit Fox military warrior society. Wooden Leg said nothing more of this warrior in the book.[97]

As I mentioned earlier, I not only asked Tim Lame Woman Sr., about Little Horse being a Kit Fox member, but also Leroy Whiteman, Linwood Tall Bull and countless other Cheyenne people. None knew if this was the same man, nor did any know if this Little Horse who fought at the Little Bighorn is indeed the man who fought at the Fetterman Fight and Battle of the Rosebud as well.

The name of Little Horse appears in the historical record from Father Peter Powell in *The People of the Sacred Mountain*. Powell lists three individuals by the name of Little Horse.

Little Horse I is said to have been a Contrary and the man who led the Cheyenne charge at the Fetterman Fight, also called The Hundred-Soldiers-Killed-Fight, or One-Hundred-White-Men-Killed.[98]

Little Horse III, might just be who Tim Lame Woman Sr., spoke of. This Cheyenne warrior was said to have had a Crow mother and an Arapaho wife. Tim Lame Woman Sr., told me that Little Horse had been in several Cheyenne camps that were attacked by the U.S. Army. Perhaps then this is the warrior who Tim mentioned and was so instrumental in preventing the non-combatants at Little Bighorn from being taken?[99]

Father Powell first mentions this Little Horse III just prior to the Arapaho being attacked on the Tongue River in 1865 at what will be called the Battle of the Tongue River. This Little Horse and his Arapaho wife tried to warn the Arapaho of an impending attack by the U.S. Army, but were unsuccessful. Powell cited George Bird Grinnell from his book *The Fighting Cheyennes*. Grinnell stated in his footnote, "very likely the same Little Horse who was a leader of the Northern Cheyennes at the Fort Phil Kearney fight (Fetterman Fight)."[100] Grinnell made no mention in the text or footnote that this Little Horse was a Contrary. However, in the same book, now writing on the Fetterman Fight, Grinnell states Little Horse had been chosen to lead the Cheyenne charge and was a Contrary.[101]

Father Powell later mentioned a Little Horse, a, 'little chief of the Kit Foxes,' as being at the Little Bighorn. He cited Wooden Leg.[102] Powell did not state if this is the same man he had written of as being at the Battle of The Tongue River, or if this was the Cheyenne Contrary who lead the Cheyenne charge at the Fetterman Fight.

Next up, Richard G. Hardorff, and his book, *Cheyenne Memories of the Custer Fight.* The author cited George Bird Grinnell's Collection, Item 463, at the Braun Research Library. Grinnell stated he had been told that it was Little Horse who stripped a soldier, who Grinnell surmised as Captain Tom Custer, C Company, U.S. Seventh Cavalry. Grinnell said it was in 1914 that he obtained this information. He did not list his source.[103]

Serle Chapman, who wrote the book *Promise,* wrote of Little Horse, a Cheyenne warrior, and his role at the Fetterman Fight. Chapman said Little Horse had been at one time an Elkhorn Scraper Society member and led the Elkhorn Scrapers charge at the Platte Bridge Fight in 1865.[104] Chapman said Little Horse was a Contrary at the time of the Fetterman Fight. He added that Little Horse wore the Sacred Buffalo Hat of the Cheyenne Tribe as he led the Cheyenne charge on the soldiers, some of whom he got within just yards before he attacked.[105]

Chapman only mentioned Little Horse as fighting at the Little Bighorn using the information put forth by George Bird Grinnell. Chapman said nothing of where Little Horse fought at the Little Bighorn. It would appear that Chapman thought the Little Horse who is a Contrary and fought at the Fetterman is the same warrior who fought at the Little Bighorn and was said to have stripped the body of Tom Custer after the Battle.[106]

Tim Lame Woman Sr. had told Chris Dixon that the Little Horse who fought at the Little Bighorn and led the resistance in the Ford D area was a Contrary.[107]

As historians and researchers, we are always looking for more answers. Yes, it would have been fascinating if Tim Lame Woman Sr. could have told us who had told him this story, and from there, moving back in time, who told those people this story. Unfortunately, at this time, history has chosen to hold on to this part of the Little Horse story. However, just let your imagination run wild for a moment and picture this warrior, said to be a Contrary, and think about what he did that day.

~

Buffalo Bull Hump's name is mentioned by Father Powell as a chief at the Little Bighorn. There is no mention from Powell of his military warrior society or where he fought during the Battle. He is listed as a Cheyenne participant in the Battle on the document supplied to us from the Northern Cheyenne Tribe. Nothing on this document tells of where he fought or of what military society he belonged to.[108]

Bobtail Horse is in the historical record many times, and the story of where he fought at the Battle is one of the most studied and scrutinized accounts in history. Those accounts in the historical record would not seem to put him fighting in the area of the fords. He is listed as Battle participant of Cheyenne warriors on the document supplied to us from the Northern Cheyenne Tribe and he is listed as an Elkhorn Scraper military society man as well.

Tangle Hair, also known as Big Head, the Dog Men headsman, does not turn up in the historical record as having had been at the Little Bighorn. Porcupine, another member of the Dog Men, does turn up in the historical record as a Cheyenne Battle participant.[109] This information comes from the 1926 Little Bighorn Battle Anniversary event at Crow Agency, Montana.[110]

Now that we have put forth oral history and the names of warriors said to be in the Ford D fight, another question to address in this chapter, now becomes, who might the, "soldier chief" be that was said to have been hit in this part of the Battle? Is it General George Custer? Perhaps another officer of the Seventh Cavalry? Cheyenne oral history shared to myself and Donovan Taylor at times during this investigation has given us speculative pieces, but nothing conclusive. The simple fact is that history has not given up the name.

~

There is archeological evidence in the area of the fords to suggest fighting occurred. Dr. Richard Fox first linked the archeological findings with oral history and presented the fight in the Ford D environs.[111] Next came the 1994 archeological study of the Battlefield, which up to that time was the most comprehensive ever done.[112]

It was again Donahue who ventured to gather this information together so it was not lost to history. In his 2003 article, "Beyond Custer Hill," Donahue presented his findings based on extensive research of not only oral history from warriors and soldiers who fought at the Little Bighorn, but their maps as well. Based on the 1994 archeological study of the Battlefield, Donahue said, "The conclusion of the authors (of the study) was that a movement of soldiers had taken place from the Custer Ridge Extension into the ravine toward the river where warriors repulsed soldiers. Several sites included mixed artifacts that indicate both a warrior and a solider position during the fight."[113]

The Custer Ridge Extension runs north from the Indian Memorial that sits to the right of Last Stand Hill as one looks north. As stated at the beginning of this chapter, oral history stated that elements of the Custer Battalion traversed this area in pursuit of warriors who they had engaged in the area of the Luce / Blummer / Nye / Cartwright Ridge complex. After crossing the Custer Ridge Extension area and then the current National Park entrance road, some of the soldiers went further to the northwest, past the Custer Battlefield Trading Post into Crow Agency. The others, as Donahue pointed out, followed a ravine (Crazy Horse Ravine) to the Little Bighorn River and the area of the fords.[114]

Some key points to note from this 1994 archeological survey, which were published in the book *A Good Walk Around the Boundary*, showed that at least six different Colt revolvers (these were used by soldiers) had been fired and left cartridge cases in the area of the Crazy Horse Ravine. The authors stated that the area where these cartridge cases were found was a protected site, out of view from Last Stand Hill. It may be the case that soldiers fired these rounds as they retreated from the Ford D environs.[115]

Lastly, the authors stated, "There is clear evidence for combat actions on the northern extension of Custer Ridge, in the ravines below the Custer Ridge Extension of Cemetery Ridge adjacent to the old park entrance road. There were over 40 .45/55 cartridge cases found in this area."[116]

Don Rickey did follow the trail John Stands In Timber set him on in 1956 and he had the area north of the cemetery along the Custer Ridge Extension metal-detected. Ten fired cartridges, all the caliber of .45/55, used by the Seventh Cavalry in their Army-issued

Springfield Carbine rifles, were found. Ricky noted these cartridges could not have been fired at Custer Hill, but instead towards the direction of Crazy Horse Ravine.[117] Ricky also metal-detected west of the current railroad bridge next to U.S. Interstate 90, in the valley near the Willy Bend's Crossing. Artifacts were found. Donahue again had to dig through the archives housed at the Little Bighorn Battlefield National Monument to find the Rickey findings. All he found from Rickey's notes and letters, stated, "shells found near the present bridge and those you found north of the cemetery on the ridge."[118]

Donahue also presented a strong case for the fact that a tombstone for the lone reporter with the Seventh Cavalry, Mark Kellogg, at one time was set in the Ford D environs. Donahue presented this and his findings again in "Beyond Custer Hill." Donahue presented that this tombstone for Kellogg was, in fact, put close to the original park entrance road.[119]

All of this now brings us to the present.

In the Summer 2023 edition of *Greasy Grass Magazine,* Donahue, Jason Pitsch and archeologist Doug Scott submitted the article, "*John Stands In Timber and New Concrete Evidence.*" Written by Donahue, it features Jason Pitsch, a local researcher and rancher, who is an avid historian on the Battle. We featured Pitsch in chapters 4 and 9. He has always been gracious helping us with our research.

Pitsch was investigating in and around the area in and around the Willy Bend's Crossing that Dr. Fox labeled Ford D 1. Pitsch found 12 army .45-55 fired cartridge cases.

Now, here is where this gets really interesting. At an area near the terrain Pitsch found the 12 fired army casings, Donahue said, "Across the river within site of the army casings, Pitsch also found four warrior casings near the western riverbank 130 yards away."[120] Archeologist Doug Scott was then able to do analysis on the army casings and determined that they were fired from five different Springfield Carbines. Scott found that one Springfield fired five of the casings, another Springfield fired two.[121]

In Summary: Ford D

The culmination of our investigation in the Ford D fight tells us the following: Oral history shared with us from 10 Cheyenne tribal members, one man adopted by a Cheyenne family, one Minnikojou Lakota tribal member and one Crow tribal member, told us that the U.S. Seventh Cavalry was repulsed and then attacked.

The Cheyenne war chief Two Moons in 1886 and then again 1909, put forth the movements of the U.S. Seventh Cavalry to the Ford D environs. Two Moons told how the soldiers had initially moved past the famous Last Stand Hill, where today the monument to commemorate their deaths still stands. His map produced from his testimony in 1913 showed soldiers had lost their horses in the area close to the fords. It also showed where a man in a buckskin coat was wounded, which was noted near the area near the fords as well.

In 1956, Cheyenne historian John Stands in Timber presented history from a Cheyenne warrior, Hanging Wolf, who told of warriors stopping soldiers from crossing the Little Bighorn River. This fighting took place at a ford called Willy Bend's Crossing near the old railroad bridge on the west side of U.S. Interstate 90. Hanging Wolf also told of a soldier's horse hit in this fighting and the soldiers having to bring this soldier along atop his horse after this soldier had been thrown off. This sounds very similar to the history told by Tim Lame Woman Sr. and Dennis Limberhand.

Archeological evidence has been found, with more very recently. These findings seem to lend credence to the fact that soldiers from the Custer Battalion did in fact come to the area where a ford was found, and the recent finds near the Willy Bend's Crossing show five different Springfield Carbines, those issued to the U.S. Seventh Cavalry, were fired in this area, strengthening the Stands In Timber, Don Rickey, Tim Lame Woman Sr. and Dennis Limberhand histories of Seventh Cavalry soldiers, at the very least, in the Ford D environs. Stands in Timber told of these soldiers retreating out of the area of the fords as well. These new archeological findings should give historians, students of the Battle and future researchers, inspiration to do more than simply entertain the theory that something went on in the Ford D area.

Tim Lame Woman Sr. puts Little Horse, a Cheyenne warrior, as the leader of the resistance efforts to the fighting near the fords. This Cheyenne Contrary remains a bit of an enigma. We cannot at this time be certain the Cheyenne Contrary Little Horse who fought at the Little Bighorn is the same Contrary who led the Cheyenne at not only the Fetterman Fight in 1866, but the Elkhorn Scrapers at the Platte Bridge Fight in 1865.

While the Fetterman Fight and the Battle of the Rosebud and Battle of the Little Bighorn are ten years apart, it bears mentioning that several noteworthy Cheyenne warriors who fought at the Fetterman did in fact participate and fight at the Rosebud and Little Bighorn. These are Ice, Crazy Head, and Lame White Man. It should not be forgotten that from the Lakota, Crazy Horse and White Bull both fought at the Little Bighorn and Fetterman Fights as well.

Could it be a possibility that Little Horse fought at both the Fetterman Fight, the Rosebud and the Little Bighorn? Yes, it would not be out of the question. Could there have been two different Cheyenne warriors by the name of Little Horse, and both be a Contrary and both be at the Fetterman and Little Bighorn? The answer would be yes.

Now, ask yourselves what are the odds that between two different Cheyenne Contrary warriors, both with the name of Little Horse, one leads the Cheyenne charge at the Fetterman Fight and the other leads the Cheyenne resistance at the Little Bighorn. That would seem rather remarkable.

Now we should ask ourselves the odds that Dr. Charles Eastman mentioned the name Little Horse as leading the Cheyenne at the Battle of the Little Bighorn? Clearly, Dr. Eastman could have read what George Bird Grinnell had said on Little Horse and Ice. That much we know. However, Grinnell's mentioning of Little Horse was not until 1914. Eastman had long since published his piece in 1900.

Keep in mind the following: If U.S. Seventh Cavalry troopers from the Custer Battalion had reached the non-combatants in the area of both fords and captured a number of them, the Battle of the Little Bighorn very possibly turns out differently. This Cheyenne warrior, Little Horse, then becomes a much bigger part of history at the Little Bighorn for his part played there that day.

The name of Little Horse at the very least should be mentioned when warriors are talked of as having led the resistance in the Ford D fight. For that matter, warriors who were veterans of the Little Bighorn Battle and who gave their accounts are not always looked at when the Battle is studied. Perhaps it is time to look more closely at these men and their actions. After all, they were the victors. We just might possibly learn more of the events that transpired there that day and gain a better understanding of what happened.

~

Cheyenne tribal members said that the Medicine Arrows of the Cheyenne Tribe were at the Little Bighorn on June 25th, 1876. The history shared states the Medicine Arrows are close to the Ford D area, which is where soldiers of the U.S. Seventh Cavalry, presumably those from the Custer Battalion, got close to the Cheyenne camps and non-combatants.

The Cheyenne historian John Stands In Timber said that the Custer Battalion were in the area of the fords and were headed for a Cheyenne camp. He gave no exact location for this camp, unfortunately.[122]

Linwood Tall Bull, Rufus Spear and Dennis Limberhand, all told that the Cheyenne camps locations are much closer to the Ford D area than is noted in the historical record. Both Leroy Whiteman and Doug War Eagle said a warrior-only camp of some sort was said to be north of the Cheyenne camps as well. This seemingly also puts the two sacred covenants of the Cheyenne close. The sacred Medicine Arrows would not need to be moved a great distance to put them in the general area of action in the area of both fords.

Gilbert Whitedirt, Scott Doser and Rufus Spear said the Medicine Arrows were at the Little Bighorn. Both Gilbert and Scott said the Medicine Arrows were used to protect the Cheyenne people during the Battle, in an impromptu blinding ceremony. Florence Whiteman, Vernon Sooktis and Chester Whiteman, all said the

Medicine Arrows of the Cheyenne were at the Little Bighorn during the Battle in 1876 as well. That's five Cheyenne tribal members and one adopted man of a Cheyenne family, for the historical record now, all stating the Medicine Arrows were at the Little Bighorn during the Battle on June 25th, 1876.

In chapter 8, we put forth history told by John Stands In Timber and Young Two Moons. Both said the Medicine Arrows were at the Little Bighorn during the time of the Battle. On the other side of this issue, Wooden Leg and Father Peter Powell both said the Medicine Arrows were not at the Little Bighorn.

From history shared with us regarding the Ford D fight and the Medicine Arrows of the Cheyenne, we are being told this part of the Battle is a culmination of a Cheyenne prophesy evoked in 1869 by Stone Forehead, who was then the Keeper of the Sacred Medicine Arrows. He warned General Custer what would happen if he should attack the Cheyenne again.

In chapter 8 we introduced this history between General Custer and the Cheyenne People in 1868-1869. Stone Forehead, the Keeper of the Medicine Arrows in 1869, said, "If this soldier chief (General Custer) broke his promise and harmed the People again, then he, their Keeper, begged the Arrows to bless the People as they avenged all the wrongs the white man had done to them." Stone Forehead it is told offered a pipe to Custer, which he smoked. "Stone Forehead spoke to him (Custer) quietly, saying in Cheyenne if you are acting treacherously towards us, sometime you and your whole command will be killed." When Custer was finished, Stone Forehead emptied the pipe's ashes onto Custer's boots and said, "Thus will the Arrows destroy the soldier chief if he ever walks contrary to the peace pipe again."[123]

Lastly, the history shared states that the Medicine Arrows were used against the soldiers of the U.S. Seventh Cavalry on June 25th, 1876. If it is the case that the Cheyenne Medicine Arrows are used to defend the Cheyenne People at the Battle of the Little Bighorn, and if soldiers from the Custer Battalion were in the Ford D area, then the Medicine Arrows and their history are now at the forefront of the Battle of the Little Bighorn.

The Medicine Arrows and their use would be a

significant event at the Battle of the Little Bighorn, made even more fascinating when we have been told that they were in close proximity to the Ford D area. Based on our investigation regarding the fight in the Ford D area, the prospect that the Cheyenne Medicine Arrows were, in essence, responsible for stopping the U.S. Seventh Cavalry from getting non-combatants who had gathered in the Ford D area, should be entertained.

Donovan and I are forever grateful to the many individuals who shared with us pieces of history that helped shape this chapter. This chapter would have never been completed with this new information without their help. Special thanks to the trail set forth by Tim Lame Woman Sr., Chris Dixon, Mike Donahue, Jason Pitsch, James "Putt" Thompson, Faron Iron, Steve Andrews, Linwood Tall Bull, Dennis Limberhand, Frenchy Dillon, Dwight Bull Coming, Leroy Whiteman, Alberta American Horse, Rufus Spear, Gilbert Whitedirt, Scott Doser, Steve Littlebird and Doug War Eagle.

Notes

1. See the Clark map and the history regarding it in Donahue 2009: 96-104, i; Fox 1993: 175-181; Powers, Thomas 2011: 200-201, 282-301. Donahue 2018: 189-190, see endnote 59, pp 321-322.

2. Fox 1993: 175-181; Interview of John Stands In Timber by Don Rickey from notes dated August 18, 1956, Little Bighorn Battlefield National Monument. Rickey traced over a National Park Service pamphlet that had a map of the Battlefield on it. It accompanied the Stands In Timber interview. See Donahue 2009: 96-104.

3. Personal communications with Chris Dixon, Steve Andrews, Michael Donahue, Tim Lame Woman Sr.-Cheyenne, Leroy Whiteman-Cheyenne, Dennis Limberhand-Cheyenne, Donovan Taylor-Cheyenne, Faron Iron-Crow and Doug War Eagle-Minnikojou Lakota. Interview of John Stands In Timber by Don Rickey from notes dated August 18, 1956, Little Bighorn

Battlefield National Monument. See the Two Moons account from 1909 with him at the Little Bighorn Battlefield in Dr. Joseph Dixon's, *The Vanishing Race* 1909: 181; and in Hardorff 1998: 130-131; See John Stands In Timber and Liberty 1967:191-202; See Fox 1993: 175-181; Donahue, "Beyond Custer Hill," 26-35; Liddic 2004:143-147; Donahue 2009: 241-247, iv. Donahue 2018: 189-190, see endnote 59, pp 321-322; Donovan 2008: 262, 266-268.

4. Ibid.

5. Personal communications with Chris Dixon.

6. Ibid. Personal communications with James "Putt" Thompson and Faron Iron-Crow. See Interview of John Stands In Timber by Don Rickey from notes dated August 18, 1956, Little Bighorn Battlefield National Monument. See Fox 1993: 176-180; Donahue 2009: 241-247.

7. Ibid. For Willy Bend's Crossing reference, see Interview of John Stands In Timber by Don Rickey from notes dated August 18, 1956, Little Bighorn Battlefield National Monument. John Stands in Timber in Donahue 2009: 241-247, iv. For the Dr. Fox map, see Fox 1993: 176-180.

8. Personal communications with Chris Dixon. For references of Little Horse, see Eastman, "The Story of The Little Big Horn," 354, 356-358; Hanson 1910: 288; Graham 1953: 96-97, 131; Marquis 2003: 212, 244; Hardorff 1998: 58-59; Chapman 2004: 85-110.

9. Personal communications with Tim Lame Woman Sr.-Cheyenne.

10. Ibid. Personal communications with Chris Dixon. Regarding Little Horse, See Powell 1981: Vol. 1, 451-461; Marquis 2003: 212, 244; Chapman 2004: 85-110.

11. Personal communications with Tim Lame Woman Sr.-Cheyenne.

12. Ibid.

13. Ibid. Personal communications with Chris Dixon.

14. Ibid.

15. Personal communications with Gilbert Whitedirt-Cheyenne and Scott Doser.

16. Ibid.

17. Ibid.

18. Personal communications with Linwood Tall Bull-Cheyenne.

19. Ibid.

20. Personal communications with Rufus Spear-Cheyenne.

21. Ibid.

22. Personal communications with Dennis Limberhand-Cheyenne.

23. Ibid.

24. Personal communications with Dennis Limberhand-Cheyenne, Tim Lame Woman Sr. -Cheyenne and Chris Dixon.

25. Personal communications with Linwood Tall Bull-Cheyenne, Rufus Spear-Cheyenne and Dennis Limberhand-Cheyenne.

26. Personl communications with Gilbert Whitedirt-Cheyenne and Scott Doser-Cheyenne.

27. Donovan Taylor Personal communications with Florence Whiteman-Cheyenne, Personal communications with Vernon Sooktis-Cheyenne and Chester Whiteman-Cheyenne.

28. Personal communications with Donovan Taylor, concerning his interviews with Steve Littlebird-Cheyenne. Personal communications with Tim Lame Woman Sr.-Cheyenne and Dennis Limberhand-Cheyenne.

29. Ibid.

30. For Tangle Hair, see Powell 1981, Vol 2: 735, 1420. Father Powell lists a man named Porcupine as being married to a Cheyenne woman and living with the Cheyenne People. See Powell 1981, Vol 2: 1425. Personal communications with Dwight Bull Coming - Cheyenne.

31. Personal communications with Donovan Taylor, concerning his interviews with Alberta American Horse-Cheyenne.

32. Personal communications with Leroy Whiteman-Cheyenne.

33. Ibid.

34. Ibid.

35. Personal communications with Doug War Eagle-Minnikojou Lakota and Leroy Whiteman - Cheyenne.

36. Personal communications with Donovan Taylor, concerning his interview with Alberta American Horse and personal communications with Leroy Whiteman-Cheyenne and Doug War Eagle-Minnikojou Lakota.

37. Personal communications with Donovan Taylor, concerning his interview with Frenchy Dillon-Crow. Frenchy is the great-grandson of Thomas Leforge.

38. Ibid.

39. Personal communications with Steve Andrews and Frenchy Dillon-Crow.

40. Personal communications with Victor Douville-

Sicangu Lakota Tribal Historian.

41. Ibid.

42. Personal communications with Sam High Crane-Sicangu Lakota.

43. Personal communications with Wayne Goodwill-Dakota/Lakota.

44. Personal communications with Rufus Spear-Cheyenne. For the White Eagle interview, see Bureau of American Ethnography No 2811, 1910. Dr. Truman Michelson. Bureau of American Ethnology Catalogue of Manuscripts, National Museum of Natural History. https://edan.si.edu/slideshow/viewer/?damspath=/Public_Sets/NMNH/NMNH-RC-Anthropology/NMNH-RC-Anth-Archives/NMNH-RC-Anth-Archives-NAA/NAA-MS/NAA-MS-2811.

45. Ibid.

46. Personal communications with Mike Donahue and see Donahue, "Beyond Custer Hill." James "Putt Thompson," Faron Iron-Crow, Steve Andrews, Bob Snelson and Chris Dixon.

47. Personal communications with Mike Donahue and see Donahue, "Beyond Custer Hill," 35-36; Personal communications with Leroy Whiteman-Cheyenne, James "Putt" Thompson, Faron Iron-Crow, Steve Andrews, Bob Snelson and Chris Dixon, Tim Lame Woman Sr. - Cheyenne, Rufus Spear-Cheyenne, Dennis Limberhand-Cheyenne, Alden Bigman Jr.-Crow, Gilbert Birdinground-Crow.

48. Personal communications with Tim Lame Woman Sr.-Cheyenne, Dennis Limberhand - Cheyenne, Alberta American Horse-Cheyenne and Leroy Whiteman-Cheyenne.

49. Personal communications with Doug War Eagle-Minnikojou Lakota.

50. Donahue 2009: 324-331.

51. Ibid.

52. Donovan Taylor's personal communications with Alberta American Horse-Cheyenne and my personal communications with Leroy Whiteman-Cheyenne. Personal communications with Doug War Eagle-Minnekojou Lakota.

53. Interview of John Stands In Timber by Don Rickey from notes dated August 18, 1956, Little Bighorn Battlefield National Monument. Stands In Timber and Liberty 1967: 196-200.

54. Donahue 2009: 324-331. Personal communications with Dennis Limberhand-Cheyenne, Rufus Spear-Cheyenne and Linwood Tall Bull-Cheyenne.

55. Pennington 2005: 183-184; Donahue 2009: 367-370.

56. Ibid.

57. Ibid. See Donahue, "Beyond Custer Hill," 36-37.

58. Personal communications with Leroy Whiteman-Cheyenne. Also see Donahue 2009: Villa Louis Map, 379-381.

59. Personal communications with Doug War Eagle-Minnikojou Lakota.

60. Alberta American Horse-Cheyenne, interview with Donovan Taylor. Personal communications with Tim Lame Woman Sr.-Cheyenne and Dennis Limberhand-Cheyenne. Pennington 2005: 183-184.

61. Interview of John Stands In Timber by Don Rickey from notes dated August 18, 1956, Little Bighorn Battlefield National Monument. See accompanied map with Custer Battalions route sketched on it by Don Rickey.

62. Personal communications with Tim Lame Woman Sr.-Cheyenne and Dennis Limberhand - Cheyenne. See Fox 1993: 175-181.

63. Stands In Timber and Liberty 1967: 198-199.

64. Personal communications with Linwood Tall Bull-Cheyenne, Rufus Spear-Cheyenne, Dennis Limberhand-Cheyenne, Leroy Whiteman-Cheyenne and Doug War Eagle - Minnikojou Lakota.

65. Stands In Timber and Liberty 2013: 366; See *Cheyenne Memories* by Stands In Timber and Liberty 1967: 199-200.

66. Ibid. Personal communications with Tim Lame Woman Sr.-Cheyenne and Chris Dixon.

67. Donahue 2009: 241-247, iv.

68. Ibid. Personal communications with James "Putt" Thompson.

69. Personal communications with Tim Lame Woman Sr.-Cheyenne, Dennis Limberhand - Cheyenne and Chris Dixon.

70. Personal communications with James "Putt" Thompson.

71. Ibid. Donahue 2009: 22-23, 241-247, iv.

72. Fox 1993: 176-180. Donahue 2009: 96-104, i.

73. Personal communications with James "Putt" Thompson. Fox 1993: 177; Donahue 2009: 22-23, 241-247, iv.

74. Ibid. Stands In Timber and Liberty 2013: 366; See Liddic 2004: 146.

75. Gordon Harper posting on the Little Bighorn History Alliance board.

76. Gordon Harper's research material on a Cheyenne hunting party given to me by informant who asked to remain anonymous. Also see Harper 2014: 189-190.

77. Ibid.

78. Personal communications with Doug War Eagle-Minnikoujou Lakota.

79. Hardorff 1993: 89-91.

80. Personal communications with Donovan Taylor regarding his interviews with Alberta American Horse-Cheyenne.

81. Donahue 2009: 195-2004.

82. Ibid. For the Two Moon's account at the tenth year anniversary of the Battle, see Ricker 2005: 143; For the 1909 account, see Joseph K. Dixon's, *The Vanishing Race* 1909: 181.

83. Personal communications with Tim Lame Woman Sr.-Cheyenne and Scott Doser - Cheyenne.

84. Donahue 2009: 195-2004; Also see Donahue, "Beyond Custer Hill," 31-32.

85. Hardorff 1997: 94-95; Donahue 2018: 190.

86. Donanhue 2009: 382-385; Donahue 2018: 322, note 63.

87. Donahue 2009: 195-2004. Personal communications with Leroy Whiteman-Cheyenne, Doug War Eagle-Minnikojou Lakota and Tim Lame Woman Sr. See the John Stands In Timber account in Stands and Timber and Liberty 1967: 199-200; Stands In Timber and Liberty 2013: 366.

88. Ricker 2005: 143. See Donahue, "Beyond Custer Hill," 31-32; Donahue 2009: 195-2004, 382-385. Hardorff 1997: 94-95.

89. Ibid.

90. Personal communications with Chris Dixon and Tim Lame Woman Sr.-Cheynne.

91. Ibid. Eastman, "The Story of The Little Big Horn," 353; And see chapter 3. Personal communications with Mitchell BigHunter-Santee Dakota.

92. Ibid. Eastman, "The Story of The Little Big Horn," 354; See Chapter 10, notes 10-15, regarding Ice the Cheyenne medicine man and holy man.

93. Donahue, "Beyond Custer Hill," 31-32; Donahue 2009: 195-2004.

94. Greene 1994: 65; Hardorff 1998: 37-40, 79-81.

95. Hanson 2003: 288.

96. Ibid.

97. Marquis 2003: 212.

98. Powell 1981, Vol 1: 457-459; See Little Horse I, Powell Vol 2: 1424.

99. Personal communications with Tim Lame Woman Sr.-Cheyenne and Chris Dixon. See Little Horse III, Powell Vol 2: 1424.

100. Powell 1981, Vol 2: 379-381, 1424. Grinnell 1955: 210.

101. Grinnell 1955: 241-244.

102. Powell 1981, Vol 2: 1005, endnote 7, 1367.

103. Hardorff 1998: 58-59.

104. Chapman 2004: 71-72.

105. Ibid. 92, 95.

106. Grinnell 1955: 234, 383; Powell 1981, Vol 2: 1004, 1422; Hardorff 1998: 37.

107. Personal communications with Chris Dixon.

108. Powell 1981, Vol 2: 1021; Michno 1997: 103-104, 118-119.

109. See www.American-Tribes.com website for listing of both Tangle Hair and Porcupine as Cheyenne Dog soldiers.

110. For Porcupine listed as a Battle veteran, See Upton 2006: 114.

111. Fox 1993: 173-194.

112. Scott and Bleed 1997: 13, 27, 41-46.

113. Ibid. Donahue, "Beyond Custer Hill," 26-41.

114. Ibid. See endnote 25 in Donahue, "Beyond Custer Hill," 35-37. Personal communications Chris Dixon, Steve Andrews, Tim Lame Woman Sr.-Cheyenne, Leroy Whiteman-Cheyenne, Dennis Limberhand-Cheyenne, Gilbert Whitedirt-Cheyenne, Scott Doser-Cheyenne, Donovan Taylor-Cheyenne, Faron Iron-Crow and Doug War Eagle-Minnkojou Lakota.

115. Scott and Bleed 1997: 13.

116. Ibid. 42-43.

117. Donahue, "Beyond Custer Hill," 35 and see endnote 25.

118. Ibid.

119. Donahue, "Beyond Custer Hill," 36-37.

120. Donahue, Scott and Pitsch, "John Stands In Timber and New Concrete Evidence," 8-9.

121. Personal communications with Jason Pitsch. See

Firearm Examination of the Zier Area Ammunition Components Associated with the Battle of the Little Bighorn. Prepared by Douglas D. Scott. Revised November 5, 2022.

122. See the Stands In Timber account in Stands In Timber and Liberty 1967: 198-199.

123. Powell 1981, Vol 2: 706-711.

17
Re-examining the Last Ghastly Moments at the Little Bighorn

What follows is a reconstruction of the Custer Battalion's movements out of the Ford D environs, as well as events related to the other three companies, C, I and L, at or about the same time. This comprehensive scenario is based on many scholarly works, such as those by Mike Donahue, Dr. Richard Fox and Bruce Liddic, to name a few. All three used Native accounts extensively throughout their work. A special note of interest should be applied towards Donahue's scholarly piece, "Beyond Custer Hill."

This chapter's title pays homage to John Stands In Timber, the Cheyenne historian who figures prominently throughout the above mentioned works and this book as well.

In 1966, the magazine *American Heritage* printed an article by Margot Liberty entitled, "Last Ghastly Moments at the Little Bighorn." This is what *American Heritage* said about Stands In Timber's account.

"A Cheyenne historian whose grandfather was in the battle sheds new light on the slaughter of Custer and his troopers."

Liberty and Stands In Timber had already been working together for a number of years recording Stands In Timber's account of the Battle, which was later published in the 1967 book *Cheyenne Memories.*

Our intention is to give the reader the best possible understanding of how events unfolded that day, to better understand the oral history which will be presented in chapters 18 and 20.

As with any reconstruction of events from long ago, historians and researchers are forced to look for answers in documents. What should always be remembered is just how these questions were asked, or framed, and how the answers were recorded and left for the historical record.

~

In chapter 14, we presented oral history to the effect that warriors had engaged the Custer Battalion in the environs of the Luce / Blummer / Nye / Cartwright Ridge complex. Oral history told of how elements of the Custer Battalion had driven these warriors away and then followed some of them, only to be mirrored themselves by the same warriors they had dispersed. The group of warriors the Custer Battalion chased eventually made their way along the backside of Custer Ridge (Battle Ridge) which is to the east, and then past, what is today known as Last Stand Hill. These warriors raced for the area of Ford D and the Little Bighorn River. Of the Custer Battalion, it is thought the headquarters unit and E and F Companies were now in pursuit. Some of these two companies rode over the very area where the monument to commemorate the U.S. Seventh Cavalry members killed in Battle of the Little Bighorn stands today.

Last Stand Hill looking towards the Visitors Center and Cemetery. -- *Photo courtesy of the National Parks Service.*

Next, oral history from chapter 16 revealed that soldiers from the Custer Battalion may have split up in order to probe and reconnoiter for a tactically sound ford to cross the Little Bighorn River. Their intended target: the Native American non-combatants. Some soldiers, one of which might have been an officer, were shot off their horses and were possibly casualties. The lone reporter, Mark Kellogg, might have been a casualty here too.

As these two companies and the headquarters unit attempted to retreat out of the area where both of the fords, labeled Ford D are located, they came under attack. Some soldiers lost their horses, presumably the troopers of F Company. This happened in part due to the soldiers having to fight dismounted and subsequently being surprised by non-combatants, who then scared the horses away from the horse holders. With the horses went the trooper's extra ammunition as well.

The situation had become a worst case scenario for General Custer and his two companies. It was time to move.

It's not known who was in the lead of this retrograde movement. What oral history, the historical record, and pieces of scattered archeological evidence tell us is that the soldiers moved in the direction of where the Little Bighorn Battlefield National Monument Cemetery was later established. There first rendezvous point was a ridge situated in front of where the current Stone House sits.

Little Bighorn Battlefield National Monument Cemetery. -- *Photo courtesy of the National Parks Service.*

Company E, still on their gray horses, may have reached the ridge in front of the Stone House first and covered the retreat of the F Company soldiers who had lost their horses. The companies had tried to cover one another as they advanced up a ravine along with the Seventh Cavalry's headquarters unit. Forced to cover the back of the retreat, the headquarters unit may have had to do this dismounted.

Once the headquarters unit made the ridge near the Stone House, the retreat continued through the area of what is today the Little Bighorn Battlefield National Monument Cemetery. Here the soldiers under General Custer regrouped. General Custer and his officers would have certainly known by now that their only hope was to continue with the retreat and link up with companies C, I and L. Those still with extra ammunition gave some to their fellow troopers in need. You would have to be naïve to presume that at this very moment, these soldiers, led by officers that were veterans of the Civil War and General George Custer himself, did not realize they were now fighting for their very lives!

Oral history told that the two companies were still in tactical stability at this point. There is evidence that at least two skirmish lines existed in the cemetery as the two companies and the headquarters unit moved through.

The troopers of F Company, some who had lost their horses in the Ford D fight, now advanced for Last Stand Hill. The headquarters unit might have been with them and tried to cover them on this desperate sortie that took them through an area where today the National Park Service Visitors Center / Museum stands. In doing so, these soldiers had to engage and then drive away warriors who previously had taken up positions there on what would come to be known as Last Stand Hill!

At the same time, part of E Company moved into the foreboding terrain that is below Last Stand Hill. These troopers of the gray horse troop had left their horses in the cemetery with the company's horse holders. This less-than-desired position of holding the reins to four horses, fell to one trooper out of every four. What was left of E Company now moved onto the area that today is called Cemetery Ridge.

The other three companies of the Custer Battalion, C, I, and L, were now fully engaged by warriors on the other end of Custer Ridge (Battle Ridge). Had these three companies in fact been part of an earlier retrograde maneuver started by E and F Companies a few miles to their northwest near the Little Bighorn River, when they began their retreat out of the Ford D environs? The lead elements of C, I and L companies might have gotten close to parts of the Battlefield that are now known as Deep Coulee and Medicine Tail Coulee before being stopped themselves. Perhaps this retrograde was really an attempt to open a corridor up in an effort to link up with the Reno and Benteen Battalions and or to clear a path for

Little Bighorn River at Medicine Tail Coulee Ford. Elements of the Custer Battalion may have gotten this far in an attempt to link up with the Reno and Benteen Battalions.

them to come on as well?

When this retrograde movement of sorts was stopped, the three companies seemingly did an about face and moved back to join up once again with the headquarters unit and E and F Companies. The historical record says companies C, I and L took up positions at three different areas of the Battlefield. The companies were strung out in a backwards "L" formation.

By this time, F Company and the headquarters unit had cleared and taken Last Stand Hill. For their efforts, they were greeted with the unmistakable roar of C, I and L Companies gunfire to their south, along Custer Ridge (Battle Ridge). Nothing was visible through all the gunpowder smoke. In a matter of just minutes, the headquarters unit and F Company started taking fire from long range. Then, the arrows started to come.

Below Last Stand Hill, E Company was in a skirmish line that extended to Cemetery Ridge. E Company also

Underneath Custer Ridge, looking to the northwest from the Little Bighorn Battlefield National Monument Cemetery towards Crow Agency. -- *Photo courtesy of the author.*

still had to protect their horses and horse holders still in the cemetery. That they were stretched too thin at this critical juncture is undeniable. The entire valley below had come alive. Hundreds of warriors had gathered and swarmed like ants towards Last Stand Hill.

Eventually, warriors overran companies C, I and L. C Company was destroyed at an area called Finley-Finckle Ridge. Named for two of the company's sergeants, Sergeant Jeremiah Finley and Sergeant August Finckle. L Company perished in and around Calhoun Hill, named

Near the Little Bighorn River where Captain Myles Keogh may have been shot off his horse Comanche. Native American oral history tells that a soldier rescued another here and then of the heroic horse that carried both soldiers up and past this steep bluff.

after Lieutenant James Calhoun. I Company was scattered throughout what is known as the Keogh Sector. Here, Captain Myles Keogh's troopers were cut down. Only I and L Companies were in relative supporting distance to one another. The three companies were not in any type of defensive formation, which would have included overlapping fields of fire.

A few soldiers managed to break out of the carnage of C, I and L Companies destruction. These few surviving soldiers sought refuge on Custer Hill (Last Stand Hill). Gunfire from F Company kept the warriors from chasing the survivors from the three companies.

Now, the final climatic scene unfolded. Anywhere from 500 to 800 warriors converged from all directions on what was left of the Custer Battalion. Warriors stealthily concealed in the terrain, but well within striking distance, poured arrows on the soldiers and their horses. It must have seemed as if the sky had opened up and the arrows came like rain.

It would have presumably been at this time that the worst order any cavalry commander has to issue was given by General Custer and his officers: kill their beloved horses in order to hide behind the bodies. Ammunition was too scarce to waste a bullet, so many had to resort to using their large hunting knives.

For many horses, repeated stabs to the neck were required. The horse's screams would have been enough to unhinge most, but that wasn't the worst of the situation at hand for the remaining troopers of the Custer Battalion. What had to be abundantly clear now was that this was a fight to simply postpone the inevitable. Their only hope was that the Reno and Benteen Battalions were on their way.

Up to this point, the fighting below Last Stand Hill and in the cemetery had been a long-range affair. Several warrior charges were unsuccessful in dislodging E Company Troopers positioned in the cemetery. The situation changed when young Cheyenne and Lakota warriors, those who had vowed to fight and protect their people, even if it meant death, now came onto the scene. These young warriors hit the E Company horse holders, and some warriors rode into the fight at Custer Hill (Last Stand Hill). The Company E horse holders panicked, letting go of the gray horses, which now ran for the Little Bighorn River. The troopers from Company F on Custer Hill (Last Stand Hill) were engulfed by charging warriors. Hand to hand combat broke out.

Last Stand Hill fell first. Warriors used their war clubs to finish off the wounded and those few defenders still alive. A handful of troopers made a dash for the Little Bighorn River before being cut down.

Those E Company troopers still in the cemetery area were now isolated and would have witnessed this horrific scene. What was left of E Company pulled their revolvers and fled for their lives toward Deep Ravine. The gauntlet they undertook just to get to the Deep Ravine must have been harrowing. The real terror began when they jumped into this deathtrap and realized it was much harder to scramble out of than imagined. Within seconds, they would have been swarmed by warriors and young boys shooting arrows at them. Their only sanctuary was to go deeper into the brush at the bottom of this ravine.

In a very short time, all were killed.

Oral history in the historical record says fighting was still going on in Crow Agency. Were these soldiers who had fled the fighting from Last Stand Hill? Or were these soldiers who had been separated during the Ford D fight? Maybe these were some of the soldiers who had lost their horses? Regardless, these soldiers, not those on Last Stand Hill, were the last to die.[1]

Notes

1. Burst, James. Pohanka, Brian and Barnard, Sandy. *Where Custer Fell*; Donahue, Michael N. "Beyond Custer Hill." *Drawing Battle Lines: The Map Testimony of Custer's Last Fight Where the Rivers Ran Red: The Indian Fights of George Armstrong Custer*. Donovan, James. *A Terrible Glory: Custer and the Little Bighorn*. Fox, Richard. *Archaeology, History and Custer's Last Battle*. Greene, Jerome A. *Evidence and the Custer Enigma*. Grinnell, George. *The Fighting Cheyennes*. Liddic, Bruce R. *Vanishing Victory: Custer's Final March*. Michno, Gregory F. *Lakota Noon: The Indian Narrative of Custer's Defeat*. Miller, David Humphreys. *"Echoes of the Little*

Bighorn." Powell, Peter J. *Sweet Medicine: The Continuing Role of the Sacred Arrows, the Sun Dance, and the Buffalo Hat in Northern Cheyenne History*; People of the Sacred *People of the Sacred Mountain, Vol* 2. Ricker, Eli S. edited by Richard E. Jensen. *Voices of the American West of Eli S. Ricker,* 1903-1919: *The Settler and Soldier Interviews.* Stands In Timber, John and Liberty, Margot. "Last Ghast Moments at the Little Bighorn" *Cheyenne Memories; A Cheyenne Voice: The Complete John Stands In Timber Interviews.*

18
Deep Ravine and Battle Ridge: Prodigious Elkhorn Scraper Society Men, Cheyenne Youngsters and Some Kit Fox Society Members

Mouth of Deep Ravine, where Cheyenne Elkhorn Scraper Society members and other Cheyennes crossed the Little Bighorn River and went into the Battle. Last Stand Hill Monument is in far background.

The following individuals pointed us on the trail we followed for this chapter: Leroy Whiteman - Cheyenne, Gilbert Whitedirt - Cheyenne, Eddie Whitedirt - Cheyenne, Scott Doser, Keith Spotted Wolf - Cheyenne, Frank Long Jaw-Cheyenne, Wallace Bearchum - Cheyenne, Roger Red Hat - Cheyenne, Eugene Limpy - Cheyenne, Dennis Limberhand - Cheyenne, Dwight Bull Coming - Cheyenne, Tim Lame Woman Sr. - Cheyenne, Nadine Weasel Bear - Cheyenne, Chris Eaglenest - Cheyenne, Victor Douville - Sicangu Lakota Tribal Historian, Doug War Eagle - Minnikojou Lakota, and independent researcher Chris Dixon.

It was in June of 2014, while standing in the Little Bighorn Battlefield National Monument Cemetery, that I first heard vestiges of a story regarding a Cheyenne warrior told to me by veteran researcher and scholar Chris Dixon. The story seemed so alive and mysterious. The veil which has concealed much of the Native People's exploits from that day had been pulled back, and I caught a glimpse into the hidden and untold history to the Battle of the Little Bighorn. This story set me on the trajectory to do this book, as I hoped to find other stories like this one and, hopefully, bring them to life on paper.

Later that afternoon, Dixon and myself walked the trail that starts at the National Park Service Museum and Visitors Center. The trail runs below Last Stand Hill, all the way to Deep Ravine. The National Park Service has worked hard to keep the landscape much the same way as it was that June, of 1876. As one walks this trail, the terrain feels foreboding. You can become a bit disorientated among the hillocks and knolls. It would have been lethal to the soldiers, who by this time, had either lost their horse, or worse, had had to kill it for a breastwork of sorts. To compound matters, most were presumably running low on ammunition. Amid the smoke from the gunfire and all the dust from horses running loose, the soldiers were now confronted by warriors who were dangerously close. Within these environs, close quarters and hand to hand combat erupted.

Cheyenne Elkhorn Scrapers Headmen Wild Hog, and Lame White Man (seated). (1873.)

The story Chris Dixon shared which so captivated me is of Lame White Man, a Cheyenne war chief, leading Cheyenne warriors at the Battle of the Little Bighorn. What made this story so fascinating was that Lame White Man was also said to have also led youngsters, some of whom were no more than 12 years old, into the Battle. While doing so, Lame White Man was said to have worn a special and honored article of clothing afforded to him due to his membership in the Cheyenne military society, the Elkhorn Scrapers.

~

It is imperative the reader understands what was put forth in the previous chapter concerning the companies of the Custer Battalion and their movements from the Ford D fight, as well as the movements of companies C, I and L. This will give the reader a better picture to interpret the oral history we now put forth.

Donovan Taylor and I followed the trail Chris Dixon's story first set me on. In doing so, bits and pieces of long-kept history fell into place after countless interviews. This history, some of which has never before appeared in print, revealed the names of the participants in this episode at the Battle of the Little Bighorn.

This oral history told of warriors coming from Deep Ravine to engage soldiers from companies C, I and L, who had taken up positions on parts of Custer Ridge (Battle Ridge), which today includes Calhoun Hill and the Keogh Sector, on the back side, or east, of Custer Ridge (Battle Ridge). Included is oral history that coincides with the fight in and around Deep Ravine with the soldiers from E and F Companies, who had been repulsed in the Ford D fight. Some of this fighting happened below and south of the famous Last Stand Hill.

~

Chris Dixon said at the onset of the Battle, Lame White Man took his family down river, presumably within close proximity of Squaw Creek. This area, later to be known as Ford D, was considered safe, and many non-combatants had gathered there only to find themselves dangerously close to soldiers from the Custer Battalion.

Lame White Man told his wife he must, "follow his boys." Dixon interpreted this to mean that Lame White Man was telling his wife he must get back to his younger Elkhorn Scraper military society proteges. He presumably knew they would be headed to battle the soldiers in an effort to protect their people.

Dixon said Lame White Man caught up with and / or returned to some type of warrior-only encampment, where he got himself ready to go into battle by putting on his Elkhorn Scraper military society clothing. This included a blue U.S. Army coat, one like many U.S. Soldiers on the frontier might have.

At the time of the Battle, Lame White Man was an Elkhorn Scraper military society war chief. He had taken the blue U.S. Army infantrymen's long winter coat from the dead soldiers at the Fetterman Fight in 1866. This battle is also called The Hundred-Soldiers-Killed-Fight, or One-Hundred-White-Men-Killed.[1]

A contingent of warriors now stood at the ready to follow Lame White Man. A few were presumably fellow Elkhorn Scraper society men, mixed with other Cheyenne fighting men. The youngsters were also there too, though at this time we do not know how many rode with the men.

Lame White Man and his warriors then crossed the Little Bighorn River. Dixon thought they crossed near the mouth of Deep Ravine. After climbing out of the mouth of the ravine, they dismounted somewhere on the flats just above the Little Bighorn River. Leaving their horses there with some of youngest of this fighting force, they moved on foot through the environs of Deep Ravine.

With Lame White Man in the lead, the warriors smashed into parts of the Custer Battalion. Dixon thought this episode happened near the head of Deep Ravine and below Battle Ridge.

The current National Park Service Road is for all intents and purposes Custer Ridge (Battle Ridge). Dixon said he had been taken to the exact spot of Lame White Man's death site. He said it was very close to where Lame White Man's tombstone rests today.

This marker, which bear's Lame White Man's Cheyenne name, was placed by the National Park Service according to information supplied by John Stands In Timber, Lame White Man's grandson. Dixon said the site he was taken to was just a little to the left of Lame White Man's tombstone, which is south, as one looks down on it from the National Park Service Road.

When asked, Dixon told me most of this information regarding Lame White Man came to him from the late Tim Lame Woman Sr. Other parts of this story were told to him by Lakota people. Dixon stated that two Lakota families he interviewed had told him that their ancestors were at the Little Bighorn and were involved in the fight where Lame White Man lost his life. Both families mentioned the blue soldier coat Lame White Man had worn into the Battle that day.[2]

Tim Lame Woman Sr., said to me that Lame White Man was an Elkhorn Scraper society war chief. Tim said Lame White Man led some young Cheyenne at the Battle, and was killed close to the site where his tombstone is today. Tim had heard stories that Lame White Man wore his Elkhorn Scraper society regalia that day, which included his blue soldier coat. Tim said the Elkhorn Scrapers had taken the blue coats, which were long infantry coats, from those soldiers that the Elkhorn Scraper military society members had killed at the Fetterman Fight.

Tim did add that the Elkhorn Scrapers came up through Deep Ravine during the Battle of the Little Bighorn. When asked, Tim could not recall any stories told to him that told of any other Elkhorn Scraper warrior's names in this part of the Battle.

I asked Tim specifically for clarification regarding these Elkhorn Scraper warriors coming into the Battle of the Little Bighorn. Tim finished that the Elkhorn Scrapers at times rode single file, or two by two. He told me this was done because elks, when traveling in herds, walk in single file. He added that at some time in history, after many fights with the U.S. Soldiers, the Elkhorn Scrapers would travel two by two. Whether this was done to imitate the soldiers, or for some other reasons, he did not know.[3]

~

The first clues regarding the Cheyenne warriors who rode with Lame White Man into the fighting in Deep Ravine came from Cheyenne elder and historian Gilbert Whitedirt. Scott Doser, adopted by the Whitedirt family, added to this history as well.

Gilbert and Scott said that Crazy Head, a renowned war chief and a member of the Elkhorn Scraper military society, rode with Lame White Man's contingent. Crazy Head was the highest-ranking Cheyenne council chief at the Little Bighorn. No specific stories were ever told to Gilbert, nor Scott, of Crazy Head's actions during the Battle.[4]

Spotted Wolf and Crazy Head.

Gilbert then added history that has never before been told, except among Cheyenne people, nor has it ever appeared in print until now.

He said Crazy Head's 14-year-old son, Ho'vese, rode with this contingent of prodigious Cheyenne warriors and his father. Tragically, Ho'vese was killed in the Battle. Scott Doser confirmed this story to me as well. Neither Gilbert nor Scott knew where or how Ho'vese was killed.[5]

The Whitedirt family are descendants of Crazy Head. The family kept the history of Crazy Head and his young son alive in an effort to never forget Ho'vese and his sacrifice for the Cheyenne people that day.

Ho'vese is not in the historical record as a listed Cheyenne casualty from the Battle. The reader will see as we continued with our investigation that Ho'vese will not be the only new addition we present to the list of Cheyenne casualties not in the historical record.

Gilbert Whitedirt added another name to the warriors riding with Lame White Man: Spotted Wolf.

Known more for his prowess as a medicine man and holy person than for his fighting record, Spotted Wolf

Ice / White Bull -- Cheyenne.

had adopted two Cheyenne warriors, Yellow Nose and White Shield, some years before the Battle of the Little Bighorn. Spotted Wolf was instrumental in preparing both of his adopted sons with spiritual protection and the making of their shields before the Rosebud and Little Bighorn Battles.[6]

Keith Spotted Wolf, a descendent of Spotted Wolf, had been told stories pertaining to Spotted Wolf's powers as medicine man and holy person. Specifically, Keith said that before the Battle of the Rosebud, Ice and Spotted Wolf took the Cheyenne contingent to Butterfly Creek, which is near Rosebud Creek and the Rosebud Battlefield. It was here that Keith said these two venerated and powerful Cheyenne holy men prepared not only the Cheyenne warriors, but their horses as well. Keith said Spotted Wolf painted White Shield's Horse, as well as Yellow Nose's horse. He was said to have painted these horses in Butterfly Creek the night before the battle. Keith said Spotted Wolf painted the horses in the water, so they would be regenerated with energy and protected because as Keith told, "moths are the butterfly of the night." He added, "the horses would move like a dragonfly, butterfly and moth, which would be hard to hit."[7]

Yellow Nose is in the historical record as having fought at the Rosebud and then capturing a guidon from one of the companies in the Custer Battalion at the Little Bighorn.[8] White Shield is noted for his bravery at the Rosebud Fight, as well as for being at the Little Bighorn.[9]

There is more to tell regarding these prodigious Cheyenne warriors and this episode regarding their involvement in Deep Ravine. Rodger Red Hat, a Cheyenne tribal member and the great-great grandson of Lame White Man, said he had been told that Ice, Spotted Wolf and Crazy Head, all Elkhorn Scraper military society men, rode with Lame White Man's group.[10]

The Elkhorn Scrapers are one of the Cheyenne Tribe's four original warrior societies. The Elkhorn Scrapers rose to prominence among the Cheyenne tribe because of their exploits fighting at The Hundred-Soldiers-Killed-Fight, also called The-Battle-of-One-Hundred-in-the-Hands, or the One-Hundred-White-Men-Killed (Fetterman Fight).

The historical record says the Elkhorn Scrapers secured their blue coats, some being long infantry coats, from dead U.S. soldiers at the Fetterman Fight. This was first noted by George Bird Grinnell in 1923. Grinnell listed one of the names for the Elkhorn Scrapers as Blue Soldiers, and at one time they were called Blue Bellies.

Grinnell was told that after the Fetterman Fight, the Elkhorn Scrapers said, "You have called us Blue Bellies; now, from this time on, we will call ourselves Blue Soldiers, from this clothing were are wearing. They did so, and used to ride two-by-two like soliders."[11]

The historical record says three prominent Cheyenne warriors who were or had been Elkhorn Scraper military society members did in fact fight at the Fetterman Fight. They were Ice (White Bull), Crazy Head and Lame White Man. The historical record says the same thing about all three as having been at the Little Bighorn. Now, according to Cheyenne tribal members, all three and Spotted Wolf are or were Elkhorn Scraper military society members, and now they are all cited as riding together at the Little Bighorn.[12]

Ice, sometimes called White Bull, had been an Elkhorn Scraper military society man and war chief. He had been at the forefront of the fight against the U.S. Government to stop white encroachment across the U.S. Plains. By the Summer of 1876, he was a renowned medicine man and holy person, capable of great feats. Ice was also the son of Dirty Black Moccasin, one of two Cheyenne Old Man Chiefs present at the Little Bighorn.[13]

Roger Red Hat continued to add more long-kept Cheyenne history of the Battle.

Roger said he was told that Dog Soldiers rode with the Lame White Man contingent as well. He did not know specifically if these Dog Soldiers were Cheyenne, Lakota, Arapaho, or a mixture of all. Roger had been told that Cheyenne Kit Fox military society men either also rode with this group or had fought near Deep Ravine.[14]

There was even more intriguing and fascinating history from Roger that has been kept quiet by the Cheyenne People for the most part. This history had to do with young Cheyennes riding in and fighting with the Lame White Man group. Roger called these youngsters, "Cheyenne young suicide warriors." He said some were as young as 12 and 13 years of age. Roger said some were killed during the Battle, and that one of these youngsters killed was, in fact, a young woman! Roger unfortunately, had never been told any of their names.[15]

~

Next, Leroy Whiteman shared some important pieces to the trail regarding the fighting around Deep Ravine and Battle Ridge and more long-silent Cheyenne history. This history had to do with the fact that more Cheyennes were killed at the Battle of the Little Bighorn, or died, as a result of wounds suffered there, than is told in the historical record.

Leroy specifically shared with me that he had always been told that, "Nine suicide boys," (his exact terminology), died in this phase of the Battle. Leroy said that it was 16 Cheyenne warriors and youngsters in total that were either killed at the Little Bighorn and or died later as a result of their wounds.[16]

Leroy said that in this part of the Battle some young Cheyenne women rode with these warriors as well. He didn't know if they rode with Lame White Man out of Deep Ravine, or with those warriors, some of whom he had been told were from the Cheyenne Kit Fox military society, fighting on and around Battle Ridge. Leroy then added that he had been told that in the Battle, two Cheyenne women died, which would put the total at 18 Cheyenne people killed at or as a result of the Battle of The Little Bighorn.[17]

Leroy stated that the last young Cheyenne warrior to die as a result of the Battle died some days afterwards from wounds he sustained to his throat and neck during the fighting. Leroy said this brave youngster was ceremoniously left for his journey to the camp on the other side somewhere near or on Otter Creek. This Otter Creek comes off the Tongue River and is just southeast of Birney, Montana. Birney sits just outside the boundary of the Cheyenne Reservation.[18]

Leroy also added to the information about the Kit Fox warriors and their role at the Battle of the Little Bighorn. The Kit Fox are another of the four original Cheyenne military societies.[19] Leroy said he had been told that some of these Kit Fox warriors fought up on Battle Ridge. Leroy specifically put this fighting south of the Lame White Man's tombstone, but could give no specific distance to it. He put the names of Red Bird, Ridge Walker and Kills Night (Kills In The Night) fighting here. All three, he said, were Kit Fox warriors.

He added another Kit Fox warrior, Weasel Bear, to this

group. Leroy said Weasel Bear stood out on this day for some feat of extra ordinary bravery. Leroy made it very clear to me that this long kept silent history was very important and sacred to Cheyenne People. He wanted me to know that he had been told this information from Willie Whitehorse, Red Bird and Black Bear.[20]

~

Dwight Bull Coming, a Cheyenne tribal member, related information regarding the noted Cheyenne warrior, Yellow Nose. This Cheyenne warrior, who much has been written about regarding his fighting at the Little Bighorn, is said to have gotten a guidon in the fighting on Battle Ridge. When Dwight and myself were on the Battlefield in 2021, he specifically put this event between the Finley-Finckle Ridge fight site and the Calhoun Hill area.[21]

Frank Long Jaw, another Cheyenne tribal member, shared information regarding his relative, Long Jaw, with Donovan Taylor. Long Jaw was a Kit Fox warrior who fought at the Battle of the Little Bighorn.

Frank told Donovan that, "Yellow Nose picked up a flag on Battle Ridge and that Ice's son, Noisy Walking, was close behind Yellow Nose, as was Long Jaw." Noisy Walking was a Cheyenne warrior and the son of Ice. He is listed as a suicide warrior in the historic record. He died a few days after the Battle from wounds he suffered there.[22]

Cheyenne elder and historian Eugene Limpy added to Leroy Whiteman's story of "Cheyenne suicide boys." Eugene's relative, Limpy, fought and was wounded at the Battle of the Rosebud. Eugene had been told that the first attack of what he called the, "young Cheyenne suicide warriors," took place very near where the Lame White Man tombstone sits. Eugene added the name of Dives Backward to the list of Kit Fox warriors fighting on Battle Ridge. Eugene then said that Noisy Walking, the son of Ice who was killed at the Little Bighorn, was an Elkhorn Scraper military society member.[23]

Before we go any further with our investigation regarding these warriors riding with Lame White Man, it is important to clarify who these youngsters were and why some have been labeled, "Cheyenne suicide warriors" or "suicide boys."[24] It was the noted Cheyenne historian John Stands In Timber who first told of these youngsters and the "Dying Dance." Stands In Timber had said that the night before the Battle, "Some Sioux boys had just announced that they were taking the suicide vow, and others were putting on a dance for them at that end of the camp." He added, "This meant they were throwing their lives away-they would fight till they were killed in the next battle."[25]

It was first from Dennis Limberhand, then Leroy Whiteman, and finally Donovan Taylor, who all cautioned me on the exact meaning of calling these young Cheyennes, "suicide warriors." All three said that these youngsters were committing suicide was misinterpreted by western historians. Writers and historians had run with the sensational aspect of it without asking the Cheyenne People its true meaning. Dennis and Leroy said these youngsters were not suicidal, but instead, had pledged to fight and protect their people until they could fight no more. They were courting death, so to speak, in this process, and if they should be killed, then they died admirably protecting their people.[26]

Chris Dixon, who had spent a great deal of time among Native People, eloquently explained who these youngsters were. "The fact that life was so highly valued, especially the life of fit and healthy young Cheyenne men in their society, is something you have to grasp in order to understand the enormity of the commitment to 'throw away a life' in defense of the people. Within the Cheyenne warrior societies, the rank-and-file members pledged to 'throw away their lives' in defense of the people. You might regard that as effectively the oath of allegiance on joining the society."[27]

These Cheyenne youngsters were not going to and did not commit suicide at The Battle of The Little Bighorn. They had vowed to protect their people, even if it meant death. Sadly, for some of these Cheyenne youngsters and for that matter, Lakota youngsters as well, this in fact occurred.[28]

What is in the historical record and how do these stories match up against it?

John Stands In Timber first brought attention to the actions of his grandfather, Lame White Man, at the Little Bighorn. In 1956, Stands In Timber told Little Bighorn Battlefield National Monument Historian Don Rickey, "The first fighting in the Battlefield vicinity was at the ford on the west side of the valley. Lame White Man and most of the Cheyennes crossed here after the troops were driven back."[29]

A few years later, Stands In Timber told anthropologist Margot Liberty details regarding Lame White Man's death from family history shared to him by his grandmother, Twin Woman, Lame White Man's widow. Stands In Timber said once Lame White Man saw his family to safety, "He did not have time to get dressed himself, or put on anything. He just wrapped a blanket around his waist and moccasins, and a belt, and a gun."[30]

According to Chris Dixon, the following points should be examined when studying the Stands In Timber account.

"These are all things that his grandmother saw. She (Twin Woman) does not make anything up; nor does she extrapolate, hypothesize or imply anything about what becomes of him (Lame White Man) after he has left her sight. Female relatives are not the transmitters of Cheyenne men's war stories.[31] Dixon emphasized, "For those who are members of warrior societies, their societies are the transmitters. The Elkhorn Scrapers, who continue in existence on the Northern Cheyenne reservation have numerous war stories about Lame White Man. The story of his death is one of many. The blue soldier coat is in a number of these stories which are not written down.[32]

Based on the information and analysis from Chris Dixon, this means that, at a minimum, two Lakota families related to the people who were in the fight and area where Lame White Man was killed have kept this history alive for 147 years. Based on Dixon's and my conversations with the late Tim Lame Woman Sr., the same could be said for Lame White Man's military society, the Elkhorn Scrapers.[33]

Rick Two Dogs, an Oglala Lakota elder and historian, told me Charles Whitedirt, father of Gilbert Whitedirt, told him the Lame White Man story; specifically, that Lame White Man was in fact wearing his blue U.S. Army soldier coat when killed.[34]

Dennis Limberhand, Cheyenne elder and historian, shared with me that he had been told the Lame White Man story. Dennis stated Lame White Man wore his blue soldier coat into the Battle.[35]

Roy Dean Bull Coming, Cheyenne tribal member, shared with me that they had been told of Lame White Man wearing his blue solider coat at the Little Bighorn. Roy Dean told me that back in the 1960s and even into the 1970s, on the Cheyenne Reservation in Oklahoma, the elders always mentioned Lame White Man when talking about the Battle of the Little Bighorn. Roy Dean said the elders always wondered, "what those soldiers of Custer must have thought when they seen Lame White Man and those others coming, wearing their soldier coats."[36] Based on Roy Dean's story, one now has to wonder if some of the other members of the Elkhorn Scrappers wore their blue soldier coat into the Battle?

Two noted Cheyenne warriors, Yellow Nose and Wooden Leg, both veterans of the Little Bighorn, talked of Lame White Man and what he wore at the Little Bighorn. Yellow Nose said through interpreter Edward Guerriere, "Lame White Man a Cheyenne put on a soldier's coat that he found. A Sioux, thinking that Lame White Man was soldier, killed him."[37]

Wooden Leg, himself an Elkhorn Scraper society member, said, "We knew he had gone with the young men in their charge upon the soldiers there." He added, "A bullet had gone in at his right breast and out his back. He also had many stab wounds. He was still dressed in his best clothing, none of it having been taken." Wooden Leg added to the ferocity of the fighting there. "Of these fifteen or so killed by the Custer men, there were more of them fell during the first close fighting, when Lame White Man led us and himself was killed, down toward the river, than fell at any other one section of the field."[38]

Father Peter Powell putting Lame White Man with another contingent of Cheyenne warriors at the Little

Bighorn needs to be addressed here.

Powell, based on information from George Bird Grinnell, said Lame White Man was in fact the warrior Mad Wolf, who rode with a contingent of Cheyenne warriors. This group included Roan Bear, Bobtail Horse and Calf. David Humphreys Miller later added a Lakota warrior, White Cow Bull, to this group. These warriors were said to have spotted soldiers from the Custer Battalion in the Medicine Tail Coulee environs and rode out to stop them from crossing the Little Bighorn and gaining access to the camps.[39]

Powell again cited George Bird Grinnell, who interviewed the Cheyenne warriors and veterans of the Little Bighorn Little Hawk and White Shield. Both inferred Lame White Man was in fact known by several different names, one of which was Mad Wolf.[40] However, the Mad Wolf who rode with the Cheyenne contingent at Medicine Tail Coulee was the Cheyenne Dog Soldier who fought at and survived the Battle of the Little Bighorn. It is not Lame White Man, who Wooden Leg never mentioned as riding with Roan Bear, Buffalo Calf or Bobtail Horse.[41]

It was David Humphreys Miller's informant, White Cow Bull, who told of this Mad Wolf and his hesitancy to engage the soldiers during the Battle. Clearly, this is not the determined and defiant Lame White Man, who had fought and distinguished himself at the Fetterman and Rosebud Battles.[42] Nor is it the man Young Little Wolf said, "was the head chief at Little Bighorn."[43] and was described by not only Wooden Leg but by Kate Bighead (Antelope) as haranguing warriors to quit running away from the soldiers and to follow him in attacking them![44]

There is no question that Lame White Man was called Mad Wolf and described using this name by not only Little Hawk but White Shield as well. Both said Lame White Man and Noisy Walking were killed in the same segment of the Battle, which had nothing to do with action in and around the ford at Medicine Tail Coulee.[45]

~

We continued on with our investigation regarding this group of renowned Cheyenne warriors who were, or had been, Elkhorn Scraper military society members, and the youngsters they led at the Battle of The Little Bighorn.

First, there is a map from John Two Moons, also called Young Two Moons. A nephew of Chief Two Moons, Young Two Moons was a Cheyenne warrior who fought at the Rosebud and Little Bighorn.

Researcher and writer Stanley Vestal interviewed Young Two Moons and sketched a map based on the information obtained. Vestal wrote, "Walking White [Man's] party made first charge, on side of hill. Yellow Nose was close by." Young Two Moons said a warrior who he called, "Walking White," thought to be Lame White Man, led a charge that was just below and ran parallel to Battle Ridge. The charge moved west and bisected near Last Stand Hill. On the map, Vestal put numeral "1."[46] Based on the location John Stands In Timber showed National Park Service personnel of Lame White Man's death site, the "1," looks to be in close proximity.[47]

There is one other reference in the historical record that says Lame White Man was also known as Walking White Man. This account comes from Willis Rowland, who was also known as Long Forehead. Rowland simply told that, "a son of Chief White Bull (Ice) and Walking White Man rode into the midst of the troops while the fight was raging and fell headlong from their horses."[48] All of this becomes even more interesting when you recall that Frank Long Jaw told Donovan, "Yellow Nose picked up a flag on Battle Ridge and that Ice's son, Noisy Walking, was close behind Yellow Nose, as was Long Jaw."[49]

To recap, Young Two Moons puts Yellow Nose and the taking of a guidon near the death site of Lame White Man. Frank Long Jaw puts Noisy Walking (the son of Ice), a young Cheyenne suicide warrior and casualty of the Battle, here as well. Frank Long Jaw said his relative, Long Jaw, who was also in this area, was in fact a member of the Kit Fox military society.[50] Leroy Whiteman put four members of the Kit Fox military society, Weasel Bear, Red Bird, Ridge Walker and Kills Night (Kills In The Night), fighting on Battle Ridge.[51] How close to the area where Lame White Man fell these Kit Fox warriors were, we do not know or would try to surmise. Eugene Limpy added the name of one more Kit Fox warrior, Dives Backward, fighting in this area.[52]

John Stands in Timber told anthropologist Margot Liberty that Cheyenne veterans showed him the death sites of Lame White Man and Noisy Walking in 1926, at the 50th anniversary of the Battle.

Liberty said, "At the third site Stands In Timber said his informant told him of a warrior named Yellow Nose counting coup on a soldier with one of the troop guidons. The incident took place below and to the left of the Lame White Man marker, a place pointed out to Stands In Timber by Tallbull at the 1926 ceremonies, when Stands In Timber was taken over the field and also shown the death sites of Lame White Man and Noisy Walking."[53]

We finish up with some accounts recorded by researcher, writer and painter David Humphreys Miller from Cheyenne veterans of the Little Bighorn, Black Wolf, Eagle Nest, Files Across, Frank Pine and Rising Sun. Each told Miller they fought under Lame White Man.[54]

Then there is the account Miller said he was told by John Dives Backward "*The son of Chief Ice sang out encouragement 'only heaven and earth last long: I do not.' This got us to our feet and running up the slopes. Poorly armed, I knew I would fight to the death, if I had to, even with my quirt.*" Miller then finished with, "He later fought valiantly with other youngsters under the Cheyenne Chief Ice."[55] This is the same Dives Backward that Eugene Limpy informed me fought at the Little Bighorn and on or near Battle Ridge.[56]

This may be the only account in the historical record of the mindset of one of the so-called suicide warriors during the Battle of the Little Bighorn. This account Dives Backward gave Miller is the only account in the historical record that tells of youngsters fighting under the leadership of Ice at the Battle of the Little Bighorn.[57]

Writer and historian George Bird Grinnell interviewed Ice about the Battle of the Little Bighorn. Grinnell simply said Ice took a carbine (rifle) from a soldier and that he lost his son, Noisy Walking, who was mortally wounded.[58]

Cheyenne historian John Stands In Timber said that according to Ice, Noisy Walking had been in many fights prior to the Little Bighorn. Ice also said Noisy Walking had fought at the Rosebud Battle as well.[59]

Interestingly, it was Ice's sister, Kate Bighead (Antelope) who gave an account of the Battle to Dr. Marquis in 1927. Kate had told how she went looking for her nephew, Noisy Walking. In the process she watched Lame White Man lead a charge on the soldiers of the Seventh Cavalry. In her account she never mentioned Ice fighting at the Little Bighorn. She never mentioned her other brother, White Moon, as fighting either.[60]

There is documentation in the historical record stating Ice, was in fact, the leader of the Cheyenne at the Battle of the Little Bighorn. We told of this in the previous chapter, that in 1900, Dr. Charles Eastman's account of the Battle of The Little Bighorn claimed Ice led the Northern Cheyennes.[61]

One account Peter Powell found from the Cheyenne warrior White Elk to George Bird Grinnell in 1914 said, "The commander in the fight [was] not Two Moon—[but] White Bull."[62]

A Yanktonai Sioux warrior, Thunder Bear, gave his account to Edward Curtis, the acclaimed writer and photographer. Curtis said Thunder Bear told him, "Ice, a medicine man, was chief of the Cheyennes."[63] Here too, it should be noted that John Stands In Timber said that when working to heal wounded warriors from the Rosebud fight [Battle], Ice evoked Cheyenne spirits from Bear Butte. These spirit beings told Ice of the impending Cheyenne victory at the Little Bighorn.[64]

There are glimpses in the historical record of Crazy Head and Spotted Wolf's participation at the Battle of the Little Bighorn. Wooden Leg told Dr. Marquis, "Old Bear and Dirty Moccasins, old men chiefs. Next to them, Crazy Head was considered the most important tribal big chief."[65] David Humphreys Miller learned from his Cheyenne informants that the leading Cheyenne war chiefs at the Little Bighorn were Crazy Head and Lame White Man.[66]

Lastly, regarding Crazy Head, John Stands In Timber said Crazy Head was actually Crow by birth, having been captured by the Cheyenne as a young child. Stands

In Timber listed Crazy Head as a, "chief" at the Little Bighorn.[67]

There is one piece from historian Renne Samson Flood regarding Spotted Wolf. His descendants told her he lost an eye in the Battle. Plus, the day after the Battle, Spotted Wolf was honored in a ceremony for his bravery and made a war chief. He and another son, White Elk, were said to each have taken a soldier's pistol from the Battle as well.[68]

John Stands In Timber said Spotted Wolf was actually a Ute Indian by birth. He didn't know if Spotted Wolf had been captured or not. Stands In Timber did mention that Spotted Wolf had only one eye and wore dark glasses. "They say chief Spotted Wolf was one of the bravest warriors in the tribe before he became a chief."[69]

The historical record does not offer much regarding the Kit Fox warriors fighting on Battle Ridge and / or near Deep Ravine. Kills Night (Kills In the Night) was said to have chased one of the last surviving soldiers from the Battle and overtaking him.[70]

Ridge Walker (Bear Walks On A Ridge) is listed as a little chief of the Kit Foxes at the Little Bighorn.[71] Ridge Walker (Bear Walks On A Ridge) was the brother of Young Two Moons, nephew of Two Moons and later, the father-in-law of John Stands In Timber. This becomes even more interesting because we highlighted the map from Young Two Moons earlier in this chapter. Now we possibly have two brothers fighting within close proximity of one another, or Ridge Walker (Bear Walks On A Ridge) simply mentioned his brother of this part of the Battle.

Ridge Walker (Bear Walks On A Ridge) was said to have become a powerful medicine man later in life.[72]

Weasel Bear was also listed as a little chief of the Kit Foxes at the Little Bighorn. That much we have from the historical record.[73] As for his exploits at the Little Bighorn that Leroy Whiteman mentioned, nothing could be found.

There is nothing in the historical record that told of Red Bird and his fighting at the Little Bighorn.

~

Oral history we collected pertaining to the number of Cheyenne killed at the Little Bighorn does not match the historical record. Seven Cheyenne are listed on the historical record as having died at or because of wounds suffered fighting at the Little Bighorn.[74] Let's examine some pieces found regarding Cheyenne and Lakota causalities mentioned at the Little Bighorn.

One account comes again from Thunder Bear. This Yanktonai Sioux warrior and veteran of the Battle told Edward Curtis that, "Nineteen Sioux and seventeen Cheyennes were killed."[75]

Certainly, the historical record contradicts this claim of only nineteen Sioux killed at the Little Bighorn. What is interesting is that this number of seventeen Cheyennes, as told from Thunder Bear, is close to what Leroy Whiteman told me and was stated earlier in this chapter. Leroy said sixteen Cheyenne warriors and youngsters died as a result of the Battle and wounds suffered in it. He added that two Cheyenne women were killed in the Battle and should be added to the number of Cheyenne casualties at the Little Bighorn, therefore putting the total at eighteen Cheyenne.[76]

The following account from Kill Eagle, the Sihasapa (Blackfeet) Lakota Chief we previously mentioned him in chapters 9, 12 and 15, is compelling in conjunction with what Leroy Whiteman said.

"There was a Cheyenne woman who had a revolver strapped on her and went into the fight and got killed!"[77] Here again, we have history presented and saved in the historical record that has clearly been ignored, but kept well alive by the Cheyenne People and others who were at the Little Bighorn.

Roger Red Hat said that he had been told that some young women rode with these Cheyenne youngsters fighting at the Little Bighorn, one of whom was killed.[78] Maybe the Kill Eagle account and Roger's now give us the two Cheyenne women said by Leroy to have been killed in the Battle?

Add to this what Florence Whiteman's grandfather Louis Dog, a Cheyenne veteran of the Battle, said regarding young Cheyenne men dancing and pledging to be "suicide warriors." "Some young women, when they saw their brother dancing, why they said, 'I'm going to go join my brother. I'll die with my brother today.' Some of the first ones did that, not that many."[79]

Returing to Michael Reynolds' research: Reynolds was present when his father interviewed Cheyenne, Lakota and Crow veterans of the Battle. He was said to have ridden all over the Battlefield by the age of seven. In fact, in 1977, Reynolds submitted a piece titled, "*The Custer Story*." In it he said, "The War Women of the Cheyenne caught the cavalry horses of Calhoun and Keogh on the Eastern slopes of Battle Ridge."[80]

Can anything definitive about who these Cheyenne War Women were, or did, be obtained from this? The obvious answer is no. However, considering what Leroy Whiteman said, as well as Roger Red Hat, and Florence Whiteman's account from her grandfather regarding Cheyenne women and young women fighting and riding with warriors during the Battle, this is interesting, to say the least.

~

In the previous chapter we described three instances where it is said the Cheyenne had casualties in the fighting near the two fords labeled Ford D.

The first came from the Cheyenne Dog Soldier White Eagle. He said that 6 Cheyenne fell in the fighting in and around Crow Agency.

Doug War Eagle told of Cheyenne casualties among the group of Cheyenne who hit members of the Custer Battalion as the soldiers retreated out of the Ford D area.

Lastly, Gordon Harper had information from the Minnikojou Lakota that there were four Cheyenne casualties among a hunting party that had come back from the northwest. As stated earlier, the Doug War Eagle and Harper accounts might very well be the same account.[81]

There are other accounts in the historical record. Mrs. Spotted Horn Bull, mentioned in chapter 10, was in the encampment on the Little Bighorn and her husband fought in the Battle. It was said she was a cousin to Sitting Bull. Here she is telling of casualties the Sioux had at the Little Bighorn.

"The Sioux lost thirty killed and more than twice as

many wounded. Among the killed were boys of twelve and fourteen, who in the ardor of young warriorhood, rushed across the river on their ponies and into the thickest of the fight."[82]

This account sounds strikingly familiar to the accounts of Roger Red Hat and Leroy Whiteman. Both said young Cheyennes fought and died at the Little Bighorn, some as young as 12 and 13 years of age.

Mrs. Spotted Horn Bull added, "Two Cheyennes tried to cross the river and one them was shot and killed by Long Hair's men." From her narrative, it appears this was not in the Valley Fight with the Reno Battalion, but instead she told this after she had mentioned, "I saw Crazy Horse lead the Cheyennes into the water and up the ravine."[83] However, it could be the young Cheyenne warrior Hump Nose, also called Roman Nose, who was killed near the Little Bighorn River, when the Reno Battalion retreated back across it.[84]

Oglala Lakota warrior Red Hawk said, "three hundred Indians had been killed during the Battle and two hundred more died from their wounds while moving back to the agencies."[85]

There are two very interesting accounts from Kill Eagle.When asked how many wounded resulted from the Battle, he said, "600 wounded in every way, head, hands, arms, body, etc.—nearly all I saw were wounded more or less." He then added, "there were twenty-seven on travois and thirty-eight (Ogalalla Sioux) on horseback."[86] Kill Eagle also told of a wounded Cheyenne warrior from the Battle, brought back to the camps on the Little Bighorn. "At first a Cheyenne Indian came in with a war bonnet and proclaimed: 'I have killed three soldiers but they have killed me at last.' He was wounded in three places." The historical record has no record of who this Cheyenne warrior was and if he died or survived the Battle.[87]

Cal Thunder Hawk, a Sicangu Lakota man, told me of some of his family's history as it pertained to the Little Bighorn. Cal told me that his relative Thunder Hawk, a Sicangu Lakota warrior, fought and was wounded at the Battle of the Rosebud. Thunder Hawk was rescued and carried off the Rosebud battlefield by a Cheyenne warrior, who was known as, Wears The Iron Shirt. The ironic twist to this story, is that this Cheyenne warrior,

Wears The Iron Shirt, was one of Thunder Hawk's wives' brothers-in-law. Thunder Hawk's wife was a Cheyenne.

Because of his wounds suffered at the Rosebud, Thunder Hawk was not able to fight at the Little Bighorn. He was present in the Native Peoples Coalition encampment as the Battle went on. As the Battle raged, Thunder Hawk's Cheyenne wife, informed him that the Cheyenne warrior Wears The Iron Shirt who rescued Thunder Hawk at the Rosebud, now had been either killed or mortally wounded. To honor this brave Cheyenne warrior, Thunder Hawk named one of his sons as, He Rescues Him.[88]

This Cheyenne warrior who was named Wears The Iron Shirt and died either at the Little Bighorn or as a result of his wounds suffered there, is not in the historical record. He is not listed as a Cheyenne casualty, nor is he on any other lists pertaining to those killed at the Battle of the Little Bighorn. Could the Cheyenne warrior Wears The Iron Shirt who rescued Cal Thunder Hawk's relative, be in fact the Cheyenne warrior Kill Eagle told of?

We certainly realize there are number of accounts contrary to the few we presented that puts the warrior casualties at much lower numbers. This was just a glimpse from a cursory search.

~

We turned our attention to the story of a warrior-only camp from which these Lakota and possibly the Cheyenne contingent under Lame White Man may have come. Leroy Whiteman told me he was not exactly sure of where the Cheyenne camps were. He did state that he was told there was a warrior-only camp of sorts somewhere down river (north) of the Cheyenne camps. He didn't know if it was only Cheyenne, or were others there as well.[89]

In the previous chapter, Doug War Eagle put a warrior-only camp of some sort north of the Native Peoples Coalition encampment on the Little Bighorn River. Doug felt some of these warriors were those who hit the Custer Battalion as they retreated from the Ford D fight.[90]

These stories of a warrior-only camp were the only

two shared with us.

The Canadian researcher Gordon Harper had been on this trail since 1960. "Actually, the camps extended well north of Ford B (Medicine Tail Coulee), almost as far as the Ford D area, where the last of the Cheyenne camps was located, and there probably was another small camp still farther downstream and close by, occupied only by warriors. There was another warriors-only-camp, considerably larger, upstream, west of Hunkpapa camps. I hope to pin down the specific locations of these two warrior camps, but there is no question but that they did exist [in my mind anyway], based on Indian histories, both Lakota and Cheyenne. Cheyennes pointed out the location of their camps to me in 1960."[91]

~

Let's now look at the possibility that some of the warrior societies of the different tribes at the Battle of the Little Bighorn fought as cohesive units, at times separately from their fellow tribesman.

For historical context, we present what George Bent, a historian of Cheyenne history, told veteran writer and researcher of Native American history George Hyde. Bent, it was said, rode with the Dog Soldiers after the Sand Creek Massacre, and was said to have been a member the Elkhorn Scraper military society.[92]

Bent told Hyde there were three thousand warriors, some Lakota, some Cheyenne and Arapaho in the Battle of the Platte Bridge. This fight occurred in 1865 outside of Casper, Wyoming.[93] In a map Hyde gave to Bent, Bent noted where the Cheyenne military warrior societies were stationed. He then talked about the military societies attacking the U.S. Army soldiers. "Bent indicates the locations of the Crooked Lances (Elkhorn Scrapers), the Bow Strings, the Foxes, and near Casper Creek, the Chiefs. He locates the Dog Soldiers along the river west of the bridge and at the mouth of Casper Creek, Bent places an 'X' where Collins [soldiers] was attacked. Below that, he writes 'this band made 1st charge,' indicating the Dog Soldiers concealed along the bank of the river. This is reiterated by the memo written across the bottom of the page: 'Note: D. Soldiers were closer to Collins [soldiers]than other bands.'"[94]

This map clearly shows where Bent annotated the Cheyenne military societies were stationed by each society, separate from one another, and then attacked together as a military society.[95]

Shifting our focus back to the Little Bighorn, we look at Walking Hunter, a Hunkpapa Lakota warrior and veteran of the Battle who belonged to the Fox warrior military society. He told David Humphreys Miller an interesting story pertaining to Fox warriors fighting the Reno Battalion in the Valley Fight. The Fox warriors were the military society chosen as the Akicita, or camp police, prior to the Battle. Walking Hunter told Miller that the Fox warrior's headsman, a war chief known as Black Moon, was killed in the Valley Fight. Walking Hunter said, "Furious at the killing of Black Moon, we Foxes charged north, chanting our society songs."[96]

In chapter 15 we told the story from Kill Eagle, the Sihasapa (Blackfeet) Lakota Chief. His was the only account I found in the historical record that told of Dog Soldiers fighting at the Little Bighorn. Regarding the Valley Fight, he said that Sitting Bull himself told him that Reno attacked on the right near Sitting Bull's tipi and was immediately engaged by the famous dog soldiers. To be clear here, we do not know if he is stating the Cheyenne Dog Soldiers, or is he referring to warriors from the Dog Soldier Band, which was at one time a band among the Cheyenne tribe,comprised of Cheyenne, Lakota, and Arapaho people.[97]

The famous Cheyenne warrior Brave Bear added some information to the history of Cheyenne military societies during the Battle of the Little Bighorn. Brave Bear fought against the Reno Battalion in the Valley Fight and later against the Custer Battalion. "We were all singing our different society songs, some singing death songs, as this is the custom among all the Indians in going into battles. They also sing these songs when they are attacked and [are] in tight places."[98]

In 1927, Kate Bighead, the sister of Ice and aunt of Noisy Walking, told Dr. Marquis she begged Ice to give her a horse during the Battle so she could go and find Noisy Walking. She wanted to go and watch the Battle, as well as sing strong heart songs for him. She said, "The

Indians mostly were in warrior society bands at different places, because the men of each warrior society understood each other's ways. But all of them I could see on that side were Sioux, not Cheyenne."[99] Later in this same account, Kate described Lame White Man leading Cheyenne warriors to attack the soldiers. She never mentioned the Elkhorn Scrapers.

In Summary:

We have put forth oral history told to us that said four prominent Cheyenne warriors, Lame White Man, Ice (White Bull), Crazy Head, and Spotted Wolf, all fought in the Battle of the Little Bighorn. The oral history states all four were at one time Elkhorn Scraper military society men and that they led youngsters, some of whom were young Elkhorn Scraper society members, at the Battle of the Little Bighorn as well. Oral history and the historical record put these men fighting in and around Deep Ravine, Battle Ridge and near Last Stand Hill. One of these warriors, Lame White Man, was killed in the Battle, as was Ice's son, Noisy Walking. The historical record verifies this by way of testimony told from warriors who were veterans of the Battle. Oral history tells that Crazy Head's son, Ho'vese, was killed in the Battle as well. We have now introduced Ho'vese in the historical record as a listed Cheyenne casualty at the Battle of the Little Bighorn.

There is yet another Cheyenne warrior to introduce to the historical record as a casualty of the Battle. The warrior's name was Wears The Iron Shirt. Their history has been kept by the Thunder Hawk family from the Sicangu Lakota people, on the Rosebud Reservation in South Dakota.

We presented three oral history accounts that put six Cheyenne Kit Fox military society men fighting on what is called Battle Ridge (Custer Ridge) and within relatively close proximity to where Lame White Man and those who followed him engaged soldiers. While the historical record does confirm these six Cheyenne Kit Fox men fought at the Little Bighorn, coupled with one warrior's account of fighting with Lame White Man, no accounts were found to confirm that the Cheyenne Kit Fox military society members were fighting together as a unified force at the Little Bighorn.

Oral history long kept by the Cheyenne regarding their dead is now on the historical record. Oral history pertaining to this part of the Battle tells that more Cheyenne warriors were killed at the Battle of the Little Bighorn than previously recorded. Oral history also reveals that some of the Cheyenne who fought at the Little Bighorn were not only very young, but that some were young women as well. Oral history from Cheyenne People brought attention to the fact that possibly two Cheyenne women were killed fighting or as a result of their wounds suffered at the Battle of the Little Bighorn. The historical record turned up one account to confirm this.

We received more oral history regarding the number of Cheyenne and Lakota casualties, but at this time, we are unable to investigate and confirm all of the accounts. By simply looking at what is now known of the Cheyenne history, it is logical to more than entertain the notion and give serious consideration to what the historical record states about the number of warriors wounded and killed at the Battle of the Little Bighorn.

For instance, look at the Brings Plenty family history, which told of five brothers -- Brings Plenty, Plenty Holes, Medicine Cloud, White Coyote and Low Dog -- all fighting at the Battle. Add to it the untold history, which is not recorded in the historical record, that states Plenty Holes, Medicine Cloud and White Coyote were all killed during the Battle or died later due to wounds suffered. This is just one family's story.

We will continue to explore this history in the next chapter, with more untold history that pertains to more Cheyenne people being killed at the Battle than is recorded and in the historical record.

Only one account was found in the historical record that told of the warrior societies of the different tribes at the Little Bighorn fighting separately from their fellow tribesmen and by their societies at times during the Battle of the Little Bighorn. This came from Kate Bighead.

Notes

1. Personal communications with Chris Dixon. See Grinnell 1972, vol 2: 58-59. Chapman 2004: 109-110. There are many accounts in the literature of the Battle that seemingly coincide with Dixon's account. These include: Interview of John Stands In Timber by Don Rickey from notes dated August 18, 1956, Little Bighorn Battlefield National Monument. Stands In Timber and Liberty 1967: 197; and 2013: 365-366; Donahue 2018: 188-190.

2. Personal communications with Chris Dixon.

3. Personal communications with Tim Lame Woman Sr.- Cheyenne.

4. Personal communications with Gilbert Whitedirt-Cheyenne, Scott Doser, Eddie Whitedirt, Roger Red Hat-Cheyenne. See Crazy Head in Powell 1981, Vol 2: 1004-1005; Hardorff 1998: John Stands In Timber interview pp 167; Marquis 2003: 211.

5. Ibid.

6. Personal communications with Gilbert Whitedirt-Cheyenne, Keith Spotted Wolf-Cheyenne. Grinnell 1955: 337; Powell 1981, Vol 2: 956-962, 1000-1001 Hardorff 1998: 49, 53.

7. Personal communications with Keith Spotted Wolf-Cheyenne.

8. For Yellow Nose, see Grinnell 1955: 350-352; Powell 1981, Vol 2:1023-1024; Hardorff 1998: 53, 62-63.

9. For White Shield, see Grinnell 1955: 350-352; Powell 1981, Vol 2: 1000-1001; Also see Grinnell 1955: 350-352; Hardorff 1998: 48-53.

10. Personal communications with Roger Red Hat-Cheyenne. Keith Spotted Wolf told that Spotted Wolf

was an Elkhorn Scraper member.

11. Grinnell 1972, Vol 2: 59; Powell 1981, Vol 1: 451-461; Chapman 2004: 71-110, 171-173.

12. Ibid. For Lame White Man fighting at the Little Bighorn there are a number of sources to see: Stands In Timber and Liberty 1967: 194-205; Michno 1997: 195-213; Marquis 2003: 211, 231. Personal communications with Gilbert Whitedirt-Cheyenne, Scott Doser, Roger Red Hat-Cheyenne and Dennis Limberhand-Cheyenne.

13. Regardind Ice, see Powell 1981, Vol 2: 747-757, 774-776; Hardorff 1998: 37-40; Chapman in Promise 2004, was told Ice was Elkhorn Scraper society member at the Fetterman Fight in 1866, pp. 71, 86. For more examples of Ice's feats, see John Stands In Timber and Liberty 1967, *Cheyenne Memories*, pp. 105-106 and Grinnell 1923, Vol 2, pp. 115-117.

14. Personal communications with Roger Red Hat-Cheyenne.

15. Ibid.

16. Personal communications with Leroy Whiteman-Cheyenne.

17. Ibid.

18. Ibid.

19. Grinnell 1923, Vol 2: 48-50, 57.

20. Personal communications with Leroy Whiteman-Cheyenne.

21. Personal communications with Dwight Bull Coming-Cheyenne. For Yellow Nose accounts see Grinnell 1955: 351; Liberty 1996: 135; Hardorff 1998: 53-54, 62-66.

22. Personal communications with Donovan Taylor regarding his communications with Frank Long Jaw-

Cheyenne. See Hardorff 1998: John Stands In Timber interview pp 168; See Marquis 2003: 241, 255-256.

23. Personal communications with Eugene Limpy-Cheyenne.

24. Ibid. Personal communications with Chris Dixon, Leroy Whiteman-Cheyenne, Roger Red Hat-Cheyenne, Donovan Taylor-Cheyenne and Doug War Eagle-Minnikojou Lakota. See Stands In Timber and Liberty 1967: 194; 2013: 366-367, 374.

25. Stands In Timber and Liberty 1967: 194.

26. Personal communications with Dennis Limberhand-Cheyenne, Leroy Whiteman-Cheyenne and Donovan Taylor-Cheyenne.

27. Personal communications with Chris Dixon.

28. Personal communications with Doug War Eagle-Minnikojou Lakota.

29. Interview of John Stands In Timber by Don Rickey from notes dated August 18, 1956, Little Bighorn Battlefield National Monument.

30. Stands In Timber and Liberty 1967: 197; and 2013: 367. For Lame White Man fighting at the Little Bighorn there are a number of sources to see: Powell 1981 Vol 2: 1025-1028; Michno 1997: 195-213; Marquis 2003: 211, 231.

31. Personal communications with Chris Dixon.

32. Ibid.

33. Ibid and personal communications with Tim Lame Woman Sr.-Cheyenne.

34. Personal communications with Rick Two Dogs-Oglala Lakota.

35. Personal communications with Dennis

Limberhand-Cheyenne.

36. Personal communications with Roy Dean Bull Coming- Cheyenne.

37. The Yellow Nose narrative was originally published by an unknown author in the Chicago Record-Herald, September 1905. Re-published in The Indian School Journal in November of 1905 (6:1-2; 39-42). In 1912 published in the Chicago Inter-Ocean. Lastly, in 1992, published in the Bighorn Yellowstone Journal, 1, No. 3 (Summer 1992): 14-17.

38. Marquis 2003: 242, 379.

39. Powell 1981 Vol 2: 1020-1028, see note 7, pp. 1370; Grinnell 1955: 350; Miller 1985: 123-126; Michno 1997: 138-139, 195-201, 209-213.

40. Ibid.

41. Ibid. See Marquis 2003: 380-381.

42. Miller 1985: 125.

43. For Young Little Wolf, see Hardorff 1998: 90-92.

44. See *Wooden Leg* in Marquis 2003: 231; and see Kate Bighead in Marquis 1967; 87-88.

45. Powell 1981 Vol 2: 1020-1028, see note 7, pp. 1370; Grinnell 1955: 350; Miller 1985: 123-126; Michno 1997: 138-139, 195-201, 209.

46. Hardorff 1998: 152-156; Donahue 2009: 219-223.

47. Donahue 2009: 222-223.

48. Hardorff 1998: 143.

49. Donovan Taylor personal communications with Frank Long Jaw-Cheyenne.

50. Ibid.

51. Personal communications with Leroy Whiteman-Cheyenne.

52. Personal communications with Eugene Limpy-Cheyenne.

53. Liberty 1996: 135.

54. See the David Humphreys Miller collection, Faces of The Little Bighorn, Survivors, at https://davidhumphreysmiller.org.

55. Ibid.

56. Personal communications with Eugene Limpy-Cheyenne.

57. See the Dives Backward David Humphreys Miller collection, Faces of The Little Bighorn, Survivors, at https://davidhumphreysmiller.org.

58. Hardorff 1998: 37-38. Hardorff cited the Grinnell collection at the Autry Museum, Los Angeles, CA, Item 497 regarding Ice.

59. Stands In Timber and Liberty 2013: 378.

60. Marquis 1967: 80-96.

61. Eastman, "The Story of The Little Big Horn," 354, 357-358.

62. Regardind Ice, see Powell 1981, Vol 2: 747-757, 774-776. For Ice as the leader of Cheyenne at the Battle of the Little Bighorn see White Elk note 5, pp. 1367, to George Bird Grinnell, in Powell 1981, Vol 2.

63. For the Thunder Bear account see Hardorff 2005: 91.

64. Stands In Timber and Liberty 1967: 106, note 19.

65. Marquis 2003: 211.

66. Miller 1985: 48.

67. Stands In Timber and Liberty 2013: 276. Hardorff 1998: 167, from John Stands In Timber's Interview in 1956 with Little Bighorn Battlefield historian Don Rickey.

68. Personal communications with Renee Samson Flood. See https: //www.astonisher.com/archives/museum/spotted_wolf_little_big_horn.html.

69. Stands In Timber and Liberty 2013: 458-459.

70. Grinnell 1955: 353; Powell 1981 Vol 2: 1027.

71. Powell 1981 Vol 2: 1005.

72. Stands In Timber and Liberty 2013: 145, 205; Marquis 1967: 19, 94.

73. Powell 1981 Vol 2: 1005; Hunt 1987: 216-217, 221-222.

74. Stands In Timber and Liberty 1967: 204; Hardorff 1999: 78-82, 147-15; Marquis 2003: 267-269.

75. Hardorff 2005: 91.

76. Personal communications with Leroy Whiteman-Cheyenne

77. Ibid. Graham 1953: 54.

78. Personal communications with Roger Red Hat-Cheyenne.

79. See Florence Whiteman's account from her grandfather, Louis Dog, in Viola 1999: 47-49.

80. Pennington 2005: 188.

81. For the White Eagle interview, see Bureau of American Ethnography No 2811, 1910. Dr. Truman Michelson. Bureau of American Ethnology Catalogue of Manuscripts, National Museum of Natural History. https://edan.si.edu/slideshow/viewer/?damspath=/Public_Sets/NMNH/NMNH-RC- Anthropology/NMNH-RC-Anth-Archives/NMNH-RC-Anth-Archives-NAA/NAA-MS/NAA-MS-2811. Personal communications with Doug War Eagle-Minnekojou Lakota.

82. Graham 1953: 85-87.

83. Ibid.

84. Powell 1981 Vol 2: 1015-1016.

85. See the Red Hawk account in Hardorff 1997: 39.

86. For the Kill Eagle accounts see Graham 1953: 53-54.

87. Ibid.

88. Personal communications with Cal Thunder Hawk-Sicangu Lakota.

89. Personal communications with Leroy Whiteman-Cheyenne.

90. Personal communications with Doug War Eagle-Minnikojou Lakota.

91. Gordon Harper email on The Little Bighorn Proboard website, Jan of 2009.

92. Hyde 1968: 168-170, 200-201.

93. Hack 2010: 12.

94. Ibid, 20.

95. Ibid.

96. See the David Humphreys Miller collection at https://davidhumphreysmiller.org .

97. For the Kill Eagle account see Milligan 1976: 74. See chapter 16, note 33.

98. Hardorff 2005: 83.

99. Marquis 1967: 86.

19
The Family of She Bear and Nokotamae: One Family's Story of Sacrifice at the Little Bighorn

This following history came from Dayton Raben and his wife, Ann Strange Owl-Raben, both now deceased. Their daughter, Nico Strange Owl and their late nephew, Al Joe Strange Owl, then picked up the trail. Ann's sisters, Ruthie Shoulderblade, Florence Running Wolf, her husband Mike Running Wolf, and Charlotte Rockroads helped finish the story of this family's long-kept story of bravery and determination at the Battle of the Little Bighorn. Help and assistance came from Pauline Highwolf - Cheyenne, Donovan Taylor - Cheyenne, Vernon Sooktis - Cheyenne and James "Putt" Thompson.

Many names and stories related to the Battle of the Little Bighorn have yet to appear in print. That does not mean they have not been told.

What follows is just one family's history. After reading this incredible story, let your imagination run free and wonder how much more is out there.

~

The history of the Old She Bear and Nokotamae family's involvement at the Battle of the Little Bighorn first appeared in 2017, in *Ann Strange Owl: A Northern Cheyenne Memoir,* co-authored by Sharon L. Arms.

Ann referred to family history that her paternal grandfather, Strange Owl, was just a baby at the time of the Battle of the Little Bighorn. An older brother, Young She Bear, age 13 or 14, was in the Native Peoples Coalition Encampment as the Battle was fought, as was his older sister, White Face Woman, said to be 17 or 18. Young She Bear had been told to stay with his mother

Dayton Raben and Ann Strange Owl-Raben.

and take care of her. He didn't listen. Instead, he got a horse and rushed into the Battle. His sister, White Face Woman, got herself a horse, too, and went to chase him down. She is said to have actually ridden into the Battle. Young She Bear found his way into the fighting and was mortally wounded in the stomach.[1]

Three days after the Battle, Young She Bear died from his wounds. The family was moving towards where the town of Kirby, Montana, currently sits. Some years later, Ann's family built a rock cairn, where Young She Bear's head fell when he finally died.[2]

I first met Dayton Raben in 2019, then his wife Ann and their daughter, Nico. I had been given Ann and Dayton's names from James "Putt" Thompson. I had no idea of the Strange Owl family history Ann had published in 2017. After several phone calls, Dayton dropped the bombshell and told me the story Ann had put in her book. But he said, there was more!

Dayton told me the Young She Bear story and how the family marked his death site near Kirby, Montana. He then added that he had been told by Ann's family that Young She Bear had been left in the ceremonial way, to make his journey to the camp on the other side, near Birney, Montana. Dayton then provided me the family tree of Strange Owl, She Bear and White Face Woman's family. This document added much, much more to the family history. We were now on their trail.[3]

The family story starts with a Sans Arc Lakota warrior by the name of She Bear (Old She Bear) and his Southern Cheyenne wife, Nokotamae. They had four boys, She Bear (Young She Bear), Yellow Woman, Big Man and Strange Owl (John), and one daughter, White Face Woman (Blanche Smith).[4]

Old She Bear fought at the Battle of the Rosebud. He was mortally wounded there, shot through his hips. He was subsequently brought back to find the Native Peoples Coalition as they moved towards the Little Bighorn River. The historical record says Old She Bear was received by his family before he made his journey to the camp on the other side. After he was given his ceremonial burial rites, he was left in a tipi on Reno Creek.[5] Nokotamae led her family to catch up with the rest of the Native Peoples Coalition as the camps began to settle on the Little Bighorn River.

Up to this point on the research trail, Donovan and myself thought we had a good grasp of the Strange Owl family's history, until Al Joe Strange Owl started on the trail with us. It didn't take long for Al Joe to inform us of how little we really did know regarding Old She Bear and Nokotamae's family.

Al Joe Strange Owl.

As it turned out, Al Joe had been raised by his grandmother, Grace Strange Owl, the mother of Ann Strange Owl-Raben. Grace had married David Strange Owl and they had 11 children. David was the son of John Strange Owl, who as a youngster was in the Native Peoples Coalition encampment on the Little Bighorn, on June 25th, 1876.

According to Al Joe Strange Owl, whose Cheyenne name was Big Man,[6] Cheyenne tribal member Pauline Highwolf told him his namesake, Big Man, the brother of Young She Bear, Strange Owl and White Face Woman, son to Nokotamae and Old She Bear, fought at the Little Bighorn like his brother Young She Bear and was mortally wounded as well!

Al Joe was told the same story by his uncle, Mike Running Wolf, a Minnkojou Lakota Tribal member married to Florence, one of David and Grace Strange Owl's 11 children. Al Joe was told that Big Man eventually succumbed to his wounds and died. Big Man

Pauline Highwolf and Donovan Taylor at the death site of Big Man.

was ceremonially left to make his journey to the camp on the other side where he died, which is between Busby, Montana and Crow Agency, Montana.[7]

Up to this point, we knew:

- Old She Bear, mortally wounded at the Battle of the Rosebud.
- Left in a tipi on Reno Creek.
- Old She Bear and his wife, Nokotamae, as it now turned out, had two sons who died from wounds suffered from fighting at the Battle of the Little Bighorn, on June 25th, 1876. They were Young She Bear and Big Man.

There was more.

Ruthie Shoulderblade was one of David and Grace Strange Owl's children and sister to Ann Strange Owl-Raben, Florence Running Wolf and Charlotte Rock Roads. What Ruthie told Al Joe and Donovan Taylor (another relative to the Strange Owl family) was historical, to say the least.

Ruthie Shouldberblade -- Cheyenne

Ruthie Shoulderblade's mother, Grace Strange Owl, told her Nokotamae, the wife of Old She Bear and mother to Young She Bear and Big Man, herself died at the Little Bighorn! In fact, Ruthie showed them where Nokotamae's death site was at the Little Bighorn

Battlefield National Monument. Nokotamae was said to have fallen within a ravine that runs from the old buffalo trail, which is U.S. Highway 212, and goes up to the ground near the Indian Memorial and Last Stand Hill. Ruthie said Nokotamae was said to have fallen three quarters of a mile from Highway 212.[8]

Neither Ruthie, nor her sisters, Florence Running Wolf and Charlotte Rock Roads, knew how Nokotamae died. Was she killed fighting? Was she riding with the warriors and got too close? Or, perhaps, maybe it was the shock she experienced when she learned and possibly saw her two sons, both severely mortally wounded from fighting in the Battle? No one knows.[9] What we do know is that no Cheyenne women are known in the historical record as having died at the Battle of the Little Bighorn. This is historical.

Young She Bear and his brother, Big Man, are not in the historical record as listed Cheyenne casualties at the Little Bighorn either.

~

We have two more stories to add to the history of the Old She Bear and Nokotamae family.

The first is from Cheyenne tribal member and historian Vernon Sooktis, who informed me that his relative Black Horse, a renowned and powerful Cheyenne medicine man, was at the Battle of the Little Bighorn. Vernon's family history told that Black Horse, in the midst of doctoring and taking care of the wounded and dying Cheyenne after the Battle, was brought two young Cheyenne warriors to heal. Black Horse looked each over and then sadly informed those caring for these two youngsters that there was nothing he could do for them. Vernon informed me that protocols as to how to care for the wounded until a medicine man or woman could administer to them had to be followed at all times. In the rush to get these two young warriors help, these protocols had not been strictly adhered to.

Vernon was not ever told that these two youngsters were in fact the relatives of the Strange Owl family. However, when I shared the story of Young She Bear and Big Man with Vernon, his first thought was immediately to wonder if these were the two youngsters brought to Black Horse.[10]

Recall that Pauline Highwolf first told Al Joe about his namesake, Big Man, and where this young warrior had been buried. Donovan was able to track down Pauline, who graciously shared some interesting pieces pertaining to Big Man and his death site.

Pauline is a descendant of Susie Shot-In-The-Eye, a Lakota woman mentioned in chapter 12 who rode into the Battle and fought in the Valley Fight against the Reno Battalion. Pauline informed us that her father, Laverne Killsontop Wallowing, was in fact raised by David Strange Owl.[11]

Pauline Highwolf said that her father Laverne and her grandfather, John Killsontop, told her that Big Man had fought at the Little Bighorn and was mortally wounded. Those who were caring for him brought him as far as his condition would allow. When the Cheyenne with Big Man stopped by a spring that is just below a ridge which sits between Crow Agency, Montana and Busby, Montana, the young warrior died. Big Man was ceremonially placed here for him to start his journey to the camp on the other side. Rock cairns marked his death site for years.

When Pauline was a young girl, her family routinely traveled the road where Big Man was laid to rest. A wagon road of sorts had been made close to the rock cairns next to the spring. Pauline's family and many other Cheyenne People made it a priority to stop and pray for this young warrior, so he knew he was not forgotten by his Cheyenne people.[12]

As for Nokotamae and her history at the Little Bighorn, Pauline had been told that Nokotama had died there. Pauline was never told how Nokotamae died, or where she fell. Pauline had been told that Nokotamae was Big Man's mother.[13]

What is in the historical record and how do these stories match up against it?

The historical record does state Old She Bear was mortally wounded at the Battle of the Rosebud and it is recorded that he made his journey to the camp on the other side after he was brought back to his family. The historical record states he was left in a tipi on Reno Creek. One such account comes from Michael Reynolds, who was raised in Crow Agency and who rode over the Battlefield with countless Native and Army veterans of the Battle.[14] There is nothing found that told of the Old She Bear and Nokotamae family history.

David Humphreys Miller, who told the Old She Bear story in his book *Custer's Fall,* never mentioned Old She Bear's family. However, many years later he painted a John Strange Owl. In the subsequent story regarding John Strange Owl, it was said he was a warrior who fought at the Little Bighorn. There was no mention he was the son of Old She Bear, or the youngest child of the Old She Bear and Nokotamae family.[15]

The family tree supplied to us by Dayton Raben and his wife, Ann Strange Owl-Raben states John Strange Owl was born in 1872. John Strange Owl was an army scout at Fort Keogh, Montana. His U.S. Army records, also supplied by Dayton and Ann, state he was born in 1870.[16]

Could there have been another Cheyenne by the name of Strange Owl, who fought at the Little Bighorn? That would seem logically to be probable. Father Peter Powell listed a warrior by the name of Strange Owl as having fought at the Dull Knife/Mckenzie Fight, in Kaycee, Wyoming, in November of 1876.[17] There is no warrior by the name of Strange Owl, listed as a Battle participant on the document supplied by the Northern Cheyenne tribe.

Did John Strange Owl, the youngest child of Nokotamae and Old She Bear, fight at the Little Bighorn, with his two older brothers, Young She Bear and Big Man? The answer would be no, based solely on his age. This from the documents supplied by Dayton Raben and Ann Strange Owl-Raben.

The historical record has nothing to offer on Young She Bear, Big Man, their sister White Face Woman and another brother, Yellow Woman. None are listed on lists of warriors who fought at or were killed fighting at the Little Bighorn. There is nothing on this family from the Cheyenne Tribes document listing warriors who participated at the Little Bighorn.

There is nothing in the historical record on Nokotamae and her death at the Little Bighorn. In the previous chapter we presented history from Cheyenne tribal members like Leroy Whiteman and Roger Red Hat of Cheyenne people killed at the Little Bighorn and never in the historical record. It was Leroy who specifically said two Cheyenne women were said to have been killed at the Battle of the Little Bighorn.[18] Kill Eagle, the Sihasapa (Blackfeet) Lakota Chief had said, "There was a Cheyenne woman who had a revolver strapped on her and went into the fight and got killed!"[19] Is this Nokotamae? At this time, we can only present the history from the family and hope more families might come forward and add more.

In this and the previous chapter, we told of Michael Reynolds, who was present when his father, a government employee of the Crow Agency, interviewed many Native veterans of the Battle of the Little Bighorn. Reynolds, who certainly would have heard a number of stories from Native veterans, said in 1977 that there were, "War Women," of the Cheyenne at the Little Bighorn.[20] He said nothing more regarding the "War Women" of the Cheyenne, nor elaborated as to who told him such history.

Donovan Taylor interviewed Cheyenne Tribal member Steve Littlebird in 2019. Steve told Donovan, "There was talk there might have been secret woman warrior societies." That was all Steve knew and he could give no other Cheyenne tribal members names to follow up with.[21]

Lastly, there is this account in the A.B. Welch Dakota Papers. Welch had interviewed a man by the name of Bill Zahn in 1921, who told him, "This woman, Cow Boy, rode with the Indian warriors at the Battle of the Greasy Grass. She was the only woman in the surround." Welch then noted that she was the wife of Blue Thunder. A search for Blue Thunder in the historical record of listed warriors who fought at the Little Bighorn turned up no information and nothing was found on the woman, Cow Boy, related to the Little Bighorn.[22]

In Summary:

Nokotamae and Old She Bear's family history pertaining to their involvement at the Battle of the Little Bighorn is now in the historical record. Old She Bear, the father, died from wounds fighting at the Battle of the Rosebud. Nokotamae, the mother, died during or after the Battle of the Little Bighorn. Her family's history puts her death site within the Little Bighorn Battlefield National Monument's boundary.

Young She Bear and his brother, Big Man, are now on the historical record. We know their history and of their sacrifice. We now know these two youngsters fought at the Little Bighorn and died later because of their mortal wounds suffered fighting in the Battle. We now know where these two young warriors were laid to rest as well. Based on this one family's story, I feel confident in saying that among the Cheyenne and Lakota, at least, there would be many more like this. Perhaps others will come forward to share and add the names of their ancestors to the historical record.

While the accounts we presented do not present clear and precise details confirming that Cheyenne and other Native woman fought and died at the Little Bighorn, they certainly should open our eyes to more than just speculate about the possibility.

We are eternally grateful to the late Ann Strange Owl-Raben and her late husband Dayton Raben and late nephew, Al Joe Strange Owl. Many other family members have graciously helped this history come to life on paper. They are Nico Strange Owl, Ruthie Shoulderblade, Mike and Florence Running Wolf, Chalotte Rock Roads and Donovan Taylor. A big thanks to Pauline Highwolf, for her contributions that helped tell this family's history.

Notes

1. Strange Owl-Raben 2017: 2-3.

2. Ibid.

3. Personal communications with Dayton Raben, Ann Strange Owl-Raben-Cheyenne and Al Joe Strange Owl-Cheyenne.

4. Ibid.

5. Ibid. For accounts regarding Old She Bear, see Graham 1953: 98, the Feather Earring account. See David Humphreys Miller 1985: 75-76.

6. Personal communications with Al Joe Strange Owl-Cheyenne.

7. Ibid. Personal communications with Donovan Taylor-Cheyenne, Pauline Highwolf-Cheyenne, Mike and Florence Running Wolf-Minnikojou Lakota and Cheyenne, Ruthie Shoulderblade-Cheyenne and Charlotte Rock Roads-Cheyenne.

8. Ibid.

9. Ibid.

10. Personal communications with Vernon Sooktis-Cheyenne.

11. Personal communications with Pauline Highwolf-Cheyenne.

12. Ibid.

13. Ibid.

14. For accounts regarding Old She Bear, see Graham 1953: 98, the Feather Earring account. See Pennington 2005: 186, for the Reynolds account. See David Humphreys Miller 1985: 75-76.

15. For the Strange Owl account from David Humphreys Miller see the David Humphreys Miller collection at https://davidhumphreysmiller.org. Strange Owl is listed as an informant by Miller his book, in *Custer's Fall,* as well 1985: 263.

16. Personal communications with Dayton Raben and Ann Strange Owl-Raben-Cheyenne and their Daughter, Nico Strange Owl-Cheyenne.

17. See Strange Owl in Powell Vol 2. 1981: 1061, 1426.

18. Personal communications with Leroy Whiteman-Cheyenne and Roger Red Hat-Cheyenne.

19. For the Kill Eagle account of him telling of Cheyenne woman fighting at the Little Bighorn and carrying a revolver, see Graham 1953: 53-54.

20. Pennington 2005: 188; Donahue 2009: 367-370.

21. Donovan Taylor personal communications with Steve Littlebird-Northern Cheyenne.

22. Welch Dakota Papers 2017: 58. www.welchdakotapapers.com.

20
Last Stories and Last Stand Hill

This following history came from Jim Red Eagle - Nakota/Lakota, Dwight Bull Coming - Cheyenne, Vernon Sooktis -Cheyenne, Chester Whiteman - Cheyenne, Richard Iron Cloud - Oglala Lakota, Doug War Eagle -Minnikojou Lakota, Joe Brings Plenty - Minnikojou Lakota and Chris Dixon -independent researcher.

We are now at the point of our journey to put forth history told to us pertaining to the fighting near Last Stand Hill. Included is oral history of the fight in and around Deep Ravine with soldiers from E and F Companies who had been repulsed in the Ford D fight. Some of this fighting happened below and south of the famous Last Stand Hill. What follows is a brief summary to give you a firm grasp as to what happened at this final climatic part of America's greatest mystery.

Before proceeding, consider the following to understand what happened at the Little Bighorn. It comes from Native American people and First Nations people:

When one comes to the Little Bighorn Battlefield, one is inexplicably drawn to Last Stand Hill. As readers of American history, we were taught that General Custer and his heroic band of cavalry troopers chose this hill because it was a good defensive position against overwhelming numbers of warriors.

What if, it was just the opposite? What if the Seventh Calvary could go no further and Last Stand Hill chose them, instead? This sums up the feelings of the tribes, bands and descendants of those Native American People and First Nations People who had been at the Little Bighorn.

~

It was Chris Dixon who first shared history with me regarding Crazy Horse and his involvement with fighting near Last Stand Hill. Dixon had been told that after fighting the Reno Battalion in the Valley Fight, Crazy Horse came back through the Native Peoples coalition encampment. He splashed across the Little Bighorn at the crossing at Medicine Tail Coulee. Right behind him were Cheyenne and Lakota warriors, some of whom belonged to his warrior society, the Last Born Child Society.

Crazy Horse was now in the area called Greasy Grass Ridge. From here, according to Dixon, Crazy Horse and his followers moved closer to the Seventh Cavalry Troopers of L and I Companies. L Company troopers were now on what is called Calhoun Hill, while behind them, below Custer Ridge (Battle Ridge), I Company and the horses of I and L Companies were held. Crazy Horse and his followers were now joined by White Bull, the Minnikojou war chief and his followers. Between these two formidable groups, they assaulted I and L Companies. White Bull and Crazy Horse were said to have done bravery runs right among the troopers of both companies.[1]

After scattering and for all intent purposes destroying I and L Companies, Crazy Horse and his followers continued on and rode behind Last Stand Hill. Crazy Horse and his followers continued through the cemetery enroute to fight below Last Stand Hill. After fighting in this area, Crazy Horse, according to Dixon, was now in or near Deep Ravine. Twice on this journey, Crazy Horse and his men had run into Cheyenne warriors who had fought in the area of where both of the fords labeled D are located. It was here that Crazy Horse and his followers ran into the Cheyenne warrior Little Horse and some of his followers -- the very same Little Horse Tim Lame Woman Sr. claimed led the resistance efforts in the area of the fords labeled Ford D.[2]

Jim Red Eagle, Nakota / Lakota historian, shared an account of Crazy Horse that seemingly picks right up along with what Chris Dixon had been told. Jim had been told there was a Cheyenne warrior by the name of Black Bear riding with Crazy Horse when he led the last charge against the soldiers defending Last Stand Hill. Jim knew nothing more about this Cheyenne warrior.[3]

~

Oral history pertaining to fighting in and around Deep Ravine and Last Stand Hill comes from two Minnikojou Lakota men.

The first, Doug War Eagle, who we have featured throughout this book, shared some lore regarding Sans Arc Lakota and Minnekojou Lakota warriors fighting near Deep Ravine. Doug said Minnikojou warriors crossed the Little Bighorn River close to the mouth of Deep Ravine and engaged what he called the "gray riders," near Deep Ravine. The "gray riders" would be the troopers of E Company, U.S. Seventh Cavalry, whose gray horses stood out among the other companies of the Seventh Cavalry. These Minnikojou were led by Spotted Elk, who was also called Big Foot, as well as Lights, Hump and Touch the Clouds. The Sans Arc were led by Spotted Eagle.[4]

Doug War Eagle said that these Minnikojou and Sans Arc warriors suffered many casualties during this part of the Battle. Doug stated that in the Deep Ravine fighting and then the subsequent assault of Last Stand Hill, no fewer than 163 Lakota were wounded. Many of these warriors never known by whites or listed in the historical record died after the Battle as a result of their wounds. Doug said a big proportion of these wounded were Sans Arc and Minnikojou Lakota.[5]

Joe Brings Plenty, a Minnikojou Lakota Tribal member, added to this history of the Minnikojou fighting near Deep Ravine and below Last Stand Hill. Joe Brings Plenty's family story told of five brothers, Brings Plenty, Plenty Holes, Medicine Cloud, White Coyote and Low Dog, who all fought at the Little Bighorn. These brothers ended up fighting near Deep Ravine and below Last Stand Hill. Sadly, Plenty Holes, Medicine Cloud and White Coyote were killed in the Battle or died from wounds suffered there. These three brothers are not listed in the historical record among the warriors killed at the Little Bighorn.[6]

~

There is some interesting oral history from Cheyenne people when it comes to the fighting in and around Last Stand Hill. One such story has remained quiet and out of the historical record, despite it involving General George Custer himself.

The first history to add comes from the Cheyenne tribe and the document supplied to us listing their warriors who fought at the Little Bighorn. A Cheyenne warrior by the name of Chief Comes In Sight and some of his followers had joined the Native Peoples coalition as it moved for the Little Bighorn. Chief Comes In Sight had fought at the Battle of the Rosebud, where he was unhorsed and then subsequently rescued off the battlefield by his sister, Buffalo Calf Road Woman. To the Cheyenne People, the Battle of the Rosebud is called, "Where the Girl Saved Her Brother."[7]

Chief Comes In Sight is listed as the first Cheyenne warrior to have ridden over Last Stand Hill during the fighting there at the end of the Battle. He is said to have charged right into the soldiers from atop his horse. Miraculously, he survived this heroic deed, and the Battle.[8]

Chris Dixon had been told this history as well.[9]

Cheyenne Tribal member Dwight Bull Coming informed me that a Cheyenne warrior by the name of Porcupine had in fact captured a guidon from one of the companies of the Seventh Cavalry during the Battle. Porcupine was a Dog Soldier. In chapter 16, Dwight shared that he was told Porcupine had fought in the Ford D fight. Dwight said Porcupine got this guidon somewhere near and below Last Stand Hill.[10]

Another well-kept piece of Cheyenne history was shared by Vernon Sooktis and Chester Whiteman. Both said that a Cheyenne woman by the name of Scalp Woman had in fact been the woman responsible for puncturing General George Custer's eardrum with her bone sewing needle.[11] While the story does not tell who killed General George Custer, it does give a glimpse into the events that happened to his body after the Battle was over.

~

Richard Iron Cloud, Oglala Lakota, told a story from his late cousin, Manuel Iron Cloud, of Eagle Bear, a Lakota warrior, as being the warrior who killed Mitch Bouyer, the scout for the Seventh Cavalry. This event happened somewhere towards the end of the Battle.[12] Eagle Bear was the son of Knife Chief, an Oglala war chief, who was also the camp crier for Sitting Bull.[13] Knife Chief had been wounded in the Valley Fight with the Reno Battalion and was said to have been administered to by a Cree medicine man.[14]

Veteran researcher and historian Michael Donahue was told a story by Manuel Iron Cloud about the killing of Mitch Bouyer. Donahue worked as a seasonal interpreter at the Little Bighorn Battlefield for 35 years. Manuel Iron Cloud worked as a seasonal interpreter for the National Park Service at several different locations, one of which was the Little Bighorn Battlefield.[15] He and Donahue became friends and discussed the Battle at length. Manuel told Donahue that at the end of the Battle, a soldier pleaded for his life and that this soldier spoke the Lakota language. Donahue could not recall at this time if Manuel had specifically said this was Mitch Bouyer.[16] It has been said and written that Bouyer could speak the Lakota and Dakota dialects.[17]

~

What is in the historical record and how do these stories match up against it?

There is an abundance of stories regarding the fighting near Last Stand Hill in the historical record. What follows are just a few we found as we followed the evidence from the oral history shared with us.

Regarding Mitch Bouyer and his death: Thomas Leforge, as we wrote in chapter 16, was a dear friend of Bouyer who took in Bouyer's widowed wife, Magpie Outside, after the Battle. Some years after the Battle, Leforge had been told by a Sioux warrior who was said to be a veteran of the Battle of the Little Bighorn that Bouyer was found wounded at the end of the Battle. He had been shot in the back. Bouyer was subsequently killed by the Sioux near the Little Bighorn River and been thrown into the river, where his vest was later found.[18]

As researchers we must ask ourselves how can this account be analyzed. Knowing that Leforge and Bouyer were close, that Leforge took in Bouyer's widowed wife, and assuming Leforge simply wanted to know the truth of what happened to his friend, we can reasonably assume this account has merit. If Leforge thought it was not true, why would he have told it?

Frenchy Dillon, Thomas Leforge's great-grandson, had been told the same story. So, the trail continues to move forward.[19]

Then, you have the account from Sage, also known as Well-Knowing One, an Arapaho warrior who fought at the Battle. At this time, I can only cite Bruce Brown and his Astonisher webpage, 100 Voices From the Little Bighorn. Brown stated Well-Knowing One's account was strikingly very similar to what Leforge had said: that a wounded Bouyer was found at the end of the Battle by Sioux warriors, killed, and then thrown into the Little Bighorn River.[20]

This is as far as we could take the account of Mitch Bouyer. The family of the warrior who is said to have killed Bouyer still keeps this story. Thomas Leforge told a story that is relatively the same. Lastly, an Arapaho warrior who fought at the Little Bighorn told this story and it is remarkably the same story as well.

~

We continued to look for more information about the Minnikojou Lakota and Sans Arc Lakota who fought near Deep Ravine and below Last Stand Hill. While nothing was found in the historical record, there is this account from the Minnikojou Lakota Warrior, Flying By. A member of Crazy Horse's Last Born Child society, Flying By was also the son of Lame Deer, a Minnikojou Lakota war chief. Lame Deer fought at the Little Big Horn and, I was told by Sicangu Lakota Tribal Historian Victor Douville, led Dog Soldiers there.[21]

Flying By said, "More Sans Arc killed than any other tribe. Sans Arc were next in numbers to the Minniconjou."[22]

A further dive into the Sans Arc and Minnikojou Lakota presence at the Little Bighorn, namely a search for the Brings Plenty family history, produced two accounts. The first came from Iron Hawk and was found in the book, *Black Elk Speaks.* Iron Hawk simply mentioned Brings Plenty as a warrior who fought at the Battle and who killed a soldier with his war club.[23]

In the second account, which comes from David Humphreys Miller, Brings Plenty is said to have unhorsed a soldier and then killed him with his war club. In the next sentence, Miller wrote, "Almost the entire gray-horse troop was now wiped out."[24]

The statement about the gray horse troop would be in regards to E Company of the Seventh Cavalry. E Company was one of the five companies in the Custer Battalion believed to have fought in the area of the two fords labeled Ford D, before retreating to the current Little Bighorn Battlefield National Monument Cemetery. From there, elements of E Company fought below Last Stand Hill, on Cemetery Ridge, and some stayed in the Cemetery, where they watched as Last Stand Hill fell. They certainly would have realized how desperate a situation they now were in and vacated this area. Their only hope, an attempt to run for the Little Bighorn River.

This history from Miller looks to match that from Doug War Eagle. Doug put Minnikojou and Sans Arc warriors fighting in this episode.[25] There was no mention of Brings Plenty's four brothers fighting at the Battle, three of which, family oral history states, were killed and are not in the historical record.[26]

With the above information from the Brings Plenty family and Doug War Eagle, it is time to return to an account from the Minnikojou Lakota, Red Horse, mentioned in chapter 11. Red Horse said, "We lost 136 killed and 160 wounded." This number is strikingly close to the number of Lakota Doug War Eagle said were wounded, which was 163, and in just one part of the Battle.[27]

James H. Howard received history from Dakota People while in Canada doing field work. One such account came from Pete Lethbridge, which was in regards to his mother, who as a youngster was in the encampment at the Little Bighorn. This very detailed and very possible never before told event that took place involved General George Custer.

'My mother was in the camp at the Battle of the Little Bighorn. She was nine years old at the time. She remembers one young man, a crazy boy, who stripped Custer's uniform from his body and put it on. He also had a bugle he picked up on the battlefield. He got on his horse and paraded around, but when he blew the bugle his horse bucked him off.'[28]

The historical record has told that General Custer wore a buckskin outfit on the Little Bighorn campaign. Could this account simply mean the buckskin outfit was the General's uniform? Regardless of your interpretation and supposing it was another officer or soldier of the Seventh who was stripped, this account is still one of most detailed ever told.

~

Tall Bull, a Cheyenne Dog Man military society member, shared an account of the Cheyenne warriors who charged Last Stand Hill and just how deadly an undertaking this was. "The horse I was riding had seven balls in him and dropped dead under me just before I got to the monument." This would be reference to the current monument on Last Stand Hill to commemorate the U.S. Seventh Cavalry dead.[29]

Here is an account that warrants a look for the detailed description of the warrior said to be the killer of General George Custer. As if that it is not enough, the account comes from none other than the noted and renowned Hunkpapa Lakota warrior, Rain In The Face. De Cost Smith took this account from Rain In the Face in 1890.

When I told him (Rain In The Face) the white people believe it was he who killed General Custer, his answer was, "No that is not so. I did not kill him. It was a young Cheyenne named Tce-tan' (Hawk) who killed Long Hair." This youth, according to Rain In The Face, crossed into British Territory with the rest of the hostiles, but did not come back to this side at the time of the surrender. Rain In The Face told me he knew this young Cheyenne killed Custer because he was near enough to them both to see what occurred, and added that he (Rain In The Face) and the young Cheyenne were, as it happened, painted and ornamented in a similar manner, and rode horses of the same (buckskin) color. It was this resemblance, he thought, which must have given rise to the mistaken report. According to his story, he and the young Cheyenne both wore long war bonnets. They were both stripped to the breechclout, with their bodies painted yellow, and each had a blue shield."[30]

There is much detail in this Rain In The Face account. Both he and the young Cheyenne named Hawk are near one another at the last brutal fighting on none other than the famous Last Stand Hill. Both are painted, not only that, but both painted yellow. Both ride buckskin horses and both have blue shields. What are the chances of all of those being the same? Is it a little too detailed, perhaps?

There is one account in the historical record of a Cheyenne warrior named Hawk fighting at the Little Bighorn that claims Rain In The Face said Hawk did kill General Custer. There is no warrior by the name of Hawk in the document listing Cheyenne warriors who fought at the Little Bighorn provided by the Northern Cheyenne tribe.

I am not sure what to make of Rain's story, even after all these years of reading it over and over. There is nothing in any of his other interviews mentioning a young Cheyenne warrior named Hawk, nor did Rain In The Face ever mention he had painted himself yellow that day.

~

It's time to look at Crazy Horse and the story from Jim Red Eagle regarding a young Cheyenne by the name of Black Bear. Jim Red Eagle had been told that Black Bear rode with Crazy Horse and those warriors who followed him at the Little Bighorn when they charged Last Stand Hill.

No accounts from other historians or from known warriors said to have fought and ridden with Crazy Horse at the Little Bighorn contain any mention of a Cheyenne warrior by the name of Black Bear. Searching Cheyenne accounts, some interesting pieces that have been hidden in the historical record showed themselves.

It was Cheyenne war chief Two Moons who mentioned a Cheyenne warrior by the name of Black Bear in 1909.

"Then I rode on up the ridge to the left. I met an Indian with a big warbonnet on, and right there I saw a wounded soldier. I killed him and jumped off my horse and scalped him. The Indian I met was Black Bear, a Cheyenne."[31]

Two Moons said nothing more regarding Black Bear. What is so interesting here is that of the Cheyenne "suicide boys" killed at the Little Bighorn in the historical record, one was named Black Bear. This youngster was also called Crippled Hand or Closed Hand.[32] What is even more interesting, albeit extremely sad, is the fact that Black Bear was killed in the fighting near Last Stand Hill with another young Cheyenne "suicide warrior," Limber Bones.[33] Another of the young Cheyenne "suicide warriors," Cut Belly, also called Open Belly, was mortally wounded in the fighting in the cemetery, very near where today the Stone House sits. He was rescued off the Battlefield by fellow warriors, but died later.[34]

Today, Black Bear's (Crippled Hand or Closed Hand) and Limber Bones' tombstones rest near one another at the Battlefield. They sit next to Last Stand Hill, but more comforting now is the fact that they sit near the Indian Memorial as well. Today there is also a tombstone in the Little Bighorn Battlefield National Monument Cemetery to remember Cut Belly.

In Summary:

We were very fortunate to catch some hidden and unique stories of Cheyenne and Lakota history as it pertains to the fighting near Deep Ravine and Last Stand Hill. These may not add a great deal to the study of the Battle; however, we hope that by sharing these hidden treasures, those who the story told of are now on the historical record, and their families and loved ones can rest a little easier knowing they won't be forgotten.

Notes

1. Personal communications with Chris Dixon.

2. Ibid. Personal communications with Tim Lame Woman Sr.-Cheyenne

3. Pesonal communications with Jim Red Eagle-Nakota/Lakota.

4. Personal communications with Doug War Eagle-Minnikojou Lakota.

5. Ibid.

6. Personal communications with Joe Brings Plenty-Minnikojou Lakota.

7. For the Chief Comes In Sight account of his fighting at the Battle of the Rosebud and rescue by his sister, Buffalo Calf Road Woman, see Powell 1981 Vol 2: 954-1002.

8. Chief Comes In Sight is listed as first Cheyenne warrior to ride across Last Stand Hill during the assault of the Custer Battalion who taken up positions here. This document was supplied to us by the Northern Cheyenne Tribe.

9. Personal communications with Chris Dixon.

10. Personal communications with Dwight Bull Coming-Cheyenne. Porcupine is listed as a Cheyenne warrior on the document of Cheyenne warriors said to have fought at the Little Bighorn by the Northern Cheyenne Tribe.

11. Personal communications with Vernon Sooktis-Cheyenne and Chester Whiteman-Cheyenne.

12. Personal communications with Richard Iron Cloud-Oglala Lakota.

13. Hardorff 1997: 42-48; Hardorff 2005: 146.

14. Mails 1979: 37-38.

15. Personal communications with Richard Iron Cloud-Oglala Lakota.

16. Personal communications with Michael Donahue.

17. Personal communications with Frenchy Dillon-Crow. Frenchy is the great-grandson to Thomas Leforge, the scout. See Donovan 2008: 161.

18. For the Leforge account, see Brue Brown's Astonisher website at 100 Voices from the Little Bighorn. www.astonisher.com/archives/museum/thos_laforge_big_horn. Brown cited *The Custer Battle Book* by Herbert Coffeen, A Reflection Book, Carlton Press, Inc., New York, 1964 p 47 -- 48.

19. Personal communications with Frenchy Dillon-Crow. Frenchy is the great-grandson of Thomas Leforge.

20. For the Well-Knowing account, see Brue Brown's Astonisher website at 100 Voices from the Little Bighorn. www.astonisher.com/archives/museum/thos_laforge_big_horn.

21. Personal communications with Victor Douville-Sicangu Lakota Tribal Historian.

22. Flying By account with Walter Mason Camp July 27, 1912, at Standing Rock Agency. See Gordon Harper Appendices 3.23.

23. See the Brings Plenty account in Neihardt: 1972: 127; and DeMallie 1984: 192. Personal communications with Joe Brings Plenty Sr.-Minnikojou Lakota.

24. David Humphreys Miller 1985: 137.

25. Personal communications with Doug War Eagle-Minnikojou Lakota.

26. Personal communications with Joe Brings Plenty-Minnikojou Lakota.

27. For the Red Horse account, see Graham 1953: 60.

28. For the Pete Lethbridge account, see Howard 2014: 44.

29. See Tall Bull's account in Hardoff 1998: 46-47.

30. See Rain In The Face in Smith 1949: 233-234.

31. Hardorff 1998: 132.

32. See John Stands In Timber and Liberty 1967: 194, 204; Hardorff 1999: 71-73, 82, 148-149; Marquis 2003: 268.

33. Ibid.

34. Ibid.

Afterword

Leroy Whiteman -- Cheyenne

It was the 100th year anniversary ceremonies to commemorate the Battle of the Little Bighorn, and Leroy Whiteman finally had had enough. Fed up with the treatment that Native People received when they visited the Battlefield and the lack of acknowledgment that National Park Service gave to the victorious side of the Battle of the Little Bighorn, especially Leroy's Cheyenne people, this tough and determined man decided he was going to do something about it.

Today, once the ceremonies draw to a close, riders from the assorted tribes and bands who fought at the Little Bighorn charge from U.S. Highway 212, up a ravine, all the way to the ground that runs near the Indian Memorial. These riders are not permitted to charge the famous Last Stand Hill.

What Leroy Whiteman did on June 25th, 1976, still resonates to this day. There was a great deal of media coverage that year, with the 100th year anniversary and the presence of AIM. That didn't bother Leroy. He and his family brought around 20 horses to the Battlefield that day.

Once the talks, ceremonies and excitement settled down from the festivities that day and with the overflow crowd still in attendance, Leroy struck. He and his family released the horses, which, by the way, had no riders. Pandemonium was the order of the day among National Park Service officials and the like, but not so for the Native American People in attendance. They knew what was happening.

The horses Leroy and his family let go were to honor the real number of the Cheyenne dead from this Battle. If a Native person caught one of these beautiful horses, they got to keep it.

~

At the fiftieth anniversary ceremonies to remember the Battle of the Little Bighorn, two Cheyenne warriors were thrust to the forefront of history. These two veterans of the Battle had been honored by their fellow Cheyenne veterans at this significant event. Both warriors were bestowed the honor of, "about one of the first to make attack on Tom Custer in Battle of Little Bighorn, June 25, 1876." Their names were White Horse and Black Whetstone. Both of their names were recorded at this event and finally captured by history.

The subsequent search for these two warriors has proved elusive. Neither warrior was on the list of known warriors at the Little Bighorn provided by the Northern Cheyenne Tribe.

Wallace Bearchum, Northern Cheyenne Tribal member and Tribal Services Director, informed us that it was his belief that White Horse was in fact an Elkhorn Scraper military society warrior at the time of the Battle.

All that could be found regarding Whetstone is in Father Peter Powells Vol. 2 of *People of The Sacred Mountain*. Powell said Whetstone was a, "Northern warrior." There is no mention of him as fighting at the Little Bighorn.

What does this mean at this point? After being on this trail for over 30 years of my life, with the last 15 extensively engrossed in this research, I have no doubt whatsoever what was told about these two warriors, especially in light that it appears to have come from and in the presence of their fellow Little Bighorn veterans, is the absolute truth. With that, it's time to re-introduce to the historic record the names of two more Cheyenne veterans of the Battle of the Little Bighorn, Whetstone and White Horse.

~

I am told by the local residents of Crow Agency that just about the time Spring comes to the North country, if one goes to the Little Bighorn Battlefield in the late afternoons you catch a glimpse of something very special. Most days the Battlefield is eerily quiet, serene, and deserted except for a few visitors just passing through this part of Montana.

The place to be is on Calhoun Hill, named for Lieutenant James Calhoun, the brother-in-law of General George Custer, who perished here with L Company. It is here that something happens as magical and timeless as the changing of the seasons.

The prairie chickens show up.

Not only that, but male prairie chickens perform their ritual mating dance, stomping their feet and raising their tail feathers to show off for any females watching.

What does this have to do with Battle, you ask?

It's very profound, actually, when one realizes what the Prairie Chicken represents to the Dakota and Lakota People.

Back in chapter 12, I wrote of Ella Deloria, a Native American ethnographer who recorded that six animal spirits, the bull (buffalo), the prairie chicken, the rabbit, the skunk, the badger, and the owl organized the first societies among the Dakota. Each had a guardian spirit. From these societies came leaders of the people, the Itaca or Chiefs, which were the bull (buffalo). The owl, called the Miwatani, provided wisdom and council. Finally, the camp police or soldiers came from the kit fox and badger, as well as prairie chickens, also called the stout-hearts.

It's really not that hard to imagine. The warriors who fought at the Little Bighorn are still there, albeit in spirit. One of which was the stouthearted Prairie Chicken.

Acknowledgments

As with any book and project of this scope, many people helped. It all started because of James "Putt" Thompson, and it all started at his place of business, The Custer Battlefield Trading Post.

From there, I was extremely fortunate to meet Mike Donahue and Chris Dixon. Very soon I got even luckier, and met Dennis Limberhand, Linwood Tall Bull, Leroy Whiteman, Gilbert Whitedirt, Faron Iron and Wallace Bearchum. Then, as fate would have it, I met Donovan Taylor, my Cheyenne brother, without whom, this book never happens.

And so, Donovan and I chased this history as best we could. Boy, did it take us for a ride! The best part we both agree on, was all the great people we met along the way and now call friends. Many, have sadly left this realm for their journeys. With that being said, we want to say thank you, thank you, to you all who helped. We both want to say a big sincere thank you to our wives, who we both agree that we have a great deal of time that we need to make up to. For me, it's Melinda and for Donovan, it is Charie Mae and their son, Deanjravon.

Thank you Matthew Wayne Selznick for putting this book together and everything else along the way. To the great ledger artist and friend, Linda Haukaas, for the book cover and other art featured in the book, many thanks dear friend. And to Peter Gibbs, a friend a friend would like to have.

It was Ben Rhodd who first helped me get going on the trail to find this oral history. He took the time and introduced me to Victor Douville. Next came Phil Two Eagle, Sam High Crane, Garvard Good Plume Jr., Basil BraveHeart, Harold Salway, John Eagle Shield Sr., Henry Quick Bear, Ronnie Cutt, Chico Her Many Horses, Jim Red Eagle, Frenchy Dillon and Rick Two Dogs.

Paula and Arvol Looking Horse have been our biggest fans and I can never thank the both of them enough.

To my Dakota friends, thank you to Akisa Peters, Vine Marks and Dianne Desrosiers.

To the Great Cheyenne people, I want to say thanks to Keith Spotted Wolf, Dwight Bull Coming, Chester Whiteman, Roy Dean Bull Coming, Rufus Spear, Eddie Whitedirt, Vernon Sooktis, Ruthie Shoulderblade and Pauline Highwolf.

Over in Arapaho country, a big thank you to Bill Goggles, Martin Blackburn, Marcus Dewey, Cletus Yellow Plume and Devin Oldman.

To those just across the Medicine Line, a thank you to Mitchell BigHunter, Rod Alexis, Joanne Pompana, James Desjarlais and Ozzie McKay.

Back in Montana, a special thanks to Gilbert Birdinground, Alvin Windyboy Sr., Michael Black Wolf, and Jimmy Stgoddard.

Thank you to Steve Andrews, Will Hutchison, Don Fisk, Bob Snelson, Randy Tucker, James Ritchie, Mark Lee Gardner and Inkpa Mani

About the Authors

Lance J. Dorrel

Lance J Dorrel is a Native American and First Nations Ethnographer, historian and writer.

His first book, *A Dance With Death: An Irish Soldier of Fortune At The Little Bighorn,* was published in 2019. Dorrel has had an interest in the Battle of the Little Bighorn since childhood.

Donovan Taylor

Donovan Taylor is a Cheyenne Tribal member and historian. He has lived in the shadow of the Little Bighorn Battlefield his entire life. A member of the Dog Soldier warrior society himself, Donovan holds the prestigious position as Drum Keeper today within the Dog Soldiers of the Northern Cheyenne People.

Bibliography

Books

Afton, Jean, Halass, David Fridtjof and Masich, Andrew E.
1997 *Cheyenne Dog Soldiers: A Ledgerbook History of Coups and Combat*. Denver: Colorado Historical Society and the University Press of Colorado.

Amos Bad Heart Bull, Amos and Helen H. Blish
2017 *A Pictographic History of the Oglala Sioux*. Drawings by Amos Bad Heart Bull. Lincoln: University of Nebraska Press, 50th Anniversary Edition.

Bailyn, Bernard
2012 *The Barbarous Years: The Conflict of Civilizations, 1600-1675*. New York: Alfred A. Knope.

Berthrong, Donald J.
1963 *The Southern Cheyennes*. Norman: University of Oklahoma Press.

Bourke, John G.
1971 *On the Border With Crook*. Lincoln: University of Nebraska Press.

Bray, Kingsley M.
2006 *Crazy Horse: A Lakota Life*. Norman: University of Oklahoma Press.

Brill, Charles
2001 *Custer, Black Kettle, and The Fight on the Washita*. Norman: University of Oklahoma Press.

Burst, James. Pohanka, Brian and Barnard, Sandy.

2005 *Where Custer Fell*. Photographs of the Little Bighorn Battlefield Then and Now. Norman: University of Oklahoma Press.

Carver, Jonathan
1956 *Travels through the interior parts of North America, in the years* 1766, 1767, *and* 1768. Minneapolis: Ross and Haines.

Chapman, Serle L.
2004 *Promise: Bozeman's Trail to Destiny. Park City, UT*. Pavey Western Publishing.

Clark, Ella E.
1988 *Indian Legends from the Northern Rockies*. Norman: University of Oklahoma Press.

Clark, William Philo.
1982 *The Indian Sign Language*. 1885. Lincoln: University of Nebraska Press.

The Edward Clown Family as told to William B. Mattson
2016 *Crazy Horse: The Lakota Warrior's Life & Legacy*. Layton, UT: Gibbs Smith.

Cowdrey, Mike
2006 *American Indian Horse Masks*. Nicasio, CA: Hawk Hill Press.

Curtis, Edwin S.
1908 *The North American Indian. Volume Three. The Teton Sioux, Yanktonai, and Assiniboine*. Cambridge: The University Press.

Deloria, Vine Jr.
2006 *The World We Used to Live In*. Golden, CO: Fulcrum Publishing.

DeMallie, Raymond J., ed.

1984 *The Sixth Grandfather: Black Elk's Teachings Given to John G Neihardt,* Lincoln: University of Nebraska Press.

DeMallie, Raymond J. and Parks, Douglas R., ed.
1987 *Sioux Indian Religion*. Norman: University of Oklahoma Press.

Denig, Edwin Thompson, Edited by J.N.B. Hewitt
2000 *The Assiniboine: Forty-sixth Annual Report of the Bureau of American Ethnology*. Norman: University of Oklahoma Press.

Densmore, Frances, Edited by Joseph A. Fitzgerald
2016 *World of the Teton Sioux Indians: Their Music, Life and Culture*. Bloomington: World Wisdom, Inc.

Dixon, Chris
2018 *Crazy Horse and the Cheyenne*. The Brian C. Pohanka 32nd Annual Symposium, Custer Battlefield Historical and Museum Association.

Dixon, Dr. Joseph K.
1909 *The Vanishing Race: The Last Great Indian Council*. New York: Bonanza Books.

Dooling, D. M., Editor
2000 *The Sons Of The Wind*. Norman: University of Oklahoma Press.

Donahue, Michael N.
2009 *Drawing Battle Lines: The Map Testimony of Custer's Last Fight*. El Segundo, CA: Upton and Sons, Publishers.

2018 *Where the Rivers Ran Red*: The Indian Fights of George Armstrong Custer. Montrose, CO: San Juan Publishing Group.

Donovan, James.
2008 *A Terrible Glory: Custer and the Little*

Bighorn. New York: Back Bay Books.

Dorrel, Lance J.
2019 *A Dance With Death: An Irish Soldier of Fortune At The Little Bighorn*. Self-Published: Amazon.

Dorsey, James Owen.
1894 *A Study of Siouan Cults*. Eleventh Annual Report of the Bureau of Ethnology to the Secretary of the Smithsonian Institution, 1889-1890, Government Printing Office, Washington, 1861, pages 351-544.

1905 *The Cheyenne*. Field Columbian Museum Anthropological Papers 99, Vol. 9, No. 1.

Dusenberry, Verne
1962 *The Montana Cree: A study in religious persistence*. Stockholm: Almqvist & Wiksell.

Eastman, Charles
1918 *Indian Heroes and Great Chieftains*. New York: Little and Brown.

Ewers, John C.
1958 *The Blackfeet*. Norman: University of Oklahoma Press.

Farlow, Edward J.
1998 *Wind River Adventures: My Life in Frontier Wyoming*. High Plains Printers.

Gibbon, Guy.
2003 *The Sioux: The Dakota and Lakota Nations*. Blackwell Publishing.

Goodman, Ronald
2017 *Lakota Star Knowledge: Studies in Lakota Stellar Theology*. 3rd Edition. SGU Publishing.

Graham, Col. William T.

1953 *The Custer Myth: A Sourcebook of Custeriana.* Harrisburg, PA: Bonanza Books, Crown Publishers.

Gray, John S.

1988 *Centennial Campaign: The Sioux War of* 1876. Norman: University of Oklahoma Press.

1991 *Custer's Last Campaign: Mitch Boyer and the Little Bighorn Reconstructed.* Lincoln: University of Nebraska Press.

Greene, Jerome A.

1979 *Evidence and The Custer Enigma: A Reconstruction of Indian-Military History.* Reno: Outbooks.

1994 *Lakota and Cheyenne: Indian Views of the Great Sioux War,* 1876-1877. Norman: University of Oklahoma Press.

2008 *Stricken Field: The Little Bighorn Since* 1876. Norman: University of Oklahoma Press.

2008 *The Washita: The U.S. Army and the Southern Cheyennes,* 1867-1869. Norman: University of Oklahoma Press.

Grinnell, George B.

1955 *The Fighting Cheyennes.* Norman: University of Oklahoma Press.

1961 *Pawnee, Blackfoot and Cheyenne.* New York: Charles Scribner's Sons.

1972 *The Cheyenne Indians: Their History and Ways of Life. Lincoln and London: University of Nebraska Press* 2 *Vols.*

2008 *The Cheyenne Indians: Their History and Lifeways.* Edited by Joseph A. Fitzgerald. Bloomington, IN: World Wisdom, Inc.

Hall, Robert L.

1997 An Archaeology of the Soul: North American Indian Belief and Ritual. Urbana and Chicago: University of Illinois Press.

Hammer, Kenneth, ed.
1976 *Custer in '76: Walter Camp's Notes on the Custer Fight*. Norman: University of Oklahoma Press.

Hanson, Joseph Mills.
1910 *The Conquest of the Missouri*. Chicago: A.C. McClurg.

Hardorff, Richard G.
1991 *Lakota Recollections of the Custer Fight: New Sources of Indian-Military History*. Lincoln: University of Nebraska Press.

1997 *Camp, Custer, and The Little Bighorn: A Collection of Walter Mason Camp's Research Papers on General George A. Custer's Last Fight*. El Segundo, CA: Upton and Sons, Publishers.

1998 *Cheyenne Memories of the Custer Fight*. Spokane: Arthur H. Clark Co.

1999 *The Custer Battle Casualties, II: The Dead, The Missing, And a Few Survivors*. El Segundo, CA: Upton and Sons, Publishers.

1999 *Hokahey: A Good Day to Die*! Lincoln: University of Nebraska Press.

2001 *The Death of Crazy Horse: A Tragic Episode in Lakota History*. Lincoln And London: University of Nebraska Press.

2002 *The Custer Battle Casualties: Burials, Exhumations and Reinterments*. El Segundo, CA: Upton and Sons, Publishers.

2002 *On The Little Bighorn With Walter Camp: A Collection of W. M. Camp's Letters, Notes and Opinions on Custer's Last Fight*. El Segundo, CA: Upton And Sons Publishers.

2005 *Indian Views of the Custer Fight: A Source Book*. Norman: University of Oklahoma Press.
Harper, Gordon.

2014 *The Fights on the Little Horn: Unveiling The Mysteries of Custer's Last Stand*. Philadelphia and

Oxford. Casemate Publishers.

Harrod, Howard L.
1995 *Becoming and Remaining a People: Native American Religions on the Northern Plains.* Tucson: University of Arizona Press.

Heobel, E. Adamson
1960 *The Cheyennes: Indians of the Great Plains.* New York: Holt, Rinehart And Winston.

Hoig, Stan
1976 *The Battle of the Washita: The Sheridan- Custer Campaign* Of 1867-1869. Lincoln and London: University of Nebraska Press.

Howard, James H.
2014 *The Canadian Sioux.* Lincoln: University of Nebraska Press.

Hultkrantz Ake
1980 *The Religions of the American Indians.* Berkeley, Los Angeles. London: University of California Press.

1992 *Shamanic Healing and Ritual Drama: Health and Medicine in Native North American Religious Traditions.* New York: Crossroad Publishing Company.

Hyde, George, E.
1968 *Life of George Bent: Written from His Letters.* Edited by Savoie Lottinville. Norman: University of Oklahoma Press.

Jablow, Joseph
1994 *The Cheyenne In Plains Indian Trade Relations* 1795-1840. Lincoln and London: University of Nebraska Press.

Kadlecek, Edward and Mabel
1981 *To Kill An Eagle: Indian Views of The Last Days*

of Crazy Horse. Boulder, CO: Johnson Books.

Kammen, Robert and Lefthad, Frederick and Marshall, Joe
1992 *Soldiers Falling Into Camp: The Battles at the Rosebud and the Little Bighorn*. Encampment, Wyoming. Affiliated Writers of America, Inc.

Kracht, Benjamin R.
2017 *Kiowa Belief and Ritual*. Lincoln: University of Nebraska Press.

Kuhlman, Charles
1940 *Custer and the Gall Saga*. Los Angeles: Haynes Corporation.

1951 *Legend into History*: Harrisburg, PA: The Stackpole Company.

Laubin, Reginald and Gladys
1980 *American Indian Archery*. Norman: University of Oklahoma Press.

Lapointe, James
1976 *Legends of the Lakota*. San Francisco: Indian Historian Press, Inc.

Leforge, Thomas H. and Marquis, Thomas B.
1974 *Memoirs of a White Crow Indian*. Lincoln: Bison Books.

Libby, Orin G. Editor
1998 *The Arikara Narrative of Custer's Campaign and the Battle of the Little Bighorn*. Norman: University of Oklahoma Press.

Liberty, Margot
1996 "Oral and Written Indian Perspectives on the Indian Wars." *In Legacy: New Perspectives on the Battle of the Little Bighorn*. Edited by Charles E. Rankin. Helena: Montana Historical Society Press, 1996.

Liddic, Bruce R.
2004 *Vanishing Victory: Custer's Final March.* El Segundo, CA: Upton and Sons Publishers.

Long, James (First Boy)
2004 *Land of Nakoda: The Story of the Assiniboine Indians.* Helena, MT: Riverbend Publishing.

Mails, Thomas E.
1979 *Fools Crow.* Lincoln: University of Nebraska Press.

Mangum, Neil C.
1996 *Battle of the Rosebud: Prelude to the Little Bighorn.* El Segundo, CA: Upton & Sons.

Marquis, Thomas B.
1967 *Custer on the Little Bighorn.* Algonac, MI: Reference Publications.

1978 *The Cheyennes of Montana.* Algonac, MI: Reference Publications.

2003 *Wooden Leg: A Warrior Who Fought Custer.* Lincoln: University of Nebraska Press.

McLaughlin, James
1989 *My Friend The Indian.* Lincoln: University of Nebraska Press.

Michno, Gregory F.
1997 *Lakota Noon: The Indian Narrative of Custer's Defeat.* Missoula, MT: Mountain Press Publishing.

2003 *Encyclopedia of Indian Wars: Western Battles and Skirmishes,* 1850-1890. Missoula, MT: Mountain Press Publishing.

Miller, David Humphreys
1985 *Custer's Fall: The Indian Side of the Story.* Lincoln: University of Nebraska Press.

Milligan, Edward A.
1976 *Dakota Twilight: The Standing Rock Sioux,* 1874-1890. Hicksville, NY: Exposition Press.

Milloy, John S.
1988 *The Plains Cree: Trade, Diplomacy and War,* 1790 *to* 1870. University of Manitoba Press.

Monnett, John H.
2008 *Where One Hundred Soldiers Were Killed.* Albuquerque: University of New Mexico Press.

Mooney, James
1894 "The Siouan Tribes of the East." *Bulletin* 22. *Washington: Bureau of Ethnology.* 1894.

Moore, John H.
1987 *The Cheyenne Nation: A Social and Demographic History.* Lincoln: University of Nebraska Press.

Neihardt, John G.
1972 *Black Elk Speaks: Being the Life Story of a Holy Man of the Ogalala Sioux.* Lincoln: University of Nebraska Press.

Nichols, Ronald H. Compiled and Edited
2007 *Reno Court of Inquiry: In the Case of Major Marcus Reno.* Hardin, MT. Custer Battlefield Historical & Museum Association, Inc.

Nichols, Ronald H. and Bird, Daniel I. (Editors)
2010 *Men With Custer: Biographies of the 7th Cavalry.* Hardin, MT. Custer Battlefield Historical & Museum Association, Inc.

Papandrea, Ronald J.
2020 *They Never Surrendered: The Lakota Sioux Band That Stayed in Canada.* 6th Edition Revised. La Vergne, TN: Lightning Source.

Pennington, Jack L.
2005 *Custer, Curley, Curtis: An Expanded View of the Battle of the Little Big Horn*. El Segundo, CA: Upton and Sons, Publishers.

Powell, Peter J.
1969 *Sweet Medicine: The Continuing Role of the Sacred Arrows, the Sun Dance, and the Buffalo Hat in Northern Cheyenne History*. Norman: University of Oklahoma Press.

1981 *People of the Sacred Mountain. 2 Vols*. San Francisco: Harper & Row.

Powers, Thomas
2010 *The Killing of Crazy Horse*. New York: Alfred Knopf.

Powers, William K.
1977 *Oglala Religion*. Lincoln and London: University of Nebraska Press.

1986 *Sacred Language: The Nature of Supernatural Discourse in Lakota*. Norman: University of Oklahoma Press.

Red Star, Nancy
2000 *Star Ancestors: Extraterrestrial Contact in the Native American Tradition*. Rochester, VT and Toronto, Canada. Bear & Company.

Ricker, Eli S. edited by Richard E. Jensen
2005 *Voices of the American West of Eli S. Ricker, 1903-1919: The Settler and Soldier Interviews. Vol 2*. Lincoln and London: University of Nebraska Press.

Riggs, Stephen R.
2004 *Dakota grammar, texts, and ethnography. Contributions to North American Ethnology*. Washington, D.C.: Department of the Interior.

Saindon, Robert A.
2009 *Old Fort Peck and the Custer Massacre…* The Connection. Self-published by author.

Schlesier, Karl
1987 *The Wolves of Heaven: Cheyenne Shamanism, Ceremonies and Prehistoric Origins.* Norman: University of Oklahoma Press.

Secoy, Frank Raymond
1992 *Changing Military Patterns of the Great Plains Indians.* Lincoln and London: University of Nebraska Press.

Scott, Douglas D.
2013 *Uncovering History: Archaeological Investigations At The Little Bighorn.* Norman: University of Oklahoma Press.

Shields, Kenneth Jr.
2000 *The Little Bighorn* Tiospaye. Charleston: Arcadia Publishing.

St. Pierre, Mark and Long Soldier, Tilda.
1995 *Walking in the Sacred Manner: Healers, Dreamers, and Pipe Carriers – Medicine Women of the Plains Indians.* New York: Simon and Schuster.

Stands In Timber, John and Liberty, Margot.
1967 *Cheyenne Memories.* New Haven, CT: Yale University Press.

2013 *A Cheyenne Voice: The Complete John Stands In Timber Interviews.* Norman: University of Oklahoma Press.

Stewart, Edgar, I.
1955 *Custer's Luck.* Norman: University of Oklahoma Press.

Strange Owl-Raben, Ann and Arms, Sharon L.

2017 *Ann Strange Owl: A Northern Cheyenne Memoir*. Allenspark, CO. Self-Published.

Sundstrom, Linea
2004 *Storied Stone: Indian Rock Art of The Black Hills Country*. Norman: University of Oklahoma Press.

Trenholm, Virginia.
1970 *The Arapahoes, Our People*. Norman: University of Oklahoma Press.

Utley, Robert M.
1993 *The Lance and The Shield: The Life and Times of Sitting Bull*. Random House Publishing Group.

Vaughn, J.W.
1966 *Indian Fights: New Facts on Seven Encounters*. Norman: University of Oklahoma Press.

2016 *On the Border With Crook*. Big Byte Books.

Vestal, Stanley
1976 *Sitting Bull: Champion of the Sioux*. 6th Edition. Norman: University of Oklahoma Press.

1984 *Warpath: The True Story of the Fighting Sioux Told in a Biography Of Chief White Bull. 4th Edition.* Lincoln and London: University Of Nebraska Press.

Viola, Herman
1999 *Little Bighorn Remembered*. Times Books.

Waggoner, Josephine (Emily LeVine, ed.)
2013 *Witness: A Hunkpapa Historian's Strong-Heart Song of the Lakotas*. Lincoln: University of Nebraska Press.

Walker, James R. (Raymond J. DeMallie and Elaine A. Jahner, ed.)
1982 *Lakota Society*. Lincoln and London: University of Nebraska Press.

1991 *Lakota Belief and Ritual.* Lincoln and London: University of Nebraska Press.

Warren, William W.
2009 *History of the Ojibway People.* St. Paul. Minnesota Historical Society Press.

Weibert, Don.
1985 *Sixty-Six Years in Custer's Shadow.*

1989 *Custer, Cases and Cartridges: The Weibert Collection Analyzed.* Self-published by Don Weibert.

Articles, Journals and Reports in Periodical Publications

Albers, Patricia.
Changing Patterns of Ethnicity in the Northeastem Plains, 1789- 1870, in History, Power and Identity: Ethnogenesis in the America 1492-1992. Iowa City: University of Iowa Press. 1996.

Albers, Patricia.
History and Idealism in Plains Indian Ethnography: Review Essay: The Plains Cree by David Mandelbaum. Reviews in Anthropology Spring: 215-228. 1980.

Blish, Helen, H.
"The Ceremony of the Sacred Bow of the Oglala Dakota." American Anthropology N.S., 36, 1934. Cowdrey, Mike. "The Wilkins Ledger- An Oglala Lakota Record of the 1870's." Plainsledgerart.org/essay/files/Blackroadwilkinsledger . 2015.

Deloria, Ella.
Ella Deloria Archives, Dakota Ethnography, Box 3, No. 17, "Origin of the Dakota Societies: A Legend." Dakota Indian Foundation. www.dakotaindianfoundation.org.

Dixon, Roland B.
"Some Aspects of the American Shaman." The Journal of American Folklore. Vol. XXI. January-March,

1908- No. LXXX.

Dusenberry, Verne.
"Horn In the Ice." Montana the Magazine of Western History." Vol. 6. No. 4 (Autumn 1956) pp 26-33.

Eastman, Charles A.
"The Story of the Little Big Horn." Chautauquan, no. 31 (July 1900). *Handbook of North American Indians.* William C. Sturtevant, General Editor. Vol 13, Part 2 of 2. Smithsonian Institution. Washington, D.C. 2001.

Grinnell, George Bird.
"Early Blackfoot History." The American Anthropologist. Vol. 5, 1892.
"The Great Mysteries of the Cheyenne," American Anthropologis, n.s., vol. XII, no. 4, October-December 1910, 573-74.

Hack, Steven C.
"This Must Have Been a Grand Sight: George Bent and the Battle of the Platte Bridge" (2010). Great Plains Quarterly. 2521. http: //digitalcommons.unl.edu/greatplainsquarterly/2521

Kroeber, A.L.
"Ethnology of the Gros Ventre." Anthropological Papers of the American Museum of Natural History, Vol. I, Part IV., New York, 1908.

Liberty, Margot and Wood, Raymond A.
"Cheyenne Primacy: New Perspectives on a Great Plains Tribe." Plains Anthropologist, Vol. 56, No. 218, Taylor & Francis, Ltd. (May 2011).

Lowie, Robert H.
"The Assiniboine." Anthropological Papers of the American Museum of Natural History, Vol. IV, Part I., New York, 1909.
"Dance Associations of the Eastern Dakota." Anthropological Papers of the American Museum of Natural History, Vol. XI., Part II. New York, 1913.

Mandelbaum, David G.
"The Plains Cree." Anthropological papers of The American Museum of Natural History, Vol. XXXVII, Part II, New York, 1940.

Matthews, Washington.
"Ethnology and Philology of the Hidatsa Indians." 1877.

McCrady, David G.
"Living With Strangers: The Nineteenth-Century Sioux and the Canadian-American Borderlands." 1998.

McLeod, Neal.
"Plains Cree Identity: Borderlands, Ambiguous Genealogies and Narrative Irony." The Canadian Journal of Native Studies XX, 2(2000):437-454.

Michelson, Truman.
"Cheyenne Stories and Historical Accounts." *Manuscript* 2811, *National Anthropological Archives, Smithsonian Institution*. August 1910.
"Cheyenne and Sutaio Stories and Notes." Manuscript 2828, National Anthropological Archives, Smithsonian Institution. August-September 1910.
"Preliminary Report on the Linguistic Classification of Algonquian Tribes," BAE, Twenty-eighth Annual Report (10-6-1907), Washington, 1912.
"Notes on the Cheyenne and Sutaio." Manuscript 2684, National Anthropological Archives, Smithsonian Institution. August 1913.

Miller, David Humphreys.
"Echoes of the Little Bighorn." American Heritage 22, no 4 (June 1971).

Scott, Hugh.
"The Early History and Names of the Arapaho," American Anthropologist, N.S., IX (1907).

Stands In Timber, John and Liberty, Margot.
"Last Ghastly Moments at the Little Bighorn." *American Heritage* 17, no 3, (April 1966).

Vroom, Nicholas.
"Cree, Assiniboine, Ojibwa, & Michif: The Nehiyaw Pwat Confederacy/Iron Alliance in Montana." 2014.

Waggoner, Linda M.
"Sibley's Winnebago Prisoners: Deconstructing Race and Recovering Kinship in the Dakota War of 1862" (2013). Great Plains 2486. http: //digitalcommons.unl.edu/greatplainsquarterly/2486.

Wissler, Clark.
"Societies and Ceremonial Associations in the Oglala Division of the Teton Dakota." Anthropological papers of The American Museum of Natural History, Vol. XI. New York, 1916.

Appendix A: Elders and Historians Interviewed and Name of Ancestor at the Battle of the Little Bighorn

Arapaho	
Name	**Ancestor**
Martin Blackburn	Last Bear
Marcus Dewey	Little Ant
Bill Goggles	Iron Eyes
Henry Goggles Jr.	Iron Eyes
Fred Mosqueda	
Devin Oldman	Little Ant
Ivan Posey	
Elise Sage	Powder Face
Cletus Yellow Plume	Black Coal Little Raven Waterman

Arikara	
Name	**Ancestor**
Loren Yellow Bird	

Blackfeet	
Name	**Ancestor**
Ernie Heavy Runner	
Jimmy Stgoddard	
Joe Wagner	
Souta Calling Last	

Cheyenne	
Name	**Ancestor**
Alberta American Horse	American Horse
Wallace Bearchum	Bear Chum Big Nose Buffalo Calf/Calf Coal Bear Grasshopper Howling Wolf Red Cherries Tall Bull Pawnee Wounded Thigh
Dwight Bull Coming	White Shield
Roy D Bull Coming	White Shield
Billford Curley	Ice (White Bull)
Scott Doser	Crazy Head
Chris Eagle Nest	Eagle Nest
Pauline Highwolf	Susie Shot-In-The-Eye
Tim Lame Woman Sr.	Little Wolf, Wild Hog
Dennis Limberhand	Limber Bones
Eugene Limpy	Limpy
Cleve Littlebear	
Steve Littlebird	Bobtail Horse
Manuel Little Whiteman	Crazy Head, Goes Ahead (Crow scout)
Frank Long Jaw	Long Jaw

Cheyenne Continued	
Name	**Ancestor**
Roger Red Hat	Lame White Man
Charlotte Rock Road	Nakotamae Big Man She Bear White Face Woman Strange Owl
Florence Strange Owl Running Wolf	Nakotamae Big Man She Bear White Face Woman Strange Owl
Alec Sandcrane	Standing Elk
Ruthie Shoulderblade	Nakotamae Big Man She Bear White Face Woman Strange Owl
Vernon Sooktis	Black Horse
Rufus Spear	Bites, Iron Shirt
James Spotted Wolf	Spotted Wolf, Tangle Hair Yellow
Keith Spotted Wolf	Spotted Wolf, Tangle Hair Yellow
Al Joe Strange Owl	Nakotamae Big Man She Bear White Face Woman Strange Owl
Ann Strange Owl Raben, husband Dayton Raben, and daughter Nico Strange Owl	Nakotamae Big Man She Bear White Face Woman Strange Owl

Cheyenne Continued	
Name	**Ancestor**
Donovan Taylor	Nakotamae Big Man She Bear White Face Woman Strange Owl Pine
Linwood Tall Bull	Tall Bull
Matthew Two Moons	Two Moons
Nadine Weasel Bear	Weasel Bear
Eddie Whitedirt	Crazy Head Ho'vese
Gilbert Whitedirt	Crazy Head Ho'vese
Chester Whiteman	
Florence Whiteman	Louis Dog
Leroy Whiteman	Bear Who Walks On A Ridge/Ridge Walker Red Bird

Chippewa Cree	
Name	**Ancestor**
Don Myers	
Alvin Windboy, Sr.	

Cree	
Name	**Ancestor**
Elaine Blyan Cross	Big Bear
Floyd Favel	
Murray Ironchild	
Donita Strawberry	Big Bear

Crow	
Name	**Ancestor**
Alden BigMan Jr.	
Gilbert Birdinground Jr.	White Swan-Crow Scout
Grant Bulltail	
Frenchy Dillon	Mitch Bouyer and Tom Leforge-Scouts for U.S. Army
Faron Iron	Goes Ahead-Crow Scout U.S. Army
Frederick Lefthand	Mitch Bouyer-Scout U.S. Army
Dr. Lanny Real Bird	

Gros Ventre	
Name	**Ancestor**
Davy Belgard	
Michael Black Wolf	
Terry Brockie	
Leon Eagle Tail	Red Whip
Catcher Cuts The Rope	Cuts The Rope

Hunkpapa Lakota	
Name	**Ancestor**
John Eagle Shield	Crawler, Deeds, Moving Robe Woman (Mary Crawler)
Linus Gray Eagle	Gray Eagle
Everette Iron Eyes	
Ernie La Pointe	Sitting Bull
Joanne Lethbridge Pompana	

Minnkojou Lakota	
Name	**Ancestor**
Joseph Brings Plenty Sr.	Brings Plenty, Low Dog, Plenty Holes, Medicine Cloud and White Coyote
Gay Kingman	Dogs Back Bone
Arvol Looking Horse	Looking Horse
Mike Running Wolf	
Steve Vance	
Doug War Eagle	Crazy Horse
Richard Charging Eagle	

Oglala Lakota	
Name	**Ancestor**
Lydia Bearkiller	
Vine Brokenrope	Brokenrope
Marcell Bull Bear	
Basil BraveHeart	Brave Heart, Charging A Fight
Jhon Goes In Center	
Garvard Good Plume Jr.	Little Killer, White Cow Bull
Chico Her Many Horses	Gall
Richard Iron Cloud	Knife Chief, Eagle Bear
Harold Salaway	Left Heron, Makhula
Rick Two Dogs	American Horse and sons, Thomas, Samuel, Ben and Charlie. Stands Against the Wind Woman (Susie Shot-in-the-Eye)
Wendell Yellow Bull	

Sicangu Lakota	
Name	**Ancestor**
Pauline Cloudman	Cloud Man
Ronnie Cutt	
Victor Douville	Moves Camp Woman
Louis Grassrope	Grassrope
Linda Haukaas	
Sam High Crane	Goes To War, Hollow Horn Bear, Iron Shell
Duane Hollow Horn Bear	Goes To War, Hollow Horn Bear, IronShell
Calvin Iron Shell	Iron Shell, Center Woman (She Cherishes Her Nation So Takes Care of Them)
Pat Iron Shell	Iron Shell, Center Woman (She Cherishes Her Nation So Takes Care of Them)
Henry Quick Bear	Quick Bear, Swift Hawk
Cal Thunder Hawk	Thunder Hawk
Phil Two Eagle	Two Eagles
Royal Yellow Hawk	

Nakota	
Name	**Ancestor**
Jalen Atchico	
Calvin Bear First	
James Desjarlais	Piapot and Big Bear
Tim Eashappie	
Jim Red Eagle	Shows Himself Big At Night
Tommy Christian	
Ira McArthur	
Peter McArthur	
Iris O'Watch	
Ken Ryan	
Ken Shields	Feather Earring

Nakoda	
Name	**Ancestor**
Francis Alexis	Standing Alone, Iron Head
Rod Alexis	Standing Alone, Iron Head
Ken Helgeson	
Dennis Paul	
Jaelin Rask	
Tom Shawl	

Santee Dakota	
Name	**Ancestor**
Mitchell BigHunter	Gray Earth Track
Dianne Desrosiers	
Wayne Goodwill	Two Horse Woman
Ozzie McKay	Gray Earth Track
Cody Seaboy	
Terry Was'te s'te	

Sisitunwan	
Name	**Ancestor**
Dianne Desrosiers	
Vine Marks	
Akisa Peters Manning	

Others	
Name	**Ancestor**
Rhonda Funmaker-Ho-Chunk	
Ben Rhodd-Potawatomi	

Appendix B: List of Santee Dakota, Sisitunwan, Yankton and Yanktonai Warriors at the Battle of the Little Bighorn

1. Inkpaduta
2. Red Tipped Horn-son of Inkpaduta
3. Red Horn Bull
4. Gray Earth Track, also called Mysterious Medicine
5. Joseph-Brother to Grey Earth Track
6. White Earth Tracking-son of Inkpaduta
7. Little Ghost-son of Inkpaduta
8. Little Soldier-Yanktonai
9. High Eagle
10. Charlie Cuwinyuksa
11. Bearbull
12. Spotted Horse
13. Red Horse
14. Black Face-may have died at the fight at the Little Bighorn
15. Thomas Thunder
16. Isaac Thunder
17. Sioux Ben
18. Bohpa
19. Old Bull
20. John Bull
21. Moses Bull
22. Kaiyoza
23. Shunka Ho Nahon
24. Pakadoshen
25. Akisa
26. Mazawasicuna
27. Dakota Red Cloud
28. Hdahdawanka
29. Mahpiyaska

30. Sioux Big Jack
31. Webadoza
32. Joe Patrip
33. Good Face
34. Jessie Wakpa
35. Wanbdiska
36. Chief Kicumani
37. Oi-pak-san
38. Wiyokiye
39. Hehaka
40. Kiyewakan
41. James Grey
42. Lean Bear
43. Feather Earring-Yankton/Lakota
44. Horses Ghost-Yanktonai/Hunkpapa Lakota
45. Buck Elk Bull-Yankton
46. Bighorn-Yankton
47. Sharp Eyes-Yankton
48. Half Red-Yankton
49. Black Buffalo
50. Fingers
51. Scarlet Thunder
52. Walking Road
53. White Cap
54. Yellow Bird-son of White Cap
55. Black Bird-son of White Cap
56. Enemy of the Great Spirit-Brother-in-law of White Cap
57. Nine-Yankton
58. Two Dogs-Yankton
59. Yellow Hawks-Yankton
60. Red Cloud
61. Yellow Eagle
62. Thundering Bear-Yanktonai
63. Iron Bear-Yanktonai
64. Medicine Cloud-Yanktonai
65. Long Tree-Yanktonai
66. His Road-Yanktonai
67. White Eagle
68. Holy Cloud-Yanktonai
69. Gray Whirlwind-Yanktonai
70. Shoot Holy-Yanktonai
71. Strong Heart-Yanktonai

72. Two Bulls-Yanktonai
73. Tree Top-Yanktonai
74. White Thunder-Yanktonai
75. Bob Tail Bear
76. Crazy Bull
77. Red Feather
78. Big Head-Yanktonai
79. Two Bear-Yanktonai
80. Siyaka
81. Ho Tain Mani (Walks Loudly)
82. Tiomani
83. Blue Ghost
84. Charging Cloud
85. Fire Cloud
86. Mazepewin-might be Ho-Chunk (Winnebago)

Sources:

1 - 42: Mitchell BigHunter - Santee Dakota
43 - 48: Kenny Shields - Yankton / Lakota
49 - 61: Calvin Bear First - Yanktonai / Santee Dakota
62 - 64:Robert Saindon
65 - 74: www.friendslittlebighorn.com
75 - 77: David Humphreys Miller
78 - 79: Inkpa Mani and Josephine Waggoner
80 - 81: Akisa Peters Manning and Cody Hotain - Sisitunwan
82 - 86: Dianne Desrosiers

Additional Sources:

Ozzie McKay - Santee Dakota, Jalen Atchico - Yanktonai/Nakota

Appendix C: List of Arapaho Warriors at the Battle of the Little Bighorn and their Dog Men society members.

1. Little Ant
2. Sharp Nose - Dog Men military society headsmen
3. Plenty Bear - came from Fort Robinson, Nebraska
4. Left Hand - came from Fort Robinson, Nebraska
5. Yellow Eagle - came from Fort Robinson, Nebraska
6. Yellow Fly - came from Fort Robinson, Nebraska
7. Waterman - came from Fort Robinson, Nebraska
8. Little Bird - came from Fort Robinson, Nebraska
9. Well-Knowing One or Sherman Sage - came from Fort Robinson, Nebraska
10. Little Soldier - Dog Men military society member
11. Crazy Hair - Dog Men military society member
12. Falls Off His Horse - Dog Men military society member
13. Yellow Bear - Dog Men military society member
14. Runs Behind Enemy - Dog Men military society member
15. Powder Face
16. Last Bear
17. Goes In The Lodge
18. Yellow Calf
19. Black Coal
20. Iron Eyes - Dog Men military society member

Other Arapaho at the Little Bighorn

21. North Left Hand
22. Antelope
23. Strikes on Top

24. Fighting Bear
25. Big Mouth
26. Big Crow
27. Scar Face

Arapaho Dog Soldiers

28. Sharp Nose
29. Iron Eyes
30. Falls Off His Horse
31. Little Soldier
32. Crazy Hair
33. Yellow Bear
34. Runs Behind Enemy

Sources:

1 - 14: Devin Oldman - Arapaho
15: Elise Sage - Arapaho
16: Martin Blackburn - Arapaho
17 - 19: Cletus Yellowplume - Arapaho
20: Bill Goggles and Henry Goggles, Jr. - Arapaho

Appendix D: List of Gros Ventre Warriors at the Battle of the Little Bighorn

1. Red Whip
2. Curley Head
3. Lone Fly / Flies Alone
4. Rising Cross
5. Wolf Voice
6. Eagle Child
7. Horse Capture
8. Cuts The Rope
9. Running Fisher

Sources:

Davey Belgard - Gros Ventre, Leon Eagle Tail - Gros Ventre, Catcher Cuts the Rope - Gros Ventre, and Michael Black Wolf - Gros Ventre.

Appendix E: List of Sicangu Lakota Warriors at the Battle of the Little Bighorn

1. Flying Alone
2. White Whirlwind
3. Red Medicine Woman
4. Medicine Ghost
5. Walking Bull
6. White Hawk
7. Shell Boy
8. Mollie
9. Bad Whirlwind
10. Crier
11. Lame
12. Soldier
13. Grey Cow Eagle
14. Little Wolf
15. Bear in the Woods
16. Looking Elk
17. Red Eagle
18. Eagle Woman
19. Bull Dog Running in the Midst
20. Red Buck Elk
21. No Judgement
22. White Calf
23. His Horse Chasing
24. Came and Sat Above
25. Blue Haired Horse
26. Kill the Pawnee
27. Pretty Dog
28. Yellow Horse
29. Eagle Dog
30. Crow's Head
31. Sitting Buck Elk
32. White Bull Cow
33. Ghost Head
34. Two Eagles
35. Two Bear

36. Two Strikes
37. Crow Dog
38. Woman Who Walks with the Stars (Crow Dog's wife)
39. Hollow Horn Eagle
40. Brave Bird
41. Big Turkey
42. Black Bear
43. Bear Soldier
44. Black Bird
45. Black Bull
46. Black Eye
47. Blue Shield
48. Brings the Woman
49. Buffalo Horse
50. Crazy Bull
51. Eagle Man
52. Eagle Pipe
53. Flying Chaser
54. Fool Bull with his wife Red Cane
55. Foolish Elk
56. Grass Rope
57. High Bald Eagle
58. Hollow Horn
59. Hollow Horn Bear with his wife Good Bed Woman
60. Horn Cloud
61. Iron Shell with his wife She Cherishes Her Nation
62. Knife Scabbard
63. No Flesh
64. Plenty Horses
65. Red Hill
66. Standing Bear
67. Thin Elk
68. Thunder Hawk with his wife Face
69. Bad Hand
70. White Buffalo
71. White Bird
72. Brave Hawk
73. Cloud Man
74. Eagle Bear
75. White Horse

76. Coffee
77. Yellow Cloud
78. Brave
79. Bear Shield
80. Crow Eagle
81. White Hawk
82. He Dog
83. White Lance
84. Quick Bear
85. Swift Hawk

From Bratley photograph.

86. Elk Teeth
87. Otterman
88. Horn
89. One Wood
90. With Horns
91. Yellow Cloud
92. Grey Eagle Tail
93. Turning Eagle
94. Fast Dog
95. Pulls the Arrow Out
96. James Kills Plenty (Son of Turning Eagle).
97. Brule Woman aka "Mary" Fine Weather
98. Charging Hawk
99. Crow Eagle

These Sicangu Lakota came into the Standing Rock Agency to surrender and were then sent to Rosebud. These were from the "northern" group known to have been involved in the Battle of the Little Bighorn.

Appendix F: List of Cheyenne Warriors at the Battle of the Little Bighorn

This appendix also includes the Cheyenne warrior society, as well as lists of Cheyenne casualties from the Battle.

1. A Crow Cuts His Nose - Elkhorn Scraper
2. All See Him
3. American Horse
4. Bad Horse
5. Bald Eagle
6. Beard or Mustache
7. Bear Chum
8. Bear Comes Out
9. Bear Heart
10. Bear Tail
11. Bear Walks on a Ridge/Ridge Walker - Kit Fox
12. Beaver Claws - Crazy Dog
13. Beaver Heart - Kit Fox
14. Big Back
15. Big Beaver
16. Big Crow - Elkhorn Scraper
17. Big Crow - Dog Soldier
18. Big Foot
19. Big Man - Died as a result of wounds suffered during the Battle.
20. Big Nose
21. Big Wolf
22. Bites
23. Blacksmith - Dog Soldier
24. Black Bird
25. Black Cloud 1 - Kit Fox
26. Black Cloud 2 - Dog Soldier
27. Black Coyote - Elkhorn Scraper
28. Black Crain
29. Black Horse - Elkhorn Scraper
30. Black Kills
31. Black Knife - Crazy Dog

32. Black/Dirty Moccasin - Old Man Chief of the Cheyenne Tribe. One of only 2 present at the Battle of the Little Bighorn.
33. Black Ree
34. Black Shield
35. Black Whetstone/Black Stone - One of the two Cheyenne warriors said to be the first to engage the Seventh Cavalry at the LBH. Said to be bravest of the Cheyenne Tribe.
36. Black White Man
37. Black Wolf - Elkhorn Scraper
38. Bobtail Horse - Elkhorn Scraper
39. Brave Bear - Dog Soldier
40. Brave Wolf
41. Braided Locks
42. Broken Jaw - Kit Fox
43. Brown Bird
44. Bull Head - Dog Soldier
45. Buffalo Bull Hump - Dog Soldier
46. Bull Thigh
47. Bull Wallowing
48. Bullet Proof
49. Bulls Keep
50. Calling Elk
51. Calf
52. Chief Comes In Sight
53. Closed Hand/Black Bear - KIA during the Battle.
54. Club Foot
55. Coffee
56. Corn/Charlie Corn
57. Crazy Head - Elkhorn Scraper
58. Crazy Mule - Crazy Dog
59. Crooked Nose
60. Crow Necklace - Crazy Dog
61. Cut Belly/Open Bell/Has Sorrel Horse - Died as a result of wounds sustained during the Batte.
62. Did Not Go Home/John Ghost Dog
63. Dives Backward
64. Dog Friend/Dog
65. Dog, Louis
66. Eagle Nest
67. Eagle Chasing, Joe
68. Eagle Chasing, Roy

69. Eagle Tail Feather
70. Elk River
71. Fast Walker
72. Feathered Sun
73. Fire Crow
74. Flapping Horn
75. Flat Iron
76. Fleece
77. Frog
78. Ghost Hide
79. Goes After Other Buffalo - Elkhorn Scraper
80. Good Bear
81. Goose Feathers
82. Grasshopper
83. Hairy Hand - Dog Soldier
84. Hanging Wolf
85. Hawk - Dog Soldier
86. He Dog
87. High Bear
88. High Bull - Dog Soldier
89. High Walking
90. Hollow Wood
91. Horse Road/Chicken Hawk
92. Ho'Vese - Elkhorn Scraper. KIA during the Battle.
93. Howling Wolf
94. Ice/White Bull
95. Iron Shirt - Crazy Dog
96. Issues/John
97. Jealous Bear
98. John Two Moons/Young Two Moons - Kit Fox
99. Just Walks
100. Kills in the Night/Kills Night
101. Kills Many
102. Lame Sioux
103. Lame White Bull - Dog Soldier
104. Lame White Man - Elkhorn Scraper. KIA during the Battle.
105. Last Bull - Kit Fox
106. Left Hand Shooter - Elkhorn Scraper.
107. Lightning, Frank
108. Limber Bones/Flying By/Limberhand/Loose Bones - KIA during the Battle.
109. Limpy

110. Little Bear
111. Little Bird
112. Little Chief
113. Little Coyote
114. Little Creek - Crazy Dog
115. Little Fingernail - Dog Soldier
116. Little Gun
117. Little Hawk - Elkhorn Scraper
118. Little Horse - Kit Fox
119. Little Horse - Contrary who led resistance in the area of the two Ford Ds.
120. Little Man - Dog Soldier
121. Little Shield - Elkhorn Scraper
122. Little Whiteman
123. Lone Bear
124. Lone Wolf
125. Long Roach
126. Little Whirlwind Soldier - Dog Soldier.
127. Long Sioux - Elkhorn Scraper
128. Lost Leg
129. Low Dog
130. Mad Wolf - Dog Soldier
131. Magpie-Dog Soldier
132. Magpie Eagle
133. Man Bear
134. Medicine Bear
135. Medicine Bull
136. Medicine Wolf
137. Mosquito-Kit Fox
138. Noisy Walking - Elkhorn Scraper. Died as result of wounds sustained at the Battle.
139. Old Bear - Old Man Chief of the Cheyenne Tribe. One of only 2 present at the Little Bighorn.
140. Old Bull
141. Old Man-KIA during the Battle.
142. Old Man Coyote - Crazy Dog
143. Pawnee
144. Pig - Elkhorn Scraper
145. Pine - Elkhorn Scraper
146. Plenty Bears - Elkhorn Scraper
147. Plenty Crows
148. Plenty of Buffalo Bull Meat - Kit Fox
149. Plum Man

150. Porcupine - Dog Soldier
151. Powder Face
152. Puffed Cheek
153. Rattlesnake Nose - Kit Fox
154. Red Arms
155. Red Bird
156. Red Cherries - Kit Fox
157. Red Fox
158. Red Nose
159. Red Owl - Crazy Dog
160. Red Robe
161. Rising Fire
162. Rising Sun
163. Roan Bear - Kit Fox
164. Roman Nose/Hump Nose - KIA during the Battle.
165. Roundstone
166. Samuel Shot At/ Blue Cloud
167. Sand Crane
168. Sandstone
169. Scabby Oevemana
170. Shadow Comes In Sight
171. Shave Head
172. She Bear/Young She Bear - Died later as a result of wounds sustained during the Battle.
173. Shell
174. Shield
175. Sits Beside His Medicine - Kit Fox
176. Sits In The Night
177. Sitting Bull - Dog Soldier
178. Sitting Eagle
179. Sitting Man - Crazy Dog
180. Sleeping Rabbit
181. Soldier Wolf
182. Snow Bird - Crazy Dog
183. Spotted Blackbird
184. Spotted Elk
185. Spotted Wolf - Elkhorn Scraper
186. Squint Eyes
187. Standing Elk - Dog Soldier
188. Star Ese
189. Starving Elk
190. Strong Left Hand - Crazy Dog

191. Strange Owl - Crazy Dog
192. Stump Bear
193. Sun Bear
194. Tall Bull - Dog Soldier
195. Tall Sioux
196. Tall White Man - Elkhorn Scraper
197. Tanglehorn Elk/Tangled Horn Elk
198. Ties His Hair
199. Touches His Grub
200. Tribe
201. Turkey Legs
202. Turtle Road
203. Two Birds
204. Two Crows - Dog Soldier
205. Two Feathers.
206. Two Moons - Kit Fox
207. Two Twists
208. Walking Medicine
209. Walking White Man
210. Walks Last
211. Wears The Iron Shirt - KIA during the Battle.
212. Weasel Bear - Kit Fox
213. Whirlwind/Little Whirlwind-KIA during the Battle.
214. White Bird - Elkhorn Scraper
215. White Body
216. White Buffalo
217. White Clay
218. White Cross Eye
219. White Glass Eye
220. White Eagle - Dog Soldier
221. White Elk - Elkhorn Scraper
222. White Frog - Elkhorn Scraper
223. White Hawk - Elkhorn Scraper
224. White Horse - Elkhorn Scraper. One of the two Cheyenne warriors said to be the first to engage the Seventh Cavalry at the LBH. Said to be bravest of the Cheyenne Tribe.
225. White Moon
226. White Shield - Elkhorn Scraper
227. White Whiskers
228. Wild Hog - Elkhorn Scraper
229. Wolf Chief

230. Wolf Medicine
231. Wooden Leg-Elkhorn Scrape
232. Wooden Thigh
233. 231.Wounded Eye
234. Wrapped Hair/Wrapped Braids - Kit Fox
235. Yellow Eagle - Elkhorn Scraper
236. Yellow Hair
237. Yellow Horse
238. Yellow Nose - Dog Soldier
239. Yellow Weasel
240. Young Spotted Wolf
241. Young Turkey Leg

Cheyenne Dog Men at the Little Bighorn

1. Big Crow
2. Blacksmith
3. Black Cloud
4. Brave Bear
5. Bull Head
6. Buffalo Bull Hump
7. Hawk
8. High Bull
9. Hairy Hand
10. Little Fingernail
11. Little Man
12. Little Whirlwind Soldier
13. Mad Wolf
14. Magpie
15. Porcupine
16. Sitting Bull - Southern Cheyenne
17. Standing Elk
18. Tangle Hair
19. Tall Bull
20. Two Crows
21. White Eagle
22. Whirlwind Soldier
23. Yellow Nose

Cheyenne Elkhorn Scraper Warriors at the Little Bighorn

1. Lame White Man
2. Ice (White Bull)
3. Crazy Head
4. Spotted Wolf
5. Noisy Walking, son of Ice, died as a result of wounds suffered at the Battle of the Little Bighorn
6. Ho'vese, son of Crazy Head, killed at the Battle of the Little Bighorn
7. Wooden Leg
8. A Crow Cuts His Nose
9. Big Crow
10. Black Coyote
11. Bobtail Horse
12. Goes After Other Buffalo
13. Left Hand Shooter
14. Little Hawk
15. Little Shield
16. Pig
17. Pine
18. Plenty Bears
19. Tall Sioux
20. Tall White Man
21. White Bird
22. White Elk
23. White Frog
24. White Hog
25. White Horse
26. White Shield
27. Wild Hog
28. Wolf Medicine
29. Yellow Eagle

Cheyenne Kit Fox Warriors at the Little Bighorn

1. Little Horse
2. Roan Bear
3. Two Moons

4. Mosquito
5. Weasel Bear
6. Bear Walks on a Ridge or Ridge Walker
7. Broken Jaw
8. Red Bird
9. Young Two Moons
10. Last Bull
11. Sits Beside His Medicine
12. Wrapped Hair or Braids
13. Plenty of Buffalo Bull Meat
14. Rattlesnake Nose

Cheyenne Crazy Dog Warriors at the Little Bighorn

1. Old Man Coyote
2. Strong Left Hand
3. Little Creek
4. Snow Bird or White Bird
5. Crazy Mule
6. Iron Shirt
7. Black Knife
8. Beaver Claws
9. Buffalo Calf
10. Red Owl
11. Crow Necklace
12. Strange Owl

Cheyenne Casualties from the Battle of the Little Bighorn

Those in the Historical Record

1. Lame White Man - Elkhorn Scraper Society Member
2. Noisy Walking - Elkhorn Scraper Society Member
3. Little Whirlwind
4. Roman Nose / Hump Nose
5. Cut Belly / Open Belly
6. Limber Bones / Flying By / Limberhand / Loose Bones

7. Closed Hand / Black Bear

Those Not in the Historical Record and Those the historical Record Contains, but Ignores, with Sources.

1. Old Man - KIA in the Valley Fight. Source: Powell, Peter. *People of the Sacred of the Sacred Mountain.* Vol 2, PP 1014, see pp 1369, note
2. Ho'Vese - Age 14, son of Crazy Head. Elkhorn Scraper Society Member. Source: Gilbert Whitedirt, Eddie Whitedirt and Scott Doser.
3. Nakotamae - Mother of Young She Bear, Big Man, Strang Owl and White Faced Woman. Source: Ruthie Shoulderblade, great-granddaughter and Al Joe Strange Owl.
4. She Bear/Young She Bear - son of Nakotamae and Old She Bear. Died near Birney, Montana, from wounds suffered in the Battle Source: Ann Strange Owl-Raben, Dayton Raben, Nico Strange Owl, Ruthie Shoulderblade, Florence and Mike Running Wolf, Charlotte Rockroads, Al Joe Strange Owl.
5. Big Man - son of Nakotamae and Old She Bear. Left ceremoniously where he died, between Crow Agency, Montana and Busby, Montana, from wounds suffered during the Battle. Source: Pauline Highwolf, Al Joe Strange Owl and Mike Running Wolf.
6. Young Cheyenne warrior, died from a neck and throat wound, sustained from fighting at the Little Bighorn. Ceremoniously left near Otter Creek, close to Birney, MT. Source: Leroy Whiteman.
7. Young Cheyenne woman. Source: Roger Red Hat-Cheyenne.
8. Wears The Iron Shirt. Source: Cal Thunder Hawk-Sicangu Lakota.
9. A Cheyenne woman who fought at the LBH with a revolver and was said to be killed. Source: Kill Eagle, Sihasapa (Blackfeet) Lakota Chief in Graham 1953: 54.
10. A Cheyenne warrior said by Mrs. Spotted Horn Bull who was shot as he tried to cross the LBH River. This warrior died later from his wound. Source: Mrs. Spotted Horn Bull, Hunkpapa Lakota, in Graham 1953: 85-87.

This list of Cheyenne warriors who fought at the Little Bighorn was compiled by Donovan Taylor with contributions from Lance J. Dorrel from *rosters of the*

Fiftieth Anniversary of the Custer Fight, The Battle Of The Little Bighorn and Custer's Last Fight: Remembered by Participants at the Tenth Anniversary June 25th, 1886 *and the Fiftieth Anniversary June 25th,* 1926 by Richard Upton, as well as the Friends of the Little Bighorn Participants List and Document supplied by Northern Cheyenne Tribe.

Appendix G: List of Youngsters from All Tribes Who Fought at the Battle of the Little Bighorn

Lakota

1. Chasing Hawk - Age 8
2. Grass Rope - Sicangu Age 15
3. Hair - Oglala - Age 14
4. Iron Hawk - Hunkpapa Age 14
5. Little Skunk - Minnikojou Age 16
6. Little Soldier - Hunkpapa Age 13
7. Long Elk - Hunkpapa
8. Pretty Bear
9. Elk Heart
10. Painted Brown
11. Pemmican - Oglala
12. Runs The Enemy - Two Kettle Age 15
13. Shoots Walking - Hunkpapa Age 15
14. Black Elk - Oglala Age 13
15. Standing Bear - Age 17
16. Young Eagle - Hunkpapa Age 17
17. Bear's Heart - died later from wounds sustained in the Battle of the Little Bighorn
18. Black Horn - Oglala Age 15
19. Blue Horse - Oglala Age 15
20. Cray Fish - Sans Arc Age 15
21. Eagle Bear - Oglala Age 16
22. Fools Crow - Oglala Age 11
23. William Standing Bear - Sihasapa Age 15
24. Thomas Steals Horses - Oglala Age 11
25. Peter Bear Stop - Minnikojou Age 12
26. Old Eagle - Sans Arc Age 13
27. Stands Against the Wind Woman
28. Charlie American Horse - Oglala
29. Samuel American Horse - Oglala Age 13

30. Ben American Horse - Oglala Age 12
31. Thomas American Horse - Oglala Age 10
32. John Didn't Go Home - Age 15
33. Little Warrior - Oglala Age 11
34. John Sitting Bull - Age 14
35. Joseph High Eagle - Oglala Age 16
36. Bear Horns - Age 15 KIA
37. White Eagle - Oglala KIA
38. Dog With Horns - Minnikojou Age 15
39. James Afraid of Lightening - Minnkikojou Age 14

Cheyenne

1. Ho'vese (Brown Snipe) - Age 14, Son of Crazy Head, KIA.
2. Young She Bear - Age 13 or 14, brother of Big Man, Strange Owl and White Faced Woman. Died later from wounds sustained in Battle of the LBH.
3. Big Man - Age unknown, brother of Young She Bear, Strange Owl and White Faced Woman. Died later from wounds sustained in Battle of the LBH.
4. White Faced Woman - Age 17 or 18, sister to Strange Owl, Young She Bear and Big Man.
5. Club Foot
6. Dives Backward - Age 12
7. Pine - Age 13
8. Little Whirlwind/Whirlwind - Age 16, KIA during the Valley Fight.
9. Hump Nose/Roman Nose - Age 16 or 17, KIA during the Valley Fight.
10. Old Man - KIA during the Valley Fight.
11. Noisy Walking - died later from wounds sustained in the Battle.
12. Limber Bones /Flying By/Limberhand/Loose Bones - KIA
13. Closed Hand/Black Bear - KIA
14. Cut Belly/Open Belly/Has Sorrel horse - died later from wounds sustained in the Battle.
15. Eagle Nest
16. Bear Comes Out - Age 16
17. Black Bird - Age 11

18. Black Wolf
19. Powder Face
20. Two Birds
21. Red Fox
22. Flies Across

Arapaho

1. Left Hand
2. Waterman
3. Yellow Fly
4. Well - Knowing One (Later known as Sherman Sage)
5. Yellow Eagle
6. Plenty Bear

Printed in Great Britain
by Amazon